Truth or Justice?

Dedicated to the memory of Martin Kruze and to all the others.

MARTENSVILLE
Truth or Justice?

The Story of the Martensville Daycare Trials

Frann Harris

DUNDURN PRESS
TORONTO · OXFORD

Copyright © Frann Harris 1998

All rights reserved. No part of this publication may be reproduced, stored in a retrieval system, or transmitted in any form or by any means, electronic, mechanical, photocopying, recording, or otherwise (except for brief passages for purposes of review) without the prior permission of Dundurn Press Limited. Permission to photocopy should be requested from the Canadian Reprography Collective.

Editor: Wendy Thomas
Printer: Transcontinental Printing Inc.
All photos except cover photos used by permission of the *Saskatoon StarPhoenix*.

Canadian Cataloguing in Publication Data

    Harris, Frann
    Martensville — truth or justice?: the story of the Martensville daycare trials

ISBN 1-55002-297-0

1. Child sexual abuse — Saskatchewan — Martensville. 2. Trials (Child sexual abuse) — Saskatchewan. I. Title.

HV6626.54.C3H37 1998   364.15'554'0971124   C97-931920-3

1 2 3 4 5 BJ 02   01   00   99   98

We acknowledge the support of the **Canada Council for the Arts** for our publishing program. We also acknowledge the support of the **Ontario Arts Council** and the **Book Publishing Industry Development Program** of the **Department of Canadian Heritage**.

Care has been taken to trace the ownership of copyright material used in this book. The author and the publisher welcome any information enabling them to rectify any references or credit in subsequent editions.

Printed and bound in Canada.

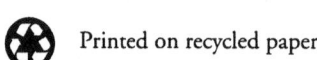 Printed on recycled paper.

Dundurn Press
8 Market Street
Suite 200
Toronto, Ontario, Canada
M5E 1M6

Dundurn Press
73 Lime Walk
Headington, Oxford
England
OX3 7AD

Dundurn Press
250 Sonwil Drive
Buffalo, NY
U.S.A. 14225

CONTENTS

FOREWORD	8
MARTENSVILLE	9
THE FIRST TRIAL	19
Muzzling the Media	21
The Prosecution	31
Ringside Seat	31
Freddy tells his story	43
Kenny tells his story	57
Rookie policewoman on trial	67
The experts aren't sure	71
A mother's love	87
The Defence	97
Competence in question	97
The scales of justice	101
A verdict to cry for	109
THE SECOND TRIAL	115
Selecting the Jury	117
The Prosecution	127
No job for a new recruit	127
A cop is cross-examined	135
Moor the mentor	167
Doubting the children	178
Tommy, Janey, and Sandy	190
Freddy speaks again	205
Kenny speaks again	216
What the doctors say	227
The enemy expert	234
The Defence	241
Expert witnesses	241
Ron Sterling testifies	249
Linda Sterling testifies	266
Travis Sterling testifies	277
Summation and charge to the jury	286
The verdict and sentence	302
AFTERWORD	309
THE LAST WORD by Sheldon Kennedy	315

AUTHOR'S NOTE

Portions of this book have been culled from the official transcripts of the two trials in question. I have doctored the quotes only to excise, for the reader's comfort, many of the superfluous sounds and pauses that litter normal human speech. I have tried to preserve the full flavour of the testimony and, where extraneous words are removed, have done my best to respect the intent of the speaker. The use of ellipses signifies for the reader where material has been excerpted.

I have documented what I heard and saw in court, but the reader must remember that I did so with my own eyes and ears — in a subjective manner. I have changed all the names of the children and of the young offender and, in some cases, created journalists who are composite characters.

ACKNOWLEDGEMENTS

I thank in particular Gerri Cook for her original inspiration; Marian Hebb for her friendship and many kindnesses; Maggie Siggins for her unflagging spirit and devotion to the project; Merilyn Simonds for her welcome encouragement; Greg Walen for his cheerful assistance with questions judicial; officials at the Department of Justice for frequently hauling the transcripts up from the courthouse basement, verifying details upon request, and other assorted kinds of help; Wendy Thomas for her intelligent questions and highly developed sense of order; and, last but not least, my dear Stephen for his computer help, flashes of brilliance, good taste, and untiring emotional support.

Foreword

A society can be measured by how it treats its very young and its very old. This book is about the very young. It is not just a story about alleged crimes against children at a daycare and whether they were actually committed, but rather an exploration of what police and lawyers and therapists did about children who said they were violated.

In general, child sexual abuse is an extremely difficult crime to prove in court. No matter how thorough or experienced the investigating police officers or how convincing the evidence, this kind of case has a rough ride from beginning to end. Even if a case makes it to court, convictions are less numerous than acquittals.

I can see why. A few years ago, between March 1993 and February 1994, I sat through two child sexual-abuse cases. During the lengthy and complex "Martensville" trials, I saw the problems child witnesses have when testifying in adult court — immaturity of language, cognitive development, and memory recall, to name only a few. The court itself had to wrestle with these difficulties in trying to decide whether to believe the children. I wrote this book, based on journal notes I made at the time, to help me reflect on the problems and possible solutions to the way child sexual-abuse cases are handled in our courts. I also wrote it to help others do the same. The way the judicial system handles cases involving the youngest, most vulnerable members of our society is of vital concern to our collective health.

I did not write this book alone. I was spurred on by small soprano voices in my head, echoes of the children I'd listened to in court. Those voices are not always easy to understand or believe but they are compelling, and I believe they have important things to say.

I hope you will listen.

Martensville

To get to Martensville, drive ten minutes straight north from Saskatoon on Highway 12. Blink and you'll miss the small green-and-white sign, though you'd hardly fail to see the Crime Stoppers billboard with its red 1-800 number. It was erected a year ago to replace the one that read "Martensville: Saskatchewan's Fastest Growing Community," which it isn't any more, not since the Sterling scandal broke.

When you hit town, you'll have trouble figuring out which way to turn because there are no signs pointing to the Sterling house, and no natural landmarks like rivers or hills to guide you. But no matter which way you choose, you won't get lost in such a small place. If you do, look for "The Hooter," the community-newspaper office, and ask for directions or go to the Chinese restaurant and sit as long as you want over a Coke. Owner Jack Wong is friendly. So is the waitress at the Adobe Inn, though you might wonder what she's got to smile about, and I doubt it's the view from her kitchen window at the end of her shift. There are no lakes in Martensville, and few trees old enough to provide shade. You won't see people strolling around downtown, for there is none. Even if there were, for most of the year it's too cold at this latitude to walk outside. Most people drive to the corner store. Or shop in Saskatoon malls. Otherwise, they spend their time fending off the ice and snow, and so do their buildings.

Some streets in Martensville look decidedly poorer, some richer. Some, in the spirit of Saskatchewan co-operatism, look both at the same time, like the one on which a handful of trailer homes squats beside a tiny house no bigger than a garage, right next to a new monster home. Among the hundreds of houses in the neatly numbered streets, I see only one with a sun room, tacked on to permit a view of the snow piles in the yard and the icicles on the eavestroughs. Most other windows in town are small, draped warily in sheers to shut out the view and prying eyes like mine. What is there to see, I wonder, from either side of the window?

There aren't any tourist attractions in Martensville, but there are eight churches. Three of them are Mennonite, one the "Old Colony" that adheres to traditional Mennonite ways. This is the Bible Belt. In summer, to the northeast of town, signs proudly proclaim Gospel Tent Meetings, Gospel Jamborees and Bible Camps. About thirty miles east of Martensville, on Highway 11, sits the Bethany Bible College. Drive another few miles up the road, past the postcard-perfect farms, and you'll come to the Mennonite Seniors' Residence. Along the way, non-denominational cows praise God's plenty beside the road as they chew their cud. The canola yellowing in the summer sun gives thanks, and billowy clouds drift in a sky without corners. When I'm out here, I feel free too, glad to be alive. If I forget all my cares for one minute and let my heart float free, I get close to God and nature. I feel blessed to see and hear, and believe that this very day — this very place — was created for me.

Maybe this was how Isaac Martens felt when, in 1939, he bought 240 acres of this land. Wanting to share his wealth, while not appreciating the consequence of impregnating the fertile soil with concrete foundations or of paving over the ancient prairie grasses, he carved up the land for lots. In 1947, the Martens family had the first road built, and the first school, and donated a large lot to the hamlet's first church, the Mennonite Mission. Martens's new neighbours wanted this God-fearing man to go down in history. So when the local newspaper announced a contest to name the place in 1953, it awarded the $40 prize to the person who suggested "Martensville." Martensville was declared a hamlet in 1958, a village in 1966, and a town in 1969. The population tripled, increasing from 1,000 in 1976 to almost 3,000 in the next ten years, during which proud parents pencilled the growth of their kids on new bathroom doors. As the children grew in size and number, Martensville did too, becoming what the billboard outside town said it was: the fastest-growing community in Saskatchewan.

During the early boom, people snapped up Martens's lots for as little as $50 each. Many of the newcomers weren't Mennonite like Martens, but Catholic, Baptist, and even those who'd never set foot inside a church. As the new, unfamiliar persuasions swelled the bedroom community with their numbers, some Mennonites moved out. The more orthodox left for other small towns where they could protect their ways and avoid the godless urban contamination creeping towards Martensville. Others stayed and married non-Mennonites. Some say the breakup of the Mennonite brethren weakened the moral fibre of Martensville. It's hard to say what Old Man Martens would have thought about the changes if he'd still been alive in the 1960s.

Originally, Grandfather Martens and his neighbours had planned a cooperative community that ran on Mennonite time. School started earlier in the year than elsewhere to allow extra days off for the Mennonite children who celebrated religious holidays throughout the year. The children's parents paid no school taxes for years because the Department of Education did, calling the Martensville school "government-aided" and using public funds to hire teachers and subsidize students to swell the ranks from nearby farms. By 1959, the student body had grown to a hundred, granddaughter Martha Martens among them, and the three small school buildings bulged at the seams. When the townspeople built their new concrete-block, six-room school, they recycled the three old buildings: one became a club house for the Mennonite Mission, one a garage, and one was used as scrap lumber.

From the start, the Martensville settlers — like the earlier Temperance Colony pioneers ten miles to the south — had frowned on the sale and public consumption of liquor. As time went on and outsiders moved in, not everyone wanted a dry town. Periodic votes on drink were held. When ballots were tallied for the 1978 campaign, the religious element carried the vote and tippling continued in the town of 1,300 behind closed doors. Then, in 1980, when 263 people voted in favour of drinking in public places and 198 voted against it, the Yes side finally got its way. One restaurant bought a licence so townspeople could order a bottle of beer or a glass of wine with their meal. The mayor of Martensville himself took a hand in the about-face, building a liquor outlet in his convenience store.

There have been other changes too. Gone is the agrarian harmony that once grew in the rich, dark soil. Now the last holdout farms at the edge of town struggle for survival as hundreds of cars belch south to Saskatoon each morning and back again at night, returning from jobs in the sprawling city to the apparent tranquillity of the tiny bedroom community. The sky arching over Martensville is just as blue as ever, but now the highway to town is flanked by a dump, a headstone maker, and the Saskatoon Pick-A-Part, a massive graveyard of cars to cannibalize.

Martensville could be any small community. I've seen it winter and summer, and it always has the same shortage of trees. On a cold February day, at recess, small children climb around on their metal "castle" in the playground of Valley Manor School. At the Sports Centre down the street, two teams of teens slip and slide on the indoor rink, trying to dunk their ball in the garbage can the goalie holds slyly out of reach. This is basketball-on-ice, the reputed invention of the teachers of Martensville. Around here, a lot of time is ice time. When school's done for the day, the kids skate or play hockey at the rink, not far from the glass cases of pee-wee team trophies, while parents curl at the club next door. The major winter pastimes — hockey and bingo — grind to a halt for midwinter "Mushermania," when the burghers of Martensville stage dogsled races and burn their Christmas trees in a giant bonfire.

When summer finally comes, for a month or two, everyone sheds their clothes as far as decency permits. Parents in jogging shorts bike on treeless streets, tots in tow proudly balancing on training wheels. The bigger kids, who've gained independence and maybe a new swimsuit, zoom along on their bikes and Rollerblades. Teens in denim cutoffs and tractor caps roar to the mall for ice cream in pick-up trucks jammed with friends. When the evening family barbecue is over, moms in shorts relax with coffee and gossip with friends, confident their kids are safe even though out of sight.

But never again will the mothers of Martensville relax quite the way they used to. Their troubles began the day the town fathers hired a policewoman. Their innocence faded the night she found a long-forgotten file. Their tranquillity ended when she launched a full-scale investigation and laid criminal charges against several townspeople, including the operators of an unlicensed daycare and five policemen.

Constable Claudia Bryden, May 29, 1993.

Her name is Claudia Bryden. When she joined the tiny Martensville force, she was fresh out of the RCMP Academy in Regina, married for the second time and the mother of two. Less than a month into her new job, Bryden heard the first complaint against a young man, Travis Sterling, did some digging, and found it was not the first on file. Within days, she received phone calls from other people alleging that children had been sexually abused at the Sterling house. She investigated the matter for weeks, spoke with children in town, and eventually accumulated evidence from half the children she spoke to. The first allegation, that Travis Sterling had sexually abused a young girl at the daycare, was just the tip of the iceberg. When, in the following months, Bryden interviewed 30 or so daycare children, some pointed their fingers at the same young man, at his parents who ran the daycare, a young woman, and five police officers.

The 3,500 residents of Martensville took sides and sought to comfort one another. Before long, they had forfeited their privacy to TV cameras and tape recorders from Saskatoon and other cities across the country. Their anger became the stuff of the national supper-hour news, their dirty linen the subject of commentary from Toronto.

Some days I feel like Claudia Bryden must have, full of uncertainty and self-doubt. A rookie policewoman and a rookie court reporter. After twenty-five years as an educator (teacher, administrator, textbook editor), I have only recently turned to journalism — and even more recently, to courtroom reporting. When you've written as many "lifestyle" magazine articles as I have, your brain turns to mush and you need some meat to sink your teeth into. Kids. Justice. These things appeal to me, especially when they go together. I'm a freelance writer, with no allegiance to any publication in particular and no idea where my next cheque is coming from. Now on my fourth career, I'm a bit wiser, a bit greener than the other reporters, and probably poorer too. So I was relieved to hear I'd have income as long as the trial lasted, and was happy I'd earn it doing something I believe in. Having just signed a contract with a Regina film company, I would soon begin to do courtroom research for a movie about the Martensville scandal. And possibly write a book of my own.

If I played my cards right, I could use the same research for both the film and the book. As with any project of this nature, there was far more research than writing involved, and so I started in Prince Albert ("P.A."), an hour north of Saskatoon. In the P.A. library I waded through stacks of old copies of the city directory to find information about some of the alleged villains in this story: Ron Sterling, Jim Elstad, and Darryl Ford. According to the directory, the Sterling and Elstad families lived in Prince Albert at the same time, from about 1973 to 1980, during which time the Fords also came and went. Coincidentally, the men in the three families worked in law enforcement — Ron Sterling at the P.A. Provincial Correctional Centre, Jim Elstad and Darryl Ford as city police officers. In itself this is not particularly compelling news, since Saskatchewan is known for its endless networks. But it comes as a surprise when the same three families live in Prince Albert in the 1970s and move to Martensville in the 1980s. By the time Constable Claudia Bryden came to Martensville in 1991, all the characters in this morality play knew one another, by accident or design.

The story that eventually made national news started in January 1988, when a child protection worker, asked by a school guidance counsellor, called the Martensville Police Department alleging that ten-year-old "Sally" had been sexually abused. The caller told Darryl Ford, then chief of police, that the abuser was Travis Sterling, the son of Ron and Linda Sterling, a Martensville couple who ran an unlicensed home daycare. The police called in the younger Sterling for questioning and opened a file on him. After talking to Travis, who was nineteen at the time, Ford put his report in a drawer. The girl's parents waited for the police to do something, but no charges were laid until Bryden came to town.

More than three years went by between the time Darryl Ford closed the file on Travis Sterling and Claudia Bryden opened it again. On September 20, 1991, her first day on the job, she met the Sterling family, when fellow officer Jim Elstad invited her to go for coffee at the Sterling house. Taking her under his wing, her "trainer" took her to meet the man and woman he'd known since his days in Prince Albert ten years ago, and the four chatted in the homey Sterling kitchen.

Bryden must have found it strange to hear about the same family just days later, under very different circumstances. That's how small-town Saskatchewan works: from one week to the next you never know with whom you'll cross paths, or swords, and there's little hope of avoiding either. Bryden was on duty when a father contacted the police to say that Travis Sterling had abused his daughter, "Janey," at the Sterling daycare. Jim Elstad talked with the man, then turned the complaint over to Bryden, who soon discovered that this was the second, not first, such complaint against Travis Sterling. After a tip from the secretary that led Bryden to search through the files, she stumbled across the three-year-old dossier, dated January 1988, crumpled and incomplete in a cardex file.

Had Constable Bryden been a long-time resident of Martensville, been male instead of female and "one of the boys," had she been less zealous and more cynical about her job, less anxious to prove herself — had she been any of these things, she might have just let this second complaint against Travis Sterling pass, too. But she was not.

Claudia Jane Bryden was born on June 3, 1959, and grew up in rural Manitoba. After attending university, in 1986, she enrolled in the RCMP Training Academy in Regina. After graduating, she was posted to Gimli, Manitoba, where she lived for a couple of years before leaving the RCMP to marry. In April 1990, she and her new husband, Dan, moved to Saskatoon, where he was hired by the Saskatoon Police Force. The following year Claudia applied for part-time work with the tiny Martensville police force, and got the job. At five feet three inches, weighing not an ounce more than 120 pounds soaking wet, Bryden looks fragile, the kind of woman men might instinctively want to protect — until she opens her mouth. When she does, you hear the willpower steady her voice and sense her steel backbone. Her fragile skin seems to contradict the impression, as does her small delicate head; and it seems unlikely her fair hair would ever be out of place or easily let down. A woman might respond to Bryden's particularity with respect, but a man might be more inclined to take her primness as a personal challenge. This woman was an outsider, and a pretty one, whom the Martensville police officers could admire. From a distance.

The Martensville force had a macho history. Former police Chief Ford had, apparently, liked to come to work in denim cutoffs and made little attempt to hide his beer belly. Mike Johnston, who served after him, was the subject of a sexual harassment complaint filed with the Saskatchewan Human Rights Commission by the station's secretary in late 1992. The following year the Martensville police adopted a personal harassment policy, and in early 1996 the Commission adjudicated $10,000 compensation to the woman for "injury to feelings and self-respect," to be paid in equal amounts by Johnston and the Martensville Board of Police Commissioners. No matter how macho some of the officers were, the last thing Claudia Bryden — or anyone — would have expected them to be accused of was molesting children. In a small town like this, she expected to encounter her fair share of high-speed drivers, break-and-enter artists, car thieves, and shoplifters. But she probably never imagined she'd investigate sexual abuse charges on such a grand scale.

When Bryden investigated the second allegation, then the first, and interviewed children who pointed fingers at her colleagues, she had a choice to make: disregard the allegations or investigate them further, in the process abandoning hope of ever being "one of the boys." Since her choice was really no choice at all, she investigated the allegations, as indeed she was required to do by law. Why she chose to do so with such vigour — as the defence lawyers argued in court — is a matter for much speculation, and it eventually landed Bryden herself in court. Her zeal ruined her police career and, temporarily, her health. But it also put an end to the alleged abuse of the children who went to the Sterling home daycare.

The Sterling house, covered in light blue siding, sits in the middle of Martensville on a regulation-sized lot on a numbered street, surrounded by other bungalows that look unremarkably like it. The front lawn now has a small flower bed and two saplings. The main entry is at the side of the house. But the driveway has different vehicles now that the Sterlings' cars and blue pickup truck are no longer there. In fact, the Sterlings themselves are no longer there. No longer do the sounds of neighbourhood children fill the house at dawn, as they did when the handful of kids ate their breakfast in the kitchen, then scrambled down to the partially finished basement to play. Linda Sterling started to run the unlicensed daycare when her own three children were young, and continued to do so when they were grown. By 1988, her husband, Ron, had his own demanding job at the Saskatoon Correctional Centre. Her oldest son had long since left Martensville for the west coast, her adult daughter had also vacated her bedroom and now lived elsewhere in Saskatchewan. Only her nineteen-year-old son, Travis, still lived at home.

When a child protection worker complained to police that Travis Sterling had molested a girl called Sally, the girl's parents must have wondered why the officers did little about it. Not until almost four years later, when the father of "Janey" reported the second complaint against Travis, did someone finally do something. If the parents of the daycare kids had seen marks on their children's bodies, they could take heart that a police investigation was now under way. If they had heard strange stories from their children, they could console themselves that Claudia Bryden was trying to find out what had really happened.

When Bryden interviewed the children, their stories trickled out, and sometimes resembled each other in detail. When one daycare boy talked about a blue building somewhere outside Martensville, the boy's father told the former mayor, who flew his private plane over the town and outlying farms. He spotted a blue building that closely matched the boy's description and told the Martensville police chief about it. The chief went to the building just north of town and took three photos. He had the film developed at the drugstore and gave the prints to Bryden. Armed with these photos, Bryden widened her investigation, interviewing more daycare children and showing them the pictures. Some immediately recognized the building and called it "The Place." Some alleged that, at The Place as well as at the Sterling house, they'd been abused by several adults: Ron, Linda, and Travis Sterling; Jim Elstad and Darryl Ford; three other police officers; and Tammy, a young woman who boarded with the Sterlings. Some of the kids identified these same people when Bryden showed them I.D. photos the police had taken.

When Bryden heard the kids accuse her own colleagues, she told her supervisor she wanted nothing more to do with the investigation, and maybe the job itself. By reminding her of the importance of the work, and agreeing to remove some of the load from her shoulders, Inspector Wayne McGillivray persuaded Bryden to stay. But she needed help, she said, which she was tired of asking for and not getting. Why, she wanted to know, had no one come to back her up the fall day she'd radioed for help from the scene of a drunk-driver accident? Why, when she sought guidance from the Saskatchewan Department of Justice in Regina — apparently making many more calls than she got in return — did she obtain neither formal assistance nor full-time guidance? Apparently no one at the department criticized the techniques she used to interview the children, though later in court they would be subject to great debate. As one police officer in Saskatchewan described the state of child sexual-abuse investigations in the early 1990s, "the expertise wasn't available in this part of the country."

It certainly wasn't available in Martensville. So Bryden called Corporal Rod Moor, a Saskatoon officer who worked on the same force as her husband and who had years of experience interviewing children traumatized by events such as sexual abuse. Moor was ordered by his superiors to help Bryden pursue the allegations of sexual abuse and, together, they questioned more kids. One boy said he'd been photographed at the daycare; another said he'd been photographed naked. The tiny Martensville force, confronted with the scope of the case, requested help from the RCMP. In late 1991, the combined squad swooped down on the Sterling house with a search warrant. The officers found a peach-coloured vibrator, forty-three videos (including three hard-core porn videos), and some skin magazines, which they seized, bagged, and photographed. When Claudia Bryden showed photos of the seized items to a few of the daycare kids, she later testified, they recognized the items at once.

Because of things the children said during the interviews and items the officers found at the Sterling house, police charged Travis Sterling, the son, with sexual assault. The following month, December 1991, they charged Linda Sterling; and a month later, Ron Sterling. In the next five months, a second raid took place on the Sterling house and more charges were laid — many of them, as it happened, on Bryden's thirty-third birthday. By June 1992, more than 100 charges of assault, including sexual assault, had been brought against the three Sterlings and Jim Elstad; and thirty-six laid against Darryl Ford and three other officers, including one officer from the Saskatoon Police Force and one from the RCMP. Tammy, the young woman who boarded with the Sterlings, was also charged.

Court dates were set for 1993 and, from the original thirty or so children interviewed, half of whom alleged abuse, seven prepared to testify. At the same time, the community held its own trial. Long before the legal trial began, many people in Martensville and Saskatoon concluded that the Sterlings were guilty, and Tammy too; those who took the opposite view accused the children of lying and said the trial would be a travesty of justice. The Martensville police force was a shambles. Months after the daycare scandal, the small force was disbanded because the mayor said the officers were "out here in left field" without the needed backup from the province. Besides, having peace officers of their own cost the townsfolk too much money.

Many Martensville residents resented the rookie policewoman for upsetting the town and their lives, and some called her names. For her part, Bryden was afraid for her own safety. What woman wouldn't be afraid if, as

Bryden later testified in court, she was stalked and received threatening phone calls? Eventually the pressure got to her.

The daycare children began intensive psychotherapy while their parents waited for the trials to begin. More and more people took sides. Some put signs in their front windows saying "We Believe the Children." Eventually, the Sterlings were ordered by the court to live with their inlaws in Prince Albert and forbidden to return to Martensville.

Did crimes take place in Martensville? Only the children will ever know for sure what happened. Whether they told the truth or not, their accusations unleashed primitive fears and irrational forces in the community, which responded to the alleged daycare crimes in as dark and mysterious a way as the crimes themselves. Those who support the Sterlings say the police brainwashed the children; those who believe the children say the Sterlings practised satanic ritual abuse.

Could such things happen in a small family town like Martensville? Could a home-daycare operator be guilty of sexually abusing children in her home? Did her husband, her son, a young female boarder, and five police officers lock kids in cages and freezers, sodomize them, and threaten to harm them if they told? On the eve of the first trial, everyone in Saskatchewan wanted answers, and I was still naive enough to think I could get them, just as Constable Bryden had once believed.

The
First
Trial

Muzzling the Media

Ron Sterling, June 4, 1992. CBC-TV photo courtesy *Saskatoon StarPhoenix*

Although the trial is months away, you'd never know it from reading the *Saskatoon StarPhoenix* over breakfast. "Martensville Nightmare" shrieks the headline today, above a photo of Ron Sterling, pudgy and handcuffed as he's led from his house by police. For what seems like forever, we've begun each morning's newscast with "... Ron, Linda, and Travis Sterling ..." — the father, mother, and son charged with more than 100 counts of sex crimes.

Here in Saskatoon, ten minutes south of Martensville, the journalists have become tightrope artists in a media circus, walking the fine line between freedom of speech and fear of libel. Some of the trial lawyers want the judge to slap a publication ban on the trial. Until that happens, the lawyers for the *StarPhoenix* are taking a liberal view of what can be printed, and so far no one has sued the paper for libelling the Sterlings. I feel manipulated by the publisher's need to sell papers, which seems to hinge on keeping readers titillated, at almost any cost.

It feels strange being a journalist when I read the daily paper because I do it very critically. I need to see why each story was written and want to be convinced that every one of them is not only important, but also fair and two-sided. When a story sounds lopsided, or smells sloppy, I get on my high horse, as I did last summer. One day I became so fed up with the *StarPhoenix* that I wrote to the publisher, complaining about the coverage of the Martensville scandal, in particular a piece on satanic ritual abuse that made it sound rampant in this part of Saskatchewan. The publisher wrote back to say the story was fair and intimated I was wrong to think it was sensationalist and one-sided. My favourite sentence in his reply about the Martensville story was: "I make no apologies for the exhaustive coverage this newspaper has provided." Nor did he make any apology for the "nightmare" headlines, which possibly contributed to whipping the community into a frenzy and jeopardizing the Sterlings' chances of getting a fair trial in Saskatchewan. Their lawyers are so worried they plan to conduct a formal poll to see where in this province their clients can get a hearing from an unbiased jury.

I sit at the computer all morning, thinking about the Sterlings. Did they really do the things they're accused of? Would a family run a daycare just to have access to kids and abuse them? Was Travis abused by his parents? Were the Sterling parents abused by their parents? What about the alleged involvement of the police? Were there satanic rituals? A kiddie porn ring? Over coffee, I ask the opinion of a real estate agent, a friend who knows the community. This man calls kiddie porn a veritable "industry" in Saskatchewan, but I don't believe a word of it. So I ask another friend, a physician who exudes an air of reliability. To my amazement, he confirms the "industry" theory, strictly off the record. Maybe the journalist who wrote the piece on satanic ritual abuse for the *StarPhoenix* knows something I don't.

I go to Regina to meet a writer to discuss the film script about the trial. The bus trip is just long enough to digest the book *Anatomy of a Nightmare*, a study of sexual abuse and a two-year-long child-custody trial in southern Ontario. I read it from cover to cover, partly to prepare myself for the trial next week, and partly to see what has already been written on the topic. The book makes me wonder: What happens to kids who are abused? Do they ever trust anyone again? Can they ever enjoy sex? Do they suffer from lifelong health problems?

The author of the book, Martyn Kendrick, learned a lot during his two years in court. Although I don't fully realize it yet, Kendrick captured the central issue in child abuse cases when he wrote these words in 1987: "As the public becomes aware that unfounded reports are falsely inflating abuse statistics, they will respond less favourably to truly abused children. And it is these children, these beaten and abused children, who need the best of our resources and directed compassion. Unless changes are made now, the potentially valuable force of public concern will serve only to increase mistrust and hysteria."

Regina. Thank God, the Hotel Saskatchewan is just around the corner from the bus terminal. I wouldn't want to have to walk very far on a day like today, when it's minus 30 but the wind makes it feel like minus 50. My writer friend is waiting in the dining room, where we eat and talk business. Naturally, she wants to know what rumours I've heard about the "nightmare." I tell her what a friend told me, that the Sterlings might have known about the police search two weeks before it took place, enough time for them to clean house and fill six or seven green garbage bags and take them to the Martensville dump. According to the friend, a daycare parent drove by the Sterling house one evening and saw several garbage bags waiting to be picked up. He picked them up himself, put them in his trunk and later rifled through them, but found nothing of much significance.

If Martensville is a goldfish bowl, Saskatoon to the south is, too. In this city of 210,000, everyone seems to know everyone and everything. Short on privacy and long on gossip, that's Saskatoon. Knowing everyone else's business might be the best thing about the place. But their knowing yours is the worst, especially if you have something to hide, or people think you do. Angry parents now accuse Ron Sterling, even before he has been tried, of being a paedophile and a liar. Now that the three Sterlings have appeared in the *StarPhoenix* and had their faces broadcast on the supper-hour news, everyone who lives in either Martensville or Saskatoon knows what the three look like. And when they drive to Saskatoon from Prince Albert, where the court has ordered them to live for the time being, I wonder if they're wounded by the angry stares on the street or embarrassed by the tongue wagging about town.

The court of public opinion has met daily, in the weeks leading to the trial. Over the back fence, almost everyone in Martensville and Saskatoon has had a say about the Sterlings and come to a verdict. "We Believe the Children" cries a crooked sign in a front window on a suburban street. "Star chamber" is how a poster stapled to a downtown lamp post labels the forthcoming Sterling trial. When you casually count the signs and posters in town, it looks as though half the community wants to lynch the Sterlings, while the other half wants to lynch the lynchers. I hope the people of Martensville and Saskatoon will have the patience to listen to the courtroom evidence, and the courage to change their minds if they learn something new.

Tomorrow, February 17, the lawyers debate the pros and cons of media coverage of the trial, and the judge decides if he'll allow reporters to stay in his courtroom. His ruling, which is his alone to make, will reach far beyond the courtroom doors and influence every page turner and channel changer in the province. After he rules on the amount of media coverage he'll allow, he will hear all the trial evidence and decide the appropriate sentence for Tammy. Now twenty-one years old, she was only a teen when she allegedly committed the crimes against the kids.

There's a lot in the news these days about young offenders. Two teenage boys in Montreal have recently bludgeoned a minister and his wife with a baseball bat because the elderly couple were "cheap" and never gave one of the boys a Christmas tip, to thank him for being their paper boy. No one ever thinks children can be that evil or soulless, but some kids live by their own set of laws. When they rape and murder, what should we do? Try them in private and give them a second chance at life, or tell everyone their names and treat them like adult criminals? I have mixed feelings.

Consider twelve-year-old Tony, a kid in my French class in the 1970s. Tony was tough. He liked to shoplift at lunch in the malls near the school. The other kids said he carried a knife. I was scared to turn my back on him. One day, after lunch, Tony didn't return to school. When I asked where he was, a classmate, clearly proud to have witnessed the event, said the police had arrested Tony for shoplifting at the mall just a few minutes before. I can't say I was sorry. It was probably the best thing that could have happened to him. It certainly was the best thing for the class because Tony hated school, my class in particular, and made everyone's life miserable. The vice principal never could understand why I had so much trouble with the Grade 8 class, and this boy in particular. One day, when my thirty classic underachievers, most of them latch-key kids, became particularly unreachable, I told them to colour in silence instead of trying to speak French. When the vice principal found out, he called me to his office and asked what I was doing with the class. I said I couldn't control the kids any more, let alone teach them. He offered to take them for a week, not out of kindness, I'm sure, but to show me the error of my ways. For those five days, he kept them in line. He didn't teach the class much French — how could he, when he didn't speak a word of it? — but he did keep the kids on their best behaviour. At the end of the week, he told me the class was ready for my return on the Monday, but said he had serious concerns about my "classroom management" skills.

And so did I. I requested a transfer when the year ended. To my horror, there were even more Tonys at the new suburban-ghetto school. I lasted another four years and then quit teaching in Toronto for good.

According to those who knew Tammy, she wasn't a menace like Tony. One woman who used to teach in Martensville told me she was a quiet girl who got reasonably good grades, despite serious health problems. According to another woman, Tammy kept her marks up by working hard and doing homework in the school library, sometimes till late in the evening. The girl boarded with the Sterlings and sometimes helped Linda look after the daycare children. I wonder how Tammy will sleep tonight. She's diabetic, and stress plays havoc with diabetes.

Under the Criminal Code of Canada, "any proceedings against an accused shall be held in open court," but all children under the age of nineteen need protection from public scrutiny. That's the question the judge will examine today: If "Tammy" abused the children she was, technically, a child herself at the time and, if her name is made public, her life would be changed forever. So the five trial lawyers, representing both the prosecution and the defence, have been scheduled to argue the matter in courtroom 5, Queen's Bench chambers in Saskatoon, at 9: 30 a.m. sharp, February 17. In turn, each will have a chance to influence the judge's interpretation of the Criminal Code and what it says about protecting children in court. Then he will decide whether to exclude the public from the courtroom, put the child witnesses behind screens, and restrict journalists from publishing the courtroom proceedings. All the lawyers want to protect the anonymity of the kids, but not all want to do it at the expense of closing the doors to the public and gagging the media. So the handful of hired guns will spend today and tomorrow haggling before Judge Albert Lavoie, to decide whose rights are paramount. After listening to their arguments, he must juggle the right to privacy of the two child plaintiffs' in question, the accused woman's right to a fair trial, her right to anonymity in view of her juvenile status at the time of the alleged crime, the public's right to hear the story, and the media's right to tell it. Good luck.

Reluctantly, Tammy walks into the courtroom, her father's arm wrapped tightly around her shoulder. It's strange to see an adult woman hugged this way by her father in public, as though she's a little girl. Though she's twenty-one years old, Tammy looks no more than thirteen or fourteen. Apparently she acts the way she looks. According to the psychologist who tested her for the court, Tammy is psychologically and emotionally immature, more like a fifteen or sixteen-year old than a young woman.

Tammy is less than five feet tall. She has shoulder-length natural blonde hair and pink cheeks that contribute to her innocent, childlike appearance —

ironic in light of the charges. She looks as though she has been crying, and, when she walks over and sits directly in front of me, I can see she has been biting her nails. The public gallery, where I sit, extends for eight or nine rows of wooden benches. The front row has been reserved for journalists — about a dozen, mostly local, except for one or two from out-of-town and a man from Toronto who says he's writing a book. Behind the media row sit twenty or thirty people, mostly middle-aged. There's an air of expectancy mixed with doubt. Tammy is about to be tried for assaulting and raping two young boys at the Sterling daycare in Martensville. She is charged with ten counts of criminal behaviour.

At 9:30 sharp, the judge enters the room with a regal flourish, as though stepping on stage. When the court clerk instructs us to stand till the judge is seated, no one makes a sound or dares to look sideways. Though this is standard procedure, my first day in court feels like a throwback to childhood. Now that I'm an adult, I'm used to sitting and standing when I please, not when someone tells me to. I've got a lot to learn.

The charges against Tammy include sexual assault, sexually touching a person under fourteen years, confinement, threatening to assault with a weapon, and uttering a death threat. She allegedly committed these offences against children from the time she was sixteen till she turned nineteen. According to the Young Offenders Act, she is eligible for a trial of her own, separate from the three accused Sterlings. And because she is considered a "Y.O.," she is not able to choose trial by jury. Judge Albert Lavoie will be her only "tryer of fact." He is middle-aged and wiry, with glasses and curly hair. He looks kind and intelligent, though irascible. I'm glad I'm not Tammy, especially when the ten counts against her are read aloud.

For the lawyers hired by the media, a lot is at stake in their push to break legal ground and establish a precedent for the press coverage of such a sensational trial. They are pitted against Tammy's lawyer, poised to protect her right to privacy, and the prosecuting lawyers who want to protect the two child victims' right to anonymity.

Judge Lavoie, like an impatient professor, removes his glasses and scowls at the lawyers as though wayward students. He asks: Have you done your homework? We have, Your Honour. We've scoured the reference books and the computerized QUICKLAW, in search of precedents to follow. We've found some, but not many. We're ready to tell you what we know about media coverage of previous trials involving children and to fight to the death for our clients.

One by one, the legal combatants draw arguments from their cases and toss them back and forth in front of the judge, who acts as referee and scorekeeper. This intricate game of ping-pong goes on for hours: Are representatives of the media also representatives for the public? Are the interests of the media the same as the interests of the public? Should the media — the local radio and TV stations, and the only local newspaper — be granted status in the courtroom? The judge, now the student, listens closely and takes notes. Whose right is greater, the children's right to privacy or the public's right to know? The right to have secrets, or the right to tell all?

Judge Lavoie knows we live in the media-dominated 1990s. Though he holds the gavel in his hands, he does not hold the microphone. Unless he lays down strict guidelines for those who do, they will invade his bailiwick and, before he knows it, undermine with their nightly news stories the ancient authority of his court. He wants to find a legal precedent to satisfy the journalists' insatiable appetite, while respecting the children's right to privacy. Failing that, he must make a ruling that will reconcile the ubiquitous nature of the media with the hermetic nature of the court. He is King Canute, sitting alone on his throne on the beach, trying to hold back the tide. If he does not succeed, he and the daycare children could easily drown in the sea of media.

After much deliberation, the judge rules. There will be no publication whatever of the courtroom proceedings or of any evidence until all the trials in this case are over, which will probably not be until 1994, at the earliest. Hordes of people who can't come to the trial — the public — will know nothing about it, while the few who do come to the courtroom every day — also the public — will know every detail. And even though journalists are not supposed to talk publicly about what goes on inside these four walls, there's nothing stopping the other people from talking once they get outside. So much for the children's privacy and protection.

By imposing the media ban, Lavoie is trying to influence not only what journalists say, but also what the public sees and hears now and in future. He hopes that if he protects the community's eyes and ears during this first trial, he will foster judicial impartiality for the second trial six months from now, especially when it's time to select the jury. Hear-no-evil-see-no-evil-speak-no-evil. I have my doubts about his strategy to keep the media muzzled till the next trial and doubt a ban will stop the public polarization or improve the local mood. Besides, the media have already done so much pre-trial coverage, the ban may lock the barn door after the horse is out. And there's always the grapevine.

On the other hand, what can the judge do? He has as much responsibility to the judicial system, and to the accused, as he has to the children. He must censor the proceedings of this trial to protect the jurors for the next trial, or there could be a miscarriage of justice. I thought the jury system operated on the premise that jurors can, and will, reach their verdict on the courtroom evidence alone and wonder if Lavoie lacks faith in it. Maybe he has been in the business long enough to know it's hard at the best of times to find twelve competent adults who can, and will, set aside their prejudices, let alone find these people when the community is highly divided. I wonder if he has discussed the need for the ban with his colleagues in the judge's private dining room, and whether he knows who the judge will be for the next trial, that of the three Sterlings.

The Charter of Rights and Freedoms gives every Canadian accused of a crime the right to a fair and public hearing, for a very good reason: to protect defendants from arbitrary or incompetent prosecution, and to expose the justice system's workings to public scrutiny. When the media are forbidden to broadcast trial proceedings, the public, increasingly intolerant of patronizing behaviour, wants to know why. Consider the Karla Homolka case in Toronto. The media ban, imposed by Judge Francis Kovacs to ensure a fair trial for Paul Bernardo, left the public in the dark, desperate to swap rumours. The Homolka ban may have silenced Canadian reporters, but not American journalists, who transmitted their stories to Canada electronically. So much for a media bans.

Secrecy forecloses the possibility of public discussion and fair criticism of the court. "Publicity is the very soul of justice. It keeps the judge, while trying, under trial," according to a former chief justice of the Supreme Court of Canada. It keeps the system honest. Everyone knows it, and people have debated the question of open court since the invention of the printing press in 1440. Journalists believe their job is to keep the public informed, and the Saskatoon journalists hate being muzzled. They've got papers to sell, and airtime to fill. I'm sure the CBC will appeal Judge Lavoie's publication ban. So far, reporters have lost the free-speech battle: We can say absolutely nothing outside Lavoie's courtroom, not even that we're here, till the entire case is closed.

Muzzling journalists is pretty cut-and-dried compared to Lavoie's next problem: our role or "status" inside his court. If he sees fit, he could kick us out of the courtroom. Lavoie listens patiently as the two lawyers for the Crown and the lawyer for the children try to convince him to do it. Then the CBC lawyer says all media outlets are not "equally representative of the public," and that perhaps the CBC has a bigger audience than Armadale Communications, the owner of the *StarPhoenix*. Ignoring the remark, the *StarPhoenix* lawyer asserts that all media are "custodians" of the people's right to know. Journalists provide the "window" for the public, testifies a reporter for the newspaper, to which a lawyer for the Crown asks how the *StarPhoenix* knows what the public should read about the trial. This causes a few ironic smiles, mine among them. When the reporter says that the *StarPhoenix*, if permitted to publish information about the trial, would steer clear of "graphic details," I want to jump up and shout, "Oh, yeah? It's not the graphic stuff your newspaper prints that offends me. It's what's between the lines. For example, that piece on satanic ritual abuse and the symptoms to watch for. Now that was a story rich in innuendo, if ever there was one."

I wonder if Judge Lavoie ever gets tired of hearing these debates. When he has heard enough, he decrees that the media have sufficient interest in the case to remain in the courtroom. The others can gripe all they like, but at least we've won the right to stay and take notes. Whether local reporters ever get to use the notes in a timely manner is another matter. Quite frankly, the gag suits me just fine, because I estimate it will be lifted at just about the time I finish writing the book, if I decide to do one. I wouldn't want readers afflicted with trial overkill before it's my turn to tell the story.

Lavoie has decided we can stay in his courtroom, but that's all. Till the day the ban is lifted, all we can do is take notes and keep our mouths shut while preparing to tell the public — after the fact — what went on in this room.

After the judge's big decision, several of us go to the Tip Top Café, to kibbitz and have coffee. The reporter for the *StarPhoenix* wryly says he can't even tell his readers that today he took the witness stand to defend their right to know. Absentmindedly, I use the real name of one of the child plaintiffs, which provokes the CBC reporter to pretend he's Judge Lavoie and to snap half seriously that I'm in contempt of court.

Lavoie has silenced the journalists. Now he has to help the children talk. What changes will be required to make the courtroom safe for them to do so?

To help answer these questions, the Crown calls on Rod Butler, an expert in child psychology. He has provided therapy to child victims and young offenders in the Saskatoon area for twenty years, and for the past year has counselled two of the alleged victims, both boys, aged nine and eleven. Butler's unlined face and full lips belie his middle-age and make him look a bit like a child himself. His voice is very soft, his manner extremely gentle, and he's tall — just the kind of friendly giant I'd want to confide in if I were a kid. As an expert witness and someone who knows two of the child plaintiffs, Butler is treated deferentially by both the defence and the prosecution. He quietly explains to the court: there are no fixed rules for dealing with sexually abused children, and you must pay just as much attention to what the children do as to what they say. He is extremely concerned about the boys' welfare and does not want to betray their trust in him. After what they've lived through, he does not want to see them "re-traumatized" by publicity of any kind, or lies. He doesn't want to "deceive" the boys by telling them there'd be no media coverage of their testimony and then have them discover there was.

I'm touched by Butler's dedication to the boys, as everyone else in the room seems to be. He says the two children in this trial disclosed they were sexually abused by numerous perpetrators, including Tammy, as many as eighty or ninety times. They were so severely abused that, in his opinion, they might be traumatized by the mere sight of the accused. Seeing her in court might even cause them to "dissociate" in order to cope with the stress. Butler tells the judge that some of the people who allegedly abused the boys were in uniform. He believes this could be a problem in court, and recommends that court officials wear casual clothes instead of the usual black robes when examining the boys. Judge Lavoie agrees.

Tim White, lawyer for Tammy, asks what kind of backdrop would be best for the boys, and Butler suggests a quiet room with no distractions, such as clocks or windows. He recommends that the boys be permitted to stand when answering the lawyers' questions, to be taller and closer in height to their legal examiners and so lessen the "power differential."

At 6:30 p.m., on February 18, 1993, the prologue is finished and the stage is set for the actual trial of Tammy. Along with the dozen other journalists, I have the right to sit in the courtroom and watch the unfolding drama, but not report what I see and hear until after all the trials are completed. Even then, I will never be allowed to disclose the real names of the young players. I'm exhausted but stimulated by my first day in court. The clerk tells us to stand as Lavoie sweeps out the side door. When he has gone, everyone starts to talk in muted tones. Tammy looks frazzled, but is probably relieved that the day is over. Her trial will begin three weeks from now, on March 8.

The Prosecution

Ringside Seat

It feels like a prizefight. Everyone in the crowd wants action; most know who they're rooting for. If everyone held up a numbered card, from one to ten, I'd be surprised to see a five among them. They would be all ones and tens for Tammy, respectively thumbs-up and thumbs-down.

Like the fans here at ringside, the community is clearly polarized and becoming more so by the day. You're frowned on if you don't have an opinion, and everybody demands to know whose side you're on — Tammy's or the kids'. The ones and tens refuse to speak to me because I'm a five, trying to stay neutral to the end. When I take my seat in the room, a colleague — a one, who swears Tammy's been framed — scowls at me. I'd like to say to her, "Look, I'm here to keep my eyes and mind open and my mouth shut. You do the same." I'm glad I won't have to sit near her constantly defending myself, but in this small room I won't be able to completely avoid her.

The audience, though energized, is sparse. Court officials had expected a large and curious crowd because of the publication ban. The trial coordinator even brought a dozen extra chairs into the courtroom. But more than half the forty-odd seats reserved for the public are empty. Maybe the press gag has dampened curiosity in the community. Most of the ringside seats, reserved for media and redeemable only with our "green cards," are occupied.

Tammy enters the courtroom and takes her place on the other side of a waist-high dividing wall, called the "bar," which is directly in front of my first-row seat. Absentmindedly, I've left my winter coat on the chair and now she sits on it, wedging it under hers for the foreseeable future. She looks preoccupied. Her face is blank, her body still, her fine blonde hair pulled tight in a ponytail.

Crown Prosecutor Leslie Sullivan, March 10, 1993

To one side of her sits a short stocky man, her lawyer, Tim White. On her other side sits a legal-aid lawyer named Don Mullord, pronounced M'lord. The court clerk opens the door at the front of the courtroom, announces the arrival of Judge Lavoie, and tells us to stand. The judge enters and sits down. Then we sit, and he calls the first witness.

Constable Jeff Keyes, a tall, handsome RCMP officer with a moustache, takes the stand. During the next few days, he and other police will describe how they took photos and looked for traces of sexual crimes at a blue building north of Martensville.

The prosecutor questioning him is Montreal-born Leslie Sullivan, who has been practising law for almost twenty years, fifteen of them for the Department of Justice. Throughout her 100 or so jury trials, the woman in her early forties has focused on the human side and, she says, does not think of her witnesses as just files. I understand she takes shark cartilege to fortify herself for this trial, the longest and possibly the most complex in the history of the province. Though I can see only Sullivan's back, I bet her forehead is creased in concentration.

Sullivan chooses her questions slowly and carefully, to help the officer methodically reconstruct his part of the story, which began on June 11, 1992, the day the police searched the blue building north of town. The search yielded five dog collars, two axe handles, a fishing rod, guns, ropes and a metal goblet. Normally, these everyday objects would not have interested police. But when the daycare kids saw the artifacts, they had things to say.

Convinced by the children's reactions that something had occurred at the blue building, which they called The Place, the police did a second search two weeks after the first. They scoured the inside of the building for evidence not visible to the naked eye. Constable Keyes, sounding like a kid with a new toy, explains to Prosecutor Sullivan how he and his colleagues searched for hairs, fibres, and body fluids using the LUMA-LITE, a high-intensity light device.

To search The Place with the LUMA-LITE, Keyes blacked out the sunlight from each room under examination, put on a pair of glasses with rose-coloured lenses, and scoured the rooms on all fours for evidence. Yet even with the help of this high-tech device, and after crawling around for hours, Keyes found no trace of any useful evidence. At the break, in the ladies' room, I tell Sullivan I'm disappointed the trial is off to such a slow start. She says she has just begun to put the puzzle together for the court and promises things will soon pick up. Be patient, she says, and all the pieces will fit together.

After Sullivan's examination of Constable Keyes comes his cross-examination, conducted by Tammy's lawyer, Tim White. The Prince Albert lawyer has pocketed his toothpick and, undoubtedly, speaks more distinctly without it. How, he asks, could the innocent-looking blue building to the north of Martensville be the site of the alleged atrocities, when the LUMA-LITE detected no evidence whatever? Perhaps nothing of the kind ever happened there, the defence lawyer suggests to the officer, and that's why the police found no traces of sperm or blood or fibre or hair.

In fact, it's a wonder the police could find a square inch of floor or furniture to focus the LUMA-LITE on, let alone walk around without tripping over themselves. The Place was a pigsty, according to Sergeant Alan Michael Gillis, the second RCMP officer to take the stand. A neat freak myself, I wonder how the owner, though frequently absent, could stand to live with clothes and papers strewn all over the place. Even in broad daylight, Gillis couldn't make sense of the place. He tried to use Auto Sketch, a sophisticated computer program for drawing diagrams of crime scenes, but because of the mess he couldn't even establish a grid for the software, the first step.

As a seasoned policeman, Gillis hates to complain. He seems embarrassed and admits with a self-deprecating laugh that he wishes he'd been assigned the simple task of photographing the interior of the building instead of trying to sketch it on the computer. Almost everyone chuckles at this, including the judge and five or six older women in the public gallery who probably hate housework. But defence lawyer White doesn't crack a smile. To him Gillis's whining is just another example of police incompetence. He plans to show the police did their job poorly.

White asks Gillis: Why did you raid that particular blue building when there are other blue buildings in the area that might have matched the kids' description just as well? Did the kids describe the building before, or after, you showed them the photos of it? But the chicken-and-egg sequence of events is not clear to me, even after he cross-examines three officers.

As each officer takes the stand, White hammers him: Although you searched the blue building three times, why did you not see fit to secure the place between searches? Why did you never take fingerprints? Why didn't you find incriminating evidence? This last one is the zinger, the no-win question, to which any answer would land the witness in hot water. Knowing this, none of the officers answers. When the three witnesses will not answer, Judge Lavoie does. Straightening his glasses for dramatic effect, he says what's on everyone's mind: Maybe there was nothing to find. Or maybe the police missed the clues. Or perhaps all the clues had been removed by the time of the police search. He has cleared the air and lightened the mood in the room.

At the time of the search of the blue building, the nine-person Martensville Police Department was in a state of turmoil, or so it appears. Between October 1991, when Ed Revesz resigned as police chief, and March 1, 1992, when Mike Johnston was hired to replace him, the Martensville police force had no permanent commanding officer.

In the fall of 1991, in the midst of this administrative mess, Claudia Bryden walked in. Depending on your view of the children's allegations, she was hired at just the right moment or precisely the wrong one. Though she lacked experience in handling sexual-abuse allegations, she didn't shirk from responsibility. By the time she was through, she'd thoroughly investigated a string of allegations. Maybe if the Martensville officers had "done their job" in the first place in 1988, when Darryl Ford was chief and took the first complaint lodged against Travis Sterling, "all this could have been prevented." At least that's the opinion of one resident of Martensville I spoke to. Because seasoned officers had not done their job, a rookie perceived that she had to. But was she qualified?

Only a handful of Saskatchewan towns the size of Martensville have their own police force. It costs money, about $300,000 a year in the case of Martensville, and managing a force can be an administrative headache. For instance, who decides what training the officers require, and who provides it? I tried to get answers to my questions by writing to the Saskatchewan Police Commission, the body that establishes protocol for the province's police officers. I asked: "What were the experience and qualifications for dealing with child abuse possessed by the Martensville and Saskatoon police officers who conducted the investigation?" The commission answered: "[This question] would best be answered by the Police Services and/or the officers in question." Not very helpful, I thought, especially since the Martensville Police Department had ceased to exist, which the commission director undoubtedly knew when he wrote back. So to whom did the responsibility fall for training the police in the fall of 1991, the town or the province? If the Martensville police were expected to deal with allegations of child sexual abuse, surely they would have received proper support and training. Some "designated municipal police officers" in the province already do, according to the same correspondence from the Saskatchewan Police Commission. And now "plans are being formulated for delivery of a non-specialist child-abuse course to all other police officers, both municipal and RCMP within the province." Police training in this subject may be taken more seriously now than it was at the time of the allegations, in the early 1990s, when no one on the Martensville force had the formal skills for dealing with allegations of child sexual abuse.

And, according to the next courtroom witness, no one on the tiny force ever acquired the skills. Inspector Wayne McGillivray, Claudia Bryden's former boss, testifies that he knew the Martensville force quite well, having been hired as acting chief for four months in the winter of 1991-92, while still doing his full-time job as police chief in the neighbouring town of Corman Park. McGillivray acknowledges to the court that he did not provide specific training for officer Bryden before or during the investigation. Nor could he justify bringing in outside help. He himself was imported from Corman Park about the same time the allegations broke, and he soon developed his own opinion of the tiny Martensville Police Department. His opinion of Bryden in particular was mixed, he tells the court, especially after receiving one or two complaints from the families of the daycare children about her manner of investigating the case and after seeing her cry and say she wanted to quit. That's what led him to believe Bryden was suffering from paranoia.

Claudia Bryden will now speak for herself. The thirty-three-year-old officer with cropped hair and discreet, almost invisible, pearl earrings, climbs into the witness box and recounts the sequence of events that brought her to the courthouse today. The witness's story tallies with what the court already knows, and contributes more pieces to the prosecution's puzzle.

Bryden tells the court that slightly more than a week after she had begun her new job and gone for coffee with Constable Jim Elstad to the Sterling house, the family came to her attention again. She was on duty the night of October 1 when a father contacted the Martensville police to accuse the Sterling boy, Travis, of sexually assaulting his daughter at daycare. Elstad talked with the man and passed the complaint to Bryden, who mentioned it to the secretary. This was not the first report about Travis sexually assaulting girls at the daycare, Bryden says she learned from the secretary. The first complaint was somewhere in a filing cabinet, dated January 1988. After rifling through drawers, Bryden found the file and discovered that parts of it were missing.

Bryden tells the court she questioned the first girl who had accused Travis Sterling of sexual assault more than three years earlier. Believing she had enough evidence against the Sterling son, Bryden arrested him and launched an investigation under the supervision of Inspector McGillivray. A few days into Bryden's investigation of the second family's complaint, which had been prompted by a redness on the baby girl's genitals, the girl's older brother said that Travis had molested him at the daycare too. On October 4, 1991, after two weeks on the job, Bryden charged Travis Sterling with one count of inappropriate sexual behaviour and arrested him. Bryden tells the court she interviewed several more children while she and her colleagues planned a search of the Sterling house, in quest of kiddy porn. The search, which took place on December 12, did not yield kiddy porn but it did provide police with incriminating evidence — three hard-core videos, six piles of skin magazines, and a Polaroid camera. Eight days later, December 20, they arrested Linda Sterling, the operator of the unlicensed daycare. Then, in light of subsequent interviews with the children, police arrested Ron Sterling the following month. Jim Elstad, the senior constable who'd introduced Claudia Bryden to the Sterling family, was arrested in April 1992.

Bryden tells the court she called, then visited, the families who used the daycare, and refers, when Lavoie permits, to the police notes she made at the time. Besides the brother and sister who complained of being violated at the Sterling house, several other children in town reported abuse to Bryden, too. When questioned in their homes and at the police station, the kids described to Bryden the assaults by Ron and Linda Sterling and their son, Travis. They also said they'd been molested by Tammy, the young woman now on trial, and by police officers too. They claimed they'd been abused at the Sterling home in Martensville, where the daycare was, and at a blue building somewhere else. They described being taken for a long, bumpy ride to "The Place" in a car or police van, usually blindfolded, sometimes gagged, hands tied behind their back.

Continuing her testimony, Bryden describes how, armed with details from the children, police went on a hunt for a blue building with windows and a large entry. The officers scoured twelve square kilometres of land while the former mayor searched the area from his plane. After hours of scrutinizing the farmland surrounding Martensville, he finally spotted a blue building that matched the kids' description. Bryden conducted more interviews with the children, hearing their stories about the events in the blue building. Police obtained a search warrant, scoured the building from top to bottom in June 1992, and took more than 100 photos of it, which Bryden used in subsequent interviews and which became the centre of much debate: did the photos trigger the kids' memories of horrors at The Place or merely give them a foundation upon which to build elaborate stories of abuse? The sequence of events and what came first — the kids' own memories or the cops' photos — is never completely clear to me, despite Tim White's meticulous cross-examination of Bryden.

Bryden is earnest and surprisingly reserved, timid even, for a woman who had unearthed the long-forgotten police file on Travis. She is quiet and evidently unburdened with airs, just as many Prairie people are who grew up in large families on farms or in small towns. According to a friend, the "angst chromosomes" are missing from the Prairie gene pool. At first, the quiet composure of Prairie people may seem boring and even slow-witted to those used to the fast lane. But when you live here for a decade, as I have, you learn that most "hicks" are pretty smart, not too different from city slickers. Bryden speaks slowly and deliberately. I want to trust her, and I bet kids would, too. From the sounds of it, some of her police colleagues did not.

For the first six months of the investigation, which was the time the force was without a permanent chief, Bryden worked alone, with little or no assistance from the other Martensville officers. In March 1992, a Saskatoon officer was assigned to help her, and in June, Mike Johnston, the new chief of police, announced that a special RCMP task force would investigate the allegations and that Bryden would no longer be the main investigator. Eight months later, in February 1993, Bryden was laid off from the Martensville Police Department.

As Bryden recounts the steps in the investigation, I begin to comprehend the strain she must have endured. A picture emerges of a woman faced with the task of investigating the children's allegations, some against her own colleagues, trying to keep her balance while treading the ever-shifting sands of the Martensville police force, without stepping on anyone's toes.

Though she lacked expertise in investigating sexual-abuse allegations, and although she didn't receive specific training during the investigation, she did take a four-day course after it, in late 1992. During the course she learned about Step-Wise, a question-and-answer technique to help kids disclose trauma that a Vancouver psychologist developed for police and social workers. Under questioning from the prosecution, Bryden admits she'd do a few things differently today, given the opportunity.

I learn that if the Martensville force had neither training nor policy for dealing with sexually abused children, the Saskatoon force had guidelines, a special interview room and an officer who specialized in working with traumatized children. Corporal Rod Moor, armed with twenty years of policing experience, became the mentor to Claudia Bryden. Though he possessed no formal training in interviewing children, he had spent five years working with traumatized children and learning through trial and error how to interview them. His boss assigned him to show the Martensville rookie how to interview them too, in the Soft Room at the Saskatoon police station.

Curious about the room, I wander over to the police station at lunch, heading straight into the north wind for the three or four blocks between youth court and the police station. The public relations officer takes the time to show me the room, adding that he's glad he never has to work there. Because interviewing traumatized children is a difficult job, the Soft Room is designed to minimize the pain for the family and to put the child at ease. It's quiet and looks like a small living room, with four pink armchairs, a coffee table, artificial plants, and pastel broadloom carpet. Two of the walls are curtained, and one is bare except for a large camera lens fitted flush into the middle of the wall, like a giant eye. On the other side of the wall, hidden from the child's view, is a video-recorder. Also hidden from the child's view are the people who wait in the next room, usually the parents, watching the interview through a one-way mirror and on the TV monitor. Before starting an interview, the officer activates the video-recorder and adjusts the TV monitor for the parents so they can watch the interview, unbeknown to their child in the next room. This is the prescribed procedure.

But, as I learn when court re-convenes, Moor didn't always follow the so-called normal procedure. When he taught Bryden how to interview the Martensville children in the Soft Room in Saskatoon, he did not record all the sessions. No one will ever hear all the questions the two officers asked the kids, or all the answers the children gave. Some sessions were videotaped, some were audiotaped, some neither. In some cases, all we have to go on is Bryden's word and her notes, which are, apparently, not enough.

Bryden has brought a black binder to court, containing interviews with some of the kids, which were transcribed for court. She will read verbatim into the trial record and, at the same time, provide a sample of the technique she learned from Moor. The first passage comes from Rod Moor's taped question-and-answer session with a boy I'll call Freddy, conducted a year ago in the Soft Room. In a quiet, almost monotonous voice, Claudia Bryden reads the transcript of Moor's and Freddy's words, as though reading the script of a play.

> Moor: So a lot of guys are really coming forward, giving us some really bizarre things, and a lot of scary things are happening to these kids. They're not just at the Sterling home — there is another place that you know about.
>
> Freddy: Yeah.
>
> Moor: And yeah, some real scary stuff?
>
> Freddy: Yeah, and that's kidnapping.

Moor: Yeah, but I mean some stuff that happened at the place — some, a lot of scary stuff going on for some of these kids...

Freddy: Uh-huh.

Moor: And some of them are policemen, wearing uniforms? Well, it's pretty hard for you to tell a policeman what's been happening... If it wasn't for you and a few of the older, really brave kids, it would have been really tough for us to do something.

I wince to hear such leading statements. As a journalist, I feel Moor was trying to co-opt Freddy, virtually telling him what to think and feel. As a teacher, I'm shocked he would conduct an interview this way when so much was at stake. Not that I totally blame the man. If the assignment hadn't been sanctioned by his boss, or if his superiors didn't think Moor knew what he was doing, I doubt he'd have been doing it in the first place. But hearing these transcripts makes me wonder if the Saskatoon police, or any others, can ever know enough about handling these sensitive cases.

Bryden looks up from the transcript and says she interviewed the children of five or six families on numerous occasions between the fall of 1991 and spring of 1992. Typically, she would interview a child in the Soft Room in Saskatoon, or go to the family home and "build rapport" by discussing sports and school. Then, when the child seemed relaxed, she asked questions. Sometimes a session took ten minutes; other times it might last two hours. Bryden holds a plastic bag containing the hundreds of police photos seized during a search of the Sterling residence, which she showed to the children during questioning. The pictures are the subject of much controversy: Were the daycare children able to recognize the items in the photos — the ropes, the peach-coloured vibrator, the Polaroid camera, the skin magazines — because they'd actually seen them at the Sterling house? Or did they "recognize" them only after Bryden showed them the photos?

As she continues to read from the transcript of the interviews, it strikes me how hard it is to get information from kids at the best of times, never mind when the very reputations of the accused are at stake. If you ask nothing and wait, the child may sit there and say nothing. If you ask anything, it must be just the right question or, sooner or later, you'll have the whole judicial system down your throat, with lawyers like Tim White and journalists like me criticizing your techniques.

If my interviews had such severe consequences, I doubt I'd ever have the courage to do one again. Interviewing is a skill, and not one you can perfect in a couple of weeks or months. It takes years to look and sound natural when doing this very artificial thing. If you really want to improve your technique, you make every interview a practice session for the next one. And you make allowance for the "X" factor: You don't always know which direction the interview will take. Nor should you. When I interview someone, I'm out to get information, but I also need to get to know the person a bit. So I try to think of each interview as a two-way rather than a one-way street. I let my subject ask me a question or two, and share the power. This means I may agree to meander and change direction if the person catches my interest. But it may mean a tug-of-war if I'm not in the mood for conversational gymnastics, or I'm in a hurry to finish. It takes time to play the game — stray, return to the straight-and-narrow interview path, and stray off it again. If you don't watch where you're headed, you can easily get lost. It can be frustrating as hell, yet more rewarding than anything else I've ever done.

Part of the thrill comes from getting people to tell you things they would not normally say, telling you stories they've never told anyone before. Sharing a never-before-told story is a thrill for the storyteller too, and confers power on the narrator as well as the listener. When you come right down to it, interviewing is about power, which is easy to abuse. When a police officer questions you, you're either a witness, an offender, a suspect or a victim. Call your lawyer if the officer wants to question you in depth. The police know the rules of the game and you, a normal law-abiding citizen, probably don't. So you'll have to do your best at playing the game, a formalized, intimidating game for the average adult. Imagine how it feels if you're a kid.

Rubbing her forearm and licking her lips, Claudia Bryden continues to read the transcript of her own taped session done the previous year with Freddy. Here are some of the things she said to Freddy to reassure him (the ellipses represent missing portions of the interview): "I can't stop you from feeling bad. All I can do is tell you that you're helping me out, and you're doing a really good job. Freddy, I just want you to understand that sometimes adults do things to people, or they touch people,... and make other people feel sad... Whenever something like that happens to a young child, it's not ever your fault... I need you to remember that you're not getting into trouble for talking to us... When the truth comes out you feel a little better... Well, you know they [the Sterlings] are in a little bit of trouble. They've done some bad things to kids... If your mom and dad knew that, they would never have let you stay there... If you tell me everything you know, then you're helping me out a whole bunch, okay?"

I'm sure her words reassured Freddy. But did they also lull him into a false sense of security and encourage the boy to say things that weren't true?

While Tim White hovers over Bryden's shoulder, she continues, coolly, to read aloud her own interview with Freddy: "Did she [Tammy] ever point the gun at you?... What kind of things did Travis [Sterling] do to Kenny?" This kind of question, depending on its context, is "leading." Kids are very suggestible to such questioning because it may plant ideas in their heads. I can hardly believe Bryden asked Freddy questions this way. On the other hand, I'm sure she thought she was doing her job.

It's easy to criticize Bryden. She'd been on the beat for little more than a week when her first big case walked in the door. It's easy to scold her for not achieving enough distance from Freddy during her interviews, for failing to show more scepticism and less enthusiasm about the boy's accusations. But when you're interviewing someone — especially someone who's accusing someone else of a serious crime — you have to challenge their credibility. However, if Bryden had challenged Freddy's credibility, he might have clammed up. If she was the first person outside his family he'd ever told his secret to, it's likely he would have detoured or withdrawn at the first roadblock.

Learning to be at one with the person you're interviewing, gaining his or her confidence so they'll talk to you, yet keeping your distance and remaining analytical: that technique takes years to perfect. Tuning in to the other person's wavelength, then turning off to see how well you did, back and forth: that process takes great courage and even greater subtlety.

I wonder what Bryden was up against. Did she dig her own grave, or did the Old Boys in Martensville dig it for her? I need a break from all this talk about child abuse. I'm desperate for fresh air and something new to think about. Maybe Judge Lavoie feels the same way because he announces a two-hour lunch break.

A magazine junkie who needs a fix, I can't wait to buy something to read over lunch. It's an expensive habit. But if you write for magazines, you read them to see what your competition is up to. In the bookstore down the street from the courthouse, a *Glamour* cover story catches my eye, as it's supposed to. "Hotter, Happier Sex: Six New Essentials," it screams in pink Day-Glo letters. The prospect of learning some new sex tips gets my attention, then I remember I don't need to know right now.

Till six months ago I was married. When I had my husband — and comfortable, conjugal sex — I would have bought the magazine and rushed home to read the piece in the bathtub, to see how to make things hotter and happier after the bath. These days, hotter and happier *is* the bath. But there's something in this magazine for everyone, even for the celibate: "Why Women Make Better Cops." Now, I think, that might be a more instructive story, with more immediate applicability to my present needs. So I buy the magazine and, to my delight, find the piece is well done.

According to the writer (a woman), being a policewoman in the United States is a nasty job. American women, for all their progress in the work world, constitute less than ten per cent of police officers in that country and about three per cent of police supervisors. Women are trying to change the face of crime-fighting. The author says they take "family disturbances" more seriously than many of their male colleagues, who still think robberies and crimes by strangers are more serious than domestic violence. Nor do policemen readily arrest the accused in a domestic dispute. This makes me wonder how Canadian women fare on our police forces.

Maclean's magazine must have heard me and, not long after, publishes a piece by Rae Corelli. It paints a surprisingly similar picture to the one in *Glamour*. Fewer than ten per cent of all police officers in Canada are women and, as of 1992, only twenty women — fewer than one per cent — were among the 2,680 police who had reached officer rank. In 1974, the RCMP Training Depot in Regina graduated its first woman; twelve years later, in 1986, Claudia Bryden joined the ranks. How many of these women are still police officers I do not know, but the *Maclean's* piece says the Ontario Provincial Police finds it helpful to provide peer support for its officers, a great deal of it to new female recruits. One anonymous constable, with more than fifteen years' experience, told the magazine, "There are women quitting all the time. A lot of them leave because you can't pay them enough to put up with what they have to put up with. We've got a lot of great guys, but we also get a lot of guys who think the uniform fits only men."

After the two-hour lunch, court re-convenes. Under cross-examination, Bryden testifies that the search of The Place did not yield the evidence police hoped to find, not even with the help of the LUMA-LITE. What kind of evidence? "Pornographic photos," possibly taken with a Polaroid camera, the witness tells prosecutor Sullivan. Some of the children told the officer they'd been photographed without clothes. One said he'd been tied up first.

According to Bryden's testimony, the four-and-a-half-hour search of the Sterling residence in December 1991 yielded no kiddie porn, though it did yield a Polaroid camera, a pile of pornographic magazines, and some homemade photos of the magazines' contents. Also found were three X-rated videos including "Sex Platoon" and "Debbie Does Dallas"; a peach-coloured vibrator; a pair of military chain anklets covered in cloth; a gun from the collection of Ron Sterling; playing cards featuring naked ladies; and an ad for an "adult" store in Saskatoon.

So this is what parents get for sending their kids to an unlicensed daycare: a pellet gun propped against the kitchen wall and pornographic magazines in the bathroom. Sure, it's a free country and people are entitled to have guns, porn mags, and X-rated videos in their homes. But not when the home doubles as an unlicensed daycare filled with children year round.

What role did Tammy play in this? What is she thinking right now? Is she annoyed that Bryden went through her things with a fine-tooth comb, searching for incriminating evidence in the bedroom she rented from the Sterlings? All I see is the back of her head, as immobile as the rest of her.

When the two search and seizures of the Sterling five-bedroom bungalow were complete, and all the questionable items stashed in plastic bags, the police photographed and numbered them. From the hundreds of photos Bryden showed the children, some sparked immediate recognition, or so she tells the court. When she interviewed a boy called Freddy, she opened the police album to pictures of the blue building and he recognized it right away as The Place, where, he told Bryden, he'd been taken with several other kids. The eleven-year-old is the first of two child witnesses to testify.

Freddy tells his story

Our judicial system is based on the right to see and hear. During a trial the courtroom doors remain open, despite noise from the hall outside. People come and go at will, bowing respectfully towards the judge every time they enter and exit. In this trial, the accused and the two young plaintiffs exercise the very different right not to be seen, either by the public or each other. No one in the courtroom can see Freddy because of his therapist's recommendation and the judge's ruling. Freddy can't see Tammy, and she can't see him. Freddy is ready to testify in a room on the first floor of the courthouse. At the back of the room sits Tammy, hidden behind a screen to avoid traumatizing the boy. The public is not allowed in that room while a child witness is there. Though we cannot see Freddy, we will be permitted to hear him on closed-circuit TV, in a small room upstairs. Into this room twenty or so members of the public and journalists are herded; it's so small there's scarcely space for elbows and winter coats, let alone the television monitor.

The only thing I can see on the monitor is what looks like the bust of Judge Lavoie, wearing a dark suit and tie. Then he turns his head to the left, smiles, and says good day to someone. I assume Freddy has just stepped into the witness box.

Does Freddy know what it means to tell the truth? Because he is still a child, not yet sixteen, the judge must determine this, as required by the Canada Evidence Act. Lavoie instructs the lawyers to test the eleven-year-old's comprehension of "truth." Tim White, lawyer for Tammy, will go first. Then

Leslie Sullivan, one of the two prosecutors, will take her turn, assisted by prosecutor Bruce Bauer.

"Do you know who'd punish you if you took an oath to tell the truth and then lied?" asks White. Freddy replies, "Yes, my teachers and my mom and dad," adding that he believes in God. Apparently, this answer is not good enough for White, who insists on knowing if the boy understands the "spiritual dimension" of telling the truth. Does White himself know, or anyone else in the room, for that matter? The question would stump a monk. It requires the appropriate spiritual training, not to mention sufficient time, to contemplate. But fifteen seconds of profound meditation is all we get before prosecutor Bauer jumps up. "Your Honour," says the greying lawyer, "I would submit that no one knows for sure whether there's going to be spiritual consequences about lying, or lying under oath." Lavoie, looking like a traffic cop in rush hour, darts an appreciative nod at Bauer then fixes his gaze on White, the signal to proceed with the truth test.

This test is not just a formality. It's a crucial test that Freddy must pass before he can tell his story. It's a test to see not only if Freddy knows what truth is, but if he has the mind and the words to tell his story in a way Judge Lavoie will understand well enough to weigh and measure on the scales of justice, before deciding "beyond a reasonable doubt" the price to be paid. If Freddy can't help Lavoie this way, as sometimes happens in court with the very young, the very old, and the disabled, the boy will have to leave the room. Freddy will have no recourse in the criminal justice system.

Freddy's testimony must be quantifiable. It won't matter how the judge feels about the boy's story, unless he gets facts to weigh and concrete details to measure. In this system the most articulate witnesses are destined to be the most successful witnesses. Just ask lawyers.

Fortunately, Freddy is no dummy. He has been prepped for his centre-stage appearance today by Linda Jensen, a blonde who looks like someone's big sister. Actually, she's a social worker, the first person hired by the Department of Justice to show a child witness the ropes in a courtroom. During the past few weeks, Jensen has had five sessions with Freddy, encouraging him to make a "fear list" admitting what scares him about going to court, helping him deal with anxiety about telling his story in public, introducing him to judicial procedure, and letting him see what a real courtroom looks like. Her play "courtroom" is a topless box the size of a dollhouse, filled with twenty or so plastic court dolls, some in black robes. Freddy got acquainted with real court by going to her office, and the boy's demeanour shows that Jensen has done her job. Though sounding annoyed he has to pass the truth test, Freddy doesn't sound intimidated. He convinces Judge Lavoie he knows how to communicate evidence, and that he knows the difference between truth and lies and understands the nature of an oath to "bind his conscience." Satisfied on these matters, the judge allows the boy to be sworn in. "Simply tell your story as you best remember it. Don't embellish it," Lavoie instructs him in a kind and fatherly manner.

The number of journalists covering the trial is more or less constant this week, and the green press passes guarantee our front-row seats. But more members of the public than expected have shown up to hear Freddy's testimony, and there aren't enough chairs. There is pandemonium outside the small video room. An incident occurs. A moment ago, a middle-aged woman insulted the commissionaire and, it's rumoured, purposely stomped on his foot while he was trying to control the crowd. Whoever assaults a court official is in contempt of court, and we'll all hear about it first thing tomorrow morning, with a long lecture from Lavoie about "improper behaviour" and a shape-up-or-ship-out ultimatum.

As we sit like sardines in the tiny video room, waiting for Freddy's evidence to begin, I wonder how he's feeling. The boy can't just mindlessly answer yes, no, yes, no to get the questions over with. No lawyer would stand for that. Nor may he simply begin at the beginning of his story and tell it to the end, without interruption. In our courts the lawyers decide what evidence will be given, which person will give it, and the order in which he or she will do so. Very organized. Very linear. And sometimes very leading, which is what Judge Lavoie wants to avoid. He wants to know if Freddy can think for himself, and see if he can tell his story so that it makes sense. So Lavoie gives prosecutors Bauer and Sullivan and defence lawyer White a pep talk: they are not to spoon-feed the boy or lead him to answers. They must ask more "open" questions than "closed" ones; in other words, no prompting, and no putting words in Freddy's mouth.

This open-ended style of questioning, more suited to a late-night talk show than a court of law, is not easy for the three lawyers to comprehend, as we shall see. In law school they learned that the shortest path to their truth is a straight line. But they will be confronted with an eleven-year-old who finds a straight line boring, and who, like most kids, prefers to meander along the path, kick stones, smell flowers along the way, and stop when he gets tired or distracted.

Before long, the trial turns into a trial about the art of asking questions. The lawyers point their fingers at the police, saying they did a lousy job of questioning the kids. The police just fold their arms as if to say, "You try it, wise guy." The old pot-black-kettle routine. To amuse myself when a lawyer's statement is disguised as a question, I imagine the courtroom as "The Gong Show." Peter Gzowski sits in Judge Lavoie's black leather chair holding the gong. He bangs it once for every good question a lawyer asks, twice for a bad or leading one. The people in the public gallery clap when they hear a particularly good question, and so do the jurors, twelve pre-pubescent children. I fantasize that every half-hour the jury foreman, a boy wearing runners and braces on his teeth, rings a bell and the court breaks for recess and snacks.

No such luck for Freddy. He must quickly adapt to the rigours of a game with hard-and-fast rules and adult expectations. The rituals of the play are strange and ancient; much of the language is formal and unfamiliar, some of it completely foreign, unless you learned Latin in school. But the boy, the youngest player in the room, does get a few concessions: no member of the public or the media will ever see his face, and no one will ever print his name. The high priests and priestess have left their black robes in the gowning room and will sometimes remain seated when questioning him; the woman whom Freddy has accused is hidden behind a screen.

But no matter how many concessions have been made to Freddy, he must stand alone. He will tell his painful stories for the umpteenth time, not in the privacy of his therapist's office, who maintains his client's confidentiality, but for the first time to faceless strangers, listening to him on closed-circuit TV.

Now Freddy has to endure the examination-in-chief with Crown Prosecutor Bruce Bauer. They discussed the material the other day in Bauer's office. Question. Answer. Question. Answer. When Freddy gets going, he sounds quite convincing, all the more because he combines good memories of the Sterling daycare with bad ones. In his memory bank, the snacks in the kitchen and the swings in the backyard are stored near the vibrator in the bedroom and the shotgun by the door. I find him especially persuasive when he simply admits he doesn't know the answer to a question or can't remember the details of an incident. I readily put myself in his place when he gets confused about the sequence of events, and wouldn't be surprised if he thought he'd seen or done things he hadn't, after all these months.

Freddy's voice is flat, without affect or feeling. I've heard such hollowness before, yet don't know where. Then the wounded sounds close in and wrap my ears in remembrance: That's my voice. That's how I sounded at 13, when my parents divorced. For three years after the breakup of our family, I punished everyone by talking as little as possible and refusing to smile. Now I think I was clinically depressed and should have had therapy, but mother was too busy with her own problems to notice mine. The teachers thought I was a problem kid, but as long as I got good grades they left me alone. Freddy must sound strange to the uninitiated: he's telling the saddest stories in a voice that cannot cry, in a tone that's flat and lifeless. But when I listen, I hear a boy stuck at the bottom of a well I once knew, struggling to get out.

Freddy knows his facts. He was babysat at the Sterlings for three years, from the beginning of Grade 2, in 1988, till the end of Grade 4, in 1991, when he and his parents moved to British Columbia. During that time, he testifies, he was subjected to all sorts of indignities and criminal acts.

The first story Freddy tells goes like this: he's in the kitchen at the Sterling daycare and Tammy comes into the room with a shotgun. She tells him to go downstairs into a room and she follows, holding the gun to his back. In a room with two beds Tammy tells him to suck on her breasts, or she'll shoot him. So he does what she says. After fifteen minutes or so, when she's had enough, she tells him to stop and puts her blouse back on. They go upstairs, he has a snack, and she goes to another room in the house.

No, Freddy answers Bauer, he doesn't remember the sounds Tammy made that time. But he does remember her breasts as a "circle with bumps on it." If his memories are true, he will never get the chance to leisurely discover a woman's body for himself. "I felt scared," he says, and "sick — like doing a play." Freddy is describing stage fright, the only other time the boy experienced this kind of fear.

Judging the down-to-earthness of Freddy's analogies, I'd say he has blended the alleged trauma very creatively into his everyday little-boy life. Sucking Tammy's breasts reminds him of an anxious moment on stage, and when he sucked her vagina the grunting sounds she made sounded "like if you get checked in a hockey game." I'd like to know what a psychologist would say about Freddy's capacity to make links between the traumatic incidents he describes and the mundane events of his life. The extraordinary coupled with the ordinary.

Bauer hands Freddy writing utensils and asks him to draw a diagram of the Sterling house basement. Freddy marks "X" for the beds where the incidents occurred. I wish Bauer would have Freddy draw a picture of Tammy and himself. Then Lavoie could add up the details of the picture and estimate the likelihood of Freddy's abuse. As mechanical as this sounds, an American professor of medicine claims she can do it. Interviewed in *Family Practice*, a doctor's magazine I sometimes write for, Dr. Linda Petersen says she sees seven constant indicators of abuse in kids' artwork. I'd expect her to pay special attention to depictions of bodies with genitalia or missing parts. But never in a million years would I guess that when a child draws a fruit tree, as she suggests, it is a clue to sexual abuse.

The Garden of Eden. The end of innocence. Whether Freddy has real memories of bad things at the daycare, or false memories the police and therapists planted in his head, no one will ever know. Either way, he has suffered things a child his age should not have had to endure. He is trying to come to grips with these memories and has seen his counsellor at least forty-five times in the past couple of years. I don't know how Freddy talked before he started seeing Rod Butler but now, on the stand, his testimony is articulate, if reluctant. He has had time to think about the time Tammy allegedly threatened to harm him and forced him to suck her vagina. He calls it "a triangle with a bunch of hair." Setting aside his confusion of the female pubis and vagina, I'd grade Freddy's observation as novel. Is Freddy making this up, or has he actually seen female pubic hair?

So far this morning he's talked about the sex acts he performed on Tammy. Now he has to tell the court what sex acts she performed on him. I read somewhere that when we have erotic dreams, we permit ourselves to dream about performing taboo acts on others but not about their performing the very same acts on us. It's certainly true of my dreams. Control is the issue. We need to think we're in control.

And Freddy was not. When it came time to tell the story about Tammy sucking his penis, he rebelled: "Do I have to? I don't really feel comfortable talking about that." Then the eleven-year-old mutineer fell silent, trying to outwait the court for a full eighty seconds. (The *StarPhoenix* reporter sitting beside me swore it seemed longer, but I timed it.) Finally, Freddy relented and gave his version of events. When Tammy sucked his penis, he stood there in the Sterling kitchen, his pants drooping around his ankles and his back against the table. "My body felt good but, in my mind, I knew it felt wrong."

Freddy is describing a deep-rooted contradiction that, whatever its origin, must have caused him years of anguish. I wonder how many therapy sessions it took to loosen the knot of emotion in his gut. While most boys his age are ribbing their friends about the secrets of sex, Freddy confides in his therapist. Circles with bumps and hairy triangles: that's all the female form meant to him when he had the precocious encounters he claims. Cunnilingus is not the normal pursuit of a grade-school boy. Moments after Tammy introduced Freddy to fellatio and de-flowered him, he went back to playing with his toy motorcycle, rolling it back and forth over the kitchen linoleum.

In his changing voice, which sometimes sounds like a boy's, then a man's, Freddy tells the court he's "a bit tense," before proceeding to recount another incident. This story, which occurred at The Place, is a bit sketchy: the flight of creaking, wood stairs with a railing on one side, the big white freezer in the basement, the blindfold, the hands tied behind his back, the "dingy black piece of cloth" that served as a gag. Freddy claims he was driven to The Place in the back of a van. He says he sometimes had trouble breathing along the way. He sounds a bit clogged up right now, and I wonder if he has allergies. If he does, reducing his air supply with a gag would terrify him.

Freddy used his other senses to compensate for the blindfold. He heard muffled screams from the other kids. He felt rough hands, which he claims belonged to Ron Sterling. Once the blindfold came off and he could see.

Someone, he says, held his arms so he couldn't squirm, and then removed the cloth from his eyes. He insists he had time to look around while the adults tried to subdue the other kids, and he caught a glimpse of The Place.

Freddy continues his story in detail. Sometimes he sat, sometimes he lay in the abducting vehicle. His shoulders got sore from having his arms tied behind his back. He couldn't squirm when strapped in with a seatbelt but, without arms for balance, he sometimes fell over sideways and hit his head on the window. Though his wrists were sore and red, his nightly bath at home made the marks go away. The gag sometimes cut the sides of his mouth a "tiny, tiny bit" and the cuts would sting if he drank orange juice the next morning.

Freddy is a wonderful story teller. Consider the account of the seatbelt, rich in detail. Most kids his age know that without their arms they lose their balance. But Freddy describes a very complex scenario. He is strapped into a seatbelt, arms bound behind his back. Unable to keep his balance, he falls sideways and hits his head on the car window. As a writer, I'm impressed. As a teacher, who has formally studied children's cognitive development, I'm struck by the young witness's grasp of cause and effect, and even more impressed that he reverses the normal sequence, creating effect and cause, wherein his morning orange juice stung the cuts in his mouth caused by the gag of the day before.

Freddy says he likes to eat and vividly remembers the times he has gone hungry. Sometimes he'd be kept at The Place till close to 5 p.m., when it would turn dark. There was no food there, so he'd miss his snack and be famished by the time he got home. Is it common for a child to imagine hunger, any more than it is to fantasize about pain?

Freddy continues his sordid tale. One day he was carted off to The Place and led upstairs to a messy room with a waterbed where Tammy, armed with the same gun as before, seduced him: "If you don't have sex with me, I'll shoot you." Freddy's detail of the incident is rich, this time in sound: Tammy's pants "scrape her skin" as she removed them. She exclaimed "Oh!" several times during intercourse. Freddy fails to mention the noises he himself might have made — how he breathed in his scared state, or the sound his hand made slapping his virgin penis. Incredibly, according to the boy's testimony, this was Tammy's prescription for making Freddy's penis stiff, before it penetrated her for the very first time.

During the fifteen-minute break, I canvas several members of the public gallery to see what they think of Freddy's evidence. Everyone has a different opinion, including Jim and Tim, two middle-aged men who always sit together in the back row. Tall Tim disagrees with short Jim today, which isn't always the case. The former, a dog breeder, thinks Freddy's stories sound far-fetched. The latter, a retired Anglican priest who likes to speak in allegories, believes the boy's stories have a ring of truth to them. I have my own doubts that Freddy's penis could have been stiffened by slapping it.

I sit in the backbreaking plastic chair in the video room, wondering why Freddy never told his parents these things. In his dead voice he tells the court, "I was scared. They wouldn't believe me," the Sterlings would "kill me, and Mom or Dad."

Maybe Freddy buried his feelings so deeply his parents couldn't see them. But how could he hide from them the symptoms that developed soon after he started staying at the Sterling house? What did they think when he insisted on keeping a baseball bat by his bed, or when his stomach began to hurt and he had bouts of vomiting? They took him to the doctor, but apparently suspected nothing unusual.

Freddy and his parents moved from Martensville to British Columbia in the summer of 1991. No sooner had they moved than Claudia Bryden called to tell the boy's parents that police had launched an investigation and that, possibly, Freddy had been involved in certain events at the Sterling house during the three years he'd been babysat there. Before long, Freddy's family moved back to Saskatchewan, this time to Saskatoon. Soon after their return, Officer Bryden began to come to Freddy's house with pictures and questions. After a couple of slow and painful sessions during which Freddy cried, as Bryden told the court earlier, the boy got the courage to talk and identify the things in her photo albums: the "waterbed" and the kitchen at The Place; the unusual rope he claimed to have been bound with, and the vibrator that he said had been placed on (and in) his private parts. Freddy also looked at police photos of porn pictures and said he'd seen them before. He now tells the court that one day when he was playing at the daycare, Travis Sterling led him into the bedroom and showed off his girlie magazines.

Once a man used his age and sex to intimidate me. I was a still a first-year university student, a virgin, meeting a third-year student to buy some used Russian textbooks. We drank coffee and agreed on the prices, book by book. Just when I thought the transaction was complete, he decided to give me a vocabulary lesson. By the time he finished fifteen minutes later, I knew the words necrophilia, coprophilia, masochism, and several others. In those days, I was too polite and afraid to be thought a prude to tell him where to get off. And I was scared of him. Finally, I got up my courage, paid him, and just walked away. I still recall the sense of defilement, the loss of innocence, I felt for months afterwards, and the fear that he might threaten or punish me if I told anyone.

It's time for cross-examination. Time for Tim White to poke holes in Freddy's story. If he can't find any, he might lose the case and Tammy might go to jail.

To protect his client, White criticizes the way police did their job. Under no circumstances should Claudia Bryden have shown Freddy photos of objects until she was certain he'd seen the real things for himself. To prove he had seen them, he should have been required to describe each item. Then, and only then, should Bryden have shown the boy the police photos. White makes himself clear: You understand, Your Honour, that Freddy's not to blame if he's hallucinating. The police officers are. If only they'd asked the boy the right questions — in the right way — he might have talked on his own about the vibrator and the porn magazines. He might have even described the unusual chain anklets seized during the house search, or remembered the special carving on the back of one of the guns. But no. The police just couldn't wait. They had to play show-and-tell, contaminate Freddy's mind, lead him down the garden path. And now no one will ever know if Freddy is telling the truth. The police co-opted the boy's mind and compromised the court's capacity to assess the child's credibility. So says White. I'm not so sure. Perhaps, as the defence lawyer maintains, the police investigation was not up to snuff. Surely that doesn't mean it's impossible to determine if the child witnesses are telling the truth.

Why would Freddy lie? White has two theories.

The Good-Boy Theory: "Did you want to please Claudia Bryden and Rod Moor?" White asks. "Not really. I just wanted to get my story out," Freddy replies in his monotone. How did you feel when Claudia Bryden and Rod Moor questioned you at the police station and told you how brave you were? "Confident," replies the boy with certainty.

Without missing a beat, White tests his other supposition, the Bad-Boy Theory: Maybe you're telling these stories, Freddy, because you don't like the people at the daycare. No, asserts the boy, he isn't telling these stories just to get revenge. He admits that Ron Sterling once caught him playing hookey a couple of years ago. But when Ron stopped his car, told the boy to get in, and drove him back to school, Freddy insists he was humiliated, not mad.

I'm impressed. Freddy, at eleven, articulates his feelings better than some adults I know. I wonder if Rod Butler, his therapist, has helped him. White continues to cross-examine the child, in pursuit of gaps in his knowledge.

White: How many times have you seen photos of The Place?

Freddy: Between March and April, 1992...

White: How many times have you seen pictures of that bedroom [at The Place]?

Freddy: Twice...

White: In the garage, was there anything besides wood...and you said there was a cage on the floor?

Freddy: Yeah. There was puddles of oil on the floor.

White: And that's all you remember about it?

Freddy: As you mentioned, there was wood propped up on the wall and the cage.

White: And there was a cage on the floor?

Freddy: Yeah, and it would get raised if you would put somebody in it.

White: And this cage, did it have chicken wire on it? Do you know what chicken wire is?

Freddy: No.

White: It's real thin wire. It has small patterns.

Freddy: Oh...

White: You say that you saw kids being put in there and get hoisted up?

Freddy: Yeah, sometimes.

White: Did you ever get hoisted up?

Freddy: Yes...not very often.

White: The waterbed. You were on the waterbed, is that right?

Freddy: Yes...

White: Is that the same waterbed you were on when you say that Tammy forced you to have sex with her?

Freddy: Yes.

White: Did you have any difficulty at all having sex on the waterbed when it was moving around?

Freddy: I'm not sure…

White: …Do you remember what kind of clothing she had on that day?

Freddy: No.

White: Do you remember what kind of clothing you had on that day?

Freddy: Sweat pants and a T-shirt.

White: Did Tammy have any underclothing on that day?…

Freddy: Yes.

White: What kind of underclothing?

Freddy: A bra and panties…

White: What colour?

Freddy: I don't know what colour the panties were…

White: …Did she point a gun at you?

Freddy: Yes.

White: What kind of gun?…

Freddy: A double-barrelled shotgun.

After a short intermission, the cross-exam continues:

White: Are you sure the stairs at The Place creaked?

Freddy: Yes, I'm sure they creaked…

White: Do you remember the kind of police van that you say you went out to The Place in?...

Freddy: Martensville police van.

White: How do you know that?

Freddy: It said "Martensville Police" on it…and it was blue and white.

Before long, White starts to gain ground. First Freddy recants and says he sucked Tammy's vagina in an ordinary twin bed, not on a big waterbed, then he doesn't remember if the incident happened at the daycare or The Place. Now he's not completely sure Tammy had a gun when she told him to suck her breasts.

Does it matter? Time after time, Freddy has told his story — to the police, his parents, psychologists, lawyers. Between the earlier examination-in-chief and the cross-examination-in-progress he has changed minor details in his story, and sometimes he leaves out entire chunks. I wouldn't remember the gaps if White didn't jump on him for every omission, every variance. Do the variations discredit the core of Freddy's story in any way? If only I could see his face, maybe I'd know if he's telling the truth. What if he's telling lies and thinks he's telling the truth? If you say something often enough, you start to believe it.

Sometimes it looks as though the limitations of the cross-exam burden White as much as Freddy. The playing field has already been defined by the prosecutor. During his examination-in-chief, Bauer asked the questions and Freddy answered them. Now White must use that information to his client's advantage. Practising what he learned in law school, the lawyer tries to box Freddy in. Sometimes he looks as though he hates feeding Freddy the questions and I wonder if he ever, just for a moment, thinks the witness is telling the truth. A bit of sympathy might make his job as defence lawyer even more difficult for him than it is. Not that anyone ever found the job of questioning Freddy easy, whether they believed him or not. Just ask Claudia Bryden or Rod Butler. The hours of taped interviews from the Soft Room will soon show how hard it was to do the job well.

Even though White has a tough job to do, he has to do his best. I don't think criticizing the police makes him look good, especially when his own cross-examination is not without fault, and when he is doing what Judge Lavoie asked the lawyers not to do, lead the witness. If White were the prosecutor instead of the defence lawyer, if he'd examined Freddy instead of cross-examining him — having *carte blanche* instead of *prix fixe* — would his questions be more open-ended and less confrontational?

Instead of: Did you talk with the police? Why? When? White asks bluntly: Did you want to please them [the police]?

Instead of broadening the field with: Did Tammy have anything in her hands? What? What did she do? he narrows it with: What kind of a gun did Tammy point?

Freddy sighs. I can hear the boy but not see him, and have become sensitive to every sound he makes. His long, stubborn silences make me want to tell White to leave him alone.

The only thing on the TV screen is White's back. When he turns to take a sip of water or reach for a document in his briefcase, I see the left side of his face. There's nothing exceptional about his appearance, but he has an intensity I find attractive. Though I never see more in court than the tip of the iceberg, emotionally, I imagine him capable of very strong feeling, and every now and then I get an actual glimpse of it, a spontaneous wave of his hands, a momentary rise in his voice. Then he reins it in, perhaps wanting to spare Freddy his full courtroom wrath. If White were Freddy's father, he might cajole or spank the testimony out of Freddy. Here he has to treat the boy ever so gently, or he will clam up. Sometimes the agendas of Lavoie, White, and Freddy complement one another; sometimes they overlap; and sometimes they openly contradict each other. The two men seem to be struggling to reconcile their natural fondness for Freddy with the jobs they must do.

White needs courage and cunning to make points against Freddy, while still playing by Judge Lavoie's rules. His job might be even harder if he had to play to a jury and not just a judge, to get twelve people onside instead of only one.

The short mid-afternoon break provides ten minutes for some fresh air. The stale air in the small video room would put me to sleep if it weren't for the testimony on the TV screen. Despite Freddy's small voice, his words are compelling.

White gives Freddy an anatomy test. Did Tammy have any peculiar marks on her body? No. Any scars? No. Any scars on her legs? No. Her tummy? No. Her upper body or neck? No. After sucking her vagina, was your face wet or dry? Wet, and I rubbed my face on my sleeve. Do you remember any particular taste in your mouth? No, says the boy. Freddy doesn't seem to mind these questions. But I do, especially when White asks, "So I gather your...nose or your face didn't stink?" And there's more where that came from: "After you had sex with Tammy at The Place, do you remember whether your penis was wet or dry on the outside?" All Freddy will say in his usual monotone is, "I can't remember."

White gathers his papers. No further questions. Prosecutor Bruce Bauer wants to do a re-exam, the last thing Freddy needs or wants. What he probably wants is his snack. It's 4: 45 p.m. But Bauer has certain things he must ask, if he is to beat White to the punch. I paraphrase the testimony:

Bauer: I'd like you to tell me what you can...about the cage?

Freddy: It has a metal bottom with a grey metal door and a padlock. The walls have a diamond-shaped pattern, like the fence on a baseball field around the dugout...

Bauer: What's the colour of the wire?

Freddy: It's silver.

Bauer: How thick? Can you remember?

Freddy: About as thick as this wire [the wire on his own courtroom microphone].

Bauer: Thank you, Freddy. Thank you, Your Honour.

Three possibilities spring to mind: Freddy saw the cage with his own eyes, he scrutinized the police photos of it, or he should consider becoming a writer where he can put his vivid imagination to good use. Outside the courthouse the snow is getting deeper and the sky blacker. Freddy's testimony is over. I hope he enjoys his supper and forgets about this day completely, as I plan to do.

Curiously, covering this trial has eased my own personal nightmare or, more precisely, put it into perspective. The aftershock of hearing my husband say, last year, that he wanted a divorce still registers nine on the Richter scale and intensifies the aftershock of the first divorce I lived through — my parents'. I eat alone, with just a bottle of wine for company. I sleep alone, if lying two inches above the mattress in a constant state of nerves is sleeping. When I do manage to fall asleep, inevitably a bad dream wakes me. Or a creak on the stairs convinces me that this time there really is an axe murderer breaking into the house.

Next morning, TV reporter Janis Crosbie tells me she has been sleeping poorly, too. Last night she dreamed about kids being tortured in cages. Her eyes are red and puffy. Another reporter says Freddy's evidence is getting to him too, and he copes with it by transforming the most lurid testimony into the blackest humour. The first time I heard his sick jokes during lunch the other day, I didn't know whether to laugh or throw the soup in his face. But unless I lighten up, I won't last through the trial. As I wait for court to resume, I sit in the upstairs video room reading the local paper. Of course it contains nothing about the trial, because of Lavoie's ruling. I have mixed feelings about the publication ban. As a citizen, I believe certain parts of the testimony should be published. As a journalist, I'm happy that the book I've decided to write won't die stillborn a couple of years from now because of media overkill. I also thank God for Debbie, the court clerk, with her corny jokes on this miserable winter morning.

The commissionaire, no longer limping, walks into the room, turns on the TV, and brings the torso of Judge Lavoie into focus. Day 4 of the trial is about to begin. But first, a slight housekeeping matter. Prosecutor Leslie Sullivan stands and, for some reason I don't understand, turns to face the camera. She's wearing, as usual, her professional frown. Then she turns away from the camera and addresses the judge, telling Lavoie that she and her teammate, Bruce Bauer, have lost one of their two copies of the Criminal Code, their Bible. Lavoie scolds the delinquents: It's their tough luck if they lost it, and they can't have another one because the court can't afford the photocopy costs. You'd better go get the one you do have, he scowls. And make it snappy.

Bauer slinks from the courtroom to get the one precious copy he and Sullivan will now share. Lavoie drums his fingers on the desk. The camera waits. We wait, in our video room, thirty bums in seats, sixty eyes not yet fully open. Five minutes pass. Bauer returns, or so we assume, not because we see him on the screen, but because Lavoie looks at his watch and smiles approvingly.

Closed-circuit court TV has its limitations. It's boring. An immobile camera stuck on a tripod, going nowhere, instead of being operated by a real person framing close-ups and panning around the room. But it's safe. Judge Lavoie will never expel the three-legged camera the way Judge Ito expelled his camera operator, twice, during the O.J. Simpson trial. Nothing exciting like that will ever happen here. I look at my notepad, the backs of Sullivan, Bauer, and White, the bust of Judge Lavoie and, occasionally, a corner of Tammy's father's back. With so few distractions, I can concentrate on Kenny's story.

Kenny tells his story

Kenny, the second child to testify against Tammy, is called to the stand. He is Freddy's young friend, who alleges that the woman abused him, too. Just turned nine in December, Kenny sounds like a chirpy little bird, in distinct contrast to Freddy's stone-flat voice. He seems happy to be here and wants to tell the truth. He knows that if you swear on the Bible and then tell a lie, you "get in heck with God...your parents...and the judge."

Lavoie chuckles and puts Kenny through the truth test: Is it true you're thirteen? Kenny says no, and Judge Lavoie swears him in. Then prosecutor Leslie Sullivan tests Kenny's memory.

Sullivan: What did you do for your ninth birthday?

Kenny: We had Michelangelo's pizza — pepperoni and mushroom — and I had a sleepover with six friends, and we played hockey.

Then she tests his long-term memory, asking him to recall the names of his teachers in kindergarten and grade school, which he remembers.
"Who's Freddy?" asks Sullivan. Kenny tells her: He's my friend, and I started to play with him in kindergarten. The first time I went to the Sterlings' I went with Freddy. What does Freddy look like? He's not very tall and he has black hair and big eyes and glasses and "he's fat, a little bit."
This is the closest I'll ever get to knowing what Freddy looks like. But quite possibly Freddy's appearance has changed since Kenny last saw him a couple of years ago. By confirming that Kenny has not seen Freddy since then, Sullivan plans to prove the boys couldn't have colluded on their stories.
Kenny likes to talk, and to draw. Sullivan has supplied him with crayons and a pad of paper, and a desk to sit at. Now Kenny can forge some evidentiary paths of his own, instead of just traipsing after Sullivan. She speaks to him like a kind but stern mother and asks him to draw his first picture of the Sterling house. Tammy's father, from what I can see of his back, is intensely making notes when not biting his nails.
When Kenny is ready, Sullivan asks him to explain his drawing in detail so that the courtroom tape can record his description. It's a task the boy is happy to perform. The Sterling house is blue, he says. There are two doors on the side of the house, but none on the front or back. The doors are rectangular. There are two sheds, some beat-up cars, a disused garden, and a swing set in the yard.
Yes, Kenny answers Sullivan, he has been inside the Sterling house, though he was never babysat there. To prove it, he draws the floor plan and signifies the kitchen "K," the family room "F." Then he describes the furniture. In the family room, there was a TV but, disappointingly, no video games. There were curtains, flowers and pictures, and behind the white couch, three tall shelves, "taller than me." In the kitchen were shelves, a table and a "cink."
What's Tammy like? asks Sullivan, sounding like a Grade 2 teacher asking him what he did during his summer holidays. Kenny responds: She's kind of short and chubby, with long hair, but I forget the colour. She did things "lots of times," he says in his little-boy voice, stressing the word "lots."

Sullivan has Kenny draw The Place and asks him to describe it. He obeys: The building had a wooden door and a garage door with windows. It was "kinda blue" and "pretty big" with an upstairs and downstairs and wood stairs. Upstairs, there was a "raggedy old desk" and a gun. The downstairs floor had sawdust and "all junk stuff" — among other things a cage and a freezer, both of which he spent time in.

Kenny then relates his version of what happened at The Place, giving light-hearted, even humorous, names to some of the incidents. I read somewhere that the childhood game "Ring Around the Rosie" dates back to the time of the Black Death and that the final line in the chant, "Husha, husha, we all fall down," refers to people dying everywhere. If children invented the rhyme, it's a testament to their eternal sense of play, even in the face of death. Most likely, the children who displayed such lightness of spirit were not yet truly acquainted with their own mortality. So it is with Kenny. His upbeat names make traumatic events sound like games, albeit macabre ones. "The First Time in the Freezer" is one such example. Tammy, he claims, put him naked in the freezer and closed the lid for about ten seconds. He remembers "ice water...little drips" and feeling "not good." He says five or six people witnessed the event, including Ron Sterling and three policemen. It must have felt like being buried alive.

Kenny has other bad memories with catchy names, like Terminator Tea Time. He had just come into the house from playing badminton and was watching "The Terminator" on TV, when Tammy entered the room and told him to take his clothes off. When he did, she — with the help of Linda Sterling, the owner of the daycare — squeezed his penis, like a "baseball bat squeeze." (Sullivan asks him to show her what he means and, as he does, she explains for the tape recorder that he's cupping one hand around a finger on the other.) Then, says Kenny, Tammy put a peach-coloured vibrator "up my bum...the part where the poop comes out." The vibrator hurt, especially when "she pulled it out hard." I squirm in my seat. He says he cried but never told anyone, for fear Tammy and Linda would shoot him. He claims that Ed Revesz, a former chief of police, was present during the incident.

He then relates The Tying Time. Freddy came to Kenny's house and begged him to go to the daycare together so he wouldn't "get abused more." After much persuasion, Kenny agreed. The two boys hadn't been at the Sterling house very long when Tammy assaulted Kenny, throwing him on the couch and touching him on the bum and penis. When Sullivan carefully narrates Kenny's live demonstration of The Tying Time for the tape machine — explaining the way he wraps one hand around a finger on the other hand, a make-believe penis — it also helps the twenty of us in the video room who can't see the demonstration for ourselves. Then Kenny resumes the narrative on his own. Travis Sterling stood in the corner of the living room, "snapping" a rope — or "rop," as Kenny labels it in his sketch.

The way the boy describes the rope makes it sound more like a riddle than a recollection: "You can feel the chains in the middle, although you can't see them... There are little hooks which you can't see when you put the parts together... You can put the chains together and take them apart."

It reminds me of a conundrum I used to love about a king, his beautiful daughter, and her many suitors. To win the hand of the princess, each had to try to answer the king's riddle: What's hot and cold at the same time, and good to eat? I spent days trying to figure it out, but never could, and finally my dad had to tell me the answer (hot fudge sundae). Kenny's riddle is about as perplexing, and has no happy ending, though everyone wishes it did. Instead of slaying a dragon or protecting a princess, Kenny had to save himself. He says Travis tried to tie him up with the chain, but, somehow, he managed to escape. He put on his clothes and "I run home... They didn't catch me that time."

Kenny sounds like one of the creatures who lives in the forest surrounding the king's castle. He has finally dared to come out of hiding, climb on to a sunny rock and tell his story. Some might call it a fairy tale, but maybe it's a cautionary tale about a land where once-upon-a-time giants stalked the young and hurt them at whim. It's a child's story, told to grownups. Is anybody listening?

Judge Lavoie is. In this trial he's the one who listens the most and says the least. He will decide if Kenny's story rings true. He alone will call the verdict. For now, he calls a recess.

In the hall, Tammy trudges up the stairs from the courtroom below. As she climbs, her knees bend, but no other part of her body moves, as though it's locked, frozen stiff, in a cast from hips to head. She's twenty-one, but now looks eighty. She was a child when she allegedly abused the boys. But was she ever really a child? I'd like to think she has enjoyed some carefree times in her life, though it must be hard when you know you could die at any time if you didn't have your insulin. I hope she was a much-loved child. I hope she has some positive memories while she munches her apple and slowly swings her short legs, waiting on the bench in the hall for court to resume.

These feelings for Tammy surprise me, and war with my journalistic, voyeuristic side. But even if I feel a sincere interest in the young woman, she may snub me. Prepared for the worst, I walk over to her.

I smile and ask what she thinks of Kenny's evidence, trying not to give anything away by raising my voice or eyebrows. In her high, little-girl voice, which I haven't heard till now, she speaks her mind: "They're getting coached real good... He's a real smart kid." Encouraged by her willingness to talk, I ask why she's wearing the Medic-Alert necklace, and she gives me a list of reasons, almost without stopping for breath.

Born diabetic, Tammy had her pancreas removed when she was still very young. She also had her left ovary and gall bladder taken out as a child, and several rounds of plastic surgery for the extensive surgical scarring. When I say I'm sorry, and mean it, she dismisses my condolence with a shrug: "It's no big deal." Tammy wants sympathy, yet doesn't. I wonder if parts of her heart were torn out too, or her soul. First she takes the time to tell her medical history, then she says it's no big deal. Push, pull. The psychologist's assessment of Tammy comes to mind, a copy of which a colleague slipped me the other day. Tammy, it says, suffers from low self-esteem and alienation on the one hand, and extreme self-centredness on the other. I'm no psychologist, but from this brief encounter I can see her conflicted behaviour. I wonder what her scars look like.

Back in court, I scribble the incident near the back of my notepad, so as not to forget. Then Kenny's testimony resumes. He tells Sullivan how to get to The Place, which he calls The Fort. "You take the road away from Saskatoon, by my right hand," begins the boy. Unlike Freddy, Kenny claims he was not blindfolded, so he could see: First we went on cement roads, then gravel roads, then we passed a gravel pit and hills. Hills? In this part of Saskatchewan? That detail alone is worth something, and should have made the police's job of finding The Fort easy. That is, if there is any such place.

If The Fort is just a figment of Kenny's imagination, he has very strong memories of it. Not only of the freezer, and Tammy's putting him in it, but also of the cage. To show what the cage looked like, the boy asks for more paper. Then he draws it and gives a private showing to Sullivan, along with a running commentary that sounds like another riddle, this one less like a fairy tale and more like the quiz show, "Jeopardy!" Kenny says: It has six sides and is hollow; it's skinny and tall, tall enough to stand in, but not wide enough to sit; it has a fence around it with "kind of diamond shapes" made of steel, like a fence surrounding a jail.

Is this the same cage Freddy talked about? The one the kids were locked in and hoisted into the air in? As I recall, Freddy likened the wiring to a baseball-field fence, not a jail. But I see striking similarities between the two boys' descriptions.

Kenny's language is less sophisticated than Freddy's. He's two years younger than his friend. The difference in development shows when it comes to frank talk about anatomy.

At The Fort, sometimes Tammy was dressed; other times she was naked and Kenny touched her boobs, her bum, and her "middle part." What do you mean by "middle part?" Sullivan asks. "The part between your legs and stomach, and by your bum. I don't know what it's called on a female." What are boobs? "Those things under their chin. They're round. Girls have them." Kenny sounds like a Martian encountering an Earthling for the first time. First I smile, then I feel angry. If his story is true, he had a brutal introduction to sex. At seven years of age, he was raped in a cruel and careless manner. If he's telling the truth and I were his mother, I'd be overcome with grief.

Which is why I didn't tell mother what Donny Burroughs once made me do. How could I when I loved her so much and knew how she'd be hurt to hear her little girl had been deceived?

When I was eleven, I went to the house of Donny, a classmate, to pick up the birdhouse he'd made me for a science project. He invited me into his backyard tent and I went in, even though I felt uneasy. Holding a flashlight in my face, Donny told me — it came as a complete surprise — that if I wanted the birdhouse so badly I would have to give him something he wanted in return. I remember feeling sick at the prospect of letting a boy see my breasts, but desperate for the birdhouse, and a bit thrilled by his interest in me. After dickering for what seemed an eternity, we compromised: I would lift my blouse briefly, but not remove it, so he could take a quick peek, after which I would get the birdhouse. Forty years later I laugh at the incident, but still remember the anger I felt at being blackmailed. The way I was trapped, and the shame I felt when I saw my mom. I couldn't tell her I was no longer her pure and innocent little girl, and decided to act as though nothing had happened. I carried the shame for years, until I was old enough to smile about it.

It's one thing to have your first sexual encounter with a peer, someone your own size, someone as innocent as you and just as inquisitive. It's normal for two kids like Donny and me to explore sexuality and make the first male-female deal of one's life: a breast for a birdhouse. It's quite another thing when an adult with urgent needs, and no regard for anyone else's, forces a child to satisfy them. Kenny says, "I was embarrassed, I was nervous," describing the time Tammy did the "limbo" and he touched his hard penis to her middle part. "How did Tammy's vagina smell?" Sullivan asks matter-of-factly. "Smooshy," says the boy, without hesitation.

Court is dismissed for the day. Janis, the TV reporter, and I go for coffee at Tip Top Café, where she keeps repeating the word "smooshy." She probably wishes she could use it for the news tonight, but no such luck because of the ban on the kids' testimony. Kenny, like other kids, probably invents words all the time. But "smooshy" is a keeper and seems based on some kind of knowledge. At least, Janis thinks so, and I see what she means. Smooshy is one of those sound-words where several meanings are rolled into one — squishy, smooth, yucky — all at the same time. A word you'd use when all others failed.

On Day 5 of the trial, the last day of the first week, Tim White will now defend his client Tammy by cross-examining Kenny. Take away the legal mumbo jumbo and what we have is a nine-year-old schoolboy in the witness box, being interrogated by a lawyer with more than twenty years of criminal-law practice under his belt. White's tough. Over the years he has cross-examined scores of witnesses to defend his clients, the country's criminals, designated the "scum of the earth" in a recent issue of a national lawyers' magazine. Now White will question a child and try to cast doubt on the boy's credibility.

White begins: If Kenny saw Tammy's body naked more than a couple of times, as he claims, it should be easy to remember the scars on her body. Maybe it should be easy, but it isn't if you don't even know what a scar is. "Like a scratch": that's Kenny's definition. After all White's years in court, I'll bet this is his first time to cross-examine a witness who doesn't know what a scar is.

Kenny may be young, but he is a fighter. At first, he sounds sure of himself, echoing the testimony of Freddy: The Fort (Kenny's name for The Place) had three storeys and stairs that "creaked." At The Fort there was a wire cage that kids were put in. (He's self-assured enough to interrupt his testimony long enough to count to six, the number of sides he claims the cage had.) Like Freddy, Kenny claims he went to The Fort in broad daylight, usually in Ron Sterling's red car but sometimes in a blue police car with white stripes, hands tied behind his back with the riddle rope. "More than twenty times," he chirps.

Preparing to pounce, White says: Kenny, let me ask you something. If your wrists were bound, how come your parents never noticed marks on them? Kenny is ready for this question: His arms were sore for a day or two after because of the chain-metal links inside the fabric tube, but no one noticed. He was very upset and mad about the incident. But he didn't tell anyone, not even his parents. He says there were many things he kept bottled up till months after the fact.

White continues: Let me ask you something else, Kenny.

White: Did she [Bryden] ever show you photographs?

Kenny: Yeah.

White: And what did she show you photographs of?

Kenny: The Fort [The Place] and the gun and the weapons and Sterlings' house and lots of stuff.

White: And after she showed you the pictures of The Fort, did that help you to remember things about The Fort?

Kenny: Yeah, that helped me a little bit.

White: Am I right in thinking that it was after she'd showed you those photographs that you started to talk about The Fort for the first time?

Kenny: Yeah...

White: I gather that when Claudia Bryden showed you the pictures you found that pretty exciting, is that fair?

Kenny: Yeah.

Fair? The nine-year-old witness thinks the word "exciting" means surprising, as we will learn later. Though handicapped in this setting by his little-boy vocabulary, Kenny wants to make sure he is not misunderstood. After his ready admissions, followed by a brief pause, he elaborates: He saw the evidence first, with his own eyes. He saw the vibrator, the ropes, the camera and "all that stuff" at the Sterling house before he ever saw them in the police photos. Then, when he saw the pictures, they helped him remember The Fort and encouraged him to talk to Claudia Bryden about it.

There are many other things Kenny remembered without the help of photos: touching Tammy's "round, fat, peach-coloured" boobs with "dark peach" nipples, touching her bum and "middle part," and getting needles in his thigh, bum, and penis. At this, Sullivan rises to object, interrupting White's cross-exam and nipping Kenny's testimony in the bud. The boy has gone too far, Sullivan says, raising a "collateral issue" to be dealt with in a later trial. Lavoie must dismiss Kenny's comment about needles, for now. Sullivan sits down.

White asks Kenny: What are your favourite movies? sounding intimate, as though swapping Hollywood titles in the playground at recess. *Aladdin* and *Terminator II*, says the boy with emphasis. Is Terminator real? asks White, who just can't seem to wait to pin Kenny to the wall. Though Kenny may not know what a scar is, he knows truth from fiction. Terminator is "not real," he says, it's just a movie. Still, he enjoyed watching it at the daycare. At the daycare? Who, I wonder, would let a nine-year-old watch *Terminator II* at the daycare? That may be my concern, but it's not White's.

He exhorts Kenny: Try to remember the first time you talked about any of the alleged events to your mom or Constable Claudia Bryden. Kenny says he told his mom about the cage long before he ever told Claudia Bryden. But by now Kenny has told so many things to so many people — his parents, the police, the lawyers — it's a wonder he keeps it all straight. Before long, he can't. In the quick-moving stream of White's questions, he begins to flounder: Which came first, going to The Fort and seeing the guns and the cage, or seeing Bryden's photos of the guns and the cage? Where did Tammy touch him, and when? Did she do it at the Sterling daycare or The Fort?

Kenny is sure about one thing and will not be budged, despite White's best attempts: Was it not just yesterday, Kenny, that you told someone for the first time Tammy put a vibrator "up [your] bum?" (The defence lawyer hopes such an eleventh-hour revelation would decrease the value of Kenny's testimony, and make it less credible.) No, it's not true, Kenny corrects his cross-examiner, sounding like an upright schoolmaster scolding a student. The truth, says the boy, is that he told several people before yesterday. Sullivan rises to corroborate the statement. Apparently, even the word of the Crown prosecutor is not good enough for the defence lawyer. White needs independent evidence, and time to get it. Lavoie permits a short break. White rushes from the courtroom.

I take my time in the washroom and wander into the hall, hoping to use the pay phone. Ron Sterling has beaten me to it. As co-operator of the daycare where Tammy allegedly abused the kids, he is scheduled for his own trial several months from now. I expect he sits in court every day to see what lies in store for him and to help Tammy. "Hi," says Sterling to the person at the other end of the phone. Where did we rent the Terminator movie for the daycare kids? He instructs the person at the other end to call the video stores and get the release date of *Terminator II*.

Something's up, though I don't know what. Now I don't need the can of Coke from the pop machine to perk me up.

Back in the courtroom, White's out to trap Kenny, with the help of the Terminator. He asks: Was it *Terminator I* or *II* you saw at the daycare, Kenny? *Terminator II*, the witness answers. Though White says nothing, I get the impression he has just learned the release date of *Terminator II*, and knows that Kenny could not possibly have seen it before then.

Kenny's vibrator-up-the-bum story depends on dates, too. White asks the boy again: Did he, or did he not, tell anyone before yesterday? Indeed he did, says Prosecutor Sullivan, as a phone call to Rod Butler, the boy's therapist, has just confirmed. According to the therapist's notes, Kenny disclosed the incident about nine months ago, on June 24, 1992, to be precise.

Kenny sounds less chirpy this afternoon. The strain is taking its toll on him, and I've heard he sometimes vomits in the downstairs bathroom before taking the stand. Now he wants his afternoon snack and a chance to watch videos in the witness waiting room. Lavoie takes pity on him and calls another short recess, during which the adults engage in their own kind of recreation, which is gossip. In the corridor a middle-aged woman who comes to court every day circulates a petition and gets eight other regulars to sign. It reads:

> Your Honour,
>
> We, the undersigned, wish to formally protest the limited seating provided for the trial of the young offender in the Martensville cases. Given your ruling that the public could view and hear the testimony of the children by way of television, it is in fact contradictory that we as citizens are denied to witness how justice is conducted in a case as important as this. Particularly in view that the media has been prevented from reporting on this case. We demand more seating will be made available.
>
> Sincerely,
>
> Evelyn Morgan et al.

After fifteen minutes or so of break, we squeeze back into the video room of "limited seating." Given the mood of the petition committee, I feel lucky to have any seat at all.

Kenny is refreshed. Crown Prosecutor Sullivan wants to re-examine the boy and clear up a few things that emerged during his cross-examination. In particular, she wants Judge Lavoie to hear what Kenny meant when he testified that he was "excited" to see Claudia Bryden with her photos. Under re-exam, the boy explains that he meant he was "surprised" to see the photos again. When Sullivan asks why he didn't immediately tell his parents what was happening to him at the Sterling house, the small disembodied voice on the TV monitor replies, "The Sterlings would shoot me if I told someone."

Still at issue is the sequence of events. Is Kenny's knowledge of The Place based on his own experience, or did Claudia Bryden plant ideas in his head when she showed him the photos during her investigation? Though the question is not resolved when the child witness steps down, he is tired. His courtroom appointment is over. "At least, I got it over now," Kenny tells the court, sighing.

No one in the stuffy video room says a word. We've been here since Kenny entered the witness box, and now it's time to hurry to the second-storey courtroom to see more police evidence with our own eyes. The next witness is Constable Claudia Bryden. Under normal circumstances she would have been cross-examined right after her examination-in-chief the other day. But the court had to revamp the schedule and decided to shuffle Bryden's second appearance so as not to interfere with the courtroom appointments made for the child witnesses. The plastic bucket chairs in this room have bent my back out of shape, and my left wrist is stiff from writing nonstop for hours. I never thought I'd look forward to another rendezvous with those hard wooden benches upstairs.

Rookie policewoman on trial

Up two flights of stairs, the RCMP officer, holster on hip, opens the door of courtroom number 8 and lets us free-for-all to the public seating. The journalists, seven or eight today, make a beeline for the front row and pile our winter coats in the corner. The writer from Toronto, who wants nothing to do with local journalists, seats himself in a back row, among the 20 people, mostly older women today. A young Native woman rolls her wheelchair in and parks by the door.

Sullivan, Bauer, and White, re-robed for their adult witnesses, traipse into the room with their heavy black bags. Judge Lavoie, the high priest, takes to his throne. He sits, we sit, and the RCMP officer goes to fetch Constable Claudia Bryden, waiting in the hall.

Bryden's identity, unlike Kenny's and Freddy's, is public knowledge. For weeks we've seen her photogenic face on the supper-hour news and in the morning paper. She sat in the witness box yesterday for hours during her examination-in-chief, and will now sit there again for her cross-exam. The honey blonde looks unassailable in her dark tweed suit, plain grey blouse, and matching leather boots. But there's a vulnerability to her small shoulders, and a world-weary expression that tells me she can't wait for her turn on the stand to be over, too.

Bryden's story may have holes and contradictions in it, and Tim White intends to find every one, as he attempted to do with Freddy and Kenny. Tammy did not commit the crimes she is accused of. Even if she had, says White, we would never know it because of the police, who acted unprofessionally, putting ideas in the daycare kids' heads.

White intends to trip Bryden up or break her down. He asks her, To your knowledge, did Kenny disclose The Fort before you recorded him on tape,

June 1, 1992? Cool as a cucumber, Bryden opens her notebook and turns to the right page: Yes, he disclosed it in the afternoon of April 11, she says. White asks for more — "What do your notes say?" Bryden reads her own writing in her police notebook: "At [Kenny's family's house], Kenny identified photos of the suspect location, and stated he had been there with Freddy. [Jim] Elstad and Travis Sterling had taken him and Freddy there via the police car and the Sterling Camaro." Making sure he gets his point across to the judge, White summarizes, "And that was the same day [April 11, 1992] that you showed him the photographs of The Place?" Yes, answers Bryden. I'm starting to doubt that I'll ever know for sure what came first, the chicken or the egg.

Bryden says that between March 31 and June 3, 1992, she had eight meetings with Kenny, two of them taped — one on audio and one on video. White asks Bryden to read the transcript from one of these two taped interviews recorded in the Soft Room of the Saskatoon police station, hoping to let the judge hear for himself how the rookie got the kids to talk. Prosecutor Bauer rises to object that the transcript is not completely correct and that it sometimes differs from the soundtrack on the tape. Bauer and White compete in a brief verbal tussle till Judge Lavoie intervenes, criticizing Bauer for not making sure before now that the two versions were identical. The video soundtrack-transcribed-to-paper is admissible, he rules, adding that merely hearing the words of the interview, without seeing the original tape of the interview, would be a bit like reading the script for a movie rather than going to the theatre. It would be "out of context." So, even though Judge Lavoie will let Bryden read some of the tapes-transcribed-to-paper, he might assign "no weight" whatever to the written dialogue when he considers his verdict.

Videotapes? I wonder when we'll see them and whether the scales-of-justice statue will remove her blindfold for the occasion. For the first time, I grasp the meaning of the blindfold. It stops the stone lady — the symbol of justice — from seeing the courtroom evidence. Unable to see it, she must weigh it, impartially and dispassionately. How rich! This is a trial about seeing and not seeing. It is a trial about boys who couldn't see because of their alleged blindfolds, presided over by a statue reputed to see the truth only when wearing one.

The room is crackling with tension. White, for one, looks as though he's about to explode. On the face of it, he just got what he wanted — a chance to show the court how suggestive Bryden's questions to Kenny were. But it's a hollow victory, if Judge Lavoie decides to give the transcripts no weight whatsoever. The defence lawyer can always hope he'll get lucky and that Lavoie will change his mind once he hears how Bryden talked to the kids. In the face of such odds, White has no choice but to proceed. He faces the constable in the witness stand and, in a resigned tone, tells her to begin.

Bryden blinks two or three times, bows her head, takes a slow sip of water, and prepares to read from the black binder transcript of her April 3, 1992, interview with Kenny. "I wish I could sound as lighthearted as Kenny," she tells the court, half-smiling. But when she starts to read, she sounds like Freddy — flat, stone-cold, and far away.

> Bryden (to Kenny): Want to scooch up a little closer?... I like to sit close to people I talk to...

In mid-sentence her words stop, her voice cracks, and she chokes back tears. The courtroom sits in stunned silence, and Tim White offers her a drink of water. I stop writing and look up. The CBC reporter chews on his pen and looks over at me, like a sheepdog begging for a day off. Lavoie removes his glasses and rubs the bridge of his nose. Bryden apologizes and asks to be excused for five minutes to "compose" herself. A break, she says, will help her read the interview with feeling, the way it sounds on tape, and capture for the court the emotional struggle Kenny experienced during the interview the previous year. Lavoie has no choice but to call a short recess, which Bryden spends in the women's washroom across the hall, splashing cold water on her eyes.

Five minutes later Bryden's five-minute reprieve is up, which Lavoie indicates by swinging open his private door to the courtroom and taking his seat. Holding our breath, we wait for Bryden to try again, all of us looking like expectant parents at a piano recital. Bryden is sensitive, probably embarrassed, and determined not to humiliate herself further. Slowly, methodically, she re-opens the binder, turning to the transcript of her April 3 meeting with Kenny. White hopes that when the judge hears how Bryden conducted the session, he judge will see how frequently the officer led the boy to provide the answers she sought. If only her techniques were that easy to dissect and analyze. As I sit there listening to Bryden read the transcript, my opinion of her interview skills shifts back and forth. If she is guilty of trying to get Kenny to talk, she must also get credit for letting him answer her questions the way he wanted.

> Bryden: ...And by being here and talking to us you're doing...a really good job, you are. Is there anything else that I should maybe know, or that you want to talk about that we haven't talked about?
>
> Kenny: I can't remember some of that stuff.
>
> Bryden: Yeah. I'll tell you something. Sometimes when things

> happen to people, whether it's little kids or even adults, sometimes when bad things happen we like to stick the memories of those things back, away in the back, of our minds in a little dresser that has a tiny, little drawer. We stick it in the drawer and we shut the drawer and we leave it there for a long, long time and we just forget about it...

Depending on your perspective, Bryden was either manipulating Kenny to say things that were false or supporting him in his struggle to tell the truth. The techniques she used with the boy on April 3, 1992, can be debated till the cows come home for one simple reason: the interview was taped.

Months before that meeting, Bryden had met Kenny for the first time. As a police officer, she knew she was supposed to tape every word the eight-year-old uttered. Yet she didn't. White wants to know why, and she gives him two reasons: She didn't want to distract Kenny. And she did not like the Martensville force's tape recorder. This dilemma is one every journalist can understand. Tape recorders create as many problems as they solve, maybe more —once I thought mine was recording when it wasn't; another time I had the tape speed button on "high," which might have made the Minister of Justice sound like Alvin the Chipmunk on radio news if I hadn't caught the error in time. After such life-shortening experiences, I've gone back to recording most interviews with a pencil, as Bryden says she decided to do. It's slower but soon you learn to write without looking at the page. Of course, your writing turns to scrawl and your shortcuts become a secret code.

When I flip through my note pad, it's hard to imagine that the quirky shorthand could ever be used to prove anything. It's even harder to imagine it ever *would* be used, with as much at stake as there is here. But no matter how indecipherable, a police officer's notes, like a journalist's, constitute *bona fide* evidence in court. Bryden's notes are the only record she has for six of her eight meetings with Kenny. White asks what exactly she did during each of these meetings. From her notes, Bryden summarizes the dates she interviewed Freddy and Kenny, and tells White which items and which photos she showed to which boy on which occasion. How will the judge ever know for sure if Kenny told Bryden about The Place before she showed him the photos? Judge Lavoie has nothing to go on but her notes and her word.

Day 5 of the trial closes quietly with witness number 7, the last one for the week. Al Bishoff is a tall, distinguished man with greying hair. By now every person in the room has heard — and some have also seen — the most intimate details of this man's life: the bed he sleeps in, the files he keeps, the state of his toilet and kitchen sink. Bishoff owns the blue building north of Martensville, the alleged scene of the crime. He isn't in the running for the

Good Housekeeping seal of approval that year, but I doubt that someone who seems so easygoing worries much about housework. The witness tells prosecutor Sullivan he knows none of the accused and explains to the court he designed the blue building — which he calls the shed — as a workshop. There he also lived, off and on, from winter 1988 till fall 1989. Though frequently absent from his property during this period for weeks at a time, the witness says his returns and departures were very predictable. Then for several months in fall 1991, he stayed away full-time. In his absence, his wife and son seldom locked the door of the building. Bishoff says that the garage door at The Place was operated manually and not, as Kenny testified earlier, by remote control. The now infamous freezer Kenny claims he was locked in was used, says Bishoff, for the animals he slaughtered. The cage Freddy and Kenny say they were put in was used to keep chicks warm, according to the man. Bishoff's long absences from his property, during which he worked in locations as far away as Yellowknife, fall within the time frame of some of the criminal charges.

The witness answers clearly all the questions put to him by Leslie Sullivan. Then he is cross-examined by defence lawyer Tim White: Did you have reason to suspect that anyone outside your family ever used the building? No, answers Bishoff, he had no reason for concern, except for the strange tire tracks inside the garage. Strange tire tracks? Bishoff says that one day his wife told him their son had recently seen a police van leaving the garage of the blue building and asked if he could explain the incident. He couldn't, he told his wife, and totally forgot about the mysterious tracks. Bishoff is convinced he always got acceptable answers from his wife and son, whenever he asked about unfamiliar tire tracks on the property. "There was never any question left hanging," he says with confidence. I wish I could say the same.

The experts aren't sure

Week 2 of the trial begins and ends with a special breed of witness: the expert. Expert witnesses answer questions and give opinions, which they are qualified to do after years of education, training, and on-the-job experience. A lawyer looks for an expert who will buttress his or her theories about the crime allegedly committed, and the process is selective. Consider the Paul Bernardo case, in which the prosecution asked two Ontario coroners to give their opinion as to how schoolgirl Leslie Mahaffy died. The first coroner said the evidence led him to believe strangulation was the cause. The second said blood loss resulted in the girl's death. Since the prosecution had already based its case on the strangulation theory, it invited only the first expert witness to testify.

For Tammy's trial, the Crown prosecutors selected their experts months ago. The medical specialists know the telltale signs of sexual abuse, at least as much as anyone can, and have scrutinized the evidence to answer two questions for the court: What is sexual abuse? How can one be sure that it has occurred?

The vast quantity of research on sexual abuse makes the "what" question easier for the experts to answer than the "how." How does one prove a child was raped when there's neither a pregnancy-in-progress nor a trace of sperm? How can there be evidence of sperm when the alleged rapist is female? The experts can only examine the behaviour of the accused and the two alleged victims, *a posteriori*, and match it to a known pattern of sexual abuse. For the next few days the experts will tell the court how many facts about Tammy and Freddy and Kenny match the "fact" pattern, how many don't, and how many gaps appear in the evidence.

Patterns, gaps, matches, mismatches. The process of expert testimony reminds me of a game my brother and I used to play. When I was eight and he was five we both got measles and Mom was told by the doctor to protect our eyes from the sun. Down came the curtain, up went a blanket, no more daylight in our bedroom. The blanket was made of brushed cotton and in the middle there was a picture of an Indian in headdress. It protected our eyes, but in the semi-darkness of the bedroom we could hardly see anything. We hated it and often pulled it off the window.

One day an aunt gave us a jigsaw puzzle with the identical Indian-head design. We discovered the puzzle pieces would stick to the blanket, transforming the Indian head from a flat picture to a sculptured one. We perfected our aim and drew up rules for Magic Blanket Bingo. Taking turns standing on the bed, we threw pieces at the blanket, quietly, so as not to call attention to what we were doing. Some stuck firmly to the cotton, others hung for hours seemingly by a thread, while most of the pieces fell to the floor. The rules prevented us from getting off the bed to move pieces into place or to try to make them stick with our hands (a rule my brother introduced since he was shorter than I, and not tall enough to reach the tip of the Indian's feathers). But it was perfectly legal to increase a piece's adhesion before throwing it. (I rubbed my pieces on my nightie, he spit on his.) The winner was the one with the most pieces stuck to the Indian head.

Sullivan and White remind me of my brother and me, competing in a stuffy room for pennies. At stake here are hundreds of thousands of dollars, a jail term for Tammy, the word of Freddy and Kenny, and the lawyers' reputations. Sullivan wants the judge to believe the boys, White wants him to believe Tammy. To help her win the case, Sullivan has called on six experts with fact patterns for sexual abuse. Each expert will hold up the pattern for the court while Sullivan and White throw pieces of evidence at it. Some pieces will match the known pattern of sexual abuse and stick; others will not fit the pattern at all and will fall on the floor; some will hang by a thread. When enough pieces have been put in place, a sculptured picture will emerge. Sullivan hopes her picture will show that Tammy is an abuser; White, that the boys have too-vivid imaginations.

Sometimes, in our increasingly complex world, covering a courtroom window with an "expert" blanket can help a lawyer win the case. But only if the blanket is just the right thickness. If it's too thin and lets in too much light the brilliance may rob the jury of its own sight. The trial then becomes trial by expert. If, on the other hand, the blanket is too thick and blocks the light, the jury may grope in darkness and lose its way. Again, trial driven by the expert. Because of this, the decision to call upon expert witnesses is a very delicate matter. They must know not only their stuff, but also how to present it clearly and plainly, shedding just the right amount of light on their area of expertise. And cost is a factor, too, when the Crown calls expert witnesses and pays the bill. Sullivan has spent a lot of time finding six people who can fill the bill without overspending the Crown's budget.

The first expert is a plump matronly woman, Dr. Eleanor Anne McKenna, associate professor of paediatrics and a paediatrician at the Royal University Hospital since 1980. Despite her credentials, the lawyers and the judge must accredit her as an expert before letting her speak like one in court. In a process that is repeated for all subsequent expert witnesses at this trial, her professional résumé is handed to the clerk and labelled as evidence. Then Dr. McKenna must prove it really is her résumé and that she is who she says she is· by answering four or five questions from the prosecution and the defence. Dr. McKenna's training, experience, and international reputation satisfy Judge Lavoie and he qualifies her as an expert witness in certain specialties, in which she will be allowed to give an opinion during Tammy's trial.

An expert in child abuse, Dr. McKenna has examined hundreds of children during ten years of practice, although Freddy and Kenny were not among them. The first medical doctor in the trial to take the stand, she confronts us with the details of what happens to a small boy's body when raped. Until now I've only considered psychological and emotional trauma. Now I must listen to the doctor explain the physical damage caused when a hard object is repeatedly thrust into the anus. It's damage you can see and touch, and from the matter-of-fact way Dr. McKenna speaks I can tell she has had to, many times.

As though lecturing first-year medical students, the doctor speaks calmly and plainly. The trauma to the anus, the dilation and pain, may lead to other serious problems. The physical pain of being anally raped, and the memory of it, may be so strong in a boy's memory that he may seek to avoid the pain at all cost, even refusing to have bowel movements. In the double negatives academics like to use, Dr. McKenna concludes that chronic constipation is a not infrequent finding in girls and boys who have been sexually abused. She has set the stage for other specialists who will follow as witnesses.

I look into space, trying to absorb the impact of this information. It's hard to imagine not wanting to defecate, or refusing to, because it hurts. Hard to imagine how strong a memory must be when you can't stop it from dominating your basic needs and threatening your vital functions.

Does the memory of rape ever fade? Does the body ever heal? Does sexual abuse rewire a child's brain? The topic holds increasing appeal for psychologists everywhere, and one of the hottest issues is False Memory Syndrome: Do individuals imagine memories of abuse? Do they know when they are making up memories? Are children suggestible enough that someone can make them believe they were abused even though they weren't? Who is qualified to judge whether a child was abused?

The next witness is Dr. John Charles Yuille, a forensic psychologist and internationally respected authority on children's capacity to remember. The middle-aged man, bearded and balding, spends his life asking these kinds of questions. As an expert in forensic psychology, a new area of expertise, the UBC professor is a pioneer. For much of his career, he has forged new ground, not in laboratories, but on school playgrounds. Bicycle thefts, premeditated and carefully staged, are his specialty. The avuncular-looking pedagogue regularly enlists kids to play-act the role of victim while others play the role of witness to a staged schoolyard theft. During each experiment, Dr. Yuille takes notes and later evaluates how much information the child witnesses can recall, how accurately they remember, and how susceptible they are to an adult's suggestion.

The professor — who stays calm and maintains eye contact with Leslie Sullivan throughout her examination-in-chief — says his experiments have shown that the younger the victims, the less they remember and the more susceptible they are to his, or anyone's, suggestion. But by the time a child is eleven or twelve, the memory is comparable to an adult's and the child is less suggestible.

How old were Freddy and Kenny at the time of Bryden's investigation? Freddy, now eleven, was nine years old; Kenny was seven. Since I can't do the math and write at the same time, I stop writing. After working nonstop for the past hour, I need a rest, or at least a change. Even a cough or whisper would be a relief. But the courtroom is absolutely still, except for the voice of Yuille, all the more compelling because of his soft-spokenness, an old teaching trick he has probably perfected at UBC.

It's so quiet I wonder who's still in court and turn to look. The pews are as full as before, but the usual fidgeting and gum-chewing have given way to rapt stillness. Clearly, the professor knows how to make his audience pay attention. Even if his lecture techniques weren't so smooth, his topic is surefire. He's talking not just *to* his listeners, but *about* them. He's giving us, his students, a crash course in human memory.

In his forensic work, Yuille concentrates on two kinds of memory storage — "episodic memory," which is the ability, apparently unique to humans, to call up specific past events; and "script memory," a behaviour guideline for ourselves and others. Violations to the behaviour code, or script, are something we usually remember with great clarity, as the psychologist proceeds to illustrate: Suppose you've been married to the same person for a long time and have a "long-term marriage sex script." Try to remember what you did in the bedroom on a particular day (or night), and you'll have difficulty because your memories of sexual events all blend together, unless you or your partner have violated the script in some way. The attentive silence in the room has changed to an embarrassed hush. Is the good doctor asking us to meditate on our sex lives? Is he trying to hold our attention with an invitation to erotic fantasy? I do that in private, not in a roomful of strangers. And definitely not in the middle of a trial about sexual perversion. My cheeks turn red.

But there is no reddening of the cheeks or cracking in the mask of Judge Lavoie. He is paid to sit stone-faced, day in, day out, listening to all kinds of things and trying to make sense of them. It's been a while since he's made any kind of joke. After all his years on the bench, he probably hears what is not said as much as what is. Right now he senses the need for a recess.

The public, about twenty today, spills into the hall. Zoltan, an out-of-town journalist I know slightly, comes over and is about to begin a post mortem of Yuille's testimony when Ron Sterling joins in, uninvited. At first I'm annoyed at being interrupted, ticked off by his pushiness. Then I realize that, no matter how he acts in this courthouse, he may actually crave acceptance. It's possible he feels like an outsider, and certain he talks like one. That stuff Yuille is saying applies to you "normal" people, not to those of us who are "abnormal," says Sterling, grinning.

I don't know what to say. Maybe Sterling is trying to second-guess Zoltan and me, or just making fun of everybody, himself included. Perhaps his cockiness is his way of clutching onto sanity in the midst of chaos. I guess I'd appreciate such bravura if I heard it over drinks in a bar. But we're standing in the corridor of a criminal court where his wife's home daycare is on trial and where, in a few months' time, he himself will be on trial for child abuse. Sterling leaves our company as abruptly as he joined it. "Go figure," says Zoltan, rolling his eyes.

We take our seats again and Yuille, in response to Sullivan's prompting, proceeds: "As long as they're carefully interviewed" children will be about as accurate as adults, which means right eighty to ninety per cent of the time. Carefully interviewed? I'm sure White will pounce on this. Yuille says adults and kids tend to make the same kinds of errors, though children exaggerate more when it comes to time, distance, weight, and height.

The professor continues: When interviewing children, one should avoid direct questions that "suggest" there should be an answer. It's important to relieve the child of the burden of trying to answer a question. After the child makes a disclosure, he says, he recommends open questions such as "Did this happen once or more than once?" "Do you remember the colour of the underwear?" The professor explains that, when a child tells a story, especially a preschooler, he will tell you the most important or interesting event first and then give the other details. The story may therefore seem jumbled to an adult.

From the sound of it, Yuille actually prefers questioning children to adults. They have less general knowledge of the world, and they can't make up credible details to fill the gaps in their stories, no matter how much you coach them. In this way, kids are better than adults, according to the expert. Unless a child has actually had the experience, he can't make it up convincingly; and if he tries to, you'll soon know it.

Yuille says that some details of a child's story come and go with each telling, even when the child is telling the truth. For this reason it's important to listen to the story more than once. If you're patient, the child tests the water, giving you fresh details each time in sequential disclosure. I wonder: What good is it, then, for a child to give evidence in court only once?

Yuille maintains that children lack the cognitive capacity to fabricate events completely. Unless they've had a particular experience, the details of their story will be scanty and fantastic, missing chapters before and after the main event. If the story is true, the child may tell you what he was doing at the time he was interrupted by the perpetrator. This is called "contextual imbeddedness." Kenny talked about watching Terminator when Tammy supposedly walked in on him. Freddy claimed he went back to playing with his toy motorcycle after Tammy had finished sucking his penis.

What about coaching the kids with photos, prosecutor Sullivan asks, anticipating that White will seize on this part of the police investigation when he cross-examines Yuille. The doctor nods. Photos, he says, could certainly have provided the source of the children's experience. But if the kids had been coached with photos, their impact would fade quickly with time, within a matter of days. He has done many experiments to measure how kids recollect events and concluded they remember a real one far more clearly than photos.

Sullivan asks, What about leading questions? Yuille tells her that a few are sometimes quite in order when interviewing a younger child, just to get the ball rolling. But the interviewer must then step back and let the child tell the story. The questioner must ask the child as few yes-no questions as possible in favour of open-ended ones, in a supportive and open atmosphere.

So ground-breaking is Yuille's research, so careful his question-and-answer techniques, that they're applied by police in some European countries, as well as several Canadian provinces. His method, called "Step-Wise," is the one Claudia Bryden learned during the four-day course. She took it after the investigation.

After the long day in court, the last thing I feel like doing is going to a lecture this evening, especially when I see frost covering most of the kitchen window. But I want to know more about the role of the expert witness in court, and Murray James Malcolm of the RCMP crime lab in Regina is in Saskatoon to talk about the subject at the library. At the last minute I dither about trading the warmth of home for a cold car, but "Science and the Law" wins out.

Malcolm is a middle-aged forensic toxicologist with a chiselled jaw his beard could never hide. His thesis is clear: The expert's primary duty is to "educate the tryer of fact" — Judge Lavoie, in this case — about designated technical matters. This puts a lot of responsibility on the shoulders of the expert witness in the courtroom, but confers no special power or privilege on him or her. In fact, no one at a trial is legally bound to believe what an expert says. And the tryer of fact is not expected to take the expert's testimony seriously, unless it's well-reasoned and defensible. In a world as complex as ours, "a truly informed response might be messy because it's very complex rather than simple," says the lecturer.

No matter how complex the subject, the expert must know what he's talking about and sound as though he does, talking in language that his non-expert listeners can understand. This may mean putting a lot of time and energy into preparing for court.

But even after all the homework is done, the expert can expect to find himself in a difficult spot, according to Malcolm. The court wants black-and-white answers, while the expert may know that there are only shades of grey. During the courtroom contest, the scientist says, the expert must try to keep his professional integrity in the face of bullying lawyers. Even when counsel tries to wring a yes or no out of the expert, he must refuse to reduce a complex topic to a simple answer.

Leaving my tea half-finished was worth it when I hear Malcolm compare the scientific to the legal mind. Scientists don't stake their careers on right and wrong. Instead of attempting to reach a verdict, the way a courtroom lawyer does, the scientist does research, publishes it, and waits for colleagues to assess it. Scientific knowledge evolves only after other scientists have questioned and accepted the research, and they are much harder to convince than lawyers. A forensic scientist in court is like a piano player in a brothel, Malcolm says, making his audience laugh: he has to stick to the music and ignore what's happening in the back room.

I'm glad I came, despite the ten minutes it takes to scrape the ice off my twenty-year-old car. I can't wait to see if Dr. Yuille stands up to the "bullying" of Tammy's lawyer tomorrow.

Next morning, Tim White walks over to Yuille on the witness stand, bids him good day and opens a book the psychologist wrote a few years ago. The defence lawyer turns to the chapter titled "General Conditions" and reads the doctor's own prescription for a proper police interview of a child: The right location and personnel are crucial, and each session should be videotaped, the interviewers should understand children, and they should be trained. Yuille calmly explains that though these are the ideal conditions, the police seldom receive appropriate training. That's why he developed Step-Wise in the first place, an interview technique with three basic goals: minimize the child's trauma, maximize the information obtained while minimizing the contamination or influence of the interviewer on the child's thoughts, and maintain the integrity of the child-care system. Yes, answers Yuille, he taught Step-Wise to Bryden. In preparing for court, he took time to review Bryden's taped interviews of Freddy and Kenny and read her interview notes. White now wants his expert opinion about her professional competence and asks pointedly, What did Claudia Bryden learn from the Step-Wise course? How well did she learn it?

Leslie Sullivan rises to object. Yuille is an expert witness, she reminds the court. His role is to comment on hypothetical matters only. Therefore, White's question is improper. Yuille stares straight ahead, calmly waiting for Judge Lavoie to rule on this matter. Unexpectedly, I see the witness not as the professor in the middle of expert testimony, but as a man in a dark suit trying hard to play a piano, straining to read the sheet music as his wire-rimmed spectacles slip down his nose and the noise in the back room gets louder.

White contends that by merely answering the question, Dr. Yuille would not "usurp" the court's role or try to do Judge Lavoie's job. Wrong, says Sullivan. If Yuille answered, he would be stepping into Lavoie's territory by influencing the judge's opinion about Bryden's competence before he sees the interview tapes for himself. Besides, the witness would be straying from the discussion at hand. Judge Lavoie is obviously perplexed and thinks out loud: How am I to relate Dr. Yuille's hypothetical knowledge to the interview tapes? I've got to have a basis upon which I can accept his opinion, don't I? Do you have any case law or evidence so that I can hear his opinion? How do I allow him to give me a general opinion so that I can weigh it? The referee needs time to rule on these matters. He calls a short break and exits with a flourish.

When we return Lavoie is ready with his ruling, the essence of which is that the cart cannot go before the horse. If he were to let Yuille answer the question and accepted his expert opinion about Constable Bryden's interview techniques, the opinion would have to be based on factual evidence that is still missing. That is to say, White's question is too general and not based on fact. The facts of Bryden's technique will come to light when the police tapes of the children's interviews are entered as evidence and examined. When Leslie Sullivan hears this, she smiles and takes a sip of water.

Having failed in his attempt to get the professor to grade Bryden's interviews of the kids, White has no choice but to concentrate on the general theory of interviewing children. White asks, What about leading questions? Yuille replies that asking a few isn't too damaging, but asking a lot of them is.

What about rewarding a child? The reward system should be balanced, says Yuille. If you're giving rewards for disclosure, you should give them consistently or not at all, even when the child doesn't tell you what you want to hear.

What about the lack of correct description, asks White. "It would raise concerns," says Yuille, but inconsistencies about peripheral details are not as important as core details.

What about remembering body scars? "What's obvious to one person is not obvious to another," answers the expert, adding that sometimes the only thing a child remembers is his or her own fear.

As White continues his cross-examination of Yuille, my opinion of the small-town lawyer's questioning skills rises. He has done his homework and, to me, sounds more like a serious student of law than a "bully."

White: Have you...ever come across a case where an adult has inadvertently encouraged a child to make false allegations?...

Yuille: The most common form I've seen is where...a well-intentioned therapist has encouraged a child to disclose abuse that did not happen...

White: What is the best way to determine whether or not an allegation of that sort is true or false?

Yuille: Conducting a good, solid, investigative interview.

White: Why is it, in recent times, that daycares seem to be the focus of sexual-abuse allegation cases? Is there any particular reason?

Yuille: I don't have that impression, so I'm — I mean there are allegations in the context of daycare, but allegations of sexual abuse occur in all sorts of context. Of course it is the case that certain people that abuse kids get attracted to those locations where there are children. Wouldn't be surprising that daycare would serve that function...

White: Let us assume that a child, upon being interviewed by someone without proper experience or training, has suggestions made to him and therefore gives a story that is not true, and then is subsequently interviewed on numerous occasions, is it fair to say that the child will develop a script which is a script of false allegations?

Yuille: It's certainly possible, if these initial interviews that you're mentioning are fairly limited, so that there isn't a lot that's suggested, and all of the subsequent interviews are quite similar, it would be possible for a script to develop then, and a pattern of repetition of what you're suggesting would be a false allegation... The more complicated the suggestions and the more different the interviews over time, the less likely that's possible.

White: Is it fair to say that, by and large, the most critical interviews for the children are the first interviews?

Yuille: The first, the earliest interviews are critical in the sense that they — what one would hope is that good interviewing is done at that point. But it isn't necessarily the case that those first interviews, if they're not well done, are going to destroy the case.

So even if the police botch the first interview of a child, it's still possible to undo the damage. Reassured that we'll still get to the bottom of all this, I eat lunch alone at a Vietnamese restaurant and enjoy my fortune cookie more than usual: "The laws sometimes sleep, but never die."

After lunch a third expert witness is called to testify — Dr. Joel Charles Yelland, born and raised in Saskatchewan. During ten years of practice, the red-haired physician has examined more than 300 children who have been sexually abused. He knows what to look for and how to carefully interpret what he finds.

I'm glad to hear that. Incorrect identification of child abuse is all too common, according to a recent piece in *Family Practice*, a trade magazine for doctors. "Young doctors frequently misdiagnose children with normal genitalia as victims of child abuse." So concluded researchers at the University of Tennessee in Memphis, after administering an exam to sixty-one medical residents to see how accurately they would identify a child's condition. Among the many photos displayed during the exam, only two photos portrayed children with normal genitalia. Dr. David Muram, head researcher of the project, disclosed the test results: "Only half the time did all residents diagnose these [the two normal ones] as normal. That's the one thing that scared the heck out of us... At best, half the diagnoses of child abuse shouldn't be there." I hope the doctors graduating from the University of Tennessee improve with age and experience. They will need a lot of practice to correctly diagnose cases of sexual abuse, for which the only conclusive proof is the presence of sperm. Any other finding may be "compatible with abuse," nothing more.

On the stand Dr. Yelland explains that, indeed, the only way for a physician to be certain sexual abuse has occurred is by finding sperm. And unless the doctor sees the victim within twenty-four to forty-eight hours of being assaulted, before the enzymes disappear, he or she is powerless to say with complete certainty what happened to the patient. He himself found no sperm when he examined Kenny on August 20, 1992. However, he did find the boy's rectum abnormal. A normal rectal diameter for a child Kenny's age, according to the physician, is no more than 0.5 cm. Yet Kenny's was 1.3 cm, two and a half times the normal size. The problem, which he says might have existed for several years, was caused either by the passage of very firm stools or by a foreign object. Either Kenny had chronic penetration or chronic constipation, but the witness can't say which. The penetration could even have engendered such fear in the boy that he became constipated, as Dr. McKenna explained the other day. Indeed, Kenny's mother once told Dr. Yelland that her son was "petrified" of going to the bathroom.

Though the boy was petrified to pass a stool, he sometimes couldn't make it to the toilet fast enough and soiled his underpants. Yelland says the decreased rectal tone and damaged sphincter muscle could not hold back the seepage. Like a baby in a dirty diaper, the then-eight-year-old Kenny developed raw, inflamed skin on his bottom.

Will Kenny's rectum ever return to normal? Will he ever manage to control his stools or will he always soil his underpants? Yelland says Kenny's rate of healing depends on several factors, including the level of resistance he put up at the time of the alleged assault. Does this mean he harmed himself more by trying to protect himself from being raped?

Long ago I thought incontinence was just an affliction of the elderly. Then I went to Uganda and came back with tropical parasites. I learned the terror of standing in front of a class, trying to concentrate on doing my job, not knowing when the amoebas would strike next and, when they did, having to bolt the room, leaving my students snickering. Fortunately the disease was curable and not a lifelong condition; my diarrhoea was caused by natural agents — the parasites of tropical flies — not by a foreign object.

I glance over at Tammy, who is nervously picking at her right eyebrow. What pleasure could she have derived from sticking a vibrator up a little boy's bum while he cried and bled?

According to Yelland's findings during his exam on March 11, 1992, Freddy, who was ten at the time, did not have parasites or any other disease. He, like Kenny, did have mild skin abrasions around his anus and was also in the habit of soiling his underpants. In summary, the physician says, none of his findings allowed him to conclude that either boy had been sexually abused.

There's a touch of black humour this afternoon. During his cross-examination, White asks the doctor, Could a boy make his penis erect by slapping it? Yes, replies Dr. Yelland, even though the boy might be in a state of fright. And could he get an erection if a gun were pointed at him? It's possible, replies the expert, though it would be less likely to occur because high levels of adrenaline inhibit male sexual response, which requires the flow of blood to the penis.

During a short break in testimony Tammy sidles up to her father, who is talking to another reporter and me. She has a bad cold, and her father tells her that's what she gets for kissing her boyfriend, who also has a cold. She replies, "I hope you haven't been kissing him." What a strange thing for a twenty-one-year-old girl to say to her dad, I think, especially in front of two journalists, in the middle of her own trial.

Day 8. I'm trying to make sense of the expert testimony, but feel frustrated. Dr. McKenna has examined hundreds of children suspected of being sexually abused and has told the court that chronic constipation is a "not infrequent finding" among them. Kenny's mother told Dr. Yelland her son was frequently constipated. Upon examining the boy, the physician found that Kenny had an enlarged rectum, perianal scar tissue, and decreased rectal tone. However, he found no trace of sperm. When Yelland examined Freddy, he found mild excoriation of the perianal area. In summary, when he examined the two boys he found symptoms compatible with abuse, but not conclusive because he did not find the one incontrovertible clue, sperm. If the presence of sperm is the only sure way to prove rape, and Dr. Yelland found none, how will anyone ever know what really happened to the boys?

I can see why the recent love affair Canadian lawyers have had with expert witnesses may have lost some of its lustre. The three experts we've heard so far have made it clear that allegations of child abuse constitute an extremely complex question, not reducible to a simple answer. And none of them has tried to do so. The court, on the other hand, wants answers. I wonder if Judge Lavoie would have enjoyed Murray Malcolm's lecture at the library. I wouldn't be at all surprised if he feels like throwing all the pianists out of the "brothel."

It's a relief to break from expert testimony and hear the down-home language of Tammy's former neighbour and old friend, Colleen Friesen, who steps into the witness box. Dressed in jeans (the official Saskatchewan uniform) the twenty-year-old woman wears her hair long, bleached, and permed. When she was twelve she lived in Martensville and Tammy, then thirteen, had just moved to town. For one or two years she was in the same class as Tammy. When they weren't at school, the two girls, best friends, would go to Tammy's bedroom in the Sterling house, where she boarded, and listen to music, play with her hamsters, and giggle at magazines, some pornographic. Colleen remembers peeking into the master bedroom, where she saw two dolls on the bed, about eighteen inches high and anatomically detailed, a male one with a penis, a female one with a vagina and breasts. "I thought it was pretty weird," says the young woman.

Colleen hasn't seen Tammy for a while and remembers her as someone who doesn't really open up to people that well. Only on rare occasions did Tammy share her darkest secrets with Colleen. Once, says the witness, Tammy was in a serious mood and told Colleen her grandpa had done "something sexual" to her.

Till now Tammy has been the alleged abuser of two young boys. Now she is declared a victim herself, in public, and hangs her head. Betrayed by her one-time best friend! She may be a third-generation paedophile who was taught by her grandfather, if what we've heard so far is true.

Tim White now cross-examines Colleen. He asks only one question, a closed question if I've ever heard one, giving the witness the answer at the same time: Did Tammy's abdomen have a "gross, large scar?" Yes, Colleen remembers Tammy's showing her the scar, but she can't say for sure where or when it was.

Colleen Friesen was not the only one who knew about Tammy's grandfather. The next witness had heard, too. Bev Hiebert, a thirty-something woman with a slight limp, lived in Martensville from 1984 till 1992, next door to the Sterlings, and "got to know [Tammy] extremely well"; the girl sometimes called her "mom." Once Tammy confided to her over the kitchen table that her own brother had forced himself on her, and while she was still a pre-teen, both grandfathers had too, during visits to Prince Albert. Fingering her cane, Hiebert says she tried to help Tammy, tried to get her to express her feelings and deal with them. But there was little she could do as long as the girl didn't want to be "responsible for breaking up her family."

Now everyone knows. Tammy looks as though she wishes she could die, and the atmosphere in the court is tense.

Lavoie tries to defuse the room by calling a short break. Out in the hall, Tammy's father paces back and forth eyeing the crowd with fire in his eye, red-faced and shouting that none of the testimony we've just heard is true. Tammy's grandfather, he rages, would die if he ever heard it. He's fed up with the whole thing, including the media. The next person who puts a camera in his face will get "decked." He'll "knock their brains out." Is that clear?

It's clear I need to escape the violence of this man and the craziness of the entire courthouse. I feel like throwing up. Instead, I go to the Tip Top Café and sit in silence for ten minutes sipping tea, my grandma's solution for all life's woes.

The tea restores me, just long enough to sit through the last witness of the day, Dr. William James Arnold, Ph.D., who is a psychologist. Head of the only adolescent sex-offender program in the province, he has assessed 142 sex offenders during the past four years, about 35 each year. I had no idea there were so many.

Leslie Sullivan approaches the witness box. (Two years from now, in 1995, when prosecutor Marcia Clark becomes a household name during the O.J. Simpson trial, some people will think of Sullivan as Saskatchewan's Clark. After seeing Sullivan here every day — short brown hair with bangs, frown, no-nonsense suits, articulate delivery — I'll think of Clark as California's Leslie Sullivan.) In her usual straightforward style, Sullivan asks Dr. Arnold to list the characteristics of sex offenders.

For every one of the sex offenders Arnold has seen so far, he has written a report, including family background, the relationship of the offender to the victim, and the risk he or she poses to the community. From his work, he says he most definitely sees several patterns. Most offenders, he says, are victims themselves, and the offender's family often has a history of sexual deviance. Male and female offenders have similar needs, but women usually don't use violence the way men do. Virtually all female sex offenders are victims, though most abused women do not become abusers, unlike men. During childhood, the exercise of sexual behaviour is learned in the home, like everything else.

Sullivan asks, How do families differ? Arnold replies, A dysfunctional family does not meet the emotional needs of the children very well. The closer the offender is to the victim, the greater the degree of trust and "the more significant" the damage to the victim.

Dr. Arnold has supplied the last few pieces to the prosecution's puzzle. When he leaves the room, the trial comes to a halt so that Leslie Sullivan can conduct a mini-trial or *voir dire*. She faces Lavoie and asks, Now that we know most female sex offenders are themselves victims of sexual abuse, and now that we know Tammy was a victim of sexual abuse, can we conclude that Tammy possesses the characteristics of a sex offender, that she bears the "mark of the badge," and that she did the things she is accused of doing?

The Crown's strategy is revealed in this trial-within-a-trial. It is based on deductive reasoning, establishing a general rule and trying to apply it specifically to the accused, Tammy. It's very logical. Arnold has shown the connection between being abused and being an abuser. Two women, Tammy's best friend and her old neighbour, testified that Tammy told them she had been abused as a child. So the evidence should be sufficient, Sullivan tells the judge, to link Tammy's own abuse to her abuse of the boys. If Your Honour can see how all this fits together, the case can be closed right now.

Not so fast, says Tim White. Like Columbo, he surprises me with his sudden cogency. (And from the slight smile on his lips, he appears to amaze himself, too.) He says, We've just heard that most abused children become adult abusers and most abused males become abusers. Most abused females do not. Therefore, Tammy's history is irrelevant to this case. Her childhood abuse cannot be used to prove she's an adult abuser. There's one more thing. If Your Honour allows Tammy's history to be used against her, Canadian women had better worry that this same cause-and-effect link may be used against them, time and time again, in sexual-abuse cases. Their childhoods may become open books. White is crafty. Lavoie announces he'll need to think all this through overnight.

Next morning the judge, looking weary, says prosecutors Sullivan and Bauer have failed to prove their argument. Just because Tammy was sexually assaulted in childhood doesn't necessarily mean she belongs to a club whose members wear the "mark of the badge." Nor does it mean she is fated to recruit new members, like a vampire. "I find the evidence is not relevant," Lavoie declares.

The psychological evidence that has taken Sullivan months to prepare is not relevant. She will not win the prize for the most perfect puzzle, at least not yet. She looks exhausted. White tries to suppress his glee, but can't, and smiles so broadly his toothpick slips from his clamped teeth and drops to the carpet.

For now, he's the winner, but I'm starting to think that ultimately no one will be the winner. When a case of this complexity is reduced to rules, to right or wrong, as it must be in our legal system, no one wins. No one gets what they need, which is help. If Tammy raped Kenny and Freddy, everyone would benefit from her acknowledging the deed and accepting responsibility for it. But support, forgiveness, healing, and rehabilitation are not simple concepts like an eye for an eye. They are much more complex than accusations, denials, and right-or-wrong verdicts. The boys' innocence can never be restored, any more than Tammy's. But the loss can be honoured and the cycle stopped.

That's not the way it works here. The ringside seats are packed. Everyone squints forward, ready for the next round. In the ring are two frozen figures, father and daughter, dressed in black from head to toe, waiting for the bell. Sullivan, down but not out, rolls up her sleeves as Dr. Zillah Ann Parker climbs into the witness box. The room quiets.

Dr. Zillah Ann Parker is the second medical doctor and fifth expert witness to testify. She looks grandmotherly, grey hair tied back in a bun, her navy dress devoid of adornment. A child psychiatrist, she has many patients who've been abused, some of them very young. One of the key issues in this trial is the credibility of the two young children, Freddy and Kenny. They tell stories, sometimes change the details, and sometimes even leave them out. How can Judge Lavoie know what to make of it all? Parker is here to help.

Before a child learns to talk, she explains, he doesn't have the words to describe events. Therefore, he doesn't think or remember in words. He records and remembers things in sensory and emotional ways. Young children do not interpret or understand what happens to them; they take a "snapshot." A child's pictures of a traumatic incident are coloured in very "sharp, bright" detail. When recalling the incident, the child may distort the details, as you would in a dream sequence. Gaps between the snapshots are normal. They're there because the child doesn't know how to fill in the blanks the way an adult does. Didn't Dr. Yuille say the very same thing?

Sullivan asks what happens to a child when he or she is traumatized, and Parker responds, The event may shatter the predictability of the child's world and make her insecure or clinging. Can you tell us, Dr. Parker, why the child wouldn't talk to her parents about a traumatic event? She responds, Perhaps the child might pretend nothing happened, in order to deal with the event. Or she might feel threatened, personally or for his parents. She might test the waters. If her parents aren't ready to hear what she has to say, the girl may say nothing.

Tim White then rises and strides to the witness box for his cross-examination of the doctor. I learn little from White's cross I haven't already heard Parker or Yuille say, with one exception. Both Freddy and Kenny previously testified they never discussed their experiences at the daycare or The Place with each other. White wants to know: Is it possible that two kids who'd been abused at the same time would never talk about it? The physician says that the children might not talk to one another about things they'd done together, if they felt uncomfortable doing so. Remembering their favourite ice cream would be one thing, recollecting abuse would be another.

A mother's love

We've all been waiting for the next witness, Kenny's mother, or "K-Mom," as I'll call her. She looks as though she's in her mid-thirties. With her long light brown hair, glasses, blue blouse, and pants she reminds me of my sister-in-law from rural Nova Scotia, the salt of the earth.

The experts who have testified had no personal stake in the damage allegedly done to Kenny. But K-Mom was "devastated" and still is, not just because someone robbed her son of his innocence, but because he was raped while she thought she was protecting him. His innocence is gone. What is there to live for?

"There have been mornings when I didn't know how I'd get through the day," she says, struggling in a husky voice. "It has shattered our whole home; it's been a nightmare." She's holding back the tears, as Sullivan may have suggested she do. But she looks and sounds all bottled up. Does she ever scream? Throw things? Curl into a ball? Cry her heart out? When she says her marital problems have been bad this past year, I wonder if she and her husband are close, and how he expresses his feelings. K-Mom's voice is small and fragile until she speaks for her son, when it gets big and strong. She kept Kenny home from school the other day, she tells Sullivan, when he vomited in anticipation of coming to court. "He was awfully nervous and scared." Then the boy was outraged when he learned many people would hear his testimony because he didn't want his friends to know he was "one of those children." Throughout her testimony I have the urge to put my arms around her and tell her it's not her fault. I doubt she'll ever forgive herself. It surprises me that K-Mom's testimony moves me much more than Kenny's, even with all his graphic details. Then it hits me: She's talking Adult; he was talking Kid. I thought I knew better than to listen in Adult mode, but I guess I can't help it.

K-Mom, her husband, and two sons moved to Martensville in 1986, when Kenny was three. Three years later K-Mom started to work, off and on, while her husband or older son babysat the boy after school. He was never home alone. And he was never babysat at the Sterling house, though she once gave him permission to go there and watch a movie. Kenny was friends with Freddy, who lived across the street, and she liked it when the two boys told her where they were going to play, which they usually did. Apparently, Kenny still tells her things and tries to protect her from pain. When he wants to talk to her in private, he says, "Mom, I have something to tell you," sits her down on her bed, and closes the door.

K-Mom knows more of her son's story now than she did that summer night in 1990 when she discovered his sore bum while bathing him after he and Freddy had played in the sand. At that time Kenny had chronic constipation and incontinence. The seeming contradiction confused her: he soiled his underpants five or six times a day but screamed when he pooped. "It hurt him so bad I had to hold his hand." K-Mom calls 1990 a "real bad year," a year when everything went wrong, from Kenny's bowels to his brain. "Quite concerned," K-Mom tackled both problems at once, taking her son to a new doctor, Dr. Yelland, and putting him in special learning Grade 1 and 2 classes. "Once he started making his disclosures, he actually graduated from that class," she tells the court.

If Kenny kept things to himself for a time, his actions spoke loud and clear. He was clingy, according to the witness, and stayed by her side so intently that he scared her and drove her to imagine he would smother her.

Although glued to his mother, the boy "withdrew" from his dad and wouldn't let him hug or play with him. To Kenny not even Santa was safe. Once, around Christmas, K-Mom wanted to have her son photographed on Santa's knee, but the boy wouldn't have anything to do with it. "Petrified," he threw a tantrum in the middle of a mall.

There were other peculiarities. Kenny refused to wear a new jean jacket she brought home because the wrists were too tight. One day the Grade 2 class went to the fire hall. Kenny "didn't want no part of it" because, she says, he knew Ron Sterling had once worked there. Then, out of the blue, he refused to go to Sunday school.

As though K-Mom didn't have enough to contend with during the day, she was kept up half the night, too, by the noise coming from Kenny's room. The boy, on all fours, would rock back and forth in his bed — so violently that he bruised his skin and rubbed patches of hair off his head. In the summer of 1994, K-Mom decided to put her son's mattress on the floor. Only then did he calm down enough to let the rest of the family get some sleep.

Why was Kenny, then seven, so agitated at night? He told his mom that the Sterlings, who lived nearby, never slept and always watched his house.

Covered in goose bumps, I try to sidetrack my imagination by doodling in my notebook. Is that what Kenny tried to do, rock in bed to sidetrack his demons? Mutilate his body to save his mind? Kenny loves drawing and seems quite creative, but he certainly outdid himself with this story. Most kids' monsters hide under their beds, just waiting for night to fall. Kenny's monsters lived in a house on the next street, and looked like you and me. Did the "monsters" tell him they'd come for him some night? Did they tell that to Freddy, too?

Kenny's pal, Freddy, still keeps a baseball bat beside the bed says his mother, "F-Mom," who is now in the witness box. She is twenty-seven years old and different from K-Mom, perhaps more in manner than appearance. The perm, the pants, the blouse, and sweater look familiar. But F-Mom seems more self-assured. She is very methodical, as evidenced by the notebook she kept of all Freddy's accounts, clearly indicating the date and time of each one. I'm surprised by such organization and doubt I'd have her presence of mind to document my child's disclosures with such precision. Throughout the testimony F-Mom frequently refers to her note pad to keep her facts straight.

Her story begins in December 1986, when she, her husband and Freddy, then five years old, moved to Martensville. The Sterlings lived on a neighbouring street and, by coincidence, F-Mom learned from her own mother, who knew Ron Sterling, that his wife, Linda, babysat for a fee. So when F-Mom went back to school in April 1988, she paid Linda Sterling to care for Freddy, then six. From that time till June 1991, Freddy went to the Sterling home, off and on, sometimes for only a few hours and sometimes for up to ten hours a day. Sometimes he left the Sterling house before his mother came to get him, and F-Mom would find him sitting on the doorstep, sometimes in 30-below weather. "I had concerns," she says, and she spoke to Linda Sterling about them. Nevertheless, Freddy continued to leave the Sterling house and sit on his front steps no matter how cold it was.

In October 1988, Freddy started vomiting after breakfast, every day, like clockwork, whether in the kitchen or at the mall. This habit lasted seven or eight months, then became less frequent. During the same time Freddy "always walked around holding on to his penis," anywhere, anytime, and would stop, briefly, only when his parents told him to. Freddy quit this behaviour for good, according to F-Mom, only when he started to talk about what had happened to him at the Sterling daycare. He also starting wetting the bed every night for about a month in the fall of 1988, when he was six. His parents took him to the doctor.

Freddy also had scrapes and bruises. F-Mom remembers one on his upper left shoulder in particular, and although she tried diligently, she couldn't convince him to tell her how he got it. From 1988 on, whether it was to avoid his parents' prying eyes or their annoying questions, he refused to go shirtless, no matter how hot it was, or try on shirts at the store. Just six years old, he routinely locked his parents out of the bathroom when he took a bath.

Freddy wasn't constipated the way Kenny was, but, F-Mom says his underwear was "usually soiled when I did the laundry." She first noticed this in November 1988, seven months after the six-year-old started at the Sterling daycare. Freddy, like Kenny, once balked at going on a field trip with classmates and had to be "pushed." However, the boy became "extremely happy" when he and his mom and dad moved to British Columbia, in September 1991.

His relief was shortlived, as was the break in his spells of vomiting. One month after the move, F-Mom's mother — Freddy's grandmother, the one who'd suggested sending him to the Sterling daycare in the first place — telephoned to say that Travis Sterling had been charged with sexual assault. Freddy's parents began to question their son. At first the boy denied everything, then he began to have crying spells, for no apparent reason, over his homework and dinner.

The witness continues: In early November 1991, Claudia Bryden called to say she was concerned that something might have happened to Freddy at the daycare. A few days later she called again to say Travis Sterling had been charged. Convinced the accusations were well-founded, Freddy's parents decided to take the bull by the horns. After just two months in small-town British Columbia, they moved back to Saskatchewan, this time to Saskatoon, "to get help" for Freddy. Before long, Freddy started to talk. One night in late November, the ten-year-old boy appeared at his parents' bedroom door and said, "Mom, I've got something to say. Get your book." From then on, F-Mom diligently recorded her son's disclosures in her notebook. She pulls these pages from her purse.

The notes, written between November 6, 1991, and January 15, 1992, document what Freddy said and how long it took him to say it. In February 1992, the boy began to see Rod Butler once a week for therapy. In April he told Claudia Bryden that Tammy had abused him.

Tim White's cross-examinations of the two mothers are fascinating. Sometimes, when questioning K-Mom, he cocks his head to the side and looks like a little boy, trying not to ruffle her feathers. White's job is to poke as many holes in her story as possible. She could be a pretty intimidating witness, sitting in the box with her arms crossed and her lips pursed, a pensive frown on her face.

> White: Okay. And had you spoken with Kenny about any of these matters before Claudia Bryden had come to see you in January of '92?
>
> K-Mom: No.
>
> White: What did she tell you that Freddy was saying?
>
> K-Mom: That the chances were that Kenny would have also been abused. [She knew] that I had given him permission to go in the house just that one time.
>
> White: Did she, at that time, tell you about the — how the rest of the investigation was going?

K-Mom: No. I just felt that she was quite concerned.

White: Did she tell you at all any of the details of what Freddy was apparently saying at that time?...

K-Mom: No, I don't remember. At one point, Freddy had mentioned that Kenny was actually being abused with him. But I don't remember exactly when that was.

White: Was that told to you by Claudia Bryden?

K-Mom: I believe — I don't — I don't remember if Kenny came out with it first or if Claudia mentioned it to me. I don't remember...

White: Let's talk about Kenny for a moment. In terms of his personality at the present time, how would you describe it?

K-Mom: Well, usually he's happy. He does get angry at times. But normally, he's a happy boy.

White: Did you ever see any bruises or odd marks on Kenny's body, whether that be his arms or his shoulders or his face, or his legs, during 1989 through to '91?

K-Mom: Oh, I'm sure he had bruises, but not that I would really suspect anything...but [that] he had fallen, or whatever... The only thing I remember one time is he had an open — it was a bruise on the back of his head, and I had asked him what had happened and he said he had fallen.

White: Particularly with his mouth, you didn't see any marks?

K-Mom: Yes, I did.

White: Oh, what did you see?

K-Mom: He was constantly licking them, like actually, his mouth was a mess. It was really chapped. It was awful looking.

White: Did you take him to the doctor about that?

K-Mom: No, I didn't.

White: What about his wrists and arms, did you notice anything peculiar about those?

K-Mom: Well, I had bought him a jean jacket about that time, and it had sort of like tight wrists, like sort of, like cuff bands on them, and he actually refused to wear that jacket because it was too tight. He didn't like it.... I couldn't understand what the problem was.

White: Okay. When Kenny was having all these difficulties with his bowel movements in 1990, and you would actually be in the washroom and holding his hand, did you ever look in the bowl to see what kind of feces he was passing?

K-Mom: They were huge.

When Freddy's mom takes the stand, White barrages her with questions about the investigation. She says that when the family returned from British Columbia to Saskatchewan, she asked Bryden to speak to her son. She believed Freddy had things to say. White wants to know what. F-Mom pulls out her notes again, takes a sip of water, and recaps the twelve or thirteen times either she or the police talked with Freddy in late 1991 and early 1992. There's little I haven't heard before, except that Freddy was interviewed five times by Claudia Bryden before being interviewed by Rod Moor.

It's late afternoon and court is over for the day. Judge Lavoie looks exhausted. His glasses rest on the end of his nose, his chin is cupped in his hand. Tammy, draped in black, stares straight ahead like a statue. Tim White looks animated but tired and rewards himself for his hard work with a fresh toothpick.

Leaving the red-brick building for the day, I see Tammy on the street corner, slouching against a fence, head down, lost in thought. She's thinking about the past, I bet, and waiting for the future. Her fiancé, a slender six-foot man with spider-long limbs, strides towards her, and wraps himself around her like a package, kissing her on the forehead. His T-shirt says, "Life is short. Play hard."

They walk hand in hand to her father's car in the parking lot. He sits in front, she in back. Her father comes running down the street and gets in, hurriedly taking the wheel. The engine is barely on before the car lurches through the deep spring ruts of the lot and out into the potholed streets of Saskatoon.

Thursday, March 18, 1993. Day 9 of the trial. Several farmers take the stand. Although I've lived in Saskatchewan almost fifteen years, I know only three farmers, none of them "typical." One (whom I secretly loved like a mother) was killed last summer in a car accident, one was convicted of second-degree murder, and the third recently opened a bed-and-breakfast with an indoor swimming pool overlooking fields of wheat. Other than these three farmers, the only ones I ever see are the women who truck my fresh milk and range-free eggs to town every two weeks and the Mennonites and Hutterites who come to Saskatoon to shop, the women dressed in scarves and aprons over their long black skirts, and the bearded men in suspenders and black pants.

Even though I don't know about farming firsthand, I can see and hear Saskatchewan farmers swaying to the rhythm of the land, gliding from season to season, eye on the sky. Farm people are tough, smart, and family-oriented, and these values suffuse not only the sprawling acreages of the province but its towns and cities too. Officially, full-time farmers constitute just four per cent of the population. But many members of my generation, who grew up on farms and moved to the city in the 1960s and seventies, brought their rock-solid values with them. The people of Saskatchewan like to see themselves as ethical, cooperative and caring. That's why the Martensville allegations come as such a shock. One day you have this nice quiet community to the north of Saskatoon, where almost everyone goes to church on Sunday. Then seemingly overnight, criminal charges are laid against people who were paid to protect the town's children and others who were hired to guard the town itself.

The blue building that police assume to be The Place sits in the middle of rich fields of wheat and canola to the north of Martensville. One of the roads that cuts through these fields used to be very bumpy, though it has recently been graded. It's called the Power Line Road and leads directly to the property the children call The Place. What we'll soon hear in court sounds like cops-and-robbers, except that the roles are reversed. Usually the police keep an eye on citizens. But on the Power Line Road, between 1990 and 1992, five locals — the ones we are about to hear — watched, perplexed, as a cavalcade of police vehicles came and went at odd hours. One of the observers, a farmer, went beyond mere wondering.

It's not every day you hear of someone who looks as conservative as Walter Enns tailing the police in a high-speed chase. A tall middle-aged farmer who has lived beside Highway 12 north of Martensville for twenty years, Enns talks in the dour, clipped way of some Saskatchewan rural people. He says he saw lots of Martensville police vehicles, including the van, ply the road in front of his farm. So concerned was Enns that he talked to the Martensville mayor in 1991. "It struck me odd they would be out of town so often."

One Sunday — June 23, 1991, to be precise, around 3 p.m. — Enns got his chance to track the peace officers down. He was on his way to visit his mother at the nursing home in the nearby town of Dalmeny, when the blue and white Martensville police van appeared out of nowhere. "You couldn't mistake that one," he says matter-of-factly. Enns's curiosity got the better of him and he started to follow the vehicle, at first doing the speed limit, and then, to keep up with the van, did a hundred kilometres an hour till, coming to the intersection at Peters' Grid Road, decided he'd given chase long enough. Besides, his mother was expecting him for tea. The van went one way, Enns the other.

Next on the stand is Neil Peters, a retired farmer and twenty-year veteran of the area, the namesake of Peters' Road, which runs by his house. Being retired, Peters has the time to keep an eye on it and can testify with authority about the "heavy traffic" between late 1991 and early 1992. He tells the court that while shovelling his driveway, he saw the Martensville police van go by quite often, heading north, usually around 11 a.m. And on his way to curl or have coffee with his buddies, which he did three or four times a week, he might meet up with the van or the police car at Thirteen-Mile Corner. His wife, Allyson, who also testifies, says she's sure she saw Jim Elstad at the wheel of the van, probably in early 1991. Unlike their neighbours, the Enns, Mr. and Mrs. Peters have said nothing to officials until now.

The next witness, Neil Laliberte, has a deep voice; he uses a green felt pen to highlight landmarks on a map and illustrate his story. One weekday morning in the spring or fall of 1990, he biked to the post office to get his mail, and then decided to visit a friend. Laliberte, a cyclist who knows a bumpy road when he rides one, says the road was full of rocks and potholes before the municipality graded it. (The ride to The Place was bumpy in the back of the police van, I remember Freddy testifying.) On the way to his friend's house, Laliberte saw the police van parked on a gravel road west of Highway 305, just north of Martensville. On his way home, fifteen minutes later, he took the same road and was surprised to see the blue and white Martensville police van again, with someone sitting in it. As Laliberte pedalled nearer, the driver turned to look in the passenger mirror, presumably to get a glimpse of the cyclist. He gave neither a word nor a wave to the passerby, even though the two were the only ones in sight.

Sherry Bohler takes the stand, appearing nervous in her fuchsia sweater and grey pants. The thirtyish witness paints a bucolic picture of life on her farm, located 200 feet from the Power Line Road. In late 1990, the Bohler family moved from the town to the country. "Not long after" the move from Martensville, where she'd worked at the Esso station and met many local police, she began to notice the police cruiser and the van. The witness says that several times a week she'd be doing afternoon chores, feeding the cattle, the goats, and the pigs, when she saw police vehicles driving back and forth on Power Line Road. "We never seen no more cruisers after the story broke on TV," concludes Bohler.

As fascinating as I find these five Crown witnesses, defence lawyer Tim White seems to think their testimony of little importance. When Sullivan has finished her examination-in-chief and it's his turn to cross-examine them, he asks a few polite questions and sits down.

The Defence

Competence in question

I haven't seen Freddy and Kenny's therapist, Rod Butler, since shopping at Safeway a month ago, when he was dressed in baggy pants and a T-shirt, looking very un-therapist. Now, in shirt and tie, slacks and navy jacket, he looks like he did a few weeks ago when he came to court to make recommendations about the courtroom setup for the boys. The soft-spoken Butler is the sixth and last expert to testify — one too many, according to the Canada Evidence Act, which stipulates a limit of five experts per criminal trial, unless the judge gives leave to call more.

It's a good thing Lavoie has that leeway because Butler has an important role to play in this trial. As an "expert" in assessing and treating child abuse, he knows the blueprint or "fact pattern" of sexual abuse; as the therapist for Freddy and Kenny, he possesses some secret pieces to the puzzle that no one else knows, which Freddy needed at least forty-five appointments to tell him and Kenny, twenty-five. During these sessions, Butler tells Sullivan, he typically would assess the situation and strive to empower each of the boys by helping them shed their victim mentality and reduce their self-blame. Freddy and Kenny have come to trust their Friendly Giant, and Butler plans to keep it that way.

I glance over at Tammy. Her face is resting on her right hand, in a seemingly relaxed pose, but her eyes are fixed on Butler. Suddenly, her cheeks flush. Does Butler tap some secret longing? Does he remind her of a Friendly Giant she used to dream would rescue her one day? I feel the urge to tap her on the shoulder and say, "Look, if you were hurt, you deserve help too. Just say so." As if it were that easy.

Although his professional specialty is pre-pubescent kids, Butler would probably know how to help the twenty-one-year-old Tammy too. In his many years as a therapist he has seen a lot of pain. "Abuse really scars the child," he tells prosecutor Sullivan. Yes, it's a tragedy. But as Tim White will now try to show, it's one kind of tragedy when a child is traumatized and driven to self-destructive behaviour, and wets the bed or soils his pants; it's another kind of tragedy when a therapist helps a child imagine things that never happened.

Did the boys have the traumatic experiences they say they did or did Butler encourage them to think so, as White contends? Did their experiences eroticize the boys and introduce them to sexual pleasure as well as physical pain? Were the erections they got when recollecting the abuse for Butler clear proof they were telling him the truth, or merely normal for red-blooded boys their age, as White maintains?

In retrospect I think the media ban has been a good idea, not just because it keeps the rhetoric off the breakfast and supper tables of Saskatoon, but because it allows court reporters more time to eat lunch instead of filing the morning's news every noon from the courthouse. On this particular lunch hour my friend Janis and I go to the Saskatoon Asian Restaurant, where we sift through the morning's evidence and lay odds on Tammy's acquittal. It's impossible to know what Judge Lavoie thinks of the evidence, though yesterday in court we got a clue when he said Constable Claudia Bryden had done an "incredible job" of investigating the allegations and interviewing the children, when "thrown into the middle of a lake without even a life raft."

Over jasmine tea, we wonder how probable it is that kids were abducted in broad daylight from a daycare, blindfolded, put into a police van and whisked to a building out in the country where they were sexually abused. Some parts of the testimony are easy to believe, while others call for considerable imagination and suspension of disbelief. Janis says she believes the kids and has since the day Kenny testified Tammy's vagina was "smooshy."

White steps up to the witness box for his afternoon cross-exam and opens fire on Butler: When and why did you talk to the police about the boys? Butler explains: On the one hand, he must protect his clients' confidentiality; on the other, he has an obligation to the police, according to the Child and Family Services Act. After interviewing the boys, he felt there was enough evidence to go on, and said so to the police. He "encouraged" them to investigate existing allegations. In exchange, the police shared some of their findings with him. For instance, Claudia Bryden gave him some notes from her interviews with Freddy. "I tried not to let them be a big factor," the therapist says of his work with the boy. But I wonder, how could they possibly not be?

Tim White asks the same question: Armed with notes during his interviews with Freddy, how could Butler behave as though he'd never seen them? Butler knows where White is headed and calmly answers, "We have to be particularly cautious in, not in any way, leading the children...because if you were to lead children in a direction, the information may have major implications for other people's lives." As White sees it, when Butler suspected the boys were victims and cooperated with police, a real victim was created — his client Tammy.

White asks Butler if he believes that children always tell the exact truth. Butler answers, "It has been my experience that most kids tell me the truth." Kids may exaggerate or brag to aggrandize themselves, but to humiliate themselves and get themselves and others in trouble is not something they like to do. White nods curtly and pours himself a glass of water as Judge Lavoie bites a fingernail and looks down at the therapist over his glasses.

Beep. Beep. The courtroom audiocassette has come to an end and breaks everyone's concentration, including White's, who stops his cross-exam just long enough for the clerk to change tapes. I want access to the courtroom transcript later and wonder if Justice personnel will make me jump through hoops to get it because of the Young Offenders Act. It would be nice to know I could have a taped version of the trial or a transcript when it's over, instead of having to decipher my messy notebook with the ripped-out pages, crossed-out sentences, and missing words. If only! As I fantasize about the perfect way to record the trial, Judge Lavoie seems to be doing the same thing, for he blurts out, "We're learning about courtroom design in this trial, and it's obvious we haven't kept up."

Maybe I underestimated his interest in courtroom technology. When the court later sold me computer diskettes of a related trial, I couldn't believe my eyes. They'd been typed by several freelance secretaries using different versions of software, and the words were not always decipherable on my computer. Nor could I believe my ears when trying to listen to audiotapes of police interviews of the daycare kids. In one tape Claudia Bryden and the teenage girl, Sally, sound more like men. Perhaps Bryden's tape recorder at the Martensville police station was unreliable, as the officer suggested on the stand, or maybe the problem lay with the compatibility of the Martensville recorder and the one at the Court of Queen's Bench in Regina, where I tried to listen to the tape. Surely, all tape recorders that are used to record police interviews should be compatible with those of the Department of Justice. If not, such technological shortcomings defy true public access to the judicial system. And at least one judge agrees with me.

Next day in court, Judge Lavoie waits to watch several videotapes of Claudia Bryden and the children, in the hope of establishing a firm "foundation" for evaluating the quality of the officer's interview techniques. He needs to watch the tapes before he can decide how much weight to assign to them when ruling. What if he decided to assign no weight at all? I wonder: how could one person watch videotapes and not be influenced in some way by what he just saw? Would such a person need two heads — one for playing videos to assess the police interview techniques and one for erasing what he saw from his mind?

The audio-visual equipment in the courtroom challenges not only the judge but also the lawyers, as Tim White discovers while preparing to prove the police investigation compromised the truth. White turns on the VCR, but he has inserted the wrong tape. Then he gets the right tape, but there's no sound. Thirty minutes later, when White finally has the tape and the sound right, he can't make the zapper work, which is odd because it works fine for the commissionaire, who goes to the exact spot on the tape White can't seem to find, and hands the thing back to White with a smile. The defence lawyer looks deflated, like a kid with a new toy that took forty minutes to master. Finally, White is ready.

So is Judge Lavoie. The TV faces his bench, away from the public gallery, thus preserving the anonymity of Freddy and Kenny, who will appear on tape. Tammy sits near Lavoie, facing the TV and the twenty or so of us in the gallery. White rolls the first police tape, which is barely audible because the quality of the sound is so poor. Lavoie, frustrated after a few seconds of static, sputters, "I don't mind putting it on the record: When is the Saskatoon City Police Service going to catch up to the real world?" He says that they just changed their name from "Force" to "Service," but forgot to change their equipment to go with the new title. I'm not the only journalist in the room who smiles at this remark.

Luckily for Lavoie, he sees the screen head on, and maybe manages to lip read what the boys say to police, even if he can't hear the tape very well. From my seat I neither see Freddy on the monitor nor hear much of what he tells Rod Moor of the Saskatoon Police and Claudia Bryden of the Martensville Police, in the Soft Room in April 1992. Nevertheless, I hear more than I want to, in the following excerpt.

Freddy: I'd like to do that to the Sterlings [electrocute them].

Moor: Good. And I don't blame you. There's a lot of people that feel just as strongly as you do, and you're looking at a couple of them... But it's because you've been able to help us. But you're not the only one that's been helping. There's been a couple of guys that's been really, really brave like you have. And what makes it even easier for them, the guys like yourselves, is knowing you're not alone doing it. That everybody is bonding together and now all of a sudden the little kids — they are able to talk.

If these portions of the tapes have a chilling effect on me, they have a surprisingly warming influence on the small crowd today. Up until now the dozen or so regulars have sat in either one camp or the other: on one side of the gallery, those who say Tammy did it; on the other side, those who say she didn't. But listening to the tapes has added a new dimension to the trial: If the members of the public in the courtroom today agree on nothing else, they may now concur that Rod Moor made leading statements to Freddy in the Soft Room.

The scales of justice

Tammy was supposed to testify today, but she's in hospital. She was taken there in a diabetic coma by ambulance during the night. The room is abuzz. White stands to read a note from Tammy's doctor to Judge Lavoie, and Lavoie dismisses us for the day.

Next day Tammy is still unfit to stand trial. Nevertheless, White tells the court, the doctors are optimistic his client will be fine. With proper diet and sufficient rest, her chemical imbalance should soon return to normal. White is visibly frustrated. He'd hoped this would be over in time for him to appear at the trial of another client, and now Tammy's trial will not resume until April 20, by which time, almost two weeks from now, she should be well enough to sit in the witness box.

On April 20, the trial resumes. Until now, all the witnesses have been examined by the prosecution and cross-examined by the defence. For the rest of the trial, the process will be reversed. The first and only witness for the defence is the defendant herself, Tammy.

The accused looks drained. I'm sure that having to take the witness stand is just as draining as having to look at pictures of her scarred body, which she must do right off the bat. The fourteen photos White gives her to identify were taken for the trial by the RCMP several weeks ago. In this room, where there are few anatomical secrets, White tells the court that the photos show how badly scarred Tammy's body is. Anyone who sees the scars, he asserts, could not possibly forget them.

Not being able to see the photos, I cannot agree or disagree with White, and wonder how it would feel to be on trial, while coping with severe diabetes and having intimate photos of my body made public property. I feel fortunate to be sitting on this side of the bar in the public gallery, in good health.

Tammy was born February 8, 1972. Since then her body, from ankles to earlobes, has been cross-hatched by scalpels and scarred by diabetic sores. White hopes the collection of evidentiary photos will convince the court that the young woman's body is unique and unforgettable.

Though I won't see the photos of Tammy's scarred body until court officials arrange a special viewing for journalists, I'm not sure they'd impress me the way they seem to White. I don't believe any body is unforgettable, including one that's very unusual, unless it's an object of love or desire: a mother's body, a lover's, one's own child. I see naked women every day in the locker room at the Y. Many have stretch marks, several have only one breast, a few have tattoos, and one has a ring through her nipple. I go by the face, not the body. Consider the grandmother who has one breast and one eye. When I think of her, I remember her sweet face. I see the black patch over her eye, not the scar on her chest. The one-eyed face is the owner of the one-breasted body, not the other way round. Somehow, I doubt that children would remember Tammy's scarred body, especially if they were being traumatized. Dr. Yuille's words ring in my ears: What's obvious to one person is not obvious to another.

The significance of a scarred torso may be controversial, but the importance of good health is not. When Tammy tells the court her story, explaining each of the scars in the photos, I realize what a difficult life she has had. Though she's just turned twenty-one, her medical history sounds like that of someone much older: diabetic; her non-functioning pancreas removed, as well as her gall bladder and one ovary; and plastic surgery to remove the abdominal scars.

Over the years, these problems have messed up Tammy's academic career, forcing her to repeat Grade 1 and possibly contributing to her decision to leave school just three credits short of a Grade 12 diploma. She has been dating the same man for the past few years and now lives with him and his parents in northern Saskatchewan. Tammy's boyfriend works, though Tammy herself is unemployed.

The accused stands at the front of the court. She is an outlaw and will be a social reject unless acquitted of the ten charges against her. The charges, read at the beginning of the trial by the clerk, are now read again by her lawyer. After every charge, White pauses to allow Tammy to deny it by quietly answering "Not guilty." Under oath, she denies ever touching Kenny for sexual purposes, or assaulting or confining him. Nor has she ever, she swears, assaulted Freddy or made a death threat to him.

Somebody's lying — either it's the two boys or Tammy, and Judge Lavoie has to decide who. White will now examine his client, to help her present her version of events.

Tammy moved to Martensville when she was twelve years old and moved in with the Sterlings, friends of her parents. Tammy testifies that her involvement with the daycare children at the Sterling house was minimal. Once in a while she helped Linda Sterling with the forty or so kids who went there over the years, but usually for no more than a half-hour at a time. Nevertheless, she remembers the children and lists their names for the court, like a roll call. All juveniles, their identities must remain confidential in compliance with Judge Lavoie's publication ban.

Tammy says Freddy was "quite a kid," who began to come to the Sterling house in 1986, when he was five. Wait a minute, that's not what I recall. Here it is in my notes, dated March 17: F-Mom said Freddy started to go to the Sterling house in 1988, when he was seven. Tammy continues: Kenny was never in the house. In fact, he never made it past the back porch. Pardon me? I thought his mother said he once went in to watch a movie. If he was never inside the house, how could he draw a correct diagram of the interior? Janis nudges me hard, almost knocking the pen out of my hand, and a woman two rows behind laughs incredulously. White stops his examination of Tammy and jerks his head around to see who is in contempt. The uniformed commissionaire, anticipating Judge Lavoie's wrath, half-rises from his chair to prepare to remove the offender. Lavoie does not scold the offender, but the commissionaire's unspoken warning stops her cold. I'm surprised, and fear that if the woman does it again Lavoie will tell her to leave, and maybe all of us with her. With the fear of judicial reproof hanging over us, complete silence falls on the room.

Some of Tammy's story corresponds to Freddy's version: usually, the boy was at the Sterling house during non-school hours, early in the morning and late in the afternoon. He was prone to upset stomach. As time went by, he seemed unhappy and became "mad with us, antsy." He was friends with Kenny.

Yes, she admits under oath, there were guns in the Sterling house, but not in the sight of kids. Tammy despises guns and killing animals and used to keep hamsters and a pet rabbit when she boarded with the Sterlings.

When White asks Tammy if she knows the way to The Place, she is adamant: "If you paid me, I couldn't tell you how to get there." When the defence lawyer shows her the anklet chain (the riddle rope Kenny described last week), Tammy says she has never seen it before. Nor has she seen the vibrator that both Freddy and Kenny recognized when questioned by police and that they identified in court. Sounding anxious, though I don't know why, White asks Judge Lavoie for a break.

Tammy returns to the stand after ten minutes in the witness room and White resumes his examination-in-chief. She answers that it was in late 1988 — not 1986 — that Freddy started to come to the daycare. That was when Freddy was in Grade 3 and seven years old, not five, she says, contradicting her previous testimony. Janis nudges me and rolls her eyes. Tammy's mistake makes me wonder about her evidence in general and leaves me with the same sinking feeling I'd have myself if I screwed up the dates in a story.

It's a kind of stage fright. And it wouldn't surprise me if Tammy's becomes more acute when White sits down and leaves her to the mercy of the Crown prosecutor. Eyebrows knit, Leslie Sullivan rises to perform her one and only cross-examination of the trial. How, the prosecutor asks the young offender, did you remember the correct dates during the break? Did someone help you? No, says Tammy, no one jogged her memory about Freddy's age or the grade he was in. It's just that, giggle, she has never been very good in math. The witness sounds like a twelve-year old and looks like one too, with her blonde hair in a pony tail and hands clasped between her knees, waiting obediently for Sullivan's next question: Tammy left her home when young to avoid domestic violence, isn't that right? No, asserts the accused, her family is pretty close, except for the occasional temper flare-up. She giggles again.

After putting months of work and years of her life into this case, Sullivan can almost see the home stretch. Destroying the credibility of this giggling adolescent girl is the last hurdle. She closes in on the witness box, crosses her arms, and scowls.

Having to look the Crown prosecutor square in the eye, the accused admits she knew about the porn videotapes in the Sterlings' bedroom. She also knew about the porn magazines. But she never, ever, looked at the videos or the magazines. She doesn't recall showing them to her friend, Colleen Friesen, nor does she remember showing Colleen the anatomically detailed dolls on the Sterlings' bed. Then Tammy softens her testimony: her used-to-be-best friend may have been telling the truth about the dolls, but she herself does not recall the incident.

The witness says that all the bedrooms in the Sterling house were off-limits to the daycare children. "Most of the kids that are involved in this were never in the bedrooms." When Sullivan asks her again, sharpening her tone and speaking each word staccato, the accused answers like a volcano about to blow: "The little kids were not allowed to enter the bedrooms."

Then, in the very next breath, Tammy says that one child sometimes slept in the bedroom of Ron and Linda Sterling while another might be put in Travis's room. The master bedroom was not off limits for the kids if they were put there for naps. And when you babysit young children for hours at a time, they need a nap at some point in the day, just as they need a bath and a change of clothes. At the Sterling house, according to Tammy, "we never, ever stripped the kids down" for a bath. Sullivan looks unconvinced.

Sullivan then questions the witness about her neighbour, Bev Hiebert, and Tammy gives her version of their relationship: "I never thought we had the mother-daughter relationship she thought we had." Nevertheless, Tammy admits, she used to call Hiebert "Mom."

Just then I happen to notice Hiebert sitting in the row in front of me and sucking on a lollipop, silently swallowing the testimony that contradicts her own and waiting for Sullivan's big question: Did you tell Bev Hiebert that either of your grandfathers... had sexually abused you in any way?

White jumps up to object.

Judge Lavoie overrules the defence lawyer's objection, making him sit in silence while the prosecutor repeats the question that Tammy will now answer, "for the sole purpose of testing the credibility of the witness." Everyone waits as Tammy takes a slow breath and says, "I can never remember telling her that, but it's a possibility due to my diabetes." She avoids perjuring Hiebert, but by not answering the question directly, Tammy calls her own credibility into question. Everyone wants a simple yes or no to the question. The tension in the room mounts. Which woman is telling the truth, Tammy or Bev Hiebert? Why would Hiebert swear that Tammy said her grandfather abused her, if she had not said it? And why would Tammy not deny that she ever told the woman anything of the kind? I'd like to cross-examine her myself.

Tammy undercuts her credibility further, by saying that if she did tell Hiebert such a thing, she may have done so during a diabetic coma. Whenever her blood sugar gets very low, she explains, she gets "really giggly." But she giggles frequently. Is her sugar low now? "I can say anything or do anything" when in a state of low sugar, or "swear at my dad for an hour." Or, she adds, make up stories. Make up stories?

Tammy's version of the story about the grandfathers contradicts Bev Hiebert's. Clearly, one of the two women is in contempt of court, and Judge Lavoie must decide which one. How? Can Sullivan, he asks, provide him with precedents that speak to this problem?

Where does the truth begin and where does it end in Tammy's testimony? If all her evidence contradicted what the other witnesses have said, Lavoie would see a pattern. But this crazy-quilt testimony sometimes contradicts the court record and sometimes corroborates it. The pattern gets craziest when Tammy's testimony does some of both, as it does now: Yes, members of the Martensville Police Service, most notably Jim Elstad, used to visit the Sterling house for fifteen or twenty minutes, on a regular basis. (This matches Claudia Bryden's testimony that Elstad took her to the Sterling residence for coffee her first night on the job.) Yes, says Tammy, guns were kept in a closet in the Sterlings' bedroom. (This tallies with the fact police found them there during a search of the house). No, says Tammy, never, never did any of the police take the kids for a ride in their vehicles and never does she remember anyone touching the guns. (This openly contradicts what Freddy and Kenny said.)

Tammy drives to court every day with her father, Ted. The trip takes twenty minutes. No, she tells Sullivan, they don't discuss what she's going to say. She has not rehearsed her lines for the day. Rehearsed? The word is like a red flag in front of a bull. Sullivan asks Tammy why she used this word, but makes no headway whatever.

Sullivan tries again: Did you ever tell your friend Colleen Friesen that your grandfathers sexually abused you? "I don't recall," answers Tammy, this time lowering her eyes. If she did say it, it would have been during an insulin reaction. It would also have been during low blood sugar that she told Bev Hiebert her brother had abused her, if she ever did. On that note, Sullivan concludes her cross-examination of Tammy, and Judge Lavoie dismisses the witness from the room.

Inconsistent evidence — that is the problem here. Sullivan hauls out her copy of the Criminal Code, Lavoie his. He wonders aloud if Tammy is deceiving the court by saying she can't recall certain things that might have occurred during insulin attacks. The judge is still uncertain about Tammy's credibility, and how he should proceed according to the Canada Evidence Act, when statements the accused has just made are inconsistent with her previous testimony.

For the past few weeks, Leslie Sullivan and Tim White have been playing an ancient game with strict rules. When the game ends, one side will win and the other lose. It's time to end the game, by arranging the pieces of the puzzle in two different ways and letting Judge Lavoie decide which picture is less flawed, that of the prosecution or the defence.

White stands and begins his summary, his voice quivering from his opening "Your Honour" while he fingers his notes. Tammy may be socially immature, he acknowledges to Lavoie, but she is credible and has tried to answer questions honestly. On the other hand, how can you believe the boys when there's no corroborating physical evidence? And how can you believe them when they had so many errors in their testimony? And let's not forget the way the children were interviewed by the police in the first place. "I submit to you that you have no option but to acquit." It would be dangerous to convict. "I'm not saying these children have not been abused by someone," but where is the evidence that points to Tammy?

Lavoie is genuinely puzzled, asking White: What do I do with the evidence? What do I do with Kenny's drawings? What do I do with the evidence of totally independent people who saw the police vehicles? And what about the evidence of these two little boys who, without talking to one another since September 1991, have still disclosed similar things?

White answers: It can't be proved the children were ever in the police cars. And they didn't even talk about the alleged events till after they saw the police photos. The police, and then their parents, formed an opinion early on and contaminated the children. In court the children made lots of factual errors in their testimony. At what point can they be called totally unbelievable? White then delivers his final point: There's a tendency today to believe children because "we want to protect [them]." But we have a "profoundly disturbing problem" here because it's hard to decide on the reliability of the child witnesses.

That's the heart of the issue, isn't it? Everyone in the room knows that the burden of proof — the linchpin of the criminal-trial system — rests with the prosecution, not the defence. The prosecution must convince the judge, beyond a reasonable doubt, that Freddy's and Kenny's stories are believable, or he will have no choice but to acquit Tammy. Perhaps burden of proof would be more aptly named acquittal by default.

"There is a reasonable doubt," concludes White, nodding to the judge and leaving the lectern.

Sullivan stands and moves the wood lectern on the table, placing it between her and Lavoie, then shuffles her papers dramatically, as though preparing to deliver a lecture. For once, she isn't frowning. For the past six weeks, she reminds Lavoie, she has attempted to prove the Crown's premise: Freddy and Kenny were abused at the Sterling house and at The Place. The pieces of evidence are numerous and, when looked at in a cumulative fashion, it's very easy to draw the conclusion the boys were sexually abused. The only question then is: Who did it? If you find as fact the events that Freddy and Kenny described, you will have to convict, Your Honour.

Sullivan recaps the evidence, like so many headlines in a newspaper: the boys' behavioural symptoms, their ability to identify Tammy, keeping their facts straight after all this time. Then she highlights parts of the story she wants Lavoie to remember: Your Honour, the police showed Freddy and Kenny photos, but the boys could not possibly have memorized what they saw. Even if they had committed the details to memory, how could they remember the details when they haven't seen the photos for two years? In fact, the things the boys don't say about the pictures, and don't consider relevant to their story, are just as important as what they do say. For instance, in some of the pictures of The Place there is a doghouse. Children love animals and a doghouse would normally be on their checklist, she continues, but neither of the boys even mentions the doghouse. Furthermore, the boys mentioned details of The Place that were not even in the photographs. For example, how does Freddy know the correct relation of the door to the bed at The Place, when he can't see the door in the photo? And how can Kenny describe the Sterling house, including the plants and photos on the wall, if he never entered the house?

Both boys gave powerful descriptions of The Place and talked about the general mess, the pressed wood floor, and the freezer. Kenny even described the freezer's inside blue lid. Both described the cage in a similar way, and yet that cage is not the one we see in the photos. It is not at all surprising, says Sullivan, that the cage the boys described was not found.

Officer Rod Moor may have offered the boys extreme encouragement when he interviewed them, but would that be sufficient to cause the boys to accuse Tammy of sexual abuse? And there's no evidence that Moor suggested the fine details of the stories to the boys, says Sullivan. If he didn't, how did they come up with their details? And what would make them tell such stories in the first place? What would motivate them?

On the other hand, Your Honour, Tammy was too often adamant and went overboard to prove that no impropriety had taken place towards the daycare children. According to the prosecutor, Tammy's testimony did not ring true at all, compared to that of the two boys. "We would ask you to convict her on the evidence before you," Sullivan concludes. Having had her say, the prosecutor shuffles her papers and leaves the lectern.

It is now White's turn to rebut. He contends that Sullivan confuses suggestion and encouragement. The police did more than encourage the boys; they polluted their minds with stories about sexual abuse. In these stories the children were the "stars" and once they had "bought into" the allegations, they couldn't back out. The boys are very intelligent, White says, and he finds it hard to believe they wouldn't know a scar when they saw one. As for Freddy and Kenny having erections in the therapist's office, White says he sees nothing unusual about that. Boys have erections all the time, so why shouldn't they have them in Rod Butler's office? With respect to *Terminator I* and *II*, any six-year-old would know the difference between the two movies and not confuse them the way Kenny did. And Kenny made another mistake too: he said the garage door at The Place was opened by remote control, but it was not. Only one thing can be said about The Place with certainty: the police found nothing there, not even with the help of the LUMA-LITE.

Sullivan retorts, in a hasty postscript: Neither police officer ever mentioned Tammy, by name, to the boys and yet they correctly identified her. White responds: The boys have trouble even remembering Tammy's name.

Lavoie says he needs time to digest the evidence and adjourns court for one month.

A verdict to cry for

On May 20, four weeks later, courtroom 8 of Youth Court is filled with many of the regulars and a few unfamiliar young faces, here to support Tammy on her big day. Instead of entering the courtroom ceremoniously at the last minute, Lavoie sits in his high black leather chair and sips from a styrofoam cup, fuelling himself for the task he's about to perform. On my left, Janis rifles through the pages of her notepad, to my right the CBC reporter stares ahead, trancelike, spiral notebook on lap, chomping on a candy. Freddy's parents are a couple of rows behind me, looking sombre, touching shoulders; Kenny's mom and dad sit further back, to the side. I wonder if the boys are at school today, and what their parents told them over breakfast. Tammy walks in with her dad's arm around her shoulder. Her hair is greasy, her face pale, looking defeated. Whatever she did or did not do to those kids, she looks as though she needs help.

At two o'clock, the appointed time, Judge Lavoie adjusts his glasses. Tension fills the room, as everyone waits to hear the end of the story that only he can tell.

Lavoie clears his throat and begins to tell the story that spans three years in the life of three children — Kenny, Freddy, and Tammy. Not only does Lavoie retell the entire saga, he also evaluates the performance of the witnesses, as though giving credit to actors in a play. The expert witnesses showed skill and sensitivity, though their testimony should not be used to bolster the credibility of the boys themselves. The neighbours who saw the police vehicles gave testimony that is more than mere coincidence, demanding that weight be attached to what they said. Without question, the boys were courageous. Although they forgot certain details, although their stories had discrepancies and some of their evidence was dubious, they stuck to their testimony and gave no evidence substantially deviating from the main plot. Their information was consistent and the cumulative effect of what each said is more than a coincidence. Their evidence is based on their own personal experience and, he says, the boys have no reason to lie.

From time to time, Lavoie hints at the end of the story. Then, just as people start to fidget, he launches into another chapter, taking his time, conveying with slow words his struggle to write the finish. Yes. No. Guilty. Not guilty.

He reminds us that medical experts talked about the many physical symptoms of the boys, not the least disconcerting of which was Freddy's erections in his therapist's office, proof that the boy had carnal knowledge. The "courts should take a common sense approach" in a case like this.

Looking over the rim of his glasses, the sole tryer of fact cuts to the heart of the matter: After examining the boys' testimony closely, he believes beyond a reasonable doubt that sexual abuse occurred.

Thud. The accused stares into space as the judge continues: The boys had known Tammy for quite some time and easily recognized her. Therefore, "identity was not an issue." Not remembering her scars may mean nothing more than that they never registered. Silence blankets the room. Though Lavoie has yet to tell the end of the story, everyone knows it now. The courts should not have the same exacting standards for children that apply in adult cases, he intones. Still, he must be convinced that the testimony he heard is beyond a reasonable doubt. He is convinced, not absolutely, but beyond a reasonable doubt.

Now the black-robed man who has sat for weeks and listened patiently to the parade of people passing through his courtroom shares his feelings. It pains him to think he will never know for sure what Tammy did to Freddy and Kenny. He will never know whose story has reached his court, the kids' or the cops', because of the way the police did their job. But the boys should not be penalized if the constabulary conducted "improper interviews." Just because incompetence occurred is no reason to assume abuse did not. We should not confuse police "incompetence" with the boys' credibility.

Tammy's credibility is another matter altogether. Most of her testimony was of little assistance. Some of it, such as blaming certain behaviour on insulin shock, was plainly suspect. And her answers were defensive, more like explanations than evidence. The Crown has proven, beyond a reasonable doubt, that Tammy is guilty of eight of the ten charges.

Two or three people in the gallery gasp. Others smile. Hearing the news, Tammy grabs the back of her right wrist with her left hand, as though already handcuffed, and drops both arms to her lap. Then, in abject humiliation, she presses fingers tight to her eyes, her body goes slack, and she sobs. Her father, who also looks ready to cry, wraps his arm around her shoulders. Her boyfriend pats her on the back. The commissionaire hands her a box of tissues. Her mother, who has come to court from time to time, stands beside the girl but doesn't touch her.

Having found Tammy guilty on eight counts, Lavoie must now decide the nature and length of her sentence. That will take time, partly because Sullivan has just requested a thirty-day psychiatric assessment of Tammy. When White asks his client if she agrees to it, she half-nods and wipes her eyes. During the assessment Tammy will live at the Regional Psychiatric Centre north of Saskatoon, a facility that houses some of the country's most dangerous criminals.

Judge Lavoie's exit from the courtroom signals to the commissionaire that it's time to clear the room. Friends and relatives leave in an orderly manner and journalists run to the nearest phone, or look for a quiet corner to use their own cell phone. Now the people who a moment ago were on one side of the door are on the other, in the tiny corridor. Noisy confusion reigns in the hall, but no one seems to mind until the person nearest the door gets bumped when it suddenly swings wide open. Through it bursts Tammy, accompanied by her red-faced father, who curses the crowd under his breath. I try to hear what he says, but am actually glad I can't quite catch it.

A month goes by. May becomes June, and light green foliage turns to dark. Tammy undergoes a psychiatric evaluation while Corporal John Popowich sweats through his own trial, the first of the five co-accused officers to take the stand. The trial is short and ends abruptly when neither Freddy nor Kenny nor a third daycare boy can identify Popowich as their abuser. The judge grants the accused officer a "stay of proceedings"; if no new evidence against him surfaces in the next 365 days, his trial will not resume.

In his three-page handwritten ruling, Judge Ted Noble apologizes to Popowich profusely, saying he is a "victim of mistaken identity," which is "related to the difficulty all of us have in recalling the essential features of another person's physical appearance." As everyone knows, it's not too difficult to alter those "essential features."

He's right. My own sister does it by cutting her hair and losing twenty pounds, and I scarcely recognize her in the bakery the day after Popowich's trial.

On June 23, the day of Tammy's sentencing, there is not a spare seat in the courtroom. The mothers of Freddy and Kenny are here, as is Rod Butler, the boys' therapist, and Bev "Mom" Hiebert. Because of the shortage of space, Tammy's boyfriend sits in the media row, beside me, his long hair and unshaved face, dirty nails, and toothpick providing stark contrast to his startlingly beautiful blue eyes. Tammy sits in front of me, flanked by her father and mother. She too has neglected to wash her long hair this morning. It's stringy and makes her look drawn. The black jersey top doesn't help much either.

The Crown prosecutor rises to speak and, she hopes, influence the sentence the judge will pass on Tammy. Sullivan does not remove her black wool legal jacket, though I'm sweltering in a loose cotton dress. Perhaps Sullivan is too intent to even notice the heat. Or maybe that's why she's frowning more than usual. Sullivan aligns her notes on the lectern, as though tidying a linen closet, and begins to "speak to the sentence."

Your Honour, a lengthy sentence is necessary to uphold community confidence in the judicial system and to "show society will no longer tolerate" such behaviour. These offences are a "plague" and are taken more seriously than they were ten years ago. Sullivan cites several benchmark decisions in other western provinces, where the maximum sentence to date is six years.

She continues: Your Honour, when sentencing, there are important criteria to consider, the most important being the "threshold level": Has the victim suffered persistent psychological problems? Was the victim abused frequently? Was there violence? The more severe the abuse, the more detrimental the effects on the victim — depression, self-esteem, self-destruction, maladjustment. And the more severe the abuse, the more difficulty the victim will experience in forming a long-term intimate relationship "without fear of abuse." In the years to come, the victim may victimize another child.

If Tammy had pleaded guilty, or shown remorse, or was willing to respond to treatment, says Sullivan, I might recommend a lesser sentence. But none of these mitigating factors is present. The Crown does not want probation now and treatment later. "The earlier treatment can start, the better." Tammy, though now twenty-one years old, has been tried as a juvenile because that's what she was at the time of her crimes. These days, Sullivan reminds the court, treatment is available right away when a juvenile is sent to prison. Therefore, she recommends a five-year sentence for Tammy, three years in closed custody followed by two years' probation.

Silence. Tammy looks at the floor. Her father places his hand on her shoulder. Beads of sweat are pooling on Sullivan's brow. She looks relieved, now that she can sit and take a drink of water.

Lavoie nods to White, who shuffles to his feet and bunches his papers haphazardly.

Your Honour, Tammy is indeed small, not just in stature, but young as well, a good six or seven years delayed in social and psychological development. According to the psychological assessment, her developmental age is somewhere between sixteen and seventeen, even though she is twenty-one years old. But she has no criminal record and she has cooperated with the psychiatrists. She's not mentally ill, but she does have health problems and problems with "low self-esteem and interpersonal relations." Your Honour, this case is "unique," and there's no real guidance as you "forge into a new area." But I'd like you to consider a "more careful balancing" when you sentence her, especially since she shows potential for rehabilitation.

During the short break, I find Tammy in the washroom sobbing her heart out. We're alone, so I hug her, rigid like a block of steel. Without notice, she breaks free, steps back, wipes her eyes with the back of her hand, and shouts, "I'm going to get sick tonight, to give them a lesson and show them what they're doing to me... How can I show remorse when I haven't done anything?" She starts to cry again. "He's going to give me six years, from the sounds of it." I don't know what to say to console her. To make matters worse, I can hardly see through my own tears. And for the first time since my husband left, they're tears for someone other than me. I want to reach out, but don't know how. I've got to find some way or someone to help her, someone like my Presbyterian Grandma Gillies, who brought me up from the time I was twelve. What would she do if she were me, and I were Tammy? She'd reach for the witch hazel, her cure-all. No, that's what she'd do for a scraped knee. For a bruised soul, she'd administer two of her oatmeal cookies and a glass of ice-cold milk. Then she'd talk sweetly to calm me down. She would not tell me any lies.

"Tammy," I begin, trying to reproduce Grandma's reassuring tone. "You don't know what the judge is going to do. Nobody does. He probably won't be as harsh as you think. Do you want something to drink?" Though she refuses the drink, she accepts the toilet paper I rip off for her to dry her eyes. After patting them, she flings open the door and storms out.

Court is in session when I return, so I do the obligatory half-bow in the direction of Lavoie. I don't know if the commissionaire keeps track of who bows at the door and who doesn't, but Lavoie is likely oblivious to such formalities when reading the eight counts on which he finds the accused guilty.

Count 1: guilty of sexual assault on Kenny
Count 2: guilty of sexually touching a person under fourteen years (Kenny)
Count 3: guilty of unlawfully confining Kenny
Count 5: guilty of sexual assault on Freddy
Count 6: guilty of sexually touching a person under fourteen years (Freddy)
Count 7: guilty of sexual assault on Freddy while threatening to use a weapon
Count 9: guilty of assaulting Freddy
Count 10: guilty of uttering a death threat to Freddy

In the middle of the last count, Tammy unclasps her gold necklace and turns to give it to her boyfriend seated beside me. She sobs.

Lavoie says that if Tammy had been tried in adult court, sexual assault would get her ten years and the additional threat of a weapon would get her four more. But this is youth court, and he is trying to strike a balance. On one side of the scales of justice, he says, he sees the need to make Tammy bear the responsibility for her contravention. On the other side, he sees the need to protect the public and maintain confidence in the judicial system, and send a "signal to all those who occupy positions of trust in relation to young persons."

Having spoken like a true judge, Lavoie gives vent to his feelings. "Quite frankly, I feel she [Tammy] is under a dysfunctional control of her parents, especially her father. I have been somewhat cognizant of the absolute constant physical presence of her father at her side. I appreciate the protectiveness of a parent's love, but this gives me an uneasy feeling that there might be something beyond that in this case." The young woman must gain personal independence from her family, and acknowledge her criminal conviction, and no amount of therapy will be meaningful and effective until she does. She displays a victim mentality as well as a perpetrator mentality. Nevertheless, her socially unacceptable behaviour must not go unpunished. The agony and revulsion of what she has done goes beyond words. The judge sounds sad when he says, "We can never truly assess the shame, guilt, emotional pain and absolute upheaval in their precious young lives that these two boys have experienced. Community support must be given, without question, in their healing process." He looks straight at Tammy and asks her to stand. She rises slowly to her feet, sobbing.

Lavoie sentences Tammy to a "fit and proper sentence" as follows: a total of three years, two in closed custody and one year on probation, and therapy till fully discharged. Hearing this, the mother of her boyfriend starts to cry. Though at first her parents stare straight ahead, dry-eyed, they cry when Tammy turns to them for a good-bye hug before being led away by a policewoman.

The prize fight is over. There's no winner and no cheering. Even though some of the people may have got what they wanted, they probably didn't expect the price would be so high. In all likelihood no one here has ever seen a sobbing young woman dragged from her family by a prison guard. Drained by the sight, I want to be left alone, in peace, to think about what I've just witnessed and try to make sense of it. I leave the courthouse and walk to my car in the parking lot, only to find the exit blocked by a small family circle — Tammy's parents, her boyfriend, and his mother. At first, I hope they'll stop talking and move out of my way. Then I see the golden opportunity to tell them what's on my mind.

"I'm sorry."

Both mothers — Tammy's own, and her boyfriend's — turn to me with tears in their eyes. Tammy's father is red-faced: "I'm going to sue that judge. Fuck." Then, through tears, the boyfriend's mother says Lavoie probably doesn't know any better than to say the things he did about Tammy and her dad because he has never seen a close family. Indignant, she blows her nose, breaks from the circle, and walks to her car, her son at her side. There's nothing for Tammy's parents to do but the same.

The Second Trial

Selecting the Jury

On August 16, 1993, citizens of all ages pack the cream-and-violet ballroom of the historic Bessborough Hotel in Saskatoon. They're here because they've won the "lottery" and the right to be members of the jury pool for the hottest trial in Saskatchewan. The Department of Justice computer picked their names at random from the province's medicare list. Of the 1,300 jury notices sent out, 97 people didn't receive the notice because they'd moved without leaving a change of address, 121 threw the summons in the garbage, and 892 came up with legitimate reasons to beg off jury duty. The remaining 190 men and women who heeded the summons are in this room.

They sense the drama they are part of. Some have brought friends. Others look around the room for relatives, once-, twice-, three-times-removed. In Saskatchewan, everyone seems to be related to or connected to everyone else. It's the best and the worst thing about living here.

Except for the climate. Though it's just mid-August, the first frost isn't far away. The last breath of summer blows across the window sills, and the sheers stir lazily in the last of the golden light. The crowd gossips in summer clothes, and their buzz rises and falls like a beehive. The more industrious ones talk about harvest, the start of school and putting up preserves. The drones who long to lengthen summer stretch in their chairs and chatter about the summer family reunion, the cabin at the lake, their golf games, and their fishing trips.

At 10:30, the chatter ceases when the black-robed clerk enters and shouts into a microphone. Even those who don't speak Old French know that "Oyez, oyez" means shut up. "State your name and save your fine," advises the clerk into the mike, which appeals to this lot who are always looking for ways to save money. So far, this summons stuff looks as easy as clipping coupons for

Superstore. When the clerk calls your name from the list of 190, you answer "Here," just like it used to be at school.

Unlike a normal school day, the judge will grant early recess because there's been an "unfortunate turn of events," as he puts it from his seat on the platform at the front of the room. There will be a week-long adjournment because the father of Ron Sterling, one of the three accused, has just died. That explains why Sterling was crying in the hall a moment ago.

On August 23, the jury pool re-convenes at the château-style "Bess" — once a CN Hotel and recently renovated to some of its original 1930s splendour.

The trial hasn't even begun and Judge Ross Wimmer looks weary already. With his bald head and remnants of grey hair, he looks like somebody's favourite uncle, all the more so because of brown eyes that twinkle behind his glasses, and make me wonder what he knows that I don't. But some of the sparkle seems to be lacking, now that he has to hold court in the hotel and sleep upstairs till the trial's over. It's too far to drive home every night to Battleford, 130 km away. How does he feel about leaving his wife for such a long time? Or about being assigned to this trial in the first place? Last week he listened to a lawyer tell him why a young man shouldn't go to jail, even though, driving drunk and way over the speed limit, the accused had maimed a young woman for life. This week and for many weeks to come, Wimmer will be paid to referee a trial in which seven sets of parents have accused the three Sterlings — father, mother, and son — of abusing their fifteen sons and daughters, including Freddy and Kenny, at the Sterling house in Martensville and an acreage outside town.

Linda Sterling, the operator of the unlicensed home daycare, is short and overweight, which can't be good for her health, since she's in her mid forties. Born in 1947, she went to high school in Prince Albert, where she and Ron were sweethearts. From the little I know, she has led a traditional life as wife and mother. But I wonder if she ever dreamed of having a career — maybe as an artist, if the palette of vivid colours she wears is a clue. Apparently, her son Travis is quite artistic.

Travis, whom I have never seen smile, strikes me as the kind of kid who'd be hard to teach. Quite the contrary, according to one of his former teachers. Travis was very well-behaved and deserved all the nineties he got. In high school he belonged to a group of good, normal kids and was popular. Unfortunately, he was the product of the small town he lived in, where many students considered reading a form of "punishment." Martensville, in the early 1980s, was apparently a place where learning was definitely not cool and many like Travis, born in the late sixties, did not go to university no matter how good their grades. The inward-looking small town failed to cultivate high aspirations and good self-esteem in many teens. This mix of factors led to Travis's frustration and eventual downfall. "Vegetating does not sit well with a creative mind," according to the teacher.

Travis was apparently not particularly aggressive when it came to job hunting and waited for jobs to come to him. In a sleepy bedroom community like Martensville he'd wait quite a while, I expect. So why didn't the son emulate his father, Ron, who seemed to have no shortage of things to do? Between his full-time job at the Correctional Centre and his volunteer role as fire fighter and emergency worker, Ron Sterling must have been a busy man. He was also, says a Martensville resident, a "caring parent" to his kids, though a demanding one.

Travis stands beside his mother and father, in a straight row at the front of the court. The co-accused have been charged together. The trio's offences, when bunched together, overlap and number twenty-six, indicting more than one Sterling at once. But when disentangled, the criminal charges against the father, mother, and son add up to sixty-one. After reciting each charge to the accused, the court clerk asks in a perfunctory tone, "How say you?" The counts range from simple sexual assault to sexual assault threatening to use a gun, to confinement and attempt to suffocate with a pillowcase, to anal intercourse. In solos, duets, and trios, Ron, Linda, and Travis plead not guilty twenty-six times.

Wimmer invites all 190 people in the jury pool to "try the case, along with me," though everyone knows only twelve will eventually do the job. Only those who are impartial will be chosen, says the judge, and only when they prove it by passing a test. "Don't be offended at being challenged," Wimmer tells the crowd. It's his job to make sure the three Sterlings get a fair trial, and that no one fakes their way onto the jury. I've got to weed out those of you who say you're ready to give the Sterlings a fair trial, but aren't, he warns. You must be honest with yourselves. If you cannot "banish from [your] thoughts" the words and pictures the media have planted there, you must say so now.

The jury test is somewhat of a novelty in Saskatchewan. It has not been used since 1920, when a Mountie was tried for murdering his first wife, who was pregnant and got in the way of his new life with the second. It is crucial that impartial jurors be found for the Sterling trial, as it was for the Mountie. But this is easier said than done because everyone in the province knows that everyone else has an opinion about the Sterlings. They either set these opinions aside, as Judge Wimmer insists, or they can't take part in the trial.

Fairness is the first basis of our judicial system and the conceptual twin of Beyond a Reasonable Doubt. Though born honestly, the siblings live in paradox. According to Columbia University law professor George P. Fletcher, in his book *With Justice for Some*, "Justice for the victim may be at odds with fairness towards the defendant. Thus to achieve justice we skew the odds in favour of acquittal. The scales of justice are not balanced. They dip heavily in favour of the defendant."

Better to let ten guilty persons go free than convict one innocent. Jurors must be ready to err on the side of caution, angelic in their purity of heart, godlike in their charity towards the most odious criminal, until they are satisfied, beyond a reasonable doubt, that the accused is guilty of the stated crime. The standards are rigorous in a criminal trial. The burden of proof falls completely on the Crown prosecutor, which means that the accused is presumed innocent till the prosecution proves otherwise. Meanwhile, the defence doesn't have to prove or disprove a thing. Jurors, the triers of fact, must be just that. They must weigh the evidence and come to a verdict based on what is put before them in the courtroom, not what they see and hear beyond it. If one juror is allowed to enter the courtroom with an attitude about the accused, or has a political agenda, that person has already skewed the outcome of the trial. The Criminal Code of Canada calls a biased juror "unsuitable."

There are plenty of those in Saskatoon, and maybe in this very ballroom: that's what the Sterlings' three-man defence team tells the judge. That's because the "most unfortunate" headlines and supper-hour newscasts of the past year have polluted the juror pool. To prove it, the defence lawyers arranged for a random telephone survey of 800 people, paid for by the taxpayers of Saskatchewan. The results, when tabulated, showed that one-third of the people polled believe the Sterlings guilty, and only one-half of one per cent — four of the 800 polled — believe they are not guilty. One of those had already come to a verdict: "Guilty based on media reports." Another was ready to pass sentence: "Hang them all."

Defence lawyers don't normally conduct a community survey before a trial, but the Sterlings' trial is not a normal trial. In light of the extensive pretrial media coverage, the lawyers believed that the public had a skewed perception of the Sterlings and they were right. When they invoked challenge for cause, the Criminal Code's litmus test to determine prejudice, they got an eye opener. A majority of those polled answered yes when asked: "Do you hold an opinion about the guilt or innocence of the members of the Sterling family?" And a majority answered no to "Will you be able to put that opinion aside and reach a decision based only upon the evidence and arguments which will be presented in court?" In a province as small as Saskatchewan, undoubtedly some of the people who said they have an opinion about the Sterlings are in this room. And very likely, some of those who said they would not be able to put aside that opinion if called for jury duty are members of the jury pool.

Therefore, say the three defence lawyers, it will be very difficult, if not impossible, to find impartial jurors in this room. They see only one solution: a fresh poll to weed out the "unsuitables." The two Crown lawyers, Leslie Sullivan and Bruce Bauer, are unhappy about the first survey, not to mention a second. They say that errors were made in the poll, and that it was not done scientifically.

Regardless of the way it was done, Judge Wimmer says, the poll is valid. The community is highly prejudiced, and the jury must not be. So the court must test potential jurors with more questions. In fact, the same questions that were used for the sampling of the 800 will be revised and put to the candidates in this room.

For anyone who wants to duck jury duty rather than relinquish normal life for four months — the expected length of the trial — now's the time to do it. Tell the lawyers you're irrevocably prejudiced when they ask. If you're too proud to admit to prejudice, pick another excuse why you'd be unfit for jury duty. There's no end to the reasons in this room.

And Judge Wimmer hears them all. When he asks who has a conflict of interest, one man stands to say he used to teach Travis Sterling, and so would like to be excused. Wimmer excuses him. Several others ask to be exempted because they're related to, or know, someone involved in the trial. Sometimes Wimmer excuses them, sometimes not, depending on the closeness of the connection. On the other hand, he readily accepts the fear of a woman who lives out of town and doesn't "highway drive" in winter. Likewise, he excuses another who is pregnant. "We can have only twelve jurors," cracks Wimmer, to the crowd's delight. Personal bias is openly declared a couple of times. "Undue financial hardship," anxiety about hearing the children's testimony, and so on and so forth. The list of potential jurors gets shorter and shorter.

Before dismissing for the day the 141 people still in the jury pool, Wimmer cautions them not to discuss what they've seen and heard in this room today, or pay any attention to what they hear outside. "It might be best if you stopped following the news altogether," he admonishes. Who's kidding whom? The potential jurors filing out of the room belong to the ninety-nine per cent of the community who, when polled earlier by telephone, said they knew about the Martensville case. How can you stop them from knowing?

All the lawyers can look for now is twelve people with open minds. That's why the jury questions have to be good. The judge and the lawyers will see to it.

No sooner has the last potential juror left the room than the lawyers set to work. The order of the questions is wrong, says Crown prosecutor Bruce Bauer. No, it isn't, retorts defence lawyer Hugh Harradence. Judge Wimmer thinks the order is fine, but that the wording of one question is not. Either it's changed or it's out, he insists. While this editorial wrangling over the six questions drags on, a handful of journalists takes notes and the three Sterlings sit in their chairs, absolutely still. I wonder what's going through their heads. On the one hand, the legal hair-splitting must be confusing; on the other, they must be glad their lawyers take their rights so seriously. Thank heavens someone in town thinks the three of them are innocent till proven guilty.

Next morning, the day of jury tryouts at "The Bess," there's not enough time to put the six questions to everyone in the room. Besides, there are almost enough people here to make up a dozen juries. So the lawyers for both the defence and the prosecution agree that the first twelve to pass the test will form the jury. No spares. The others can go home.

Now that the six questions are ready, Wimmer wonders who will ask them. It was one thing for the Saskatchewan Legal Aid Commission to hire pollsters to telephone 800 people to see if they were biased. It's another to be face-to-face in the same room with people who already have their minds made up, and to know this is your very last chance to weed them out. If the telephone results can be extrapolated, half these men and women have already reached a verdict. Too bad they're not wearing "G" or "NG" on their foreheads. You have to read the eyes to see if they match the lips.

Who's good at reading lips and eyes? Who will pick the first two jurors from the 141 candidates? By law, the lawyers are forbidden to select the first two, though they have the final say about all twelve jurors. Till recently the Crown lawyers had the power to disqualify four potential jurors for each one the defence lawyers disqualified. But the Supreme Court struck down that procedure, saying it violated human rights. So now the lawyers on both sides have the right to disqualify an equal number of potential jurors. If, for instance, the three defence lawyers disqualify one person, the two prosecuting lawyers may nix the next one, or the next, if necessary. This process of selecting and disqualifying goes on until there are twelve jurors approved by both sides. In this trial, the six questions will be asked by both sides of the court. To start things off, the judge needs two neutral people without an axe to grind.

Wimmer surveys the room, trying to find two honest faces. Come now, he urges, what could be more important than doing your duty as a citizen? And what could possibly be more important than being the first two "triers of fact" and starting the jury selection in motion? Then he ups the ante: Oh, in case I haven't mentioned it, there's a reward. As soon as the triers of fact select the first two people whom the lawyers approve as jurors, the two triers can go home and enjoy the rest of the summer. Exempt from jury duty.

When no one bites, Wimmer is forced to try a new strategy. Put your money where your mouth is, he exhorts the journalists in the front row. Janis Crosbie nudges a fellow reporter, Robert James, and, after seconds of hesitation, the two stand, for God and the Queen.

It's not every day two TV journalists help lawyers pick jurors in a criminal trial. It is even more unusual because Janis and Robert ("R.J.") are reporting the trial for the local evening news. At break, Janis tells me she answered Judge Wimmer's call as a citizen, not as a journalist. But she came to the courthouse as a journalist, not a citizen, I argue. Doesn't it seem like a conflict of interest? If she accepts some responsibility for the makeup of the jury, can she then stand back and report on the trial in a completely objective manner? Janis says she can. I thought journalists were supposed to be separate from the judicial process, not part of it, and would like to discuss the topic one day with Judge Wimmer or a professor of journalism ethics.

But this double-duty is not particularly unusual, according to A.M. Rosenthal, who writes for the *New York Times*. Commenting on the O.J. Simpson trial shortly after the verdict, he wrote, "Various journalists regularly instructed the judge on what evidence to admit or exclude... I never realized it had become a journalist's task. I worked for editors who would have hung me out like a dead chicken if I had tried." Does Rosenthal mean to say courtroom reporters were more familiar with the law than the judge? Even if the journalists were also schooled as lawyers, it's inconceivable that one person could wear two different hats in a criminal case and get away with it. I guess the court reporter for the *Saskatoon StarPhoenix* thinks so too, for he will call the jury-selection process "unusual" in his front-section story tomorrow.

On the other hand, who is better equipped than a journalist to choose jurors? Who is more able to see when eyes and lips match, or when they don't? When you've interviewed hundreds of people and peered through the windows of their soul, you do a pretty quick read of everyone you meet. I wonder if Janis and R.J. will enjoy picking the first two jurors, and whether they'll tell their audiences tonight what they did in court today.

The jury-selection process takes the rest of the morning and is done in a calm and civilized way. The first candidates are called to the front of the room, by number not name, and Janis and R.J. give each person the once-over. This takes about fifteen seconds. After scrutininzing fourteen candidates in a row, and finding them all unacceptable, Janis and R.J. reject them and inform the lawyers of their decisions. No questions will be put to these people. Then the fifteenth candidate, a woman, comes forward. To the two journalists she looks as though she'd make a good juror. They say so to the lawyers, who then proceed to ask the questions: Have you discussed the trial? Do you hold an opinion about the guilt or innocence of the accused? Will you be able to set aside that opinion? Evidently the lawyers, two for the Crown and three for defence, like the woman's answers well enough to select her as the first juror. Before long, Janis and R.J. see another candidate, also a woman, whom they think worthy of the questions. She is passed along to the lawyers and, after passing their test, becomes the second juror.

When Janis and R.J. have selected the first two jurors, their job is done. For the rest of the morning, the two jurors assist the five lawyers. By noon, more than fifty candidates have been rejected and ten more jurors selected. The six men and six women have convinced their challengers that, when sworn as jurors, they will be able to "put out of [their] mind anything [they] may have heard about the case and arrive at a verdict based only upon the evidence and arguments which will be presented in court."

If the Sterlings' trial is about to begin inside the courthouse, it has been debated for weeks outside the building. The public purging, inevitable for such a notorious criminal case, is apparently essential to the community's mental health. Columbia University law professor George Fletcher, author of *With Justice for Some*, writes that if the Rodney King trial had been heard in Los Angeles, instead of being moved to nearby Simi Valley, the city could have grieved and healed itself. "...the affected population, expressing itself through a jury, should have confronted the 56 baton blows to King's body and tried to reach a just verdict." Instead, the citizens are still licking their wounds, infecting the rest of the United States with their rage. A crime must be tried where it was committed so that justice may be seen, first-hand, to be done.

Judge Wimmer, who suggested to jurors the other day that they stop following the news, also understands the need for "public discussion of the case, according to its facts." The three defence lawyers for the accused want the public to know what the trial is about, and their three adult clients want open court, too. By contrast, the two prosecuting lawyers want the court closed to provide complete privacy for the children who will testify. The two Crown lawyers also want to ban the media from the courtroom, as do the daycare children and their parents. The five lawyers battle it out with Wimmer, while reporters scribble as fast as they can, while they still can. At the very least, local journalists will be able to report the ban and warn the public to expect the news blackout, if the judge so rules. I'm surprised there aren't more people in the public gallery today. Though their right to know is at stake, there's only a handful of citizens in the courtroom.

Judge Wimmer has his own thoughts about courtroom doors and reporters' notepads. Open is good, closed is bad. All the more so in light of the pretrial media coverage, which has fanned feeling in the community. Coverage or no coverage, the bottom line is this: the child witnesses must not be identified. They've filled out their "fear list" for the court and made it clear they don't want the whole world to hear what happened to them. Some are afraid their friends might put two and two together in the school yard, then see the trial on the supper-hour news. Wimmer must strike a balance between the children's privacy and the public's right to know. He does this by ruling as follows: Publishable material: all testimony of the adults, except for what is banned on a day-to-day basis. Non-publishable material: all testimony of the children, until after the verdict is reached; and all information of any kind that would identify the children, until further notice, which may be never. In other words, we can keep our notepads open as long as we keep our mouths shut where the children are concerned. What a break! Remember the muzzle on Tammy's trial?

It's easy for me to be smug about a partial ban. I've got time on my side and months to write a book. The teacher in me wouldn't think of questioning the confidentiality of the kids' identities. Neither would the journalist, unless she had to, or until she can. When the ban is lifted, I'll go back over my manuscript and fill in the blanks with as much of the children's evidence as possible. Isn't that what everyone is waiting to read about?

The ethical tug-of-war is one of the best and worst things about being a journalist. If you interview Santa Claus, for instance, you have to decide whether to respect his image as an icon, whether to tell if he picks his nose or scratches his crotch while he talks to you, or makes you wait while he takes ten more 1-800 calls from kids. When you tell a story about alleged child abuse at a daycare, there's not much to say that's pretty. But there's not much of anything to say if you can't report the children's side of the story and illustrate it with the ugly details of being locked in a freezer, tied up, gagged, and buggered. The ethical within me is at war with the professional. And a partial ban is even more tricky than a total one — you can say some things, but not others. What's legal to publish, what's not? Only the court knows for sure. Reporters will have to ask Wimmer, or one of the lawyers, from day to day.

The judge has certainly cramped the style of the country's radio, TV, and newspaper reporters. By laying down the law and permitting them to tell some, but not all, of the story, he has temporarily diminished their rights in order to augment those of the children's. He has forestalled reporters' hopes of titillating the community and deprived them of the thrill of testing the public taste for atrocity. Till kingdom come, rules Wimmer, none of the daycare kids will be sacrificed on *his* public altar. The journalists in the room are caught in a bind. They love their own kids and would choose anonymity for them in a case like this. But they have a job to do, and because of Wimmer's ruling, now they have to perform a balancing act.

If Wimmer's ruling has somewhat placated the journalists, it has very much displeased the parents of the children, who fear the kids will be "intimidated" when they learn that the public will hear their stories one day. That day is thoroughly dreaded by Kenny and Freddy, who ranked invasion of their privacy near the top of the fear lists they filled out for the Department of Justice. I can imagine the boys' shame and have no intention of ever divulging their identity, for my sake as much as theirs. Besides, the moral of this story fascinates me as much as its characters, and I don't need real names to write about a daycare scandal and what it means for our society. A lot of people are thinking about children these days and stories about them seem to be gaining national prominence, moving from the back page of the country's newspapers to the front. This morning, a front-page piece appeared in the *Globe and Mail*, stating that Ontario has a serious daycare crunch.

Canada does not have a national daycare policy. Does anyone want to take responsibility for developing one? Apparently not. While many provinces want the federal government to impose national standards, the federal government says daycare falls under the jurisdiction of the provinces. Is it nap time on Parliament Hill? This country needs a policy and a global scheme that includes licensing and monitoring. Ice cream vendors and shoemakers need business licences, but daycare operators and babysitters do not.

In the *Globe and Mail* piece, the author, Jane Gadd, asks, "Who's Minding the Kids?" She gets some "rude surprises." At houses around Toronto, many children are dropped off by their parents every day. The lucky ones go on day trips and eat nutritious snacks. The unlucky ones get plunked in front of the TV or stuck in a playpen. Some of them put in longer days than their parents. Gadd writes, "While there are many caring unlicensed babysitters, the informal market provides none of the protections offered by either licensed daycare centres or licensed homecare: safety standards, adult-child ratio standards, training for staff in child development and stimulation, program standards and spot checks. The caregivers do not even have to go through a criminal-record check. They are supposed to childproof their homes and limit their numbers to five, but no one checks. The only time they come under scrutiny is if a parent makes a complaint to the [Ontario] Ministry of Community and Social Services."

The Prosecution

From left to right, Ron, Travis, and Linda Sterling. September 10, 1993.

No job for a new recruit

On this warm day, September 13, 1993, courtroom number 1 is packed, even though it's the largest courtroom in the city and the largest in the grey stone building overlooking the magnificent South Saskatchewan River.

If this were a civil suit and the daycare parents were prosecuting the three Sterlings, suing them for negligence or wilful damage, they might have a good chance of winning. A civil suit is like a shoot-out between two angry *hombres* with hired guns. Most of the time the plaintiff wants money; if he's lucky, he gets it. But this is not the OK Corral. It is a court of criminal law, where the burden of proof is much higher. It is the state — as in we, the people — prosecuting the three accused adults for crimes they are alleged to have committed against children. By law, every Canadian has the right to be deemed innocent till proven guilty. The Sterlings are innocent and no one in the room is to assume otherwise till the Crown, represented by the two prosecuting lawyers, proves that they are guilty, beyond a reasonable doubt.

So what if the police found guns, a vibrator, and porn magazines at the Sterling house? The mere presence of these items in the house that doubled as a home daycare is not a criminal offence. Porn videos and pellet guns do not constitute sufficient evidence to convict the Sterlings of criminal wrongdoing. To get a conviction the prosecution must prove to the jury that the suspect items corroborate the horrendous stories the children tell — that the vibrator, the guns, and the porn material played a role in the everyday life of the Sterling house when the children were there. The Crown has already proved it once to Judge Lavoie, who convicted the young woman Tammy on eight counts of criminal behaviour. In this trial by jury, the prosecuting lawyers must convince twelve men and women of criminal wrongdoing beyond a reasonable doubt, if they are to convict Ron, Linda, and Travis Sterling.

Judge Wimmer's private door to the court opens and he enters. Then the twelve jurors file in. Until they take their seats, the three Sterlings stand in their small box, a sign of respect for the Crown against whom they are alleged to have sinned. The clerk reads the roll call of jurors, to make sure they're the right twelve, after which Wimmer welcomes them and tells them what to expect for the next several months. He explains that those who have a collective agreement in place will earn their regular income for every day of the trial, no matter how long it lasts. In addition, all of them will receive a daily rate of $40 jury pay — from this, the first day of the trial, on. Until further notice.

What will they do to earn this magnificent sum of money? Wimmer reads the job description: "You must keep an open mind until the very last word is said, because something may happen late in the trial that could change your view of the situation. You should watch the witnesses carefully, and form your own individual impressions of their testimony..." because the jurors' verdict must be based on this testimony. On the other hand, the things they think and discuss among themselves are their "secrets," as are any notes they might take, which will be kept in a vault at the end of each day.

Then it's Leslie Sullivan's turn, on behalf of the Crown, to address the jury. She speaks in her usual crisp, articulate way. As she speaks, her brown bangs stay put and her frown vanishes. Jurors listen closely, several leaning towards her. She tells them this case is all about children who've been sexually abused. You'll have to really listen to the children, she says, and enter their world as they tell us what happened to them at the hands of the Sterlings. Remember, it's been at least two years since the events, and the children were small and under stress. Think about it. Would you be able to come in here like these children and talk about your most recent sexual experience, if you were terrified that threats against you would be carried out? The bottom line is this: Were these children abused by the accused as set out in the indictment? You, the jury, must be sure that guilt is established beyond a reasonable doubt. The jury "is one of the undisputed essentials of our justice system."

The first witness called is Claudia Bryden, the policewoman who put Martensville on the map. She calls herself a "peace officer," as does the Criminal Code of Canada. How was she taught to think of her role at the RCMP Academy in Regina during her six months of training there and what, I wonder, does Claudia Jane look like in full Mountie regalia, sitting on a horse? Here in the witness box she looks calm. She sounds calm too, and talks in a soft voice. She could be a poster girl for apples, or milk, or rowing — anything wholesome. Her white cotton blouse is buttoned up to the neck and she's wearing the same pink suit she wore one day to Tammy's trial. This girl next door is "relatable," as they say in the advertising business.

Some say her life has been hell ever since the third week in September 1991, when she was sworn into office and started to work for the Martensville Police Department. Although she doesn't whine or brag, it's easy to read between the lines when she testifies about her admission to the nine-person force: "I was the first female." In the small group, four of the officers, including her, worked part-time. When she was hired, says Bryden, she didn't even know where Martensville was. So Jim Elstad, her "trainer," showed her around town her first night on the job. At 11 p.m., he drove her to the Sterling house, where the two drank coffee and chatted with Ron, Linda, and Travis, whom she would arrest before long.

Ten uneventful days followed the Sterling-kitchen coffee klatch. On the eleventh day, when Bryden was on duty, a father came to the police station to report what his very young daughter had said: Travis Sterling had assaulted her at the Sterling house. Jim Elstad, who took the complaint, handed it to Bryden.

By now, the story Bryden tells is as familiar as her face. I could almost recite it by heart, though new details will inevitably emerge during her time on the witness stand. This trial is much more complex than Tammy's, mainly because of the numbers: three people are being tried at once, each represented by a lawyer; seven children are scheduled to testify in person, and we will hear sixty to seventy witnesses. Because there are more people on trial this time and more parts to the story, I'll have to avoid getting buried in the avalanche of evidence and keep my ears open till I've heard all of it. I don't envy the jurors and am relieved for them that Wimmer will permit them to take notes in court. If he didn't, they'd have to store everything they hear in their heads.

Bruce Bauer, Leslie Sullivan's greying co-prosecutor, graduated from the University of Saskatchewan Law School in 1979 and, after articling for a year, was hired by the Crown. He begins Bryden's examination-in-chief. Question. Answer. Question. Answer. Fresh details emerge, as do charges by children who didn't testify at Tammy's trial. The false names for the first two girls are Sally and Janey.

Janey was a two-and-a-half-year-old toddler when, on October 1, 1991, her father informed the Martensville police that she'd accused Travis Sterling of sexually abusing her. Again, we hear the now-familiar tale: When Bryden heard this, she became concerned. Then, with a tip from the secretary and after digging through disordered files, she came across a report on Travis Sterling, dating from January 1988. Bryden could see that this new complaint was the second one against Travis, and that twice in little more than three years he had been accused of sexually abusing a child. According to the report, the first complainant was a child protection worker who had given the details of the assault to the police, on behalf of a then-ten-year-old girl named Sally. Reading the report and seeing that parts of it were missing, Bryden decided to do something.

Normal procedure at the Martensville police station called for officers to develop a report as soon as a complaint was lodged and assign an individual occurrence number to it. Then all complaints would be compiled and alphabetically ordered on filing cards. Following routine, Bryden opened a proper file on Janey. Then, out of the blue, the secretary gave her an existing file on Sally, dated January 1988. When Bryden searched for the matching report on Travis, which was, in her words, "not easy to access," all she found in the filing cabinet was an informal, incomplete file, consisting of a one-page police report and several handwritten notes on scraps of paper. According to the report, officers Darryl Ford and Ed Revesz had interviewed Travis at the time and taken a written statement from him. But "it could not be found," says Bryden, even though she "carefully looked through the files which were accessible to [her]." Now more curious than ever, Bryden decided to speak with the parents of the girls, and the girls themselves. Three days later, the police charged Travis Sterling with sexual assault.

Bryden tells the court she continued to investigate the allegations of sexual assault at the Sterling daycare. A short time after Bryden found the file on Sally, Sally's mother gave her names of some families, and those families gave her more names of parents who'd used the Sterling daycare at one time or another. After talking with parents and kids, Bryden laid more charges against Travis Sterling.

Two of the children she interviewed said they'd been photographed, one of them naked. Police thought they might find kiddie porn at the Sterling daycare and got a search warrant. "It was not a secret" there'd be a raid, says Bryden. On the contrary, the search was carefully planned by the Martensville police over five or six weeks and was scheduled for the morning of Saturday, December 12. A Saskatoon TV station, CFQC, got wind of it and sent a cameraman to film it.

If Ron and Linda Sterling knew too, they didn't let the raid stop them from going shopping. When Bryden and four male officers arrived at the house at 11: 10 a.m., they found the door locked and had to call a locksmith. Once inside, Bryden found a very groomed home, quite unlike the lived-in one where she'd had coffee three months before. When Linda and Ron returned home, they got a big surprise.

Though I'm trying hard to concentrate on Bryden's testimony, the story of Goldilocks and the Three Bears keeps popping into my head. Maybe it's because Ron and Linda had shopped for food, as the storybook bears had foraged for honey before returning home to find that unwelcome guests were turning the place upside down.

The five officers searched the premises for more than four hours with the curtains closed to keep out the TV cameras, but they found no home videos or pornographic photos featuring children. They did find a Polaroid camera with a couple of used flash bulbs, and mail-order porn magazines and three adult videos. These, along with the pellet gun, the vibrator, the Polaroid camera, and some strange weighted ropes, were later tagged, bagged, and, where possible, photographed.

The items found in the search, combined with the children's stories of abuse that continued to emerge, seemed to point in one direction. But to continue the investigation Bryden needed authority to do so. She received it from the acting chief, Inspector Wayne McGillivray, who was seconded from the nearby Town of Corman Park though apparently never formally added to the Martensville payroll.

In the weeks leading up to Christmas of 1991, Bryden took the following steps in her investigation: she visited and talked with several families, which now included Freddy's; had Janey's toddler clothes and hairs tested at the RCMP forensic lab in Regina; obtained from one child, whom I'll call Tommy, a signed statement of what Travis had done to him; and witnessed another child identify Travis in a photo-album lineup. Five days before Christmas, Bryden believed police had enough evidence to also arrest Linda

Sterling, and did so. When one or two more children pointed their finger at Ron Sterling, he was charged too, on January 16, 1992.

From January to June, Bryden interviewed three or four more children, including Kenny. She filled her notebooks with their stories; showed them photographs of the Sterling residence and The Place; showed them police photo lineups of eight people, including Travis Sterling, whom two more children identified; interviewed children at their family homes, sometimes on audiotape; and interviewed others in the Saskatoon Police Soft Room, sometimes on videotape. During this time, she saw the size of the job grow and knew she needed help. To make things even more difficult, the Martensville Police had no policy for dealing with sexually abused children.

While Claudia Bryden went about her business, Ron Sterling went about his. Sometimes the two agendas seemed strangely juxtaposed. For instance, Ron still occasionally walked into the Martensville police station to have coffee with his buddies, even though Bryden had arrested his son. On other days, their agendas positively clashed. One day, while Bryden was conducting a home interview with the child named Kenny, Sterling drove back and forth in front of the house, slowly, in his blue pickup truck. "I saw Ron Sterling actually looking into the house," she tells the court.

An important aspect of this trial, as with any criminal trial, is the admissibility of evidence — which evidence will be admitted, and what will not. Now, the three-man defence team tries to keep the Sterlings' porn magazines out of the courtroom: The fact that they kept porn in the same house as their daycare doesn't necessarily mean they abused little kids. Just because they ordered adult videos by mail and kept a vibrator in the dresser drawer doesn't mean they raped the kids they babysat. The two prosecuting lawyers then argue that if the police found these things in the Sterling house, the jurors should see them. The three defence lawyers say it's wrong to connect two things — in this instance, porn and abuse — unless the connection can be proved beforehand. The lawyers want to argue the matter in private, so Wimmer asks the jury to leave the room.

The three lawyers argue that even though one's choice of magazines provides a form of character evidence, mail-order magazines showing women in sexy lingerie or none at all are a private matter. In other words, the magazines police found in the Sterling house are the business of the Sterlings, and nobody else. It follows that the magazines should not be shown to jurors because they might prejudice the jurors.

In response, the two prosecuting lawyers say, Now we have to edit the investigation and censor what we show the jury. Why were these things kept in a house where children were babysat in the first place?

Judge Wimmer asks if the possession of such things shows propensity on the part of the Sterlings to abuse children. He asks for legal precedents. The defence lawyers say they've looked, but found none to guide them. In the absence of precedents, and until he has time to think about it, Wimmer tells the two prosecuting lawyers to carry on without the police photos of items such as porn magazines, found during the search on the Sterling house. That's a tough thing to do, M'Lord, says one of the two. At this, Wimmer signals the clerk to call the jurors back in and tells them, "We've hit a sticky wicket." Then he smiles at them avuncularly, dismissing court until the following morning.

Next morning, the three defence lawyers — Hugh Harradence, Earl Kalenith, and Don Mullord — come to court with two Canadian precedents they think fit. In one case, the judge ruled that just because the man on trial had been found with marijuana in his possession and was therefore guilty of "crime A," it did not necessarily mean he was also guilty of "crime B," which was also in question. In another similar case, the judge ruled that the accused's trafficking in heroin did not necessarily mean he had anything to do with other particular charges.

Drug trafficking? Are these cases the most relevant precedents these three guys can dig up? What do drugs seized at the border have to do with porn seized at the Sterling house? The moral of the story, as Wimmer knows, has nothing to do with drugs and everything to do with fairness: The court must be fair. It must not encourage jurors to stereotype the Sterlings. If they saw that the Sterlings consumed pornography, they might hastily jump to the conclusion they also consumed children. Wimmer flips through the album of photos police took during the search of the Sterling house and pauses to peer over his glasses at prosecutor Bruce Bauer. The judge reminds me of a professor, omniscient, but kindly, scolding his student for behaving presumptuously.

Bauer, sounding like a kid pleading for the keys to the car, explains the purpose of the photos. They are to corroborate the evidence of the children, not bolster it. Wimmer answers: If jurors see the photos first and hear the children second, that's not what would happen. Bauer sees a ray of hope: Can they see them later? "Maybe," says Wimmer. "I don't know how things are going to unfold." Until the judge does know, prosecutor Bauer must omit a dozen police photos from his examination-in-chief of Bryden. And he must erase the word "pornography" from his courtroom vocabulary. Wimmer tells the lawyer he must not use it in the presence of the jurors when referring to the material the Sterlings kept in their house. Wimmer has reminded everyone in the room that the Sterlings are innocent until proven guilty.

If I could raise my hand, I'd ask Judge Wimmer: What is the main difference between trial by judge and trial by jury? If my memory of Tammy's trial serves me well, Tim White did not question the admissibility of police photos of the Sterling house. And I don't remember Judge Lavoie ruling that the photos (including some of porn magazines) might prejudice him against Tammy if he saw them before he heard the children testify.

For all the differences between this trial by jury and the earlier one by judge alone, there are striking similarities. It looks as though the defence lawyers are defending their clients by putting the police on trial. Prosecuting lawyers Bruce Bauer and Leslie Sullivan know this. They saw White rake the cops over the coals at Tammy's trial. This time things will be different. They'll show, in even more detail than before, how painstakingly Bryden conducted her investigation.

Bauer asks Bryden to retrace her steps. It's like wading through gumbo. Even Mr. Justice Wimmer shows signs of fatigue at one point and wonders if the jurors are getting tired too. I feel like saying, "What about the journalists? We've had to sit through this stuff twice. For you, it's just the first time." Forbidden to speak, I write it and pass the note to Janis. She rolls her eyes and fakes a yawn. Maybe her gesture convinces the judge to call a break.

The men have no idea what goes on behind the door of the women's washroom, or that it's fast becoming a place for significant conversations. Though it's just a tiny room with two cubicles, a mirror, and a sink with very confusing taps, every time I enter I wonder what will happen before I exit.

On this particular trip I find myself alone with Bryden. Before washing her hands, she puts on the shelf a plastic bag, containing her afternoon snack of an apple and a cinnamon bun. Her eyes are cast down to avoid contact with mine, and she says nothing. I guess she has been advised to avoid journalists like the plague. But it costs me nothing to say hello and tell her she's doing a good job on the witness stand. She smiles, and says thanks. Encouraged, I press on. "We're not getting to the bottom of all this, are we?" No, she replies. For all the evidence you'll hear in the courtroom, she says, there are many more facts you'll never know. Then, to my amazement, Bryden tells me what she lived through during the investigation. She made many calls to the Department of Justice that no one returned. On the occasions she did talk with the department, she says, no one criticized the way she interviewed the children. Most surprisingly, she says, no one at the department assisted her substantially in the investigation. I can scarcely believe this and want to hear more. Just as I'm about to try to get it, Leslie Sullivan walks through the door, looking very annoyed that Bryden and I are even in the same small room together. I smile and wash my hands, slowly, like a cat, knowing that a hasty exit might cast suspicion on the two of us.

Back on the stand, Bryden provides details of her interviews with the Martensville children. Bruce Bauer wants her methods divulged now to defuse the defence lawyers later. Why, he asks, didn't Bryden audiotape or videotape every word of her interviews with the children? She explains: Neither she nor the children particularly liked the police tape recorder, but for different reasons. In her opinion it was temperamental, in theirs it was intrusive. They didn't like being taped, period. Sometimes disclosures were impossible to tape because they were spontaneous. For example, the day she drove Kenny from school to court he told her certain things. She couldn't drive and write at the same time and did not record his comments in her notebook till later.

I can relate to Bryden's dilemma: tape-less, pen-less, and on the road. I know the rigours of chronicling on site, after having interviewed people on planes, trains, and, in one case, on a patio as it was being poured. Having conducted one interview half-asleep at 2 a.m., and another half-frozen at minus 40, I know the difficulty of trying to capture the moment. And I can only imagine how hard it must have been for Bryden to try to drive Kenny to court while trying to concentrate on his disclosure of abuse.

Prosecutor Bauer asks Bryden if she broke Kenny's confidence, or told any of the children's secrets to the other daycare families. Looking him square in the eye, she answers that on no occasion did she share information about previous interviews. She told every one of the dozen or so families she talked with to play it close to the vest and not to tell anyone anything.

She also told parents to be careful not to put ideas in their children's heads. "Whenever I attended to take a statement from a child where the parents were actually physically present in the room or nearby, I explained that the interactions that were to take place were just to be between myself and the child. I asked them to refrain from making comments or interrupting and asking questions."

The defence lawyers don't buy it. Bryden was a rookie who didn't know how to proceed. She knew little about interviewing kids, or helping parents talk to their children. And she did little to discourage everyone in town from talking to everyone else.

A cop is cross-examined

Perhaps she is guilty of these things. Does she get any credit for simply having done her job to the best of her ability? Was she rewarded for doing it, as she claims, with little advice from the authorities in Regina, with little help from her fellow officers, and little formal training to fall back on? Perhaps her biggest crime of all was trying to do what she thought was her job and failing. She has paid dearly for this. Now she will pay again with a gruelling cross-examination. As we'll soon see, this is the modern-day equivalent of a flogging in the town square. The lashings will be administered not by one lawyer, but three, one for each Sterling.

How much experience do these three Saskatchewan lawyers have with this kind of case? Earl Kalenith, though peach-cheeked and seemingly unaware of the evils of the world, is very familiar with them. Just before being hired as the legal-aid counsel for Travis Sterling, he defended white supremacist Carney Nerland, convicted of killing Native trapper Leo LaChance. The balding legal-aid lawyer, though not yet forty, has been called to the bar in the three westernmost provinces. The blond-haired Hugh Harradence, though he works in private practice with his well-known father in Prince Albert, will also receive from the province's legal-aid purse a percentage of his fee for defending Linda Sterling. He says he regards the task as a challenge, all the more because he doesn't know anyone else in Canada who has defended such a complex case. Don Mullord is a chemist with two science degrees as well as a law degree. Educated in England and Canada, he has worked for the province's legal-aid department since 1991 and is the lawyer for Ron Sterling. I wonder if his rusty-coloured beard and soft English accent wouldn't be less conspicuous in Old Bailey than here in the midst of flat Prairie voices. This is his second case involving allegations of child sexual abuse.

Mullord rises to cross-examine Bryden, and Judge Wimmer turns to the twelve tryers of fact. He explains that the defence team's strategy is to play several tapes of Bryden's interviews while the jurors "focus" on her method of conducting them. They must pay attention to her questioning, but disregard the answers the children gave her. My only question is this: Are you serious, M'Lord? Do the defence lawyers think these people can focus on what Bryden said to the kids, but not what they said to her? If so, I think you should have added one more question to the challenge for cause questionnaire: "If chosen as a juror, would you be capable of listening to police interviews and weighing the questions but not the answers?" Asking jurors, as you are, to focus on Bryden's questions while disregarding the children's answers might be a reasonable expectation if the jurors were specialists — psychologists, film critics, professors, or judges — people used to distinguishing form from content. When you hired the jurors you asked six questions to determine if their prejudices would obstruct their vision. Now it looks as though they need highly specialized training to do the job. I doubt that any one of them has studied the theory of interviewing traumatized children, mastered the most up-to-date techniques for doing it, and acquired the credentials for evaluating another person's performance.

Judge Wimmer knows the jurors' task is risky and says so to the legal-aid defence lawyer: "I don't think they'll be able to disassociate this information from the real evidence." And I agree with him. So I'd like to know why the three defence lawyers are taking the risk. Maybe they think Bryden's technique so flaw-ridden that even twenty-four untrained eyes will see the deficiencies. If that's what they think, there is nothing the judge can do to stop them. He gives the go-ahead and Don Mullord rolls the tape, or at least tries to, in the face of one more technological glitch. Wimmer declares a break, at which Ron Sterling stands, turns to face the public gallery, and winks at someone at the back of the room.

After the twenty minutes required to restore the tape recorder, the crowd returns to the courtroom and Bryden climbs back into the witness box. There she sits very still, eyes down, as the tape begins to roll. The near-midnight interview we are about to hear took place on October 3, 1991, at the Martensville police station. The session with Sally took place two nights after the child protection worker called to lodge the complaint. Sally, thirteen at the time of the taping, told Bryden what Travis had done to her when she was ten. The quality of the sound is bad, and sometimes indecipherable.

Bryden: Why didn't you tell your parents right away?

Sally: I was too scared that they wouldn't believe me.

Bryden: Why did you decide to tell them?

Sally: It was gettin' too far... It bothered me a lot and I don't want other kids getting hurt, and that's why I spoke up.

Bryden: Where did he touch you?

Sally: My breasts and vaginal area.

Bryden: When did he do this to you?

Sally: Every day, between 6: 30 and 8 a.m., while I was sleeping on the couch under a blanket, waiting to go to school.

Bryden: Where was Linda Sterling?

Sally: She was asleep or somewhere else in the house. She didn't know till the police alerted her. Even then, Linda didn't believe me.

Bryden: I know this is difficult and I really appreciate your coming to tell me… Did he use anything other than his hands?

Sally: No.

Sally knew that what Travis was doing was wrong. It made her unhappy, even though she really liked being babysat at the Sterling daycare till Travis allegedly abused her. As luck would have it, she'd just seen a film at school about abuse. "I got up my courage" and went to the counsellor, she says on the tape.

Disregard what Sally said to Bryden? Scrutinize what Bryden said to Sally? I'll bet not one of the jurors can separate the two halves of the interview. Could King Solomon himself split it in two? After hearing the tape, I don't think that Sally had an axe to grind. She liked the Sterlings, and maybe she even liked Travis. But she didn't like what he did to her. And she didn't want him doing it to other kids. Listening to her, I'm left with little doubt that Travis did what Sally says he did. So why didn't Linda Sterling believe her? And why did she, the operator of the home daycare, turn a blind eye to the incident, even when police told her what her son had done? And if the police got as far as telling Mrs. Sterling, why didn't they, or someone in the community, ensure that Travis would never molest a child again?

Travis sits at the front of the court, in jeans and jacket, busily writing in his notebook. He has cut his long blond hair and shaved and the result is, well, courtworthy. Travis considers himself an artist and apparently likes to draw dragons and fantastic scenes. Yet his courtroom palette is monotonous, restricted to one colour — a yellow highlighter — with which he writes important testimony in his daily notebook.

His mother's only colour today is black, a simple suit, a sombre contrast to the eye-catching reds and blues she usually wears. She stares straight ahead, as she does every day. It's hard to say whether she's scared stiff or bored silly. If I walked over and asked, "Linda, what mood are you in?" she could answer my open-ended question any way she wanted. But if I asked her, "Linda, are you scared stiff?" my closed question might put words in her mouth or plant thoughts in her head.

Generally speaking, a closed question seeks a simple answer. To the question, "Linda, is your dress black?" there are only two possible answers. At the other end of the spectrum an open question requires the listener to think and juggle words. For instance, "Linda, what colour is your dress?" or, still more open-ended, "Travis, what are you writing in your notebook?" The open question opens the door to the unknown and invites the speaker to answer in a free-flowing and unrestricted way — in a paragraph, not a sentence; in a complete sentence, not just one word.

Claudia Bryden knew the difference, or should have. Besides having learned some interview techniques at RCMP Academy, she had taken a brief lesson from Corporal Rod Moor the day before interviewing Sally. After the Saskatoon officer explained and demonstrated his techniques for questioning traumatized kids, Bryden would have known them too. But if she did, she didn't put the knowledge to work, or so Mullord contends.

If Mullord were being paid to investigate Claudia Bryden's philosophy of motivating the kids she interviewed, he might ask, "What is your opinion about bribing a child with a reward?" But the legal-aid lawyer is paid to defend his client, Ron Sterling, and asks the witness, "Do you agree that you shouldn't bribe a child with a reward?" Bryden has two options, yes and no, and she answers, "Yes, I agree." This type of courtroom question — designed to pull answers, not thoughts, from witnesses — deprives Bryden of the chance to explain at length what she thinks about rewarding a child. It also deprives the jury of seeing how much thought she has given the matter. But this, after all, is a cross-examination, not a philosophy class. If the yes-and-no system is the most cost-effective road to a verdict, it is not the way to true understanding. Truth cannot be reduced to yes and no, nor reconstructed from these two simple words.

As long as Mullod has the woman in the witness box, there's always another question to ask and another interview tape to play. The one about to roll is a beaut. In the video you can see Bryden's methodology, not just hear it. Let's watch it now, says Mullord. But the show is not to be. On cue, the "gremlins" (Judge Wimmer's word) disable the VCR and force the judge to call a two-hour lunch break.

At 2 o'clock Bryden returns to the witness box and the VCR is fixed. The tape will show Janey, who was not yet three when she alleged Travis assaulted her. Her father lodged the complaint that sparked the investigation. Nine days into the investigation Janey's parents drove her to the Saskatoon police station where Claudia Bryden and Rod Moor took her to the Soft Room, sat her in one of the pink upholstered chairs, and asked her questions as the camera recorded her every move.

The tape of that interview is about to be projected onto a big screen that bisects the courtroom. The size of the screen reminds me of a drive-in movie, with one big difference: the majority of us sit behind the screen, not in front, and no one but "the court" — the judge, the five lawyers, the twelve jurors and three accused — can see the tape of Janey. Like a slice of cheese, the screen separates one half the sandwich — the twenty-one people on the front side of the screen — from the other half — the fifty or so journalists and members of the public seated on the backside. The video that the front side is about to see and hear, which the backside will only hear, was taped October 10, 1991, when Bryden and Moor questioned Janey in the Soft Room.

The interview in the Soft Room begins with an anatomy test, in which Rod Moor holds an anatomically detailed female doll, a "Janey doll." Moor asks the girl to name the body parts he points to. Then he gets Janey to show him on the doll exactly where she claims the man touched her. The soundtrack of three-year-old Janey captures the language of a child still learning English. The girl says things like "He hitted me" and "They hitted me," in answer to two of Bryden's questions. I imagine she has chubby cheeks and a bow in her hair.

Here in the courtroom, Bryden admits that Moor asked Janey closed questions and led the girl to answer them in a certain way. Yet the Saskatoon officer was the Martensville officer's "only guide at that time" and Moor's interview of Janey in the Soft Room doubled as Bryden's first orientation session. The rookie interviewer then returned to Martensville, where she tried to question the daycare kids on her own, equipped with a notepad and a "temperamental" tape recorder. It's impossible to know how open or closed her questions were because not all her interviews were documented. The one with Janey's older brother, Tommy, in November of 1991, was one Bryden did tape and arrange to have transcribed, and she now reads for the court what Tommy told her two years ago: Travis Sterling never touched him, but he did touch the private parts of Janey and his other sister, Sandy, at the daycare. He saw Travis do it when he spied on the man from behind the couch. He wanted to protect his sisters, but was too little and couldn't.

This story resonates. The five-year-old Tommy worried, not for himself, but for others, like Sally who, in 1988, made the first allegation against Travis to her school guidance counsellor because "I don't want other kids getting hurt." If Sally and Tommy are lying, they have very sophisticated imaginations, so much so that they can conjure up the feelings Travis might have caused them to have, not just for themselves, but for others too. This type of imagining is called emotional projection. Some people are naturally better at it than others. Playwrights and actors devote their lives to developing it, and most fiction writers would say it's the hardest part of writing.

Was Tommy lying to Bryden? When she asked him at the beginning of their interview, the boy told her, "A lie is not the truth." Then he proceeded to tell the officer his story about what happened at the daycare: "Travis took my clothes off [jeans and a blue shirt]... It made me feel sad." He was "touching my private parts with his hands." Bryden remarks to the court that, at the memory, Tommy's forehead became damp with sweat. Is it possible, I wonder, to fake sweat? Judging from the soundtrack of the tape, Tommy was certainly not faking the pleasure he derived from being play-handcuffed to the lady cop while he told her his story.

A month or so after Tommy's interview in late 1991, the first formal meeting of the daycare parents took place. According to Bryden, the parents from five different families came to the meeting to learn about the signs of abuse and the best ways of dealing with their feelings about the investigation. Bryden herself did not attend the meeting because she was busy tying up a few loose ends after the search of the Sterling house that afternoon. Five or six hours after the search, she called the mother of Janey, Tommy, and Sandy to tell her that no photos of her children, or of any other children, had been found in the house.

Here in court, Bryden's cross-examiner persists: Did you not also tell the mother that you found a vibrator and other things during the search? "No," says Bryden. Would you agree with me that before that day her children had never spoken about a vibrator? "Yes," says Bryden.

By now we've heard these same questions and answers several times, and even Judge Wimmer is starting to look frustrated. I can almost see the steam coming from his ears when he issues the warning to Bryden's cross-examiner: "Mr. Mullord, if you keep following that line of questioning, you're going to get some answers you don't want. And I'm not going to intervene again." Mullord retreats a bit, but continues to question the witness, who maintains that, publicly, she divulged nothing about the investigation and showed nothing to any of the daycare families. As for the chicken-and-egg question of all questions, the officer testifies that only after she'd taken a written statement from five-year-old Tommy on October 20, 1991, did she show the police photos to the boy. Not the other way around.

When directed to do so, Bryden reads the boy's statement, which details what happened to him and his two sisters at the daycare: Linda Sterling "kisses their bums" and "puts toys down their bums." Then Tommy told Bryden that Linda pointed a gun at him and Travis said he would shoot or stab his parents, or poison them with a snake and throw them in a volcano. Bryden says Tommy began to cry in front of her, so overcome was he remembering the assaults on his sisters and the threats towards his parents. Bryden, recollecting Tommy's tears, starts to shed her own. She reaches for a tissue from the box on the stand, limply wiping her eyes and trying to control her bottom lip. In the attempt, she becomes speechless. Clearly, the cross-examination is too much for her. Wimmer calls a short break.

The two-stall washroom has overflowed — not with water, but with a cop, a Crown prosecutor and two journalists. In this smelly six-by-ten-foot room, Claudia Bryden is in one cubicle blowing her nose and Leslie Sullivan is in the other. They emerge, seconds apart, and Sullivan makes a joke about losing one's faith in the justice system. Wiping her nose, a tired-looking Bryden quips, "Are you ready for my monotone voice?" The two exit, leaving Janis and me, lions in wait at the watering hole, to make of the scene what we will.

Bryden resumes reading the transcript, with dry eyes and a controlled voice. Then Mullord runs the videotape documenting what Tommy said Ron Sterling did to his little sister: "He put his penis inside her bum...and hurt her." Bryden told the boy, "You're a real help. That's what you're here for." Tommy's words are hard to hear, punctuated as they are by a tapping that sounds like drum playing, but perhaps it doesn't matter right now, given Wimmer's instructions to the jurors to focus on the questions, not the answers. Bryden asks the boy: Can you show me on the Tommy doll what Ron Sterling did to Tommy? She tells him he can go out to play after he tells, then points to the doll's penis and asks if anybody ever touched him there. There is no response. She persists: What did Ron ever do to you? "He kicked me as hard as a giraffe," says the boy. "What else?" asks Bryden. "That's all," he answers. "How did that make you feel?" Tommy says, "Bad."

Mullord stops the tape and says to Bryden: You say you don't agree with bribes. Don't you think telling Tommy that he was helpful was bribery? She explains that she would have told Tommy he was helpful even if he'd told her nothing, and she believes she acted in an appropriate manner. Besides, Tommy was fidgety and she needed to get him to focus.

The cross-examiner moves on. Didn't it concern you that Tommy had nothing to say, especially since the information he had given you two weeks before had led to the arrest of Linda Sterling? Bryden answers coolly: This interview was not about Linda Sterling, it was about Ron Sterling. "I believe the child was aware of what he was going to say during the interview prior to his coming to the interview. I was not aware of what the child was going to say exactly when he came in."

Mullord is trying to prove that Bryden put ideas in Tommy's head, but she says she did not. Whether Tommy had something important to say in the first place is another matter. Anyone who has ever tried to get a child to talk about a difficult topic knows it's difficult at the best of times.

Could Bryden have done a better job? Her competence is not the only thing being brought into question. Skill at doing one's job is important, but know-how must be part of a larger package, and this is tied to one's knowledge of corporate rules and held together with team spirit. From the sounds of it, the Martensville police officers didn't function as a team in the winter of 1991-92 (and were disbanded by the Saskatchewan Police Commission in April 1993). The small force had no permanent full-time chief and no clearcut guidelines for handling sexual-abuse allegations.

The witness testifies that when Travis was charged with crimes based on allegations made by Sally and Janey, she thought the other eight or nine families who also used the Sterling daycare deserved to know that police were launching an investigation, so she told them. When parents started to inundate her with an enormous amount of information, she asked Acting Chief Wayne McGillivray for help with the investigation, preferably from an "outside" police force with more experience and manpower. Without help, the sole investigator found that she was spending ninety per cent of her work time in addition to off-duty hours on the case. Then in March 1992, she "hooked up" with an outside person assigned to help her. Rod Moor was a Saskatoon police officer with eighteen years' experience, five of them in child-abuse investigations where he learned the job through trial and error.

It's one thing to question a child for the first time in a police station, where there's a fresh slate and no investigative mistakes to sweep under the carpet, another to question the same child in a criminal trial, where defence lawyers criticize the police investigation and get paid for it. If the police made mistakes, it's too late to correct them. And if you're the officer who made them, you're screwed. There's no going back for touch-ups or major revisions and no such thing as a retrial — a second chance — the way there is in court.

But suppose a new kind of expert — a referee, such as a teacher or psychologist who was accredited and designated by the court — had played an integral role in the interviews Bryden did with Tommy and the other children. He or she could have accompanied Bryden in the interviews, taken notes on her work and helped her, providing rewording for inappropriate questions and stopping her altogether from asking improper or leading ones, similar to the way Judge Wimmer now referees Mullord's cross-examination of Bryden. With more coordination of this kind, everyone would know what everyone else was doing. In some provinces, there is growing recognition of the need for coordination in cases of suspected child abuse. Applying the knowledge to changing the system is, as always, a slow and painful process.

An audio or video recorder is a good way to document a police interview, but such a device is no more than a dumb witness. A tape allows lawyers to criticize the police after the fact, but does it actually help police do their job on the spot? Taping her interviews might have helped Bryden improve her techniques, if she had received useful and timely feedback. Apparently, she did not, until the investigation was over and it was too late.

Unlike some of the previous tapes, the sound is good on the next one and I catch almost every word of Bryden's January 7, 1992, interview of Janey, then thirty months old: "His [Ron Sterling's] penis peed on me... I had a dribble" (from her bum) "and Ron cleaned it up." It sounds totally credible to me, though I hate to think that what Janey called pee was sperm. What really happened, I wonder? Bryden asks: Who else was there? The toddler says: A lion and a bear and a bad boy.

What does Janey mean? Does it matter?

Remember: It's not supposed to matter, if you're a member of the jury.

When the Janey tape is over, Wimmer turns to the jurors and reminds them: You're watching these videos in order to assess the method of the investigation, not to weigh the information.

Mullord runs the next audiotape; ten-year-old Freddy is talking with Bryden. Since Tammy's trial I haven't thought very often about Freddy, but I feel strangely at home when I hear his slow mumbling. As inarticulate as Freddy may sound, "stuffed up" might be a better way to describe his way of speaking. He's the second oldest daycare child on tape, after Sally, and the one with the biggest vocabulary and most advanced sense of time and space. On the tape, Bryden offered encouragement to the boy with comments such as "It's not your fault if these things happened to you… You're really doing well and helping me out a whole bunch." Here are excerpts from a subsequent Bryden-Freddy interview, done a few days later in January 1992, which gives the flavour of the audiotaped session Mullord now plays in court.

Bryden: (brings out photo of a vibrator) Have you ever seen this?

Freddy: I saw it on the coffee table and the kitchen table.

Bryden: Do you know what it is or what it's called?

Freddy: Travis and Mrs. Sterling called it "the thing."

Bryden: What was it used for?

Freddy: I saw Travis using it once. I saw Travis in his room. He put the thing on his penis.

Bryden: Who was in the room with Travis when he was using the thing?

Freddy: Just Travis.

Bryden: Who else did things to you at the Sterlings' that you didn't like?
Freddy: Mrs. Sterling.

Bryden: What did she do to you?

Freddy: She threatened me. I didn't like that.

Bryden: Why did she threaten you?

Freddy: I don't know. Because I was late coming home after school.

Bryden: How did she threaten you?

Freddy: She said, If you're late again, I'm going to shoot you.

Bryden: How did her threats make you feel?

Freddy: Scared.

Bryden: What else did Linda do to you?

Freddy: She pulled down my pants. Ron came in the door, so she made me pull them back up.

Bryden: What else did Linda do to you?

Freddy: She stuck her hands down my pants, down the back side. She threatened me...

Bryden: Did Linda do anything else to you?

Freddy: She made me pull my pants down about twice a week.

Bryden: When Linda made you take your pants off, would she do anything to you?

Freddy: She'd, she'd pat my butt, she rubbed my leg and then she started playing with my penis.

Bryden: What was she touching you with?

Freddy: Her finger.

Bryden: How did it make you feel?

Freddy: It made me feel really gross...

Bryden: Did Linda Sterling ever take your picture?

Freddy: Yes.

Bryden: What were you doing in the picture she took?

Freddy: Sitting on the toilet...

When the tape is finished, defence lawyer Mullord stops the machine, turns to Bryden, and asks if her method of questioning Freddy was leading. Bryden says she knew from Freddy's parents that although he had things to say, he was afraid to talk to her the first time.

The tape of the January 1992 interview of a boy I'll call Tommy is short. In it he echoes Freddy's remarks. "They touched me...with their mouths on my private parts... They told me not to tell. They all pointed guns at me."

Wimmer has cautioned jurors not to give any weight to what the children say on tape, but how can they avoid hearing Tommy and Freddy talk about the Sterlings' lips on their private parts? How can they disregard Freddy's story about Kenny's screams when Travis put his hands down the boy's pants? Or that both Janey and Freddy said police did bad things to them, and independently identified officers in a photo lineup? In fact, Freddy went one step further, saying three of the policemen had a red stripe on their pants, and one had a yellow stripe, and one had a scar by his right eye. And Freddy named names: Jim Elstad, Darryl Ford, Ed Revesz.

Whatever jurors think about the children's finger-pointing, Bryden was faced with a dilemma when Freddy identified three of her colleagues as child molesters. She tells the court, "I did not want to be involved in investigating police." Her husband was an officer on the Saskatoon Police Force, where one of the officers Freddy accused also worked. Bryden drove, in a state of shock, to the home of Martensville's acting police chief to tell him she wanted to quit the investigation. The officer, Inspector MacGillivray, persuaded her to stay on the job, but assumed responsibility for part of the file himself. Bryden tells the court that the investigation then underwent a metamorphosis. She continued to work on it, though she was not responsible for investigating allegations against fellow officers.

She worked on the case part-time, frequently putting in more hours a week than she was paid for, until June 1992, when the task force was formed to include RCMP and Saskatoon officers and she was no longer the main investigator. Among the children she interviewed during those spring months was Kenny, then eight years old, whom she audiotaped at his home on April 3, 1992.

Bryden: Do you remember why you're here?

Kenny: I'm here to talk about the bad people.

Bryden: Do you remember the first time you went to the Sterlings'?

Kenny: I went there to play with Freddy.

Bryden: What did you do there?

Kenny: I was watching a movie and Travis and Linda took my clothes off. It made me feel bad and they touched my private parts.

Bryden: (She calls the anatomically detailed doll "Zeddy Doll" and asks Kenny if he knows the parts of the body.) Can you show me where they touched you?

Kenny: (He shows her where Travis touched him.) They would touch me and go on top of me. Travis and Linda took my clothes off and no one else was there. Linda touched me with her hands and that thing.

Bryden: What did you do when they touched you?

Kenny: I screamed for help. They told me to shut up.

Bryden: What else did they do?

Kenny: Travis had two ropes. They would tie my hands and feet. They made me feel bad. Sometimes I can't remember.

Bryden: You're doing really, really well.

Kenny: Sometimes Mr. Sterling was there too. And sometimes Tammy. She would touch me here and here and here.

Bryden: Is it okay if I show you some more pictures?

Kenny: Yes.

When the taped interview is over, so is court for the day. The following morning, in the jury's absence, Judge Wimmer excoriates Mullord: "This is devastating material for the jury. I don't think they'll be able to disassociate this information [what the children say on the tapes] from the real evidence [what the children will say later, in person]. I thought you were trying to show the frailties of the interview process but you're not, in my opinion. I want this on record… I don't want it later to be said that I have failed to protect the jury. You're doing this at your peril."

You'd think this lecture — and the seriousness of the situation, in Wimmer's view — would make the defence team want to change course, but it doesn't. Don Mullord's two colleagues, Hugh Harradence and Earl Kalenith, insist that the tapes are being played so jurors can see and hear for themselves the improper methods Bryden used in her interviews. They want to convince jurors that if the officer hadn't shown the police photos to the children or put ideas in their heads, the kids would never have made the allegations against the Sterlings.

Wimmer sees it differently. The child witnesses are giving evidence to the jury on tape before being called to the witness stand in person. How can jurors be deaf to the children's taped answers and listen with fresh ears to the children when they give testimony in a few days? How will jurors reconcile the discrepancies in evidence if the boys say different things in court from what they said on tape? Wimmer is boiling. A mistrial may be in the making, and it wouldn't look good on his record if the longest trial in the province's history had to start all over again. It would be a scheduling nightmare, tying up a courtroom for several more months and booking lawyers and witnesses. He asks Bryden to leave the room and peers down at Mullord. "I really didn't see in that last videotape [yesterday] that there were any leading questions by Bryden. Have you really thought this through?" Steam rises from his head as he hisses at the lawyer: "You're satisfied that I am going to be able, in my instructions to the jury, to persuade them that they must disassociate this information from the testimony of the witnesses and only act on the testimony of the witnesses?" There is silence. The three-man defence team needs time to rethink, and Wimmer gives it to them by calling a short recess.

It turns out to be much shorter than expected. Just as I leave the ladies' room, an RCMP officer leads a handcuffed man and woman into Courtroom 1. The public rushes back in. Wimmer, called back to his chair, scolds the two for picketing in front of the courthouse to express their feelings about the verdict from a previous trial on child abuse. He says: You're intimidating the jurors and will return here Friday to show why you should not be held in contempt of court. Wimmer whisks out of the room and the gallery empties again.

The corridor fills with the public and journalists, and Bryden passes me on her way to the washroom. "Someone should make a movie out of this," she half-whispers, winking mischievously. It's funnier than she thinks, because one of the jurors told me the other day, strictly off the record, that the twelve have reached consensus on one thing — if there's a movie made of this trial, they want to play themselves.

Wimmer knows this isn't a movie, at least, not yet. He looks grave when he asks the defence team one more time if they have their clients' agreement to continue playing the tapes in front of the jury. They do, and they have the next one ready to roll: a hard-to-hear, hour-long audiotape of Bryden interviewing Kenny at his home on June 1, 1992.

Bryden: Why are we here?

Kenny: We're here to talk about that house...where a policeman lives... He's bad.

Bryden: Is he bad? Why?

Kenny: He touched my privates.

(Bryden gives him photos, but he doesn't remember any of them.)
(Bryden gives him more photos, and asks if he's ever seen any photos of "The Hideout" [The Place].)

Kenny: Nope.

(Bryden shows him more photos and asks if there's anybody he has seen before.)

Kenny: Nope, not really.

Bryden: Okay. That's good. (She takes more photos from a bag.)

Kenny: I've seen this guy. And that's about it.

Bryden: Where have you seen this one?

Kenny: Sometimes he's in cars and trucks, and stuff like that.

Bryden: (Shows him more photos.) Is there anybody you recognize?... You have to be able to tell me... you might not be... This is kind of like a test... Some of these people in these pictures you've probably never seen before. Some of them you may have seen before...okay? And this is like a test...it shows if you remember people.

Kenny: Just these three...

Bryden: Who else was at The Hideout?

Kenny: The whole Sterling family... Can I say their names? (Yes, says Bryden.) Linda, Travis, and Mr. Sterling... and Tammy...

Bryden: What happened to you at The Hideout?...

Kenny: I'd take my clothes off, or they would do it roughly.

Bryden: How did they make you do it?

Kenny: They would yell (although he doesn't remember what they'd say).

Bryden: I know this is hard... You're being a really big help. I know this is embarrassing...

Kenny: You have to do it so they can go to jail.

Bryden: That's right. You have to talk about it so they can go to jail. That's exactly right. That's why I came to see you today...

There's more, but most of it was heard at Tammy's trial: how Kenny was disrobed, touched on his privates, tied up, photographed, put in the cage and the freezer, and threatened. And how his friend, Freddy, was tied up too.

Mullord turns off the tape, and asks Bryden about Kenny. "Did you ever confront him?" he asks. Bryden says she was shocked to hear such things, and let Kenny know it. She adds that, on other occasions, she was never as aggressive about expressing her scepticism to the boy and that, generally, "I don't know if I challenged him. I often repeated back to the child what he said to me, to give him a chance to reflect."

Reflect. Reverberate. Resonate. Ring. Kenny's voice is captured on tape and lodged permanently in Bryden's head. If I were her, and Kenny had asked innocently, "Can I say their names?" I'd be stung with grief. Faced with the little boy's powerlessness — his fear of doing the wrong thing, apparently a characteristic of abused children — I would try to be his white knight. If I fell or got pushed off my own horse, I don't know if I'd have the strength to get back on.

My sitting in the front row in court has the disadvantage of not being able to see the faces behind me. I crane my neck to see the guy filing his nails by the window, and the one in the back row reading *The Racing Digest*. It's a little easier to see the woman in the second row who comes to court every day right after work in her black and white waitress dress. She looks like a grandmother.

Bryden's drawn pallor is in contrast to the apple-cheeks she came to court with the first day. Her second cross-examiner, Earl Kalenith, is fresh and youthful in appearance. The lawyer for Travis Sterling looks like a good student, the kind who always does his homework. He asks probing questions in a very gentle way.

I have to hand it to Bryden. She doesn't defend herself by pretending to be Ms. Perfect and she sounds objective, even self-critical, when answering Kalenith's questions about the daycare investigation.

Bryden: In hindsight, I mean, I learned a great deal from the interview course that I took, but if I was to conduct my interviews all over again, with the training I have now, there wouldn't be a great deal that I would do differently. There would be definitely some things I would change, but I wouldn't change a great deal.

Kalenith: And what would you change then?

Bryden: John Yuille suggests the use of guidelines — he likes to provide the child with a set of rules during an interview. For instance, he suggests the use of a Stop sign, so that if you are asking the child questions, if the child becomes uncomfortable with the question or isn't ready to go on and the child wishes to stop the interview, they have the option to hold up their sign and indicate to you that this is a point in time when they wish to stop and take a break or — I would endeavour to ask non-leading questions as much as possible, although they are necessary sometimes when information is provided by the child. Some questions asked subsequent to information being provided are naturally going to be leading in and of themselves, but they're not leading if you — if you view and review information that the child has previously disclosed.

Kalenith: Are those all of the changes that you would make?

Bryden: I'm sure there are others, but —

Kalenith: No other ones that you can think of at the moment?

Bryden: No, I'd have to give it some thought.

Kalenith: Okay.

Wimmer: Are you moving on to something else?

Kalenith: Yes.

Wimmer: This is my Stop sign.

Next day, September 23, defence lawyer Kalenith's cross-examination of Claudia Bryden continues.

Kalenith: Mrs. Bryden, would you agree that you don't have any expertise in the area of how they use leading questions or repetitive questions or suggestive techniques, such as the use of dolls or showing children things, how any of those affect the child's memory?

Bryden: No, I'm not an expert in that area.

Kalenith: Now before you conducted each interview with the child, did you have a general idea of what story you were attempting to get from the child?

Bryden: In most cases I had, through conversation with parents, learned that the child had certain information to provide to me. Sometimes it was provided in a very general way.

Kalenith: And so that outline of information, whatever it was, affected the way in which you conducted the interview with the child?

Bryden: To an extent, yes.

Kalenith: Would you agree with me that if you were to, knowing what you know now and having taking this subsequent training with Dr. John Yuille, if you were to go back and examine each of the interviews you did, that you would agree that you did something wrong in each interview that you conducted?

Bryden: It would depend on which perspective I was examining the interviews from.

Kalenith: Well, from any perspective would you agree that there were some things done wrong in each interview?

Bryden: There were some things that I would — I would try not to do in subsequent interviews, yes...

Kalenith wants to show the jurors how Bryden's interview techniques are faulty. He begins to pick apart some sessions she conducted with the children and asks for her cooperation in the exercise: "I've just randomly picked an example from each interview and I'd ask whether you agree with me that, in fact, these are examples of the leading questions you used."

Kalenith: I'm referring to the November 2 interview with Tommy and the question was "What happened to you?" Do you agree with me that question is leading or suggestive in and of itself?

Bryden: I agree with you that it is in and of itself suggesting that something happened to the child, yes, in and of itself.

Kalenith: Now, I'm going to refer to the November 8 interview. And I'm referring to page seven of that interview. And the question, "Did Travis ever use his fingers?" Would you agree with me that that's a leading or suggestive question?

Bryden: Yes, it is.

Kalenith: I'm now referring to the December 20 interview with Tommy and on page three of that transcript. And the question, "Did Linda do to you what she did to Janey and Sandy?" Is that also leading or suggestive?

Bryden: Yes, it is.

Kalenith: And [from] the January 7 interview with Tommy. The question, "Has anyone ever touched you there?"

Bryden: Yes, in and of itself, yes.

Kalenith: And the January 7 interview with Janey, on page eleven of that transcript. The question, "What else did Ron touch you with besides his penis?" Is that leading and suggestive?

Bryden: In and of itself, yes. Yes, that's following information that he provided earlier. In and of itself it's a — it can be construed as a leading question, but the child had provided information earlier, which provided me with information in that question. In other words —

Kalenith: So you're suggesting that the part that you're referring to there was a part that he'd already told you about, being touched?

Bryden: Yes, I was trying to have the child be more specific. He had been talking about being touched on the butt and I wanted to know exactly where on the butt the child was referring to...

Kalenith: On the April 3 interview of Kenny, the question, "Who else touched you there?"

Bryden: Yes, again, in and of itself it could be considered a leading question. And it was based on information that I had received through conversations with parents.

Kalenith: And on the April 5 interview with Tommy, the question, "Who else touched Janey at the devil church besides Jim?"

Bryden: Yes, the question, "Who else touched Janey at the devil church besides Jim?" can be construed in and of itself as a leading question...

Kalenith: And finally, the last one that we saw on the first of June with Kenny, the question, "What else did they touch you with?" ...Is that leading or suggestive?

Bryden: Yes, it is. However, that question was based specifically on information that the child gave me initially at the interview. And if I — if I recall correctly, the child mentioned the use of tools. He mentioned during the interview that they had tools with them or they used tools. The questions — the question, "Did they ever touch you with anything else?" I was trying to have the child be specific as to what in fact he was touched with. He had mentioned tools and I wanted to find out if in fact there was a specific object that he had generally alluded to previously in the interview that he could provide an answer to.

Kalenith: And you don't think that's more specifically covered by saying, for example, what kind of tools?

Bryden: That's a question I could have asked him.

Kalenith: Right. I mean, this certainly includes a number of things other than tools, this question, doesn't it?

Bryden: Which question are you referring to now?

Kalenith: "What else were you touched with?" It's not limited to tools, is it?

Bryden: No, it gives the child an opportunity to provide any information that he wishes to provide.

Kalenith: Or — or potentially suggest that there are other things that you would like to hear about?

Bryden: Precisely.

Kalenith: And again, as you've said, you don't have any expertise as to what effect these types of leading questions would have on a child's memory?

Bryden: No, I do not have any expertise.

Kalenith: All right. In conclusion would you agree with me that, given an opportunity to consider and reflect on the interviews that were conducted, you would have done some things differently?

Bryden: I would have done some things differently, yes, absolutely.

Kalenith: Thank you, those are all of my questions.

In other words, Bryden usually knew something about what the kids had to tell her and she was merely asking them to tell her more. So her "leading" questions, in and of themselves, must be placed in context, as Judge Wimmer reminds Kalenith.

According to Bryden, the interview excerpts we've just heard were based on an understanding that had developed between her and the children, what Bryden called "continuity," Morse-code chats in which some words took on special meaning and others were not necessary. The cop and the kids sometimes communicated twice as much non-verbally as they put into actual words. According to Bryden, tears sometimes drowned Kenny's words during interviews, and the other children cried, too. But certain things that might not have been taped did not escape Bryden's notice. The children's body language and facial expressions were as meaningful to her as what they said.

Bryden: Towards the latter stages of the investigation when information regarding allegations against police came up and especially because it was apparent to me that the children appeared to be afraid to disclose to police about police, I reassured the children at the beginning...of every contact with them for the purposes of an interview...that it wasn't important to me what they told me necessarily, but what I was interested in was just the truth. It didn't matter what the information was, but as long as they believed that what they were telling me was the truth, that's all I was concerned about hearing...

Did Bryden automatically accept what the children told her? Would this approach console the children or encourage them to tell more horror stories? This issue is of concern far beyond the town limits of Martensville, and mental-health workers everywhere are debating it.

The central question is this: Did you experience a particular event just because you think you did? Suppose your therapist encourages you to "remember" an event that never really happened at all. Suppose the investigating officer puts so much pressure on you that, before long, you actually believe something happened. Psychologists call it False Memory Syndrome. Some say it's fraudulent; others say there's no such thing as "false memory" — a memory is a memory. If you have the memory of an experience, you had the experience. As researchers probe the mysteries of the brain, they ask more questions about our capacity to remember and to write our own personal histories.

Personal history? I have trouble remembering what I had for breakfast or what I looked like months ago, when I was thinner and had not yet started to vegetate here in court. Should I worry that my memory of once being size 10 is false? But I have proof: countless photos of a slimmer me, a closetful of clothes that no longer fit, and no one who contradicts me when I say I must lose weight. My more progressive friends say it's not so much how I look as how I feel that matters. I feel like a fat person, and no matter how slim I appear on the surface, I'm fat underneath. But suppose I felt like an abused person and told a therapist or police officer I believed I'd been abused. Whether or not they believed me, I don't think it would help to tell me I was making it up. Surely, if the Martensville daycare children believed they were abused, someone had to listen to the abuse they remembered and try to locate the origin of their memories.

We are what we remember and what we perceive, about ourselves and everything else. If you believe you were raped, you believe it. The concept of memory-making-us-who-we-are is explained in *Rewriting the Soul*, a book by Ian Hacking, philosopher at the University of Toronto. According to Hacking, those who believe it has occurred "explain their behaviour differently and feel differently about themselves," whether or not child abuse has occurred. Anyone believing they have been abused will therefore "redescribe the past" and this new description, ultimately, "changes their sense of self-worth, reorganizes and reevaluates the soul." A sense of self-worth is one of the most important things you can ever give a child. That some might make it their business to destroy that self-esteem is very hard to imagine. Yet, if what the Martensville children say is true, a group of adults were doing just that on a systematic basis. Bryden was the one, for better or worse, whom the children finally managed to tell in detail. Was she ready for the disclosures? According to the defence lawyers, far too ready.

Hugh Harradence, lawyer for Linda Sterling, the third and last to cross-examine Claudia Bryden, asks, Would it be correct to suggest the investigation was "more than an investigation to you, and that you were personally committed"? The witness answers, "It was a job. But I felt I had work to do that had to be done. I felt an obligation to complete the work at hand, even though it was infringing on my time off." Harradence continues, "Mrs. Bryden, I apologize for what may appear to be the rather disjointed nature of my examination. If there's ever any of my questions you don't understand or have trouble with, please don't hesitate to seek clarification from me."

It's interesting to compare the different styles of the three defence lawyers: Don Mullord, earnest plodder; Earl Kalenith, cherubic choirboy; and Hugh Harradence, weathered prima donna. With a slight limp and granny glasses perched precariously on the end of his nose, the effect is very human, and quite deadly.

Harradence continues, Is it correct to say that the day you searched the Sterling residence was the first time you conducted a search of anyone's house? "Yes, that's correct," Bryden says simply. And the first time you ever appeared in court was for this case? "Yes." Would it be fair to say you were inexperienced when you went to Martensville? "Relative to a lot of other police officers, yes," she says cautiously. Would it be fair to say your rapport with the other officers was "somewhat strained" right from the beginning? "I was the first female," is all she will say.

Now that Harradence has reminded everyone in the room that Bryden was inexperienced, he will examine the way the new kid on the block did her job, almost from the day she arrived.

> Harradence: When the Sally file was brought to your attention, did you contact nine or ten daycare families that might be involved?
>
> Bryden: Yes.
>
> Harradence: Why?
>
> Bryden: For the purpose of advising them the police were conducting an investigation.
>
> Harradence: Would it be fair to say the families were inquisitive?
>
> Bryden: Some were more inquisitive than others.
>
> Harradence: On October 29, 1991, did you give MacNeill Clinic [in Saskatoon] a list of names over the telephone?
>
> Bryden: I supplied a list of names of people who were interested in receiving some counselling.
>
> Harradence: Although confidentiality was a concern of yours, there was still information flying around?
>
> Bryden: We were concerned about it. I could not control them [the families], but I did advise them not to discuss the issue outside the home.

Martensville being so small, it probably wasn't long before everyone in town was talking about the scandal, and rumours started flying, including some about satanic ritual abuse. Soon after Bryden had supplied the list of names to the MacNeill Clinic in Saskatoon, one of the psychologists drove to Martensville in December 1991, to meet with five of the daycare families. In January 1992, she made the short trip to Martensville again, to attend a public meeting in a classroom with ten to fifteen parents. Though Bryden didn't attend the first meeting, she went to the second, to address the parents' questions and concerns and explain how the police were handling the investigation. "They simply had questions about the justice system and how a matter like this would proceed." That evening at the school, Bryden could point to the fact that police had arrested Ron Sterling that same day.

Harradence asks Judge Wimmer to remove the jury from the room. Then he shocks everyone by asking Bryden if she told the Martensville parents at the meeting that she'd been abused as a child by her two brothers. Bryden is stunned. She stares at the clock at the back of the room. Crown Prosecutor Bauer rises to object: Your Honour, I don't think it's relevant information and I doubt that it's legitimate to delve into Mrs. Bryden's past in this way.

Silence blankets the room. No one, not even Judge Wimmer, knows what to do next. He says he needs time to digest the matter and calls the lunch break. *I need a swim to wash away the dirt of the world. If I were Freddy or Kenny or Sally or Janey right now, I'd say I feel yucky.*

The swim, as usual, cheers me up, gives me an appetite, and makes me late for afternoon court. Outside courtroom 1, Claudia Bryden is sitting alone on a bench, excused, she says, from the legal discussion taking place on the other side of the door. "What do you think of all this?" she asks. I wish she hadn't, but feel obligated to answer her question.

I thought the Rape Shield Law was introduced in the 1980s so that defence lawyers could no longer drag a woman's past sexual history into court. During Tammy's trial, I thought Tim White called on that law to remove Tammy's sexual history from the gaze of the court. He told the judge that just because Tammy may have been abused as a child did not necessarily mean she was an abuser herself, and Judge Lavoie ruled in his favour. Now, I said, we're faced with a recent change in the legislation. Months ago a new Rape Shield Law was introduced, permitting a woman's previous sexual history to be used as evidence, according to strict guidelines. Now, in this court, you're faced with a defence lawyer who may try to persuade the jury that because you were abused as a child, you were unfit to do your job. He may argue that your childhood experience affected your judgement when you investigated the alleged abuse of the daycare children. He may try to question your credibility and competence. If that's what's taking place in the courtroom right now, I think it's a risky argument. It's also primitive and discriminatory. I tell Bryden I think Harradence risks alienating some of the jury, especially the six women, if he tries to discredit her by dragging her sexual history out of the closet.

Harradence is treading on thin ice, says Bryden. She tells me that she was sexually abused as a child, and that it wasn't until a few years ago she told her husband. Now everyone will know. If Harradence gets his way, Wimmer will allow this information to be part of public evidence, which troubles her because she hasn't told her parents about it yet.

Knowing Bryden never told her own parents makes it all the more surprising she told the Martensville daycare parents, people she hardly knew, and that now she's telling me. She explains why: After thinking "very hard about whether to disclose," she finally decided to tell the people at the meeting so they'd know she knew what they were going through and that there was hope for their children. In other words, Bryden thought that if she bared her soul she'd do a better job. If she'd been a man, or a little more experienced, would she have done this?

The doors of the courtroom are flung open and the clerk tells Bryden the court is ready for her. She smiles faintly at me, rises from the bench, and walks slowly into the courtroom towards the witness stand. I'm left in the hall, stunned and sad, wishing there were something I could do. There's nothing, except my work. Head bowed in deference to the court, I enter the room and make a beeline for my spot in the front row.

Now that the Crown and defence lawyers have hashed out the legal arguments with Wimmer, and he has ruled that Bryden's personal statement to the daycare parents at Venture Heights Elementary School is relevant and therefore admissible, the jury is recalled. Harradence limps over to the lectern where his notes are and resumes his cross-examination, peering up at Bryden.

> Harradence: Can you tell us what, if anything, you said to the parents at the January 16, 1992, meeting bearing upon the topic of child sexual abuse?
>
> Bryden: I related a personal experience to the parents at that time.
>
> Harradence: And I take it, Mrs. Bryden, that was part of your presentation at that meeting?
>
> Bryden: It was not planned. My reasons for providing the information that I did provide were basically twofold. First of all, at that time it had been over a period of weeks and weeks that I had had parents

phoning me, often in tears, often in the middle of the night after dealing with a child that had just had a nightmare, for instance. They were basically calling me and they were very concerned that they felt their child, due to the allegations, they felt that their child had the potential to be affected by these experiences for the rest of their life...

Harradence: The second reason, Mrs. Bryden?

Bryden: The second reason was I had tried to explain to the parents, again, over the period of weeks that I'd been dealing with them previous to this meeting. I tried to explain to them that I appreciated the difficulties that their children faced in disclosing information to anyone, whether it be parents or therapists or police. I sensed at this meeting on the sixteenth, because of what they were telling me, that they felt that I was not completely understanding the difficulties that they faced, that their children faced. So the reason for telling them was to simply show that in fact I could definitely understand where their children were coming from in terms of fear and apprehension in disclosing. And as well to show them that just because a person is abused as a young child does not mean that it necessarily affects them for the rest of their lives.

Harradence maintains that Bryden's "personal experience" biased her investigation, gave her tunnel vision, and drove her to see abuse where none existed.

Harradence: Just out of curiosity, Mrs. Bryden, how many people were there [whose] children had actually disclosed to police, at that point?

Bryden: There were at least two.

Harradence: So two out of ten to fifteen? I believe that it was your evidence that there were ten to fifteen people there?

Bryden: Yes.

Harradence: And there were two out of these ten to fifteen that had disclosed any criminal activity to police?

Bryden: To police, yes...

Harradence: Okay. Do you believe that your personal experience affected this investigation in any way, or advised or prejudiced your outlook towards this investigation?

Bryden: No, I don't believe it did... Perhaps I was a little more sensitive to the feelings that these children may have been having and in terms of their difficulties. And also in terms of the parents' difficulties.

Harradence: But with all due respect, ma'am, are you not putting the cart before the horse? There are no allegations from most of the people in that room and you're being sympathetic to them, assuming that there's allegations of abuse there?

Bryden: Although allegations had not come from all the families present, certainly concerns were expressed to me as well as to therapists at or by that time regarding the ability of their children to overcome the experience, or the alleged experiences that they had had.

Harradence: Well, there were some concerns, but there was nothing definite, was there? And I put it to you, ma'am, that the whole point behind this meeting organized by MacNeill Clinic was to encourage and promote disclosures?

Bryden: No, that was not the purpose of the meeting.

Harradence: Then what did you understand the purpose of the meeting was?

Bryden: I was asked to attend that meeting specifically to answer the questions and address the concerns of the parents. And those concerns and questions that I was unable to address or answer at the time, I referred to the prosecutor's office and we did our best to address as many of those issues as possible... They were asking questions such as, when will matters proceed to trial or preliminary hearing... And they had a common interest in understanding how the justice system would work a case like this through. They were parents who had concerns because of information they had received from the children at that point.

Harradence: But you hadn't received the information from the children?

Bryden: At that point I had received some information from other children, but not from all of their children, no…

Harradence: And ma'am, do you remember who else spoke at that meeting?

Bryden: Heather Brenneman spoke. She reinforced to the parents as I did that some of the questions that they were asking were absolutely impossible for me to answer. Questions like "Would the accused ever be tested for HIV?" That's a question I could not absolutely answer at all. Many of the questions were very difficult and way beyond my capabilities. And those were questions that I did address with the head prosecutor at a later time…

Harradence: Do you remember any specific questions that anybody else asked that stick out in your mind?

Bryden: Questions like "What is sexual abuse? What constitutes an offence of sexual abuse?"

Harradence: What did you say to that matter?

Bryden: I don't recall my exact words, but I explained generally that it was wrongful touching.

Harradence: Would it be your observation, ma'am, that the majority of the parents present at this meeting were making the assumption, and your observations based on their questions, that some criminal conduct had occurred?

Bryden: The parents were aware that charges had been laid against some members of the Sterling family. They were aware that criminal proceedings had begun.

Harradence: But the parents whose children weren't involved in charges, could you make the observations whether they were assuming that their children would eventually disclose?

Bryden: Some of them were of the opinion that, at that point in time, that their children had not been abused. And some to this day maintain that their children have not been abused. Others later learned otherwise.

Harradence: Okay. So there were some people there that said, "Hey, these people might be innocent"?...

Bryden: Not at that meeting. No, not that I recall.

Harradence also calls into question Bryden's memory.

Harradence: Ma'am, it's my observation that you rely heavily in giving your testimony on your notebook and these summaries that you've created from the contents of your notebook. Would that be a — a fair observation on my behalf?

Bryden: Yes.

Harradence: And the problem is it's not humanly possible to record every contact and the details of every discussion in your notebook?

Bryden: The purpose of the notebook isn't to record detail, it's to record information to refresh your memory.

Harradence: Right, but it's somewhat difficult to remember hour-long conversations when you just have a note of the time in your notebook, is it not?

Bryden: I can't account for every minute of this investigation, no.

Harradence: No. And that's why, ma'am, you have referred to, in Mr. Bauer's examination-in-chief, general conversation, conversation in general terms, you use a lot of those phrases because you don't recall the whole conversation, do you?

Bryden: I don't recall all the exact words that were spoken, no...

Harradence: Suffice it to say then, ma'am, you have no idea of what was said to those parents, none?

Bryden: Well, I have a general idea of some of the discussions that went on...

Harradence: Were you...were you personally committed to this? Was it more than a job to you?

Bryden: It was a job, but I — I felt that I had work to do that had to be done. I felt an obligation to complete the work at hand, even though it was infringing on my time off...

Harradence: Suffice it to say, ma'am, that you developed a friendship with some of these families?

Bryden: I had a professional relationship with these people. I — as far as the children go, I had to get to know them a little bit and had them — I had to have them get to know me a little bit, so that we could develop a trusting relationship so that there would be something to work with down the road when it came time for disclosures.

Harradence: Do you deny, ma'am, that you developed a friendship with some of these families?

Bryden: I would not continue a relationship with these people — if this case was concluded tomorrow, I wouldn't seek out these people, no.

Harradence: Would you agree, ma'am, that in some cases and perhaps this case, that when you develop a close relationship with people it sometimes affects your professional judgement?

Bryden: I suppose it's possible, but in my case it's not probable.

Harradence: And hard decisions become harder to make?

Bryden: This was a difficult investigation whether it was with a family that I had a lot of contact with or a family that I had very little contact with. Opportunities to interview children or to talk with parents were — were always not something that I really relished doing...

Harradence: Would you acknowledge that not all your contacts with the parents were noted in your notebook?

Bryden: Yes...

Harradence: In relation to that interview with Freddy's family, there are, according to my count, forty-four words in your notebook. The notes aren't that significant, are they?

Bryden: There are general notes following that interview.

Wimmer: I think you've made your point, Mr. Harradence. She can't remember everything.

For us the trial is over for the week, but not for Wimmer. Before retiring to his chambers, the judge must decide the fate of Mr. and Mrs. Richard Klassen, the husband and wife who picketed the courthouse the other day to protest the outcome of a different child sex-abuse trial. Obedient, grateful to be free of handcuffs, they stand before him like two kids hauled in from the schoolyard. "Picketing of a courthouse is illegal," Wimmer reminds them, wearing his judge's smile. The man and woman apologize. The judge accepts, then excuses them, on condition they picket elsewhere in future. Yes, M'Lord.

But that wasn't the end of it. Now that the judge had spelled out the Klassens' part of the bargain, they expected something in return. And so it was, several days later, that Richard Klassen's four-page letter was delivered to the courthouse office of Judge Wimmer. The picketer complained about the way authorities had handled him and his wife. He wanted respect and he expected the return of the confiscated placards and leaflets.

Judge Wimmer answered promptly: The placards and leaflets, in his opinion, were confiscated because they impugned the integrity of the lawyers involved in the case. He did not take kindly to terms like "Crown rapists" and "secret trials" and "Saskatoon travesty" paraded in front of the courthouse. The Klassens, he suggested, were like two pots calling the kettle black: How could they complain about a stacked judicial deck when their own placard campaign was one-sided and defamatory?

The Klassens never did get their placards and leaflets back, as far as I know.

Moor the mentor

Claudia Bryden testified that when she'd been on the job less than a month in fall 1991 and realized the magnitude of the investigation, she discussed it with Inspector Wayne McGillivray, acting chief of the tiny Martensville force. When McGillivray testified, he explained that he had been unable to justify assigning additional officers to the case. So outside help was sought at the Saskatoon station to the south and, in March 1992, officer Rod Moor was assigned to help Claudia Bryden with the investigation.

Rod Moor now steps into the witness box, a friendly looking man with thin hair and thick eyebrows. The middle-aged Moor tells the court that after thirteen years on the police force, he had needed a break from his regular beat and asked for a transfer. Before long he was working in the Youth Section of the Saskatoon Police. He says he likes helping traumatized kids, which immediately sets him apart from the other officers who've told me they wouldn't take his job for all the handcuffs in hell. Moor testifies that his training consisted of a fifteen-week course at the Regina Police College, supplemented over the years by occasional refresher courses in statement analysis and hostage negotiation, and a four-day course in Step-Wise to help him deal with traumatized children. Other than that, Moor tells the prosecutor, he learned to question kids on the job by conducting hundreds of interviews.

From one minute to the next, the witness's world would be shattered. He would be called to court and criticized for the way he did his job — a job he thought he was doing properly, by listening to the darkest secrets of the children he interviewed and sometimes showing them the police dogs.

Moor thought he did his job well. So did everyone else, and Bryden asked him to show her how to interview children. Weeks later, in March 1992, Moor's own boss formally assigned him to the Martensville investigation. According to Moor, he certainly didn't volunteer for the job. Nevertheless, he was, he says, happy to assist Bryden, placing emphasis on the word "assist."

Moor tells the court he harboured no notions of usurping the authority of the Martensville police. At this, my ears perk up and I'm reminded of the Leslie Mahaffy-Kristen French murder investigation, where two different-sized police forces are collaborating. According to the article I read the other day, there is jurisdictional combat between the Metro Toronto and Niagara Regional police services, even as they try to work together to solve the murders of the girls.

I'm starting to feel sympathy for Moor. Don't get me wrong. I've felt no affection for the Saskatoon police force since the day one of their meter men (he must have seen me park the car) stuck a parking ticket under my windshield wiper with a handwritten warning on the back: "Don't try this again, bitch." When I called the police station, a superintendent denied that his men would ever do such a thing. Whoever did it, the proof is tacked to my office bulletin board.

When questioned by Crown prosecutor Bruce Bauer, Rod Moor testifies that he videotaped some interviews in the Soft Room but not others. The Saskatoon police force had no policy on the matter and sometimes, such as on the day new flooring was being installed, he couldn't use the Soft Room at all.

The first child Moor interviewed, in tandem with Bryden, was three-year-old Janey. Moor tells Bauer he videotaped the interview, but did not show the girl photos or any items whatsoever. During a subsequent videotaped interview three weeks later, he did not show Janey's brother, Tommy, any photos or items either. However, in a subsequent interview, Moor and Bryden did show the boy photos of items found during the search of the Sterling house. Because Moor was assigned specifically to help Bryden, and particularly to investigate the allegations of police involvement, he showed Freddy a police photo lineup during a meeting at the boy's home and a picture of The Place at a later interview.

Moor and Bryden also showed photos to Kathy and her brother, Frank. They also travelled to Alberta to interview Bill, another daycare child who'd moved there. The two officers showed the boy pictures of the Sterling house in addition to a lineup of eight people, including Travis Sterling. The boy identified Travis. Moor also interviewed Kenny several times, and once showed him a police photo lineup.

Most of the sessions with the children lasted about half an hour. Moor videotaped some and audiotaped some and recorded others only in his notebook. He maintains that, beyond the interview room, he never discussed the disclosures that children made to him and Bryden. As an additional precaution, he and Bryden discouraged the families from discussing the kids' disclosures with anyone else and encouraged parents to let their children talk only when ready.

So far, things have gone well for Moor. But now it's time for his cross-examination as Hugh Harradence limps to the lectern. Moor tells him that most children want to tell the truth. Question: Do you agree it's important not to reward the child for answering your questions? Answer: I disagree. In my opinion, the child needs to be reassured that what they're saying, when it is the truth, they are doing right.

Moor took the Step-Wise course developed by Canadian psychologist Dr. John Yuille. Like Bryden, it was only after the investigation that he took the four-day course, designed to obtain from a child the maximum amount of information with the minimum amount of "contamination." Moor tells Harradence he doesn't believe the course affected his interviewing style very much.

I'd like to review the officer's technique, says Harradence, and selects police videotapes from the collection of evidence stacked at the front of the room. He has chosen a video of Tommy, the boy who said he hid behind the couch and watched Travis Sterling abuse his sister. While the tapes are being readied, the clerk sets up the screen so that it faces the Sterlings, the lawyers, the jurors, and the judge. The judge reminds the jurors again that they are to evaluate the method of each interview, not the content. They are to concentrate on the police officer's questions, not the daycare children's answers.

Tommy: Is the TV on?

Moor: Yes, you're a star.

The boy talks a bit about his sister. Then he refers to a front bum and a back bum. A penis. Boobies. Band-aids. Car seats. Giant police. Being blindfolded.

Tommy: (Sigh.) We were going to the devil church... It wasn't me who drove... I want to be an astronaut, policeman or firefighter... If I had my bike, I'd ride home and get my sword... This gets me angry. This gets me sick.

Guy in this photo is bad. Bad guy too. (Sigh.) Bad things. Good boy. Pretend. Brave. I don't remember. Buddy. Police badge. Black hair, black moustache, blue shirt, black pants, red stripes. Colouring book. These are the words that echo in my head at the end of Moor's several taped interviews with young Tommy.

Harradence accuses Moor of "driving" the interviews, of talking about "bad people" and kids with cuts who go to the doctor for a Band-Aid solution, even before Tommy has opened his mouth. Moor explains to the court why he talked to the boy the way he did. A child may be afraid to disclose abuse, or feel guilty because the abuser could be the father or a family member. "Or it could be no one," bellows Harradence, causing Judge Wimmer to remind the lawyer he is supposed to ask the witness questions, not make statements. "Sorry, My Lord," the chastised counsel says. From the sly grin on his face, I'm sure he feels the scolding was well worth it.

Harradence wants Moor to explain why he still uses anatomically detailed dolls when interviewing children, even though the Step-Wise program advises police to avoid playing let's pretend. Dolls, the course teaches, are suggestive and toys are distracting. Nevertheless, the Step-Wise student on the stand defends the use of dolls, saying they allow the child to identify body parts without becoming embarrassed or traumatized. "Doesn't it strike you that this child was to some extent simply following a script that had been provided for him?" accuses Harradence. Didn't his parents (waiting in the next room, with Bryden) coach him? "No, I don't feel that," says Moor.

Maybe that's how it looks when, on video, Tommy runs to the room next to the Soft Room to see his mother and screams, "I'm never coming here again," to which she replies: "What do you mean, you don't remember? We came all this way so you could tell. If you can't remember his name, just tell him ... Or I'll get Janey to tell."

Maybe Tommy was so angry he didn't want to talk to anyone, least of all a policeman. And perhaps the investigation would have gone more smoothly if Moor, or an art therapist, had handed the boy a ball of clay and let him sit in a corner for a half-hour. He might have sculpted figures of the people he was angry at, then hacked them up or taken them home as souvenirs. Maybe he needed to fight back, reclaim a sense of power. In an article in *Family Practice* magazine, Ontario art therapist Louise Moore says that in the initial stages of disclosure, it's a lot easier for an abused child to deal with tangible objects than it is to talk about what's in their hearts.

There was no clay or play dough in the Soft Room. And Tommy, even though he didn't want to see the inside of this place again, was flanked by Moor and had his mother to deal with in the next room. Reluctantly, he answered Moor's questions and his feelings are captured on tape, the anger, the helplessness, the need for revenge: "If I had my bike, I'd ride home and get my sword. This makes me sick."

The videotapes, and others that the court will see in the days to come, are approximately two years old. Other tapes in the collection capture the daycare children's allegations that police officers — Moor's very own colleagues — abused them. Two of the alleged abusers are here today, Saskatoon police officer John Popowich and RCMP officer Darren Sabourin.

Popowich has already had his day in court. During the brief trial, Freddy and Kenny failed to identify him in a lineup of twenty-two police officers and civilians with similar features. When the boys flunked this demanding exercise, a journalist asked Popowich's lawyer, Morris Bodnar, if all charges should be dropped. "Is the Pope Polish?" quipped Bodnar. Soon after that the Crown, "being unwilling to prosecute further," stayed the eight charges of sexual abuse against John Popowich. Now the talk of the town is that it won't be long until the thirty-nine charges against Sabourin and the three other officers are also dropped.

In the middle of officer Moor's nervous stuttering, Ron Sterling starts to snicker, as does the brother of John Popowich. Popowich himself is dressed in a red bomber jacket and jeans. At break, he saunters over to the three

Sterlings to chat and follows them into the small room off the court that is designated the family's retreat.

On this warm sunny day, I'm curious about life beyond the courthouse walls and dying to take the road to The Place. Lawyers had wanted jurors to see for themselves the second crime scene called The Place, where the children say they were abused, but the judge thought the 150-odd police photos taken there and the detailed floor plans should inform them sufficiently. So he refused the request to transport them there, saying that it was presumptuous to scrutinize other people's property. Perhaps, but I've decided to go anyway, and Janis is coming, too.

The constant prairie wind is behind us. The trip is short, and I have enough gas to get to Martensville before filling up. The streets are empty because the kids are in school. I wouldn't want to live in such a small place, where entertainment seems limited to places like the Silver Screen store where the Sterlings used to rent videos. As we turn a corner, Janis sees a sign in the window "We Believe the Children," a reminder of why we've come here. As we drive around the east-west streets and north-south avenues, we see many more such signs. They'd be comforting if they were Block Parent signs, protecting the town's children. But they are defiant signs of protest.

The municipal office is out of grid maps, but a politician's aide in the provincial constituency office has one and gives us directions to the Storey-Bishoff acreage, "The Place," without asking questions. We drive to the unexceptional blue bungalow on 5th Avenue where the Sterlings used to live.

Our plan is to time the trip from the Sterling house to The Place, the building where the kids say they were driven in a police van and abused. If they were, we want to put ourselves in their shoes and clock the trip for ourselves. At 3 p.m. we leave. Janis navigates while I drive north on Highway 12, then left onto Power Line Road, right at the first dirt side road. There it is, in a field behind a clump of trees. A right at the second driveway on the grid road.

The driveway snakes towards the Storey-Bishoff property, which includes a plain house and not far behind it, the building that resembles the description the kids gave the police months ago. It's a two-storey structure covered with sky-blue metal siding, with few windows and a door only big enough for a car. There's a single detached garage near the house. The Place is far from the next acreage and, with all the bushes on the perimeter, neighbours would need binoculars to get a really good view of a police van pulling up in broad daylight and blindfolded children being frogmarched into the building.

I don't like trespassing any more than Judge Wimmer does, especially when I see the sign on the fence in front of the house: "Trespassers will be Prosecuted." That might be better than being mauled by the German shepherd prowling behind the fence, or being threatened with a shotgun, which I half expect to see behind the screen door at any moment. We decide to leave.

There's not enough room to turn the car around, so all I can do is put it in reverse and back down the lane slowly. This gives us more time to keep our eye on the dog and look at the blue building, You'd think the owners might have painted it some other colour after all the notoriety.

The odometer says we've driven 7.5 miles, and it's 3: 15 p.m. Freddy testified that the trip from the Sterling house to The Place took fifteen minutes. Yes, but on one of the court tapes the other day he said to Rod Moor, "Tell me where that place was, 'cause I was blindfolded... Jim [Elstad] put Kleenex balls in my mouth and blindfolded me." Maybe Moor told him. Whether he did or not, we know for certain that the police showed Freddy photos of it. But how could a nine-year-old boy know how The Place felt, that it wasn't properly heated in winter, and that it was cold? How would he know the contents of the freezer, and what would ever prompt him to say a skull was stored there? What led him to say one of the daycare boys was hosed down naked, then put in the freezer, or that he himself was stripped and thrown outside in midwinter?

When court reconvenes next morning, Hugh Harradence asks Moor why he showed pictures of the blue building to Bill, one of the alleged young victims. Surprisingly, Moor admits that he showed photos of The Place to Bill before the boy gave him a description of it. Even more surprising, he is convinced he did nothing wrong. Harradence disagrees and suggests that a better way to conduct that interview would have been for Bill to describe the place prior to showing him the photographs. Moor disagrees.

The Step-Wise program teaches practitioners to avoid contaminating the child's testimony. The interviewer must make every effort to let the child name names and provide descriptions of people and places, drawing pictures whenever possible. But Moor, rather than waiting for Bill to describe The Place, if he could, showed the boy photos of it. Harradence persists: Couldn't those photos be a source of contamination for this young lad? Wouldn't you be providing certain suggestions to Bill? Again Moor disagrees.

Harradence wants to show that Moor interviewed Bill incompetently, and in hindsight it's easy to criticize Moor. But even if he did ask the boy leading questions and do things in the wrong order, in all likelihood he conducted the interview with the best of intentions and to the best of his ability. But Harradance says the officer led the witness in the interview that was taped in March 1992, which the lawyer now plays for the court.

Moor: Did anyone touch you?

Bill: Ron and Linda did.

Moor: Very good. When did Ron touch you? How?

Anyone conducting an interview, especially when people's reputations are at stake, should know better than to congratulate the interviewee for giving you the "right" answer. Your goal is to look and act neutral, no matter what the interviewee says. Your objective is to look dispassionate, as though you're gathering information, not keeping score.

But this is hard to learn. It's normal to utter an exclamation or raise your eyebrows or gape, when you hear something unusual, and it's extremely difficult not to. The hardest task when interviewing is to engage your subject, yet keep your distance. You keep your ears open and your mouth shut and never utter, at least in the presence of your interviewee, "hot damn" or "holy shit" or "very good." If you have to hide your feelings, wear a mask. But don't expect the mask to exempt you from irresponsible behaviour towards the other person. Interviewing is work, not play, even though, when skilfully done, it may look like it. If it is a game, it's a serious one. You talk more smoothly, so that you can help someone else do it, while you watch, listen, and think. You choose the topic and, with your guidance, the interviewee helps you write the script.

Like any unwritten contract between two people, an interview can be broken or declared void at any time. It takes time and training to learn contractual laws, which we start to do the day we're born. If you're a baby and you cry when mother bends over the cradle, she'll probably pick you up. Smile and coo, and she'll reward you with hugs and kisses and a big smile. If you get really lucky, she feeds you. That's her part of the bargain and how she shows she loves you. But the line between love and manipulation is a fine one. The smile and the sucker you give your child today, to show her you love her, may look to her exactly like the smile and the sucker you gave her yesterday to stop her crying from driving you crazy. You know the difference between your two motives, but does she? And does it make any difference?

Suppose, for a moment, I put myself in the shoes of one of the daycare kids. I'm used to the adults around me treating me a certain way. I clean up my toys, they let me watch a video. I wash my hands, they give me lunch. I do this, they do that. When they stop responding to my cues, or respond in a totally unpredictable way, or bribe me, or hurt me, I get confused and no longer trust them completely. This trial is about adults who have allegedly broken their contracts with kids and breached the trust their parents placed in them.

Maybe Rod Moor felt he had a double duty to perform, to get to the bottom of the allegations while helping to restore the kids' faith in grownups.

He probably took his mission extremely seriously, all the more so because the kids said some of the culprits were police. Was he not supposed to smile in order to reassure each child that everything would soon be okay? Was Moor not supposed to say encouraging words to get the children to relax and talk? Was he not supposed to act in a fatherly way towards them? Maybe Moor cared too much about doing his job. Maybe he didn't know the job he was supposed to do in the Soft Room was not at all like tucking his own kids in at night, or coaching them at the rink. And maybe no one ever explained the difference to him until it was too late.

We get the occasional glimpse into Moor's mind during his cross-examination. He admits to Harradence, as Bryden admitted during her cross-exam, that he was reluctant to challenge the children and loath to express scepticism of their allegations, for fear of alienating them. In fact, if Moor had been cast in the role of parent or counsellor to the children disclosing abuse, he would have behaved correctly and provided the emotional support many experts think appropriate in the circumstances. But Moor was a policeman, who, it seems, felt very protective towards the kids. Was he concerned for the accused? It would have been difficult, if not impossible, to balance everyone's rights at once.

But it's important to try. Richard Gardner, an American physician and author of *Sex Abuse Hysteria*, criticizes the stance people like Moor take. In Gardner's view, accepting unquestioningly the allegations of a victim, as Moor admits he usually did, demonstrates a lack of common sense. He also labels such a stance among investigators "holier than thou" and patronizing. "They, unlike the rest of us, are there to protect children. They, unlike the rest of us, 'believe the children'... It provides these examiners with a feeling of special importance, which likely serves to compensate for basic feelings of inadequacy." I find Gardner's tone patronizing and his opinion simplistic. Is the physician suggesting that if no one took what children say at face value, the world would be a better place? Is he prescribing scepticism to cure the problem of child abuse? If we don't believe children when they say they were abused, then they weren't?

Allegations of sexual abuse are notoriously hard to prove at the best of times. When the police fail to do their job properly, victims pay — in fact, we all do, not just financially, but with the health of our society and the happiness of our children. I'm perplexed that Moor, on at least one occasion, showed apparent disregard for the confidentiality of a child witness. Completing his taped interview in the Soft Room with Bill, the officer opened the door to the adjoining room where the boy's parents sat and left the door open while he talked with them. In the courtroom, Harradence criticizes the witness for this.

Harradence: Okay. And obviously you left the door open?

Moor: Yes.

Harradence: And obviously you were talking about this investigation?

Moor: Yes.

Harradence: And obviously Bill could hear you?

Moor: I didn't realize that, but obviously he could.

Harradence: We could hear something over the tape?

Moor: Yes.

Harradence: And now that you know that he — that he could hear you, you would acknowledge that's a mistake?

Moor: Yes, definitely.

Harradence has had a chance to blow holes in Moor's story, and now his colleague, Don Mullord, questions Moor about young Bill.

Mullord: It wasn't clear to me...why you did not obtain a description of the Storey-Bishoff property before you showed the pictures.

Moor: ...Firstly, one of my concerns dealing with children is that I always have a specific area, or a specific time frame that I can interview the child and not traumatize them. Secondly, I was focusing on other areas of the investigation, matters I wished to cover, and I...[it] would be no different than getting a specific description of the accused before showing a photo lineup. I didn't do that [either].

As a police officer, Moor had a schedule. He knew that the fewer times he interviewed a child the better. So why not try to get the maximum amount of information in the shortest amount of time possible? That's fine, according to the experts, as long as you don't plant ideas in your subject's head to make the crop of allegations sprout faster. Whether you agree with Moor's methods, he sounds pretty enlightened for a policeman. Just the other day I heard a story on the radio about a Quebec police officer who says his fellow cops sometimes lie to suspects, kidnap, and even beat them to make them talk. By comparison, Moor's decision to give kids colouring books or Cokes during an interview was harmless, and letting them look at the police dogs benign.

Mullord, though not always audible through his rust-coloured beard, continues to question the officer about Bill's references to cages. According to Mullord, there was an inconsistency in the boy's evidence and he asks Moor if he tried to determine which of the two statements was true.

> Moor: No... That would not, in my opinion, be appropriate... He's a bright boy, as you saw in the video... If I begin challenging him, I'm going to... make an enemy, or at least...have him afraid of me.
>
> Mullord: Your position is that the child is always telling the truth?
>
> Moor: Yes.
>
> Mullord: The difficulty is that, in this situation, he's made two different statements, and they can't both be true. One...must be true, and one must be false.
>
> Moor: We're dealing with multiple offences, multiple offenders over an extensive period of time... I'm assuming that he's telling me the truth as he remembers it both times.

Indeed, time makes us forget. How can anyone, child or adult, remember anything that happened so long ago? But that's a question nobody asks. So let's move on, as the judge likes to say, to the defence lawyer's attempt to pillory the police officer.

> Mullord: ...Regardless of what disclosures they [the children] made, you always wanted more. There was always... pressure on the child.... And if they came forward with something... all it led to was another interview?
>
> Moor: No. I advised the child to contact me. So the child could control the pace. The child always disclosed before another interview.
>
> Mullord: So you contacted the parents and the therapists?

Moor: No. Claudia Bryden and only one therapist.

Despite Moor's good intentions, he and Bryden questioned Freddy five or six times and Kenny at least eight. Although baby Janey also had six interviews and although ten-year-old Sally had three or four, there is solid proof that both girls told their stories to others before telling the police. Before Sally told Bryden that Travis Sterling had abused her, she'd told her guidance counsellor; before police heard about Janey, the toddler had told her mother about "Ravis and Uncle." The manner of the disclosures, the steps in the police investigation, and the overall sequence of events will have a significant impact on later events.

As much as the defence lawyer likes to criticize the police officer's work, the judge feels obliged to criticize the lawyer's. "Mr. Mullord, I ask you to frame a question and not just argue with the witness," he bursts out at one point. A little later, he turns in his chair, red faced, to remind the man, "Mr. Mullord, I'm sorry to interrupt you. But I have to ask you to frame questions and not just argue with the witness... The points you are making are points...to be made later in your argument to the jury." The scientist-turned-lawyer blanches to think he's not doing a proper job in the eyes of the judge.

The witness likes to think he did a good job, too, when interviewing the children. Earl Kalenith, the third lawyer to cross-examine Rod Moor, asks the officer if he'd change a thing about the techniques he used in his sessions with the kids. Moor says, "No, I would not."

Because of Wimmer's publication ban to protect the children's privacy, journalists can't say as much as they'd like, except to each other, which makes our morning break today livelier than usual. The CBC reporter is annoyed at the recent trial coverage by the *StarPhoenix*, which he likens to McCarthyism. In turn, the *Star* reporter mocks the CBC, dubbing the public broadcaster Goliath, as in David and...

Like siblings, the reporters know they must keep their nattering to a dull roar if the courtroom "family" is to survive until the end of the trial. Petty rivalries aside, the ten or twelve of us covering the trial every day must work together. I share little of the tension that grips the local journalists who must write or say something intelligent every day when, some days, there's precious little to say. My problem is just the opposite: there's far too much to say, too many notes to take, too many details to record, too many to leave out.

The one force guaranteed to bring a truce among the journalists is the partial media ban and the shortage of publishable trial material. Like soldiers on rations, they long for substance and regularly check with the lawyers about what they can publish and what they don't dare touch. Having to beg for the occasional scrap is a constant reminder that they are not in charge of the daily news diet.

At break this morning, a creative TV reporter suggests that we just make up the stories, to which a radio reporter quickly replies that we'd all better say the same thing, if we want the public to believe us. The joker in me laughs along with the others, but my serious twin winces, remembering the last time I heard talk of fabricating stories, during yesterday's cross examination.

> Mullord: Freddy was presented with two dolls and was asked to demonstrate what Travis did to him. He whispered under his breath: "Well, oh God, what to do?" Did it occur to you at that point Freddy was making it up?
>
> Moor: Absolutely not. Children will open up to a point, and then retreat for a while. Freddy's cornered. He's feeling he's going to have to answer the question.
>
> Mullord: He was hesitating to make a disclosure.
>
> Moor: His face is at a very stressful point. He goes very beet red. He gets very uncomfortable.
>
> Mullord: He was uncomfortable at the point where you showed him the dolls?
>
> Moor: I asked him to show what Travis had done. This is a time to retreat or to open up and disclose.
>
> Mullord: He was struggling to make things up?
>
> Moor: I never got from any of the children at any time that they made anything up regarding disclosures.

Doubting the children

The three-lawyer defence team has tried to make the Martensville and Saskatoon police officers look incompetent in the eyes of the jury. Now they will attempt to make the children sound unbelievable. These kids have had their share of misery. Life has dealt them serious blows, either weakening or strengthening their character, to what extent no one will know for years. Even if I have doubts that they're telling the truth about the Sterlings, there's one thing I know for sure. These children have withstood the blows of separation, divorce, depression, and moving.

Paul is nine years old and in Grade 4 at Venture Heights elementary school in Martensville. He was five when his parents started dropping him off at the Sterling house early in the morning. Around that same time they separated for several months, though saw each other weekends. Paul's father tells the court his son became angry and started using the words "fuck," "bitch," and "Jesus Christ." He started wetting the bed and peeing on the wall, stealing from his parents' wallets and having nightmares from which he'd wake up screaming. Nightmares in the middle of the night, daydreams in the middle of the day, and screaming when the time came to go to the daycare — behaviour that lasted five or six months and finally prompted the parents to apply for child counselling at the MacNeill Clinic in Saskatoon.

Paul's mother, who now enters the witness box, tells the court she stopped taking the boy to the Sterling house when he told her he'd once played with a gun there. She called Linda Sterling but found inconsistencies in the daycare operator's explanation. According to Paul's mother, Linda was in the habit of putting the boy down for a nap in the master bedroom where, she later learned, the guns were kept.

The pre-pubescent Paul enters the witness box in the downstairs courtroom, while the public and journalists remain in the upstairs courtroom with the closed-circuit TV. The camera shows the front of Judge Wimmer and the back of Crown prosecutor Bauer who, without legs, look like talking puppets. The witness Paul, however, is but a voice, that of a child punctuated with bouts of silence and the occasional sigh. It's ironic we can't see his body when this is what the evidence is all about.

Bauer: Can you tell me what you remember?

Paul: All I remember is that Linda told me to pull down my pants. She touched me. In the private part. The peepee.

Bauer: Can you show me what happened?

Paul: No, I don't want to do it.

What kid is going to pull his pants down in front of the judge, the lawyers and the jurors? Paul continues in his birdlike voice: For several years he told no one about this incident, including his parents, because Linda had threatened to hurt him and because he forgot. His memory was not jogged till the day he watched TV news and saw the Sterlings being arrested. I wonder: Is it as improper, in the eyes of the court, for a boy to watch television and remember events as it is for him to look at police photos and get flashbacks?

Paul, like Freddy, has good memories of the Sterling daycare as well as bad ones. He tells the court that Linda, the same woman who once fondled his peepee while she held a gun to him and threatened to hurt him if he told anyone, also liked to serve him chocolate-pudding snacks and protect him. Once, on an outing to a farm, she told Paul to cover his eyes while Ron Sterling slaughtered a chicken and a pig. If the things Paul says about Linda Sterling are true, the contradictions in her character are interesting: One day she threatened to harm the boy with a weapon; another day, she hastened to protect him from witnessing a barnyard slaughter.

Bill is the next witness. Now eleven, his voice sometimes breaks, though his vocabulary is still that of a child. Like many Canadian kids his age, Bill has moved a lot and lived in four different towns, including Martensville. He tells the court he went to the Sterling daycare when he was five. Although, at the time, he and Freddy were best friends, now, just like a kid, Bill has forgotten his best friend's last name. Bill also admits to defence lawyer, Earl Kalenith, that it's hard to remember the things that happened at the Sterling house. Fortunately, a lot of people have helped him remember, including his parents and the police with their photos.

On this topic, the soft-spoken Kalenith tries to trap the boy. "Part of what you remember is because you've seen pictures? Some of it you remember because you've talked with others?" Innocently, Bill answers yes to both. Then Kalenith drives home his argument: "It's hard to remember what you remember from the beginning and what you remember from pictures you saw, and because of things that people have helped you remember?" Yes, Bill agrees readily.

But Bill is not a complete pushover, even though he's tired from throwing up all morning and making the long journey from Alberta, where he now lives. Without hesitation, he tells Kalenith he didn't need any help to remember. "All the stuff about pictures and touching me in the privates and clothes off I remember by myself." But dates are another matter. When Kalenith expects Bill to remember such-and-such a date, Judge Wimmer steps in and scolds the defence lawyer gruffly: "I don't know how you can expect him to remember dates."

Tommy, seven, is the next witness. He still sounds a bit like the five-year-old boy we heard earlier on tape, but his voice has matured and deepened since Rod Moor recorded it in the Soft Room. His vocabulary, too, has expanded and he speaks with more ease and confidence. The contrast is a reminder of the passage of time and this child's rate of growth. Like the other children in this trial, he must pass the truth test before testifying.

Sullivan: What does it mean to take an oath on the Bible?

Tommy: It means you're promising God that you'll tell the truth.

Sullivan: And what do you think would happen if you broke that promise?

Tommy: God would be sad.

Sullivan: Can you tell us the difference between a truth and a lie?

Tommy: Yes.

Sullivan: Okay. Tell us, please.

Tommy: If I said your robe was blue,... would I be telling the truth?

Sullivan chuckles on camera, and everyone in the upstairs courtroom does too. The boy has been prepared for court by learning to answer questions, not ask them. By assuming the prosecutor's role for an instant, Tommy unwittingly turns things around. But Sullivan barely misses a beat before beginning her examination-in-chief of the boy.

Tommy says that Ron, Travis, and Linda Sterling touched his "privates." Reluctantly, he answers that privates are "between my legs," but when the Crown prosecutor asks him what they're called on the back of the body and the front, the boy refuses to answer the question and, instead, makes a diagram labelling the front "A" and the back "B." Nor will Tommy answer Sullivan when she asks where Ron put his hand. "I can't tell you where he touched me. I wrote it on the piece of paper," he whispers. "Can you show us with your hand how Ron's hand was in your pants?" she persists. " No, because I don't want to." Tommy is equally unwilling to speak about Travis's and Linda's fondling. He will only say that they both touched him "under" his clothes. Linda touched his "A" and his "B."

Tommy sounds as though he's about to cry. He continues, his voice sounding strained. He tells Sullivan he also saw Linda Sterling touch his two sisters, Janey and Sandy, on their "A" and their "B." But when the prosecutor asks if Ron Sterling touched his sisters too, he doesn't answer at first. Then he mumbles, "Yes, I think so." Breaking the silence that follows, Judge Wimmer calls it a day. "This young boy seems a bit tired to me." Sullivan agrees, and court is adjourned.

Next morning Tommy tells a different story. He tells Sullivan that he never saw Ron or Travis do anything to his two sisters, although his mother once told him these two men had done something to them. The back of Sullivan's head and her marionette-like torso are all I see on the TV screen, but I know the witness's words have just deepened the constant crease in her forehead. After sleepless nights and days dedicated to clearing a path through the evidentiary swamp, she watches helplessly while Tommy changes his testimony and damages his credibility. He has just strayed unwittingly from the straight-and-narrow and Sullivan knows she may never get him back on it. She also knows that the defence team is waiting for Tommy, although he is oblivious to their snare and yawns in the middle of his next answer.

Tommy explains how he was driven to the "devil church." In some ways, it sounds like The Place the other kids have described; in other ways, it sounds like a different location altogether. Sometimes, he testifies, he went to the green house. Green? Both the Sterling house and The Place are blue. And sometimes he walked to the green house with Travis Sterling and his sisters, and went in to visit Jim Elstad or Ed Revesz, he can't remember which. Although this is the first time a child has testified about a green house, this boy echoes the other children when he talks of driving to the devil church in a two-door blue van with white stripes. Though he needs Sullivan's help to spell "blue" to label his drawing of the van, he knows very well the number of seats and windows it had, the view from the van window, and the kind of road taken. And he recalls the interior of the devil church well enough to draw the three floors, the stairs, toy boxes, and the attic. But he forgets what happened to him once he got there. On the other hand, he is certain he never saw Ron or Linda at the devil church, just Travis and other "bad" people. Why they were bad, he can't exactly say. In fact, he tells Sullivan he was "having fun." By now, the prosecutor must be tearing her hair out.

But not defence lawyer Hugh Harradence. He couldn't ask for a more perfect witness than Tommy, who forgets things and often changes his story. Faced with such an easy stalk, Harradence can be kind to his prey. "Do you need a second to finish your snack?" he asks Tommy sweetly, after a short courtroom break. "No, I'm done," answers the witness.

Harradence: You remember yesterday when I was asking you some questions?

Tommy: Okay.

Harradence: We were just touching on Sandy and Janey?

Tommy: Yes.

Harradence: Do you remember how old [your sisters] would have been when you were at Ron and Linda's?

Tommy: No.

Harradence: Do you remember them being in diapers when you were at Ron and Linda's?

Tommy: Sandy was, but Janey wasn't.

Harradence: Do you remember talking to your mom that people were killed at Ron and Linda's?

Tommy: Yes.

Harradence: Did you actually see people killed?

Tommy: Yes.

Harradence: …Were they killed with guns or knives?

Tommy: Forget.

Harradence: Do you remember telling your mom you saw dogs being killed at Ron and Linda's?

Tommy: No.

Harradence: …Do you remember telling your mom that Ron and Linda used to stuff animal parts and human parts in your mouth and in your ears?

Tommy: No.

Harradence: Do you remember telling your mom that Ron and Linda gave you an electric shock?

Tommy: No.

Harradence: Do you remember telling your mom that Ron and Linda poured poison all over a lady and it ate at her skin and you saw that?

Tommy: Don't think so.

Harradence: ...Do you remember you saw a lady on the street and you told your mom that she was one of the people that had been at the devil church? I think you were at the post office.

Tommy: No.

Harradence: Do you remember a fellow by the name of Bob Convey that came and asked you some questions?

Tommy: Yes.

Harradence: ...Do you remember telling him that you saw Jim Elstad shoot somebody?

Tommy: No.

Harradence: ...Do you remember a policeman by the name of Rod Moor?

Tommy: Yes.

Harradence: And sometimes you'd go and see the police dogs after he'd talked to you?

Tommy: No.

Harradence: ...Is it right that your mom and dad have talked to you about this a lot?

Tommy: Yes.

Harradence: ...And do you remember Rod Moor asked you a lot of questions about this?

Tommy: Yes.

Harradence: Do you know Constable Bryden or Claudia?

Tommy: Yes.

Harradence: And she's sometimes been over to your house?

Tommy: Don't think so.

Harradence: ...Can you tell me who's the first policeman or policewoman that you talked to about this?

Tommy: Claudia... She was the only one I talked to.

Harradence: You told me you talked to Rod Moor, though.

Tommy: The only police lady.

Harradence: Do you remember ever when you were talking about this sort of stuff playing with dolls?... And that was when Rod Moor was asking you some questions?

Tommy: Yes.

Harradence: And do you ever remember being confused as to why these people were asking all these questions?

Tommy: No.

Harradence: When your mom was asking you these questions, did you ask her many questions about it, or do you remember?

Tommy: No... I never asked any questions about it to her, until now.

Harradence: Can you tell me some of the good things that you did at Ron and Linda's?

Tommy: Played with toys and then watched movies and went outside to play, went to school.

Harradence: Do you remember anybody at Ron and Linda's house ever getting mad at you kids?

Tommy: Yes. When I went in the bath with Duplo and... when I took it all apart, some water spilled on the floor and Ron screamed at me.

Is it hard for Tommy to keep all the interviews from getting muddled in his mind? He says it is, and I don't doubt it, especially when two or more years have elapsed since the events he describes. As fantastic as parts of Tommy's testimony sound, other things seem very real: Spilling the water on the Sterling floor and getting yelled at; enjoying the daycare toys and playing outside. I wonder what Tommy means when he says he doesn't remember feeling confused about why police were asking him questions. Does he mean he doesn't remember anything about the police interviews, or does he mean he doesn't remember being confused? And did he even understand the question Harradence asked him? I'm not sure I do.

Earl Kalenith, legal-aid lawyer for Travis, is next. Though he doesn't have children of his own, he knows how to treat Tommy. When Wimmer says the boy isn't speaking loudly enough into the mike, Kalenith calls upon Tommy's team spirit, as a father would a son, saying that both he and the boy must remember to speak up for the court as they go through the cross-exam. Pep talk or no, I bet the net result of Kalenith's questioning is the same for the jurors as it is for me: confusion and uncertainty about what to believe. Recently, Judge Wimmer has seen that they be supplied with pad and pencil, and now some take notes busily while others distractedly chew the pink eraser with furrowed brows.

Kalenith asks Tommy, "Did your dad tell you about Jim Elstad and Ed Revesz?" Not knowing where the question could lead, Tommy answers yes, innocently. When Kalenith asks him if his assailants wore uniforms, the boy says he doesn't remember. Why, then, did you say earlier that the men were police? "I don't know." Nor does the witness know if it was his dad who told him the men were "bad police." Tommy's memory is vague: "I just found out somehow."

Kalenith has snared Tommy without a whimper. A classic example of logic that his professors could be proud of, all the more so because the witness was such a willing participant, letting the lawyer lead him from question to question and failing to see the effect of the answers when strung together. If Tommy failed to see the cumulative effect of his testimony, it will not have escaped the jurors.

Tommy is in Grade 2. He combs his hair in the morning, brushes his teeth at bedtime, eats everything on his plate, plays Nintendo, does his homework, and plays with his friends. Most important of all, Tommy tries to be a good boy so his parents will be pleased. In this room, too, he wants to do the right thing. But the questions are hard.

Kalenith: Okay. Aside from those two [Jim Elstad and Ed Revesz], were there other bad police?

Tommy: Yes.

Kalenith: Do you remember how many there were?

Tommy: No...

Kalenith: Okay. So these other people that were police, how do you know if they were police or not, Tommy, if they weren't wearing any uniforms?

Tommy: I don't know...

Kalenith: And when your parents talked about them, they told you that the Sterlings were bad people, didn't they?

Tommy: They never told me that they were bad people.

Kalenith: They never said that?

Tommy: No.

Kalenith: Okay. How about Rod or Claudia, did they ever say the Sterlings were bad?

Tommy: No. I just knew they were bad 'cause they touched our privates.

Kalenith: So no one ever told you the Sterlings were bad?

Tommy: No.

Kalenith: Did people tell you, Tommy, that bad people touch kids' private parts?

Tommy: Not all the time.

Kalenith: Okay. But did someone ever tell you that, that bad people do that?

Tommy: Don't think, no.

Kalenith: Don't think so?

Tommy: Don't remember.

    This one Tommy can't answer; he doesn't remember. Kalenith chips away at Tommy's certainty, question after question. Yes, says Tommy, he remembers saying Travis touched him. No, he doesn't remember if Travis touched him once or more than once. Come to think of it, he isn't sure if Travis ever touched him at all. He's also got new ideas about the devil church and why he calls it that: "Because lots of bad people went there." But today he has no recollection of his interview months ago with Rod Moor, though anyone can hear him say on a police tape that he didn't have any particular reason for calling it the devil church. He has probably also forgotten that he told prosecutor Sullivan earlier today he was having fun at the church. If he does remember, I'm sure he is oblivious to the inherent contradiction in his testimony.
    Tommy's credibility is further dented by Don Mullord, legal-aid counsel for Ron Sterling and the third member of the defence team to cross-examine Tommy.

Mullord: When you think about it really hard, Tommy, can you remember Ron and Linda touching you?

Tommy: Yes.

Mullord: You think you can remember that, even though you told Rod Moor on the tape before that they didn't? Are you sure about that? You think maybe — is it possible that someone just told you that?

Tommy: No.

    Now that it's time for the judge and lawyers to assess the credibility of the evidence of the young witness, Wimmer excuses Tommy for the day and reconvenes court upstairs. When will this merry-go-round stop? The bags under Leslie Sullivan's eyes are getting bigger and Bruce Bauer's hair is going greyer by the day. The three defence lawyers, though possibly pleased Tommy lacks credibility, are finding it difficult to examine such a poor witness.
    It's time for a legal huddle, so Wimmer asks the jurors to leave the room. The three defence lawyers question not only what Tommy said during the police investigation, but also when he said it. For instance, did the boy mention the green house before or after talking with police? When did he first

talk about the devil church to police, and how many times has he changed his story since then? What about the time he told his father that he'd made up the whole story? Clearly, M'Lord, some of Tommy's statements are not reliable and should not be admitted as evidence in the trial.

Leslie Sullivan rebuts. Maybe Tommy can't keep his facts straight. But, M'Lord, if you don't admit his statements about the green house and the devil church, I want you to admit certain other statements. For instance, the terrified plea he once uttered after a therapy session at the clinic: "Are you going to get rid of me?" When the boy said this, he was apparently panic-stricken that his parents would abandon him because of the evil things he had disclosed.

Judge Wimmer must adjudicate the admissibility of the boy's pathetic plea as well as his evidence about the green house and the devil church. He will base his decision on two factors, the reliability of the statements and their necessity or importance to the overall evidence. In my business, we call these kinds of decisions "editing" — what you leave out is just as important as what you leave in. I had no idea judges vetted evidence in court and have mixed feelings about the jurors' being excused from the discussion. They have a crucial decision to make, so why shouldn't they know all the facts? On the one hand, jurors could never have too much information when something as important as the liberty of three people is at stake. On the other hand, they cannot do a good job if they're overloaded by information that confuses them needlessly. Wimmer knows the courtroom rules like the back of his hand and understands them better than anyone else here. He'll need time before deciding how to balance the evidence fairly. Listen, M'Lord: if you exclude the boy's devil-church evidence, says the prosecution, it's only fair to include his post-therapy plea. The three-man defence team wants neither piece of evidence included, unless they can cross-examine Tommy in a meaningful way. Until the judge decides how to apply the rules fairly, he adjourns court for the day.

The courtroom regulars are starting to look a little the worse for wear. "Tall Tim" and "Short Jim," two seniors who come every day and who talk to me at breaks, are looking perplexed. We take advantage of the early adjournment to go for coffee nearby.

Both men, I learn, are grandfathers and Jim's hobby is trials. For fifty years he has been sitting in Canadian courts, following one criminal case after another. Until he retired, he was an Anglican minister. I don't know how many confidences he's heard during his years of service but, whatever the number, I'll bet they give him an edge listening to testimony. After years of attending criminal trials he says about the system, "At least it's out in the open." But like me, he feels a trial where the word of young children is pitted against the word of adults poses special problems. It's hard to bend down to the kids' level, he says, speaking metaphorically. "That's why we're still in the primitive stage." If you listen to a child "literally," you'll never get to the truth. The daycare kids are talking on two different levels at once, fantasy and reality. "I couldn't make head or tail of it," he says.

Tall Tim, who was born on a Saskatchewan farm, is no less critical of the Sterling trial. "The evidence isn't sharp enough," he says, sipping from his cup. Nevertheless, he hasn't lost his own capacity to focus. Or synthesize what he has heard so far. "I tend to believe the kids," he says, telling me, "Think about it: If the kids had been talking to each other, they would have had their stories straight."

Tommy, Janey, and Sandy

The next witness, Tommy's dad, has probably learned to love and hate the world since the day his fell apart. What price would he have paid, I wonder, to avoid the sacrifice of his three children? He's a regular churchgoer, and I would like to know what he asks God for when he prays. In the Old Testament, God asked Abraham to kill his own son as a sacrifice. If God was testing Abraham, Abraham passed the test when he agreed to put his son, Isaac, on the chopping block. Biblical scholars still debate this story and Leonard Cohen sings about it. Why was God testing Abraham? Maybe T-Dad takes strength from the biblical passage and believes God is testing him, too. But there is a difference between sacrificing a child to prove you love God and sacrificing the child wantonly, not in praise of the Spirit but for the pleasure of the Flesh. Not just one child, mind you, but three.

T-dad is about thirty years old, handsome and clean cut. In his dark suit, he's one of the few people in the room who is formally dressed. But then, he's a successful businessman and probably plans to go back to the office as soon as his testimony is over.

Without meaning to, Leslie Sullivan stumps the witness right off the bat when she asks: When were you married? T-Dad can't remember, and facetiously scolds Sullivan for neglecting to warn him she'd ask. The laughter in the courtroom feeds the ham in Sullivan and relaxes her, and gives the witness time to think. After a second or two, he remembers, then tells the court the names of the children: Tommy, now seven; Janey, four; and Sandy, two. All three went to the Sterling daycare.

T-Dad always forgets his anniversary but September 27 is one date he will always remember. On that day in 1991 his wife told him she suspected that Janey had been abused by a "stranger." The next day, Saturday, he had a brief talk with Janey, two and a half years old at the time. She told him a "stranger" had hurt her and pointed to her genitals and bum. T-Dad promised her the stranger would never hurt her again. The next day the family went to church, then to the family farm for a get-together. On Monday, he went to the office briefly and quickly returned home when his wife called, concerned about Janey.

T-Dad testifies he came home and talked to his little girl. Sullivan wants to know what kind of questions he asked. "It's hard to describe the kind of question, but it could be compared to asking her if she stole candies out of the candy bowl." An interesting analogy, except that, if Janey's telling the truth, she was not the thief. He now gives the court a sample of the questions he asked his daughter that day.

T-Dad: Is the stranger [who hurt you] a boy or a girl?

Daughter Janey: A boy.

T-Dad: Do you know the stranger?

Janey: Yes.

T-Dad: Do you know where the stranger lives?

Janey: Yes.

T-Dad: Have you talked to the stranger?

Janey: Yes.

T-Dad: Would you show me where the stranger lives?

Janey: Yes.

And so, he testifies, he and his daughter went for a drive around Martensville, passing the houses of friends and eventually coming to the Sterling house. "There it is," Janey pointed. Her dad took her home and asked more questions.

T-Dad: Where did the stranger hurt you?

Janey: In a car.

T-Dad: What colour was the car?

Janey: Blue.

T-Dad: Did you have a car seat?

Janey: No.

T-Dad: A seat belt?

Janey: Yes.

T-Dad contacted the police and talked to Jim Elstad, who passed the complaint to Claudia Bryden. She told T-Dad and his wife to keep notes of what their three children might say. Their kids started to talk that night at supper and again at bedtime, telling their parents a story that, under different circumstances, would have been rated "R."

T-Dad became so obsessed that one night after putting the kids to bed, he drove by the Sterlings' and saw more than the usual number of garbage bags waiting to be picked up on the front lawn. T-Dad himself picked up the eight plastic bags, stashed them in the trunk of his car, and later went through them looking for incriminating evidence. All he found were pizza boxes, beer caps, and used medical supplies. Clearly the Sterlings had cleaned house, coincidentally one week before the police raid, though T-Dad knew nothing about it at the time.

T-Dad also became obsessed with finding the devil church Tommy talked about. Late at night, when he couldn't sleep and the "household was settled down," he'd grab a coffee and drive around town in search of a building like this. Having no luck, he approached a friend who flew a plane and asked him to conduct an aerial search. The friend, who was the former mayor of Martensville, soon found himself staring down on a blue building northwest of town that looked like it might be the one Tommy had told his dad about.

The pilot gave the coordinates to T-Dad, who drove northwest from town, turning left on the Power Line Road, right onto a grid road, and right into a snaking lane where he spotted the building in the middle of the night. Sitting alone in his car under a starry sky, T-Dad shone his headlights on what he thought was The Place. Next day he and another friend, a policeman, drove Tommy back to the building. As the three drove by slowly, the boy became very agitated and restless, fidgeting and shuffling in the back seat, and finally burying his face in the car seat upholstery.

When T-Dad comes to the end of his story, Sullivan returns to her seat, looking satisfied. Defence lawyer Hugh Harradence approaches the witness box to begin his cross-exam. Harradence must raise a reasonable doubt in the jurors' minds about the witness' credibility, and starts to do so by faulting T-Dad for the way he questioned his kids and planted ideas in their heads. But T-Dad holds his ground, saying he asked his kids questions, open-ended ones as a parent, not as a professional.

Harradence gets T-Dad to agree that the more the kids talked to their therapists, the more they disclosed at home. But the witness refutes the idea that he and his wife discussed their kids' disclosures with anyone else. Why would they tell anyone when the disclosures were so personal? he asks. Harradence seems to be trying to make T-dad look hysterical, like a parent on a witch hunt. T-Dad stays calm, while acknowledging that the experience changed his life profoundly. "My kids told me they were raped. I was going to find out who."

Harradence loves a chase. Looking like a fox among hens, he taunts T-Dad: You "investigated" the matter yourself before contacting the police. The witness admits he did, and sees nothing wrong with this. But after he called the police, he did as he was told. For instance, Claudia Bryden told him to make notes of his kids' disclosures and he complied, writing down all sorts of things, including the big surprise his son gave him one day. Ever since Judge Wimmer agreed to allow as evidence a statement Tommy made to his father, the three defence lawyers have been itching to let jurors hear it, and now they have their chance. Harradence pounces: Tommy once told you he'd made the whole story up, didn't he? T-Dad admits coolly that this is so, explaining that this was his son's way of ending the uncomfortable discussion they were having. In other words, Tommy was bluffing.

If two-and-a-half-year-old Janey had also told T-dad she'd made it all up, he would have been a very happy man. But she didn't and "I believed my child." He wanted to go to police right away, but at the same time was reluctant. He procrastinated, hoping Janey would say the "stranger" had done nothing to her. But she did not change her story and her father was forced to get in touch with police.

While T-Dad drove around town with his coffee, searching for the devil church Tommy described, he also looked for the green store with elephants that Janey talked about. A lot of what she told her dad was "unclear" and the details varied from telling to telling. But the essence remained the same. T-Dad is a calm and credible witness, and a man who clearly loves his kids.

T-Mom is the next witness. Until five years ago she would not have been allowed to give "hearsay" evidence, which was inadmissible under Canadian law. In light of the ever-increasing number of cases involving children, the Supreme Court of Canada ruled in 1990 that "hearsay evidence of a child's statement on crimes committed against the child should be received," but only on two conditions: the evidence must be necessary for the court to hear, and it must be reliable. Judge Wimmer recently ruled that Janey's statement to her mother, which we are about to hear, is both necessary and reliable.

Everything about T-Mom is somewhere in the middle: height, hair length, hair colour, dress, age. Even the volume of her voice and the manner in which she tells her story to prosecutor Leslie Sullivan are measured.

T-Mom worked shifts. Because her husband had his own business and there was no one at home when she worked weekdays, the couple needed a babysitter. In early 1990, when Tommy was four and Janey two, the parents began to leave the children at the Sterling house. Shortly after their third child Sandy was born in 1991, she too was cared for by Linda Sterling. "I had some hesitation, but it was convenient," says T-Mom. She claims there was no baby-gate at the top of the basement stairs, that Linda Sterling said she never drove the kids anywhere and therefore found car booster seats pointless, and that Sterling didn't change the baby's diapers often enough, even though T-Mom left spares. If she didn't think her three kids were receiving proper care, she consoled herself that they were in Linda's care for short periods only, eight days a month on average, for four hours at a time.

One night, while T-Mom was still at work, T-Dad got home early, bathed the kids and put them in pyjamas. When T-Mom returned, she noticed that Janey had soiled her pyjama bottoms, so T-Mom bathed her two-year-old again. (She has specialized training, but if I gave more specifics, it might provide clues to her identity and that of her children. Let's just say her profession requires her to be observant.) When T-Mom undressed her daughter for the bath, she saw that the skin between the girl's legs was unusually red. The skin on the buttocks was "excoriated," so she applied a water-repellent cream.

T-Mom says she didn't tell her husband right away, but when she told Janey she would be babysat at the Sterlings' the next day, Janey started to cry. That night a nightmare woke Janey and she crawled into bed with her parents. The next day, Friday, September 27, despite Janey's story, tears, and bad dreams, T-Mom took her three children to the Sterling daycare and went to work.

It must be painful to admit this to the court, even more so to admit it to herself. Sometimes she can't, and keeps confusing Thursday and Friday when answering Sullivan's questions. When the lawyer suddenly interrupts her exam-in-chief to ask why, the witness explains she has momentarily blocked out Friday, September 27. Looking sad and angry at the same time, she says that the last Friday in September of 1991, the day she took Janey back to the Sterlings, no longer exists in her mind.

T-Mom testifies that when she picked up her kids that day, she questioned

Janey again. The girl told her there was a stranger at the Sterling house and that the stranger hit her. Then the toddler removed her doll's pants, put cream on its vaginal area, and hit her doll to show her mother how the stranger had hit her. She said the stranger did it with a pink rope, which might have been a white one: Janey didn't know her colours very well and confused these two at that stage of her development.

Janey also confused the concept of "stranger," or twisted it to match her training. T-Mom testifies that she and T-Dad had taught Janey not to trust people she didn't know, and encouraged her to trust the ones she did. Perhaps when Janey was molested, her little-girl logic took a 180-degree turn that might have gone like this: Mommy and Daddy taught me that strangers are the only ones who hurt you, and a man I know has just hurt me. Therefore, he must be a stranger and not someone I know. How else could she understand what had happened to her, except by taking her parents' training literally? The man who used to be on her "familiar" list was moved to a "stranger" list, even though she'd seen him several times a month for at least a year. According to T-Mom, Janey told her that the stranger, or strangers, were "Ravis and Uncle."

The best defence is a good offence. Prosecutor Sullivan has learned to second-guess her opponents and anticipate the defence team's strategy. In this case, she knows they will try to prove that everyone in Martensville from the parents to the police gave the children clues and put ideas in their heads. So the question they're bound to put to T-Mom when they get their chance is the one Sullivan must present now. She asks the witness: Why did you question Janey so many times? T-Mom replies: "As a mother I was not able to accept that I might have put my children in a position where something had happened to them." She stops, unable to continue until she takes a sip of water. "I needed to hear it repeatedly until I was able to accept what had happened."

She heard Janey's news, but blocked it out of her mind. Maybe, she hoped, if she clasped her daughter's disclosure to her breast and hid it there long enough, it would disappear. T-Mom wiped a day off the calendar, told herself that nothing had happened, and spoke to no one. She hid the news from her husband for a day. While she kept her silence she also held out hope, which never came. T-Mom starts to cry and Sullivan hands her a tissue.

Everyone needs a break, including Judge Wimmer, who's writing as fast and furiously as the journalists and the defence. He grants a ten-minute break, long enough for Janis and me to decide where we'll go for lunch.

When court reconvenes, T-Mom testifies that by the time she took Janey to the doctor several days later, much of the redness on the girl's buttocks and genitals had disappeared. But Janey was still upset. With her security blanket in one hand and a thumb in her mouth, Janey resisted her mother's attempts to undress her for the doctor's exam and lab tests.

According to the witness, Janey would sometimes lapse into "trancelike states" over the next few months, drop her head, and sob, "Mommy, I'm not a bad girl." Perhaps T-Mom wondered why she said these things and why her son begged her not to give him away for being bad, all the more so because she and her husband avoided labels like "good" and "bad" when disciplining their children. It sounds as though the T-parents had to cope with at least two things at once, their kids' strange behaviours, and the way the behaviours jeopardized their own self-esteem as parents. The parents tried to maintain their composure and kept reassuring Janey with hugs and kisses that she was a good girl.

The physical findings were bad enough without being compounded by a set of behavioural changes that T-Mom now rattles off for prosecutor Sullivan: inappropriate touching of the genitals of each other and their parents; Tommy's persistent bedwetting and diarrhoea; nightmares; destructive play; depression; withdrawal; Janey's exceeding compliance; and Tommy's compulsive disorder, which required that the stuffed toys in his bedroom always be arranged in the exact same order.

Therapy has helped the children, says T-Mom, and it has also helped her and her husband. The children's symptoms come and go. Much of the children's therapy depends on their capacity to communicate. At the time of the alleged incidents, Janey had just learned to talk but Sandy, still in diapers, had not. Did anything happen to her? And if it did, does she remember anything now?

Sullivan continues the examination-in-chief, and the witness says that Janey and Tommy, her two oldest children, still exhibit a great deal of anxiety. After one session with the therapist, Tommy started to cry and asked his parents if they planned to give him away. Because Tommy is not here in person, the parts of his evidence he gave to his mother will now be given to the court by her as hearsay. Fortunately for the family, Judge Wimmer decided Tommy's emotional outburst about being given away was an admissible piece of evidence, like Janey's assertion "I'm not a bad girl." Had he ruled these inadmissible, or had the legislation not recently been changed to permit parental hearsay, T-Mom could not have given her children's statements to the court.

Hugh Harradence limps slowly to the lectern to begin his cross-examination. Where did he learn to tack the word "ma'am" onto the end of every other question? It sounds so condescending. If I were T-Mom, I'd add "sir" to my answers, in just the right tone to avoid being found in contempt. But Harradence is a man you wouldn't want to annoy with wisecracks. As a witness, you wouldn't want to let your guard down for one minute by paying too much attention to his obvious vulnerability and not enough heed to your own. If you did, this defence lawyer would take you by surprise, with his sly humour and keen intelligence. Just think of him as a cross between Maxwell Smart and Lucien Bouchard, and you get the picture. I bet he's an excellent lawyer to his clients; I can see he is deadly to a witness.

He asks T-Mom the question everyone in the room wants answered: If things were so bad at the Sterling daycare, why did you take your children there? T-Mom answers calmly, "I had some hesitations, but it was convenient. The kids didn't want to go back — they were fighting me." If I read between the lines, neither the children nor the mother much liked the Sterling setup. But T-Mom regarded Janey's anxiety as normal. "We had a new baby, Mom was going back to work, and she [Janey] was going back to the babysitter's."

Few mothers want to leave their children regularly in someone else's care. Most Canadian women would prefer to stay home with their children rather than put them in daycare, according to a 1991 Decima poll. But T-Mom may not have had much choice if her family needed the money, and if she wanted job security, seniority, and her own pension at the end of her career. She faced the dilemma that confronts many women in this country: who looks after their children if they go to work?

T-Mom has brought her notepad to court. Harradence knows what her journal says because he read it in preparation for his cross-exam. He reminds her that she once wrote, "Explained to Tommy that Travis had been touching Janey's private parts... Asked Tommy if Linda touched their private parts." Harradence makes it impossible for T-Mom to deny ever making the notation, when he cites the date: "October 28, 1991...on page 4 of the notes, ma'am." He continues, "Before he [Tommy] told you anything, you told him?... Despite...explicit instruction from Constable Bryden that you were not to lead these children?" Judge Wimmer interrupts, "I don't think that's leading him." Harradence apologizes to T-Mom.

T-Mom's diary helps her keep her dates straight during the cross-exam. On April 1, 1992, Tommy first talked to her about the devil church. On April 11, she noted her son's "bizarre" stories about poking out the eyes of live dogs and cutting their heads off. Before long, her son graduated to tales of killing children at the devil church and at the Sterling house. Sometimes the entrails were put in his mouth, a detail his sister Janey corroborated. Brother and sister also told their mother about getting electric shocks from Ron and Travis Sterling.

How is it possible, Harradence asks, peering over his reading glasses, that you and Claudia Bryden once spent ninety minutes together over coffee at her place, yet did not discuss the investigation at all? T-Mom stays cool and maintains that she and Bryden talked about "kid things," looking at Bryden's children's baby albums and discussing how their children played together, as mothers will. She explains that even if she had wanted to discuss the investigation, Bryden refused to, fearing that eventually it could be used to hurt the case. Harradence doesn't buy that, but he lets the matter drop. Ma'am, what about this book? Harradence continues, handing her a copy of *The Secret of the Silver Horse*. Yes, she remembers reading the book, published by the federal government, which encourages children to disclose abuse and which Bryden gave to T-Mom during the early stages of the investigation.

After pausing long enough for jurors to absorb the answer, Harradence asks, Isn't it true that you were with your son at the post office April 30, when he saw a woman he said he'd seen before at the devil church and she "had a knife and cut a lady's arm off." At the mention of this, Ron Sterling's neck turns red and his ears go flat to his head. Flattening their ears is a thing scared cats and angry dogs do, but very few people do. In our family, my sister inherited the trait from our maternal grandfather and, on command, wiggles them as a joke. But this is no joke.

"Thank you, ma'am." Harradence has completed his cross and gives way to his colleagues, Earl Kalenith and Don Mullord. When Kalenith quizzes T-Mom about Ravis and Uncle, she says she'd taught her children to have "their own personal space and that their body is their own, and people other than their mom and dad, or doctors...shouldn't be touching them, and shouldn't be doing that without permission, and it shouldn't be in a forceful manner. And we always told them that it would be a stranger. We always referred to the [offending] person as a stranger." In other words, she taught her daughter to mistrust strangers because only strangers would hurt her. If T-Mom had known more about child molesters, she might have taught her daughter that an adult who abuses female children is usually known to the victim, and may even be a member of the family. In light of T-Mom's teaching, Janey must have been very confused if two men she knew, Ravis and Uncle, acted like strangers.

Mullord, the last of the three lawyers to cross-examine T-Mom, asks the witness when she actually recalled Janey's reference to "Ravis and Uncle." She says it was just last week, going through her notes in preparation for court. Mullord stares at her in stony silence, hoping the jurors will have as much trouble believing the witness as he does, then asks, Do you remember showing your kids a photo of a vibrator in a Consumer's catalogue? T-Mom answers no, though she does remember looking with her children through a Christmas catalogue and coming across a vibrator. When Janey saw it, T-Mom testifies, she said it looked like the one she'd seen at the Sterling house.

In fact, T-mom knows the incident occurred on December 16, 1991, because she wrote the date above her diary entry. Mullord pounces. Were you aware that a vibrator had been photographed at the Sterling residence during a search on December 12? No, answers the witness. And no one told you that? No, she says.

If Mullord were a writer instead of a lawyer and examined the vibrator stories closely, he'd marvel at how they mirror each other: Janey, a two-and-a-half-year-old girl, apparently saw a real vibrator before seeing a picture of one in her mother's catalogue. Claudia Bryden, an adult, testified that she'd seen pictures of vibrators in catalogues long before seeing the real thing at the Sterling house during the raid. If this were a work of fiction instead of a criminal trial, readers might think the author invented these things to keep them turning the page.

The cross-examination is finished. Even if it weren't, Judge Wimmer would have to call a break because a juror is having a coughing fit. T-Mom steps down from the witness box and, as she does, Ron Sterling stops writing in his notepad and lowers his gaze. Then he purses his lips and begins to tap his pad on his knee, as though venting excess energy.

Noon, as usual, meant spicy food served on the cheap at Saigon Rose. Janis and I picked a corner table for a bit of privacy, but no sooner had we ordered and begun to re-hash the morning's testimony than Ron Sterling walked in with one of the defence lawyers. We kept our heads and voices down and continued to talk shop. When it was time to pay — I still don't know how it happened — Ron Sterling materialized at the front of the line, holding a five-dollar bill, asking Rose how much my lunch was. I was trying to fish some money out of my purse, but Rose was in a hurry and Sterling's money looked good to her, so she took it despite my protests. When I did get my wallet out of my purse and tried to pay Sterling back, he refused to take it. I was annoyed, but couldn't imagine running up behind him in court stuffing money in his pocket. So much for my journalistic integrity.

Back in court, it's time to hear, though not see, the next child witness. Until now we have heard T-Mom speak on behalf of her daughter, Janey. But that testimony is less valuable than the girl's own words because, on the scales of justice, hearsay evidence weighs less than direct evidence. But direct evidence is difficult to obtain from a child as young as Janey, and Wimmer must test the four-and-a-half-year-old to see if she's capable of speaking for herself. If she is, it will definitely help the court. Though Janey has given evidence to the police three times before, this is her first time in court, and at least two years have passed since the alleged events.

What will Janey remember? Can she communicate it? She was little more than two when she told her story to her mother for the first time, and had just turned four when she told Rod Moor at the police station in Saskatoon — twenty months later. The unreasonably long time until the formal statement on tape, when combined with uncertainty about the time of the alleged crime, has produced what Judge Wimmer calls a police tape "of little or no value" in telling the girl's side of the story.

It would be a pity for Sullivan if Wimmer ruled the tape inadmissible. I've heard through the informal network that she is dying to play it for the jury. Apparently, it captures Janey saying things a four-year-old never would have said unless she knew what she was talking about. Unfortunately, it also captures Rod Moor saying things he never would said have if he'd known more about proper interview techniques. Sullivan is willing to pay the price of letting jurors hear Moor's interview, in return for letting them hear Janey's recorded disclosures. But Judge Wimmer doesn't like the tradeoff. Citing an Ontario precedent he found while doing his research, he says a taped disclosure as belated as Janey's might have been rehearsed. At the very least, he doubts it is meaningful, especially since the tape shows how Rod Moor "put words in [Janey's] mouth." After a few minutes' more reflection, he reaches a decision: Because the time lapse was not reasonable, the prosecution falters. In other words, because police did their job neither expediently nor well, their tape is not worth a tinker's damn. "So there you have it. I don't think the tape should be played," says the judge. "That's fine, M'Lord," responds Sullivan, frowning. Having made the ruling, Wimmer calls for a break and whisks through his private door.

I'm glad we have gun control in this country. One of the reporters tells me he's afraid to come to court the day of the verdict because he fears an irate parent will hold us all hostage in the name of justice. I think he's getting paranoid, and tell him so. But I'll bet T-Mom and T-Dad are fuming, asking themselves what they could have done differently. T-Dad went to the police soon after Janey told him her story. But because they delayed unduly in taping her disclosure, the court has denied jurors the chance to hear it. Now the preschooler must climb into the witness box and tell her story one more time, or whatever parts she remembers, this time to strangers.

Let me get this straight. Janey's taped statement to police, made more than a year after the alleged incident at the Sterling house, is useless to the court. The lengthy lapse was not "reasonable" and she might have had time to "rehearse" her performance before taping it in the Soft Room. Here in the courtroom, a year after the taping and possibly more than two years since the alleged crime, Janey will get another crack at telling her story. Wouldn't this longer time lapse cause an even greater lapse of memory? Putting Janey on the stand to give direct testimony and be cross-examined may make legal sense, but does it make common sense?

Wimmer sends for the jurors, whose minds are uncluttered by knowledge of the tape. Janey enters the witness box. The moment she opens her mouth to take the truth test, she becomes "Polliwog" to me. The preschooler sounds like a tadpole lounging on a lilypad, so enchanting is her tiny voice. Her mastery of English, even after three or four years of practice, is still developing, and her pronunciation is careful and deliberate. Like all the child witnesses, Polliwog is not seen by anybody but the court — the judge, lawyers, jurors, and the accused — though all of us in the upstairs courtroom can hear her. In front of the closed-circuit TV, we listen intently to Polliwog as she tries to prove to the judge she can perceive, recollect, and communicate evidence. On the one hand, I feel like cheering her on; on the other, I wonder if her effort is worth all the fuss.

Sullivan thinks it's worth it. She has to. "Watcha got in your hand?" she asks Janey in her best girl guide leader voice. Janey answers, "Pink, my teddy bear." What's your mom's name? "Mom." I bet everybody wants to hug her, even the defence lawyers. Polliwog remembers her age; her birthday; her last birthday party; her address; the names of her playschool teacher, her playschool friends, and her playschool activities. She remembers her brother's name — changed here to Tommy — and "Sandy," her baby sister's name. She also knows what it means to tell the truth. When questioned by Sullivan, Janey asserts that her teddy bear is pink, not blue. The defence is sceptical that the young girl can truly recollect, but Judge Wimmer is satisfied that, in general, she can perceive and recollect events and communicate them, and that she knows what it means to tell the truth. Now he must establish her understanding of the word "promise."

Wimmer turns his head in the direction of the little girl and asks, "Can you look at me for a minute?... Will you promise me that you'll tell the truth?" The tadpole voice has a smile in it: "Yeah." It's not the traditional hand-on-the-Bible commitment, but it's good enough. And it's the closest thing to an oath Wimmer is going to get. Sullivan steps up to the witness box and, with her back to the camera, proceeds to examine the girl, "Janey, what are you here to talk about?" Polliwog answers, "The truth." The prosecutor then asks the witness to recollect her days at the Sterling house. Janey says, "My mom took me and she thought it was a good place." She remembers the bacon-and-toast breakfasts, the cartoons on TV, the bathroom and the kitchen, and the sword. The sword, she claims, was silver and had a face on the handle. Ron Sterling waved it back and forth and almost hit her with it, saying, "I'm going to kill you." It happened in a room made of cement. She felt "sad." She says Ron and Linda "used to be good people, now they're bad people... They did bad things."

Before long, Janey tells the Crown prosecutor she needs a short break, before anyone else asks her questions. It's a good time to call my dentist, who says the pain in my jaw may come from clamping it at night, and that maybe I need a plastic retainer to relax it while I sleep. "Have you been experiencing stress lately?" he asks.

Hugh Harradence cross-examines the preschooler: Janey, you said that Ron and Linda used to be good people. "Yeah," she answers. And somebody told you they're bad people now? "Yeah," she answers. Did your mom tell you they were bad people? "Yeah," she answers, oblivious to the leading nature of the question. And did your mom tell you that they did bad things? "No," Janey replies. The defence lawyer concludes: Other than what you've told us today, you don't remember anything else bad that might have happened there? Harradence realizes the question is leading and rephrases it: Do you remember anything else bad that might have happened there? "No," she replies. Thank you very much, Janey. I have no more questions.

Don Mullord, stroking his red beard, which looks black on TV, begins his cross-exam: Can you remember any good things at Ron and Linda's? "No," answers the girl. Do you think the room made of cement might have been a dream? "No," she answers, but not till after Mullord explains to her the word "dream."

If the almost-five-year-old Janey is the youngest witness to take the stand, Sally is the oldest at fifteen. The two girls bracket the other five children like bookends. And like bookends are their allegations, which stand on their own. Why? Both girls claimed Travis Sterling abused them, and both reported the abuse to adults they trusted. The adults, in turn, went to the police before the police came to them. This chain of events distinguishes these two girls from the other child plaintiffs in this case, on whose doors Claudia Bryden knocked and in whose minds she and Rod Moor planted unsavoury thoughts about Travis and Ron and Linda Sterling, according to the three-man defence team. As we shall soon see, the procedure the two girls followed when alleging sexual assault will be critical to the jury's eventual outcome.

In June 1988, when Sally told her school guidance counsellor about Travis, she wanted to save herself, and others, from Travis Sterling. According to the testimony of Sally's high school counsellor, who is now in the witness box, the girl seemed emotionally conflicted when she came to her office, wanting to tell what Travis had done to her without having to betray him. The counsellor, professionally trained in such matters, immediately arranged for a child protection worker to hear the girl's story and take it to the police. Next day Darryl Ford, then police chief, came to the school to talk with Sally in the counsellor's office. Now that the ball was in the court of the Martensville Police, why did they drop it?

Three years later, in 1991, after Janey told her mother about being abused by "Ravis and Uncle," T-Dad spoke to police. Claudia Bryden then learned it was the second complaint against Travis Sterling, and removed the shroud from Sally's long-buried file. Thus Janey, then the youngest daycare child except for her baby sister, provided the spark that ignited the investigation. Out of the mouth of babes...

If the allegations are true, Travis Sterling, a fully grown adult, molested Sally when she was ten years old and, three years later, Janey when she was just over two. Now fifteen-year-old Sally is a much more articulate witness than the almost-five-year-old Janey.

Sally tells the two courtrooms, upstairs and down, that her family moved to Martensville when she was three. When she started kindergarten, her dad would take her to the Sterling house at 7 o'clock in the morning, where she'd nap on the couch till it was time to go to school. Linda Sterling, after tucking the girl in, would go back to sleep. For a few years, nothing unusual happened at the Sterlings' and Sally says she liked going there. When she turned ten everything changed. Linda Sterling still came to the door to let Sally in each morning, and returned to her bedroom and shut the door. But Travis started a new habit.

In the spring of that year — Sally remembers that the ground was still covered with snow — Travis "started touching me where he wasn't supposed to." The young man, then nineteen, began his new routine by sitting on the couch where Sally lay sleeping, and lifting the blankets and her shirt to rub her breasts. Not discouraged when she turned her back to him, Travis began to fondle her bum, first outside her panties then inside. Once, he tried to rub her vagina. "I was really scared," the girl says. Yet, she was worried that if she said anything, "he might hurt me." So for a while she told no one.

The ten-year old girl hoped that Travis would go away if she said nothing and pretended to sleep, but her passive resistance seemed to encourage him. Nestled up against her on the couch, he violated her boundaries with increasing interest, every day for five or six weeks. If she was wearing a dress, he lifted it. Sometimes he unzipped her pants and spread her legs. Once he even tried to insert his finger in her vagina. She knew for sure it was Travis because she sometimes opened her eyes. When she saw him molesting her, time stood still. All the more so because the hands on the clock of the living room wall seemed to take forever to reach 8 o'clock, the time the other daycare kids began to arrive. With the first knock on the door, Linda came running and Travis went to his room to get dressed for work. Sally knew that what he did was wrong and that she must put a stop to it. She was afraid to tell her parents but knew she had to talk to someone. The previous year, in Grade 3, she'd learned that kids should not blame themselves if this sort of thing happened.

"Feeling Yes, Feeling No" was the name of the sex-education course the guidance counsellor regularly taught at Sally's school. Produced by the National Film Board, the six-hour video program helps teach children to trust their feelings, to know the difference between someone's good touch and bad touch, and to learn about sexual abuse and what to do about it. The videotapes empowered Sally to pluck up her courage and talk to her guidance counsellor, though not without difficulty. She tells the court, "I felt confused...angry... He had no right doing that to me." While she was putting up with Travis Sterling's abuse, her parents were in the midst of separating. Her grades dropped dramatically and she sought counselling.

Sally's personal trials are history, and if you're a defence lawyer like Earl Kalenith, the passage of time can be your friend, or so you hope. Kalenith bounds to the witness box and begins to cross-examine the witness: "Would you agree with me that it's difficult to remember everything exactly right that happened five years ago?" The girl agrees. But she doesn't let Kalenith change her position, and although her memory is sometimes shaky, she appears confident. Sally's age and burgeoning maturity provide a remarkable contrast to Polliwog, and her articulateness and cognitive development make her sound more credible than the younger kids.

At fifteen, Sally knows how to talk precisely about anatomy, even if she doesn't like to in public. When asked what a bum is, she explains to the court that it's just below the waist and just above where the legs come together at the back. How different this description is from the one Polliwog might have given and the one Kenny did give to the court. Yet Sally is still a child and frequently sounds like the younger witnesses when she echoes their mixed reviews of the Sterling care. She remembers Travis abusing her one minute and Ron putting Band-Aids on her cuts the next. Kalenith says to Sally, "Now in what you were describing...I take it that at no time did Travis ever hurt you... And nothing that happened there during those times ever made you cry." Sally answers no to both. Pardon me? I feel like jumping up and shouting: What Travis allegedly did to Sally went far beyond tears, and Band-Aids.

But there's not a peep in the upstairs room as Kalenith continues his cross-examination. Do you know if your counsellor contacted your parents that day? Yes, she did, says the witness, because my parents talked to me about it that night and I hadn't told them, and she was the only one who could have told them. Was it your understanding that no charge was proceeding because they (police) didn't think there was enough evidence? The teen answers yes.

Freddy speaks again

It's been months since I heard Freddy's voice, though I certainly haven't forgotten it. When he is examined by prosecutor Bruce Bauer, the eleven-year-old tells the same story he told at Tammy's trial, in the same way, pulling up dry words. This time Freddy is an old hand at courtroom procedure, and more sure of himself, though he sounds tired and worn out. If only he blew his nose during one of the frequent breaks he asks for, maybe he'd stop sniffling into the mike .

Freddy clearly recalls his snapshots of the Sterlings: Travis Sterling forcing him to look at *Penthouse* magazines with "naked men and women"; the "whiplike thing"; the cage; the pillowcase over his head; being shoved outside, shirtless, in midwinter; Travis fondling him; Travis sodomizing him; Travis making him perform fellatio on his "big" penis; Ron Sterling tying his arms, blindfolding and gagging him, and driving to The Place; watching Travis hang Tommy up by one arm; seeing Travis fondle Kenny and hearing Kenny's "high-pitched shriek"; seeing Ron Sterling hose down Frank and shut him in the freezer at The Place.

The stress of telling all this to the court gives Freddy a headache. Judge Wimmer dismisses him even though prosecutor Bauer hasn't completed the examination-in-chief. He also dismisses the jury, then proceeds to discuss the witness order and whether it's proper to let Freddy's father go next, even before Bauer has finished questioning the boy, not the usual procedure.

The defence team argues this point of law, debating whether the interruption of Freddy's testimony might confuse jurors. Judge Wimmer decides that in keeping with the witness-order list drawn up by prosecutors Bruce Bauer and Leslie Sullivan, the son's testimony will be suspended so that the father can go next. F-Dad did not testify at Tammy's trial.

The witness is thirtyish and handsome, even more so when he smiles, and it's obvious he loves his son Freddy. During the three years the child went to the daycare, F-Dad sometimes picked him up at the end of the work day. But on three occasions when he went to the Sterling house to get his son, Freddy was not there and Linda Sterling said he was at the house of a friend. On those days, F-Dad testifies, he was greeted by Linda Sterling and her son, Travis, who was dressed in a housecoat even though it was midafternoon. F-Dad says he met numerous guests at the house, including police officers.

F-Dad recalls that, at some time after Freddy began to go the Sterling house, the boy began to wet his bed at night and vomit early in the morning. He became "very emotional and easily upset by trivial things," and would cry over problems with his homework or having to eat a plate of liver. Freddy smiled when his parents told him, in fall 1991, that the family was moving to a small town in British Columbia. The boy's happiness was cut short the day Claudia Bryden called from Martensville to announce the daycare investigation and Freddy's possible involvement. This prompted his parents to move back to Saskatchewan just several months after leaving, so that Freddy could get professional help.

I read somewhere recently that a father has more trouble than a mother accepting that his child may have been abused, especially when it's his son. The male ego balks at the aggression of other males whereas the female, even if she detests aggressive behaviour, may respond more pragmatically. F-dad says that after that hearing Freddy might have been abused, he "hadn't really accepted that this was a possibility yet" and it took him a month to come to terms with the possibility. During this time he and his wife often questioned Freddy. F-Mom took notes, even if the child got up in the middle of the night to talk. The following year, 1992, they arranged for Freddy to start therapy. The boy seemed to benefit from his sessions with Rod Butler, as F-Dad explains: "He would be quite tense before and he'd tell us that he was relieved afterwards."

Hugh Harradence has listened to the examination-in-chief. He insists that F-Dad, F-Mom, and Freddy returned to Saskatoon because of Claudia Bryden. F-Dad insists they moved back because of work opportunities and for Freddy's well-being. F-Dad is polite towards Harradence, though clearly frustrated by the lawyer's badgering. Harradence barks, "Sexual assault" — when did Freddy start using the term? and where did he learn the meaning? F-Dad says he doesn't know. Nor does he remember when Freddy first said that Linda Sterling, who is Harradence's client, had done things to him. Harradence baits the witness: Would it be fair to say Freddy's disclosures took on a "snowball effect"? F-Dad admits his son's disclosures became more numerous with time, and that his son never looked unusual when he returned from daycare. How the boy acted was another matter.

Hugh Harradence is a hard act to follow because his cross-examination of F-Dad was very provocative, keeping the witness on his toes and the public on edge. Don Mullord, the legal-aid lawyer for Ron Sterling, now rises to cross-examine F-Dad in a completely different manner — one I would classify "thorough" rather than exciting. If the thirty or so members of the public are not all listening to Mullord, I hope Judge Wimmer and the jurors are. It's one thing for the folks in the gallery, including some heavy-lidded journalists, to let their attention wander and quite another matter for a court official to snooze in the middle of someone's testimony. To stay awake Wimmer may resort to pinching himself or calling a break soon. For now, he removes his glasses and rubs the bridge of his nose while Mullord continues.

My mind wanders to the pretty Native woman in the wheelchair who comes here every day. What would it be like to be paraplegic, dependent on other people for everything? What would it be like to be the middle-aged farmer by the window, who shifts in his seat as though he has back problems? Farmers have all sorts of back problems, though newer tractors with hydraulic springs aren't nearly as hard as the old ones. "New Diesel" says another guy's tractor cap, obediently removed and put on the bench beside him, like in church. Mullord, the high priest in black who is schooled in Latin, is still attempting to discredit F-Dad's story in front of the twelve apostles. Suddenly, into the sepulchral silence and the sonorous snoozing breaks the unexpected rumbling of my stomach. Speed it up, Mullord.

In the witness box F-Dad testifies that although Freddy looked "normal" and insisted that he was fine, he and F-Mom "believed something had happened" because the boy's body language was "angry." He would "jump at any opportunity" to keep from going to the daycare.

At 2 o'clock, Freddy takes the stand again while, on the upstairs court monitor, we watch prosecutor Bruce Bauer reviewing his list of questions. In all likelihood, Freddy would like nothing better than to thumb his nose at them. On this brilliant winter day, a boy his age should be in school thinking about playing hookey instead of cooped up in a courthouse.

Freddy sighs and hesitates when it's time to resume the examination-in-chief, cut short so his dad could testify. The first story he recounts goes like this: He and Ron Sterling were at The Place, in the bedroom. Ron Sterling pulled Freddy onto the bed and then knelt beside him. He began to suck the boy's stomach. "I felt sickened," is all the boy can say. There are more stories about sucking, and Bauer wants Freddy to tell them. The boy sighs again, then proceeds: He and Ron Sterling and a daycare chum, Tommy, were at The Place. Ron ordered Tommy to suck on Freddy's penis. When Tommy did, Freddy admits, his penis got hard. While the two boys did as they were told, Ron Sterling watched and, according to Freddy, said nothing. On another occasion Ron Sterling, double-barrelled shotgun in hand, ordered Freddy to suck his penis. The boy complied while the man's penis got hard and he groaned.

Freddy's doing pretty well remembering these details, a bit too well for the defence's liking. Hugh Harradence complains that the boy's testimony is a script, not a recollection. He is referring to the special list Freddy made for court, which he reads from when he forgets something. Rebutting this, Bruce Bauer replies, It's true Freddy didn't make his list until well after the events, so it's more like a memory aid than a genuine past recollection recorded. The deadlock is settled when Wimmer rules that Freddy can continue to use his list. If in future the defence team wants to let a witness use a list, he says he'll allow that too.

A criminal trial is a contest at the end of which the side with the strongest story or the greater credibility wins — usually, though not always, the same thing. This win-lose strategy strikes me as counterproductive at best, primitive at worst, and makes me wonder why winning seems more important than uncovering the truth. I'd like to start wearing my new T-shirt to court that says, "Jury: 12 persons chosen to decide who has the better lawyer," but Wimmer would probably find me in contempt and throw me out.

The more enthusiastic the lawyer, the more incompetent he or she may try to make the police look. Blaming someone else is easier than examining the complexity of a problem. If the police investigation was poor, we should learn why it was. It's time to examine the pressing social problems facing the Canadian community now that mothers and fathers spend all day at work and leave their preschool children in the care of others. Either our society has obligations to protect children or it doesn't. It isn't good enough to come to court just to prove that my lawyer is better than yours.

Childhood is not a commodity. Innocence cannot be measured. So how can anyone prove these things were stolen, when even the expert witnesses don't agree on the signs? A loss like this is hard to prove, so stealthy is the thief's leavetaking and so indecipherable his fingerprints. But the jurors get no respite. They must reach a verdict and decide whether one or more of the Sterlings stole the innocence of the children. Even if the kids are telling the truth, and even if the prosecutors prove it and the jurors find the Sterlings guilty, the damage has been done. How can the court compensate a child who has been robbed of innocence?

Freddy is in the middle of his examination-in-chief, clutching a piece of paper, the list of events he has been permitted to keep. I hope it gives him courage and puts a bit of distance between him and the story itself. The court should give him a medal for bravery. Where does he find the courage to tell the judge, lawyers and jurors — all strangers — that Travis Sterling used to fondle him, that Ron Sterling once made him perform sodomy, telling Freddy to put his little-boy penis in his grown-man's anus. He testifies that Linda Sterling once demanded that he rub her labia and on another occasion told him to urinate in her mouth, on pain of death. It takes courage to say such things in public, whether he's telling the truth or not.

If he isn't, it's hard to explain why his testimony echoes that of the other children. If he is, it's hard to stomach the things he says. His words sound like a cry for help. Throughout his testimony, his plea keeps growing louder in my ears, sometimes deafening me to the voices of the other kids: Sally, Janey, Tommy, Frank, Paul, Bill. Echoes of Kenny's voice resonate when Freddy says Ron Sterling grabbed him once and shoved a needle filled with watery fluid into his arm. That's exactly what Kenny said at Tammy's trial, but there weren't any jurors to hear him at that trial.

Freddy doesn't know how to describe the way he felt when Linda Sterling took him into her bedroom and put the vibrator on his penis. He tells the court it's too hard to describe because he can't find the right words. Who could?

Maybe Freddy does the court a kindness every time he fails to describe an incident, for I wish I'd never heard the ones he talks about next. Once Linda Sterling forced him to have anal sex with Kenny, he claims, and another time in the master bedroom she made him mount Kathy, a five-year-old daycare girl. When I hear this, hatred tightens my chest. I'd scream if I could, to let the anger out. But I can't and choke it down in silence.

Linda Sterling was supposed to be running a babysitting service, where kids could play games, sing songs, read books, have snacks and, above all, be safe. She was a surrogate parent, hired by real parents to do her best for their children. Everyone in town trusted her. But she allegedly took their wholeness and broke it in pieces. Not only did she prey on Freddy, but she also forced him to prey on a younger girl, if we are to believe what Freddy says. He says that because he was bigger than Kathy, when he put his penis in her vagina his chest came to her face, and that his chest rubbed against her face as he "started to go up and down." Freddy says he did it because he was scared of Linda. Now he is consumed with guilt about what he did to Kathy.

Either Freddy is telling a finely crafted lie or he's telling the truth. Presumably, the eleven-year-old boy is not experienced enough in normal sexual relations to re-create such striking mental images of copulation. And he remembers his feelings too, testifying that during the assaults he sometimes felt scared, sometimes guilty, sometimes bad, and sometimes good. Particularly compelling is his recollection of the mixed pleasure he experienced from sex, something I can relate to if I think back to my first sexual encounters, when the Dionysian ecstasy of the sixties was tinged with the Presbyterian guilt bequeathed by my grandmother. I hope he won't always associate sex with anger and evil, or continue to confuse his own pleasure with another person's perversion.

> Bauer: Can you tell me when you'd have good feelings about these things that were happening?
>
> Freddy: I don't know when it would happen.
>
> Bauer: Where would you have these good feelings?
>
> Freddy: What do you mean?

Bauer: Where in your body? In your mind, or somewhere in your body? Do you recall?

Freddy: My penis.

Bauer: Do you remember how that made you feel when you'd have good feelings in your penis?

Freddy: In a body sense it felt good, but in my mind I knew it was wrong.

Bauer: Do you remember any feelings about knowing it was wrong?

Freddy: I did, but I don't know the right words for it.

Bauer: Can you give me any kind of description?

Freddy: No, it's too hard.

Bauer: Would it make you feel sad, or happy or angry?

Freddy: It would be a cross between sad and angry.

For the next few hours the three defence lawyers will question eleven-year-old Freddy, trying to dent his credibility and prove he made up his entire story. Harradence will go first. But before cross-examining the boy, he tells the court, "If it's of any comfort to the Crown, it is not my intention to confuse the child." To which Judge Wimmer replies, "Yeah. It's difficult with young children. We just have to do our best and, in the end, the jury is going to have to try and sort it all out."

Harradence: You told me a couple of minutes ago that the more memories you told people about, the more attention they gave to you.

Freddy: Yes.

Harradence: Okay. And that made you feel good?

Freddy: It made me feel good that I got this off my chest and they're doing... and they were doing something about it.

Harradence: I see. Okay. But did the attention that you got also make you feel good?

Freddy: Sort of...

Harradence: Okay. And I take it when you were remembering these things... you got help from your parents and [Rod] Moor and [Claudia] Bryden and Rod Butler?

Freddy: Sometimes.

Harradence: Okay. And I take it also that, at least to you, it seemed like they were pleased. When you'd remember certain things, you'd remember additional things?

Freddy: Yes.

Harradence: Okay. And quite often, Freddy, they offered suggestions or helpful hints for you... I take it that one of the [helpful] things... would have been the pictures.

Freddy: Yes.

Harradence: And they help you, as you say, to remember some of these things?

Freddy: Yes.

Harradence: And in a lot of ways, Freddy, these things are difficult for you to remember?

Freddy: Yes.

Harradence: And in a lot of ways, Freddy, it's hard to distinguish between what actually happened and what didn't happen?

Freddy: No.

Harradence: It's hard to distinguish whether it's a bad dream or whether it actually happened, isn't it?

Freddy: No.

Harradence: It's fairly clear in your mind?

Freddy: Yes.

Harradence: I see. Now, would it be fair to say then, Freddy, that you've obviously talked to a lot of people about these things?

Freddy: Yes.

Harradence: Okay. And does that amount of talking to people... does that confuse your memory at all, perhaps?

Freddy: No.

Harradence: You keep things fairly clear in your mind, you think?

Freddy: Yes...

Harradence: Okay. You have a notebook, do you, that you keep notes in?

Freddy: I got a note folder...

Harradence: And I take it these notes were made — as you remembered things you'd jot them down?

Freddy: Yes.

Harradence: Okay. And you looked at them and then made this list. This list is kind of a condensed version of things, is it?

Freddy: Yes...

Harradence: Okay. And those notes are in your handwriting, are they?

Freddy: Yes.

Harradence: Okay. And are you telling us, Freddy, that Mrs. Sterling had sex with you on the day that she — you say she stripped for you?

Freddy: I can't remember.

Harradence: Thank you, Freddy. Do you remember seeing that in your notes when you were preparing for court?

Freddy: Yeah.

Harradence: Is there some particular reason, Freddy, why you didn't tell us about that?

Freddy: Forgot to make a name for it.

Harradence: But you did make a name for Mrs. Sterling stripping for you?

Freddy: Yes.

Harradence: Did you think, Freddy, maybe that some people might have trouble believing that Mrs. Sterling had sex with you...and that's why you haven't told us?

Freddy: No...

Harradence: Has anybody said, "Hey look, Freddy, that sounds a little bizarre to me. Are you sure that's right?" Has anybody ever said that to you?

Freddy: I can't remember.

Harradence: You can't remember?

Freddy: No, I can't.

Harradence: Thank you very much, Freddy. Those are my questions for you.

Whatever else Harradence has accomplished, he has dented Freddy's credibility and shown him to be an unreliable witness. Earl Kalenith continues on the same tack. To avoid intimidating the boy, the defence lawyer is seated, his back to the camera, holding a copy of *The Secret of the Silver Horse*, a book designed by the federal Ministry of Justice to help children disclose abuse. The defence lawyer begins his cross-examination.

> Kalenith: Remember that you were talking to Claudia Bryden about [this] book?
>
> Freddy: Yes.
>
> Kalenith: And do you remember that in [this] book it said something about a big person putting their hands down a little person's pants?
>
> Freddy: Yes.
>
> Kalenith: Okay. And it was shortly after that then — in that same interview, I guess — that you told Claudia about Travis doing that.
>
> Freddy: Yes.
>
> Kalenith: And in that [interview] do you remember that you said that Travis never did anything to Kenny?
>
> Freddy: Yes.
>
> Kalenith: Now was that true at the time that you said it?
>
> Freddy: No.
>
> Kalenith: Can you remember whether then you knew that Travis had done something to Kenny or not?
>
> Freddy: Oh, I didn't remember then.
>
> Kalenith: You didn't remember then. So that was something you remembered later?
>
> Freddy: Yes.
>
> Kalenith: And could you remember how much later you remembered it?

Freddy: No.

Kalenith: Is the reason for not telling about Kenny at that time because you didn't remember it?

Freddy: Yes.

Kalenith: All right. And you've said that at some time later you remember something with Travis and Kenny. Is that right?

Freddy: Yes.

Kalenith: All right. And at that time...this incident with Travis and Kenny happened, was there any reason you didn't tell anyone then...that it happened?

Freddy: I was scared.

Kalenith challenges the boy: Scared? That no one would believe you? Freddy calmly answers: his greatest fear was not that no one would believe him, but that someone would kill him and his parents. Kalenith reads Freddy's comments made during other earlier police interviews, and asks Freddy if he remembers making certain statements. Sometimes the boy does not. For instance, he doesn't recall ever telling police his friends had told him where The Place was. Yet the notes of Rod Moor and Claudia Bryden, now in the possession of Kalenith, apparently reveal just that. They also show that Freddy doesn't remember telling Claudia Bryden and Rod Moor that Travis "put his dink in my butt." Not only does Freddy forget certain things, he also changes his facts. Today, for instance, he testifies that he was at The Place thirty or thirty-five times. When he testified at Tammy's trial, he said he was there "probably ten times," which Kalenith draws to everyone's attention. Today Freddy says the other kids being transported to The Place in the van never screamed or said boo. At Tammy's trial, Kalenith informs jurors for the first time, Freddy testified: "I could hear them screaming." But the witness doesn't remember ever saying this either. The defence lawyer is sceptical about the witness's memory and openly disdainful of the list of events the boy holds in his hand. Defending his paper prop, Freddy says that without it he would still remember all the incidents, though perhaps not all the details. Smart boy, I think to myself, just as Judge Wimmer intercedes and, with an avuncular smile, critiques Kalenith's questions as "too convoluted for an eleven-year-old boy."

I wonder what the jurors make of the defence lawyers and their cross-examination of Freddy. Tough? Fair? Ruthless? Disorganized? Boring? Wimpish? None of the lawyers asked Freddy to repeat certain evidence he gave at Tammy's trial, such as the taste in his mouth after oral sex with the young woman. Freddy sounds exhausted after being cross-examined time after time.

Kenny speaks again

Kenny is the next witness. He is probably exhausted too, though he hasn't even started his testimony. After giving him the truth test, prosecutor Sullivan begins her exam-in-chief. Kenny tells the court he was never babysat at the Sterling house. (In fact, he is the only child witness in the trial who wasn't.) And he testifies that the only reason he went there in the first place was because Freddy, his best friend, begged him for protection. Other than that, Kenny says, he and Freddy never discussed what took place at the hands of the Sterlings, even though "every time mostly something happened." Prosecutor Sullivan asks: Why didn't you talk about things with Freddy? Kenny answers, "I just don't feel like it sometimes." Even if he did, there'd be "too much" to say.

Some of what Kenny has to say I remember from Tammy's trial, and the rest comes back when Leslie Sullivan questions the nine-year-old. Having promised to "tell the truth to God," the witness claims Linda Sterling hit him with the axe handle and shoved it up his bum. She also shoved the vibrator "up my penis and my bum"; put a needle in the cheek of his bum; and told him to strip, then took Polaroid pictures of him naked. Sullivan asks him to explain how a vibrator could go up his penis, and he demonstrates off-camera. She asks him to describe the vibrator. He says it was peach-coloured and about six inches long, the distance from his wrist to his elbow. Several people in the upstairs court look down at their arms. I do too, and mentally measure my forearm to be nine or ten inches long. Sullivan asks the witness, Do you know what the word "position" means? Kenny answers, using a hockey analogy, "The coach tells you to go to left wing, and you do." Sullivan wants Kenny to explain the position he was in when Linda Sterling used the vibrator. Lowering his voice and speaking quickly, as though trying to throw the words away, he answers, "I was bent over...my bum was sticking up...my hands were down...I was looking down... I was crying and trying to get away."

According to Kenny, Ron Sterling abused him too. On more than one occasion the man sodomized him; put him in the freezer, where "it was dark and it was cold... I felt like I was gonna die"; put him in the cage on the floor and shoved the vibrator through the cage holes; shoved the axe handle into his bum "near the hole," and shoved the vibrator up his bum and penis; slapped him on the bum and penis; and injected a needle in his bum. "I was crying and felt I was never going to get away," he tells Sullivan. As for his "position," he bent over when the vibrator was shoved up his bum, and stood up straight when it was put "in" his penis.

And yet, says Kenny, he told not a single person because Ron would have held a gun to his head. Besides, "I felt bad, so I didn't tell." But there were witnesses, according to the boy. One of them was Jim Elstad, a Martensville police officer, who was also the driver of the vehicle that transported the kids to The Place. Sullivan asks, How did you know it was Jim? Kenny says he saw the car keys in Elstad's hand.

That's a convincing detail. Just as good as when Freddy told the court he knew Elstad from school because the officer sometimes came to talk to kids about bike thefts. I find tiny details like these very convincing and wonder where Freddy ever got the idea of the orange juice stinging the cuts in his mouth. That's the kind of thing you can't make up on the spur of the moment, unless you're a good liar, or an extremely observant writer, or ready for the question. I wonder if anyone discussed this with Kenny ahead of time.

Kenny says Travis Sterling also abused him, by sucking his penis, tying him up, shoving the vibrator in the boy's "bum crack" and shoving his penis in his "bum cheeks." In answer to Sullivan's question, the witness says he knew it was Travis's penis because he looked back and saw the man naked, his feet planted on the ground and his hands hanging at his sides. Besides being "big and hard," which made Kenny cry, the penis felt "squishy." Janis pokes me in the side and underlines the word three times in her notes.

Kenny's testimony is more than a litany of assaults. It is a story, at times jumbled and strange. From time to time in the telling, it stops sounding surreal and starts to sound real. Sometimes the real and the surreal are juxtaposed in a way that makes me think of the upside-down, dreamy art of Marc Chagall, whose paintings are enigmatic, yet rooted in everyday life. One tale Kenny tells is at once tame and wild, a story of sexual perversion. One half is easy and requires no imagination to comprehend; the other half is hard, if not impossible, to believe. If Dr. Yuille, the psychology professor at Tammy's trial, were on the stand now, I think he'd say Kenny's story has contextual imbeddedness. It goes like this.

First Kenny played soccer with Freddy, then accompanied him to the Sterling house. Linda was in the kitchen, cutting apples on the table, and Ron was lying on the living room couch watching TV. Travis was there too, as were several daycare children and two police officers, Darryl Ford and John Popowich. According to the witness, Ron bent down and sucked Kenny's penis and "kind of nibbled on it," and performed other assaults on him. "I was crying. I tried to get away." By now, "every kid was crying mostly," as the "bad cops" proceeded to assault them too, in a paedophilic orgy. Meanwhile, in the next room, Linda continued to cut apples on the kitchen table.

When Kenny finishes his story, Sullivan asks how he feels about the stories he tells. "I felt lonely. It was my secret, or something like that," says Kenny, adding that it feels good to tell people what happened to him. But he doesn't want his friends to know what happened, or find out he came to court today in a police van. If they found out, says Kenny, they'd never play with me again. Just being here is risky for him. Why would he concoct his testimony, when it would virtually cost him his life if his friends ever heard it? A deep sadness washes over me, and the only thing I'm grateful for this afternoon is Wimmer's publication ban.

Lawyers are interesting people. They believe in the supremacy of law the way priests believe in the Bible. A big-city corporate lawyer, an old boyfriend, once said he believed the law is more important than the people it governs. I tried to convince him it was just the reverse, that the laws belong to the people who made them in the first place. It's a debate I return to in my head as I sit here watching the trio of defence lawyers question Kenny. Their goal is to protect their clients, and to accomplish this they must punch holes in a nine-year-old boy's credibility.

"Patronizing" is the word I'd use to describe the way Mullord starts his cross-exam. "You don't know what questions I'm going to ask… Does that make you nervous?" The young witness replies, "A little bit." Kenny is off to a shaky start, maintaining that whenever he and Ron Sterling arrived at The Place, Ron opened the garage door by remote control. (According to the owner's testimony at Tammy's trial, which neither Kenny nor this jury heard, the door to that garage is opened manually.) However, Kenny then redeems himself by giving testimony that is quite accurate: At The Place, the garage led into the main building. You went through a door, up three steps to a platform, then down three steps. That's how you got into the lower level at The Place, where there were no windows. That's where the gun was and the blue and white freezer that Ron, Travis, and some policemen put him in. Up a big flight of stairs was where the cage was, and there were windows too.

How does Kenny know these things? How could he learn these details merely from looking at police photos, and would he remember things so vividly if he'd never seen them with his own eyes?

Ron Sterling's future is on the line and his defence lawyer, Don Mullord, plans to prove the police photos and interviews gave Kenny knowledge he didn't already possess. "When you saw those pictures of [The Place] is that when you remembered going there?" asks Mullord. The boy answers, "No.

Just that I couldn't tell anybody. That's why. And she needed my help, that's why I told her [Claudia Bryden]." The cross-examiner continues: "Now if you couldn't remember [The Place] the first time, and then you could remember with the pictures, did the pictures help you to remember?" Kenny says, "Yeah, a little bit." Who doesn't remember things better when someone or something jogs your memory? When you look at the pictures of your summer holidays, you remember the fun.

Mullord, pleased with his all-purpose theory, suggests that Kenny's therapy sessions also helped improve the boy's memory. "Did he [Rod Butler] tell you that, if you kept seeing him, you'd remember more and more things?" No, says the boy flatly. "But you did remember more things, didn't you, after you...started to see him." Mullord makes this a leading statement, not a leading question, and Kenny responds as expected, "Sometimes, yeah." Who doesn't remember things better when they've had time to think? And why would Kenny tell his therapist his innermost secrets the first time they met? I'm sure therapy did help Kenny "remember" things, and start to talk about them. I'm also sure the boy controlled the process almost as much as the therapist did.

Which is a lesson Mullord is about to learn. Kenny is a smart, stubborn kid not easily cowed by adults. When Mullord tries to push the boy further, to get him to agree that the therapist planted false memories in his head, Kenny maintains the memories were already there just waiting for the right person to dig them out. Emphasizing the last word of his answer, Kenny describes how he acted in his early sessions with Rod Butler: "I didn't tell him anything." He says he remained cautious for a long time and gave his therapist obvious answers such as "cold," when Butler asked how it felt to be put in the freezer. After all these months, the boy is still reluctant to talk about his feelings and refuses to tell Mullord what he talked about in therapy. He answers the cross-examiner's questions with non-committal answers like "yeah." Kenny may be a kid, but he's complex and he's got steady nerves.

I think he must have compassion too, or why would he have agreed to accompany his friend Freddy to the daycare? He says he did it in the hope Freddy wouldn't "get abused more," even though he knew his mother would be angry if she found out he was lying to her. In for a penny, in for a pound — having agreed to protect Freddy he then had to protect his mom, to the point of lying, telling her he was playing happily somewhere with Freddy when he was actually at the Sterling house. There are two ways of looking at it — either Kenny is a little liar or he is a very courageous son and friend. Either way, his character has landed him in big trouble.

Hugh Harradence follows Mullord. A lot is at stake for Harradence's client, Linda Sterling, and the lawyer now has to highlight the contradictions in Kenny's testimony. One minute the boy says the Sterlings' front curtains were usually open; in the next breath, that they were usually closed. Sometimes the boy has trouble remembering things he said earlier to the police, the therapist, and the court, things that are documented in official records Harradence used to prepare himself for court. For example, on several occasions in the past the boy sometimes had trouble remembering who took the Polaroid pictures of him; yet today he knows for sure it was Linda Sterling. Harradence asks the boy when he remembered it was Linda. Not surprisingly, he can't say, any more than he can tell the court why he told his therapist he'd been put in a fridge at The Place, when today he knows it was the big freezer. Harradence's next question perplexes Kenny: "Is it correct that the more people you talked to, the more you could remember"? The boy stumbles: "What do you mean there, like?" Harradence rephrases the question, omitting the sarcasm. Now that Kenny understands the question, though not its implication, he answers yes — the perfect note for Harradence to end on. Thank you very much, Kenny. Those are all my questions.

Earl Kalenith, the third cross-examiner, dents Kenny's credibility further. The boy admits it's hard to remember who did what and who said what. When asked if he made mistakes about remembering what happened, he grudgingly answers, "Maybe, I'm not sure."

Now it's time to hear what Kenny's mother, K-Mom, has to say. Witness 52 is a Mennonite, though she dresses in pants and blouse, not the traditional long skirt, apron, and head cover. Soft-spoken, she testifies that she has been married eighteen years and has two sons, six years apart, Kenny being the younger. He was her baby, she says, though he has taken care of her just as much as she has of him. When he first told her certain things had happened at the Sterlings' she was "shocked." Seeing this, her son quickly softened the blow by telling her nothing had actually happened to him, and this made her "happy." Having tested the waters and found them treacherous, he clammed up, even after Claudia Bryden brought the Secret of the Silver Horse to the house and K-Mom read it to Kenny twice.

But before long, the book had its intended effect. A week after the second reading, Kenny led K-Mom to her room, closed the door, sat her down on the bed, and began to tell his story. They both cried. Dredging this up for the court makes her cry again. Leslie Sullivan hands her a box of Kleenex, and says, "Just take a deep breath. Have a drink of water, okay?" I wonder if K-Mom can see past her own tears to the two or three people in the public gallery wiping their eyes. The tissue and Sullivan's sympathy seem to fortify K-Mom enough to help her stop crying.

There's plenty of ground to cover if Sullivan is to keep K-Mom ahead of the three defence lawyers who are waiting to tear her story apart. The Crown prosecutor probably expects them to try to make jurors think that K-Mom badgered her son into confessing imagined atrocities, and that she went on a witch hunt with Claudia Bryden, the other parents in town, and Rod Butler, the therapist. So Sullivan hastens to ask K-Mom about her relationship with Claudia Bryden. The witness answers that the Martensville policewoman advised her to hope for the best and take Kenny at his word when he said nothing had happened to him. Wait and see, Bryden told K-Mom. Above all, don't give the boy ideas or mention any names. That's exactly what K-Mom did, or so she says. Since the beginning, her only source of information about alleged events was Kenny himself, not Bryden or Butler. She says she never talked with other parents about their children's disclosures.

K-Mom seems to brighten a little when she talks about the changes in her son during the past year or so. His symptoms and his grades have improved, thanks to the therapy. But the cause of his misery has not been eradicated. Kenny is still, she frowns, an angry little boy. His memories cause the temper tantrums that make him slam doors and throw things and swear, though cursing is not allowed in her Mennonite house. Determined to mutilate himself, Kenny uses nail clippers four or five times a day to cut the balls of his fingers and feet until they bleed. When she confiscates the clippers, he gets scissors to continue the job.

Kenny has never been one to wet his bed. How could he, she asks rhetorically, when he hardly ever sleeps the night through? His insomnia was especially bad in summer 1990, when he'd been friends with Freddy for about a year. Often, in the middle of the night, Kenny would rock in bed on his hands and knees till he rubbed the hair off his head and grazed his forehead. Once he even put a hole in the drywall. After a night of self-abuse and little sleep he had puffy, tired eyes and bruises on his body. The court doesn't have to take the witness's word for it because the prosecutor produces proof in the form of a school photo of Kenny, taken around the time in question, that K-Mom uses to point out the hair loss and scrapes and bruises on her son's forehead. When it comes to Kenny's constipation, however, the only evidence is K-Mom's word. She held his hand once, as he tried to have a bowel movement and "actually screamed" in pain. This mystified K-Mom because he also had diarrhoea and soiled his underpants, as often as five times a day. Finally, when Kenny complained of a sore bum, K-Mom examined him and saw the broken skin around his anus. She testifies that she took Kenny to the doctor immediately.

During a short break, several reporters gather in the hall for this morning's topic, which is constipation. Who among us doesn't know the feeling? You have to be careful not to strain too hard, for fear of doing damage to your body, possibly even the blood vessels in your eyeballs that feel as though they're about to pop. None of us, it seems, has ever had constipation so bad it makes you scream. None of us ever had constipation and diarrhoea at the same time. Trying to make sense of Kenny's predicament, we do a re-hash of the medical evidence at Tammy's trial. The boy may have been so terrified to pass a stool that he held it in as long as possible and by the time he reached his limit of endurance, the size and firmness of the stool made passing it extremely painful. Yet Kenny couldn't completely control his bowels and hold in his poop. It leaked out because, as Dr. Yelland testified months ago, the boy's sphincter muscles were stretched to almost three times normal and didn't function properly.

Kenny's behaviour was just as conflicted as his bowels, says his mother from the witness box. When not slamming doors and swearing at her, he stuck to her like glue. She first noticed the clingy behaviour in 1989, when Kenny entered kindergarten and started to play with Freddy, who went to the Sterling house. Her son didn't want her to leave the house, even though his father or brother was always at home, and he wouldn't leave her side even to go to a public washroom. She was stymied about her son's behaviour, because the domestic environment was safe and secure and there had been no trauma in the house that would upset him. She often imagined he might smother her with clinginess, but she could not understand his problem. On the verge of tears, she swears to the court she knew nothing of the alleged incidents at the daycare until a year or two after Kenny began to act strange. Not until the end of 1991 did she get a clue when, just before Christmas, Claudia Bryden came to the house to question Kenny. Then in January, K-mom heard about the meeting for the daycare parents. She decided to go, even though Kenny had never been one of the daycare kids at the Sterling house.

What could she have done differently to protect her baby? Once wasn't enough, now she has to go through the trauma all over again. Not just think about what happened, over and over again, but come to court to talk about it without forgetting any details. The toll shows on her face and in her voice.

Hugh Harradence stands in front of K-Mom. Did the police give you photos of the inside of the Sterling house to show to Kenny? She remembers neither receiving such photos nor showing them to her son. Does she remember, then, being advised by the police to take notes? Yes, she remembers that, but she didn't do it because she was under a "lot of stress." Oh, so there was a lot of stress in your house, Harradence repeats her words, trying to lodge his foot in the evidentiary door. "Yes, there was lots of stress," K-mom answers, because of the investigation.

Were you "overly strict" with Kenny? the defence lawyer asks. Now I've heard everything. To my surprise, Judge Wimmer doesn't question the relevance of this line of cross-examining. "Is it true that when Kenny wasn't in your line of vision, you wanted to know where he was and what he was doing?" Yes, says K-mom, it's true. Thank God she didn't say no, or Harradence would be calling her negligent.

Despite herself, K-Mom forgets things, as Don Mullord now tries to highlight. He asks, How often did Kenny play away from the house with Freddy for more than an hour? She can't remember back that far. Mullord insists that she remember. Okay, she says, about ten to fifteen times. She remembers clearly that the two boys once went into the Sterling house, ostensibly to watch a movie, and stayed for just twenty minutes. Mullord then asks when she first met Claudia Bryden. K-Mom's answer differs from Bryden's earlier testimony. In fact, the witness can't even remember going to the Martensville police station in December 1991. Nor does she remember delivering a signed statement to the police station several weeks after that. Why not? asks Mullord. "I was under a lot of stress... I was concerned about my child."

K-Mom's eye muscles twitch, and the courtroom is thick with tension. Now that her cross-exam is over, the Mennonite woman climbs down from the witness box, while across the room Travis Sterling sits in the prisoner's dock, fidgeting with his hands. Both he and his father are dressed in black suits, but his mother wears a bright pink outfit. I wonder why they look more formal today than usual.

By contrast, the next witness to climb into the box is dressed casually in shirt, pants, and sweater. K-Dad, Kenny's father, has a moustache and receding hairline. He tells the court that his son has never told him the details of his alleged trauma. Kenny talks to his mother instead. But Kenny doesn't sleep well, his father says. He still has nightmares after all this time, though not every night like he used to. And when Kenny goes to court, he gets more upset than usual. K-Dad testifies that certain things stand out in his mind more than others, such as the day he took Kenny, who would have been six or seven then, to Lakeview pool in Saskatoon. Inexplicably, the lights in the change room went out. Kenny "went hysterical" and his father had to rush him from the change room to the hall. Kenny's reaction surprised K-Dad because he had never been afraid of the dark.

K-Dad and Kenny are working on their relationship now and it's pretty good. They've gone through phases: good, bad, good again. Kenny entered the bad phase about the time he started kindergarten, refusing to let his father hug or play with him or tuck him in at night and clearly preferring his mother. No stranger, not even Santa Claus, was safe in Kenny's eyes, and he screamed when his parents put him on Santa's knee for a Christmas picture.

Apparently nothing is the same any more in the witness's home: his son's hair, skin, and bedroom walls, and the harmony he used to share with his wife. "We probably don't get along as good as we used to," K-Dad says, admitting that Kenny has seen him argue with K-Mom.

Kenny's parents have given their version of things, and they also let Kenny speak for himself. It never occurred to me they didn't have to. Now that the courts recognize parents' right to speak on behalf of their children, they can shield their kids from the courtroom. The parents of Kathy, nine, and Frank, thirteen, have apparently told the court they will not subject their children to the pressure of testifying about the three years they spent at the Sterling house. Instead they will take the heat themselves.

Visibly pregnant, Kathy and Frank's mother stands to tell her story to the judge alone in a *voir dire* so that he can decide if its prejudicial value outweighs its probative value. In other words, he will rule whether the story does nothing but cast the Sterlings in a negative light so as to prejudice the jurors, or whether her tale sheds new light on the case, and possibly adds important proof which the jurors should see and hear. Only when he has made that decision will the jurors hear what she has to say. For now, the judge asks them to leave the room, and the mother of Kathy and Frank begins her chilling story.

After work one day she went down to her basement to get something from the freezer for supper, and her son Frank, who was two or three at the time, toddled after her. When she opened the freezer lid, Frank said several times — here, the mother imitates her son's way of talking — "You can put people in there." She asked Frank why he said that, but he refused to answer. Shocked, she told her husband and they kept a lock on the freezer for the next couple of years.

Opening a fridge or freezer and finding your child dead inside is every parent's nightmare. This is pretty incriminating stuff for the Sterlings, if the prosecution can ever prove the incident is related to things that happened at The Place. Of all the evidence I've heard since the beginning of Tammy's trial, the freezer stories tap my deepest fears. Sexual abuse is one thing; murder, accidental or otherwise, is a crime of a completely different order. What will the defence team do with this hearsay evidence? It's certainly prejudicial. What will the jurors think if they ever get to hear it?

Heavy-hitter Hugh Harradence goes first. Could you tell us, ma'am, when exactly the home-freezer incident took place? The mother can't pinpoint the year, though it was while her children were going to the Sterling house. She kept notes when her kids began to disclose, but didn't write immediately about this incident. In fact, she didn't even remember it and failed to see its significance until months later. Then, when she did, she made notes. But, by then, months had elapsed since the occurrence and the kids were older. Harradence, who has copies of her several sets of notes, questions her: "How did it come to you, ma'am, that the freezer was important to this case...or not important?" She replies, "I was asked if there was anything unusual that I remembered from my children during the time period they were babysat by the Sterlings, and that's one of the things I recalled as being unusual." Like any good journalist, the defence lawyer puts the question another way: "Did someone ask you specifically about a freezer?" No, she answers, and is then asked to leave the room.

The defence team is fired up: M'lord, this evidence is hearsay and should not be admitted. But if you admitted part of the story and jurors heard only that the parents locked the freezer without being told why — that is, if they didn't hear what Frank said to his mother — they might assume one of the Sterlings had actually put Frank in the freezer at The Place. M'Lord, we believe that your choices are to admit either all the evidence — what Frank said, and what his mother did — or absolutely none of it.

Why am I not surprised when the defence team tells Wimmer the jury should not hear the freezer story because it is more prejudicial than probative? Why does this mini-trial look more and more like a game of chess than a path to truth?

Prosecutor Leslie Sullivan can't bear to see this evidence ruled inadmissible and starts to flip frantically through the chapter about hearsay rules in her copy of *Canadian Criminal Evidence*. Wimmer has just said he will let the jury hear the freezer story on one condition, that the prosecution prove it relevant.

Relevant? To what? Isn't the story relevant simply because it corroborates evidence already given by other kids? Does Wimmer mean that what Frank said to his mother is, in itself, irrelevant unless Sullivan can show its specific bearing on the case? How can she show that further, when the relevance is obvious to her? In order to prove the relevance to you, M'Lord, would you have her investigate why young Frank made the statement to his mother in the first place? The police tried to investigate why the daycare kids said and did certain things, and look where it got them. "Why" questions don't get asked much around here, do they? But I guess it would be difficult to weigh the answer to why on the scales of justice, designed as they are for who, what, when, and how.

Court is adjourned for the day, and I'm looking forward to a long, quiet evening with Judge Harold J. Rothwax, author of *Guilty: The Collapse of Criminal Justice*. Though I've had no formal legal training, I have just spent the past five months in court. And what I've seen has made me cynical. I'm in good company. Judge Rothwax has spent twenty-five years at law, and he sounds cynical too. He has crammed a lot of his dyspepsia into his 200-page book, which keeps me reading until way past midnight. "In reality, the law is not necessarily a search for the truth. Indeed, it is often *not* a search for the truth," he writes. Closing the book and turning off my light, I wonder if Judge Wimmer is burning the midnight oil in his room at the Bessborough Hotel, preparing to rule on the freezer story.

Next morning, before calling in the jury, he speaks. Since the parents of Frank and Kathy decided that their children would not testify, this "makes it difficult for the criminal justice system, as presently structured, to fairly operate." His sonorous voice drones on. "It has not been demonstrated that the children are incapable of testifying, and so the element of necessity [for the parents to have testified] is absent." Wimmer concludes that the statements cannot go before the jury. He also believes Frank's statement to his mother is equivocal, capable of more than one interpretation, and not necessarily indicative of the commission of a crime by any of the accused. It is impossible to ever really know what Frank meant when he said what he did at the age of two or three, and impossible to cross-examine the boy because he won't be called as a witness. Wimmer continues: To let the jury hear the freezer story might be a terrible injustice to the three accused, especially since they cannot challenge it. "The probative value...is well outweighed by the probable prejudicial effect."

The words ring in my ears: "terrible injustice," "the criminal justice system, as presently structured." Wimmer has weighed the evidence and evaluated the potential damage to the accused. When placed on one side of the scale, the weight of the child's words is too light for the court to consider their relevance and too heavy when balanced against the rights of the accused. Ironically, the boy's words are empty and meaningless. They shed insufficient light on the matter at hand, and may constitute the wrong kind of evidence, prejudicing jurors and blinding them to their task. So nothing further will be said about Frank and the freezer in this room. What, I wonder, does Ron Sterling think about this ruling? He sits in his front-row seat in the prisoner's dock, arm draped nonchalantly over the back of it, fingers drumming the wood, one pinched tight by a Masonic ring.

Wimmer calls a short break, after which jurors return to the courtroom and the trial proceeds. Freezer story on ice, the mother and father of Frank and Kathy still have lots of evidence to give, and this time the jury will hear it. Mother goes first: her son and daughter started to go, off and on, to the Sterling house when they were very young. She thought the Sterlings were "very happy, social people," but little Kathy once told her she wanted to go to another daycare and, uncharacteristically, Frank agreed with his sister. One smile leads to another in the room as the witness recounts anecdotes about her children, such as her son's claim that a computer shot him in his peepee, which she found "strange." Judge Wimmer, in a light moment, says he doesn't find it strange at all. In fact, he quips, he has a computer that shoots him, too.

When the laughter in the room subsides, the witness continues: Strange things began to happen to her children, things to which other parents have already attested. For instance, while he was still a baby, Frank once returned from the Sterling house with a red arm. Then, when he was eight or nine, he began to have nightmares and sleep problems, which continue to this day. Also, he began to wet the bed and suffer bowel problems and was "not his normal self" in the presence of Linda Sterling. The witness says she noticed, on several occasions, that baby Kathy had redness on her genital area, but thought it was because of incorrect wiping so she took appropriate measures. When she was a little older, Kathy had nightmares several times a week and showed low self-esteem. On this note, mother concludes her evidence and father steps up.

The children's father, who has dark hair, appears upset on the stand. One day, he says, while he was driving his daughter, Kathy, to daycare, she made an absolute fuss. Then, when he tried to pick her up that afternoon, she was not at the Sterling house. This was not a complete surprise to the father because "Auntie" Linda didn't always know where his daughter was playing when he came to get her, or have her ready, even when he had called ahead to say he was coming. Looking grim, the witness says, "If you're a father you try to forget a lot of these things... We've tried to put everything behind us." I can only imagine that the struggle has met with varying degrees of success from family to family.

What the doctors say

We will now hear from several expert medical witnesses, many of whom appeared at Tammy's trial. The first is Dr. Joel Yelland who, as a resource person for the Saskatoon Child Abuse Council, has examined hundreds of children, many of them abused. Though not the regular physician of either Freddy or Kenny, he once examined both boys.

The red-haired Yelland takes the witness stand and testifies that he examined Freddy in March 1992, when the boy was ten. He found little unusual about the boy's genitals, except for mild excoriation of the area around the anus. The doctor's examination of Kenny in August was a different matter. When he measured the boy "cheek to cheek," he found a 0.5 cm-deep tear in the child's rectum, extending towards the scrotum, with a small cleft that had recently healed. Besides the rip, the rectal-area skin was red and raw and Kenny's sphincter muscle could not squeeze the doctor's finger. No wonder. The diameter of the boy's rectum was 1.3 cm, almost three times normal for his age. Yelland explains that the stretching and slackness were consistent with chronic constipation or rectal penetration. The damage was caused either by natural objects that had trouble pushing their way out of Kenny's rectum, or unnatural objects that were shoved in. It might have been caused by both types of objects, in a vicious circle of destruction, fear, and further destruction of the rectal area. The doctor can't be certain. Even if he were, the court would not allow him or any other expert to state unequivocally that Kenny was abused. That is for the jury to decide.

Hugh Harradence goes to the lectern with his notes and begins to grill the physician. Would you agree that the measuring of the rectum is susceptible to subjective analysis? "No," answers the doctor. We use an objective measurement. Harradence: Do you agree that because you're dealing with a small person and small measurements, it's hard to measure? "No," replies the doctor, explaining that the tape measure he uses records to the nearest millimetre.

Harradence's third question he illustrates vividly, if unintentionally, with his forefinger crooked towards the ceiling. He asks Yelland if it is correct that he measured the child's sphincter tone by putting a finger in his anus. If the topic under cross-examination weren't rectal examinations, and if everyone in the court weren't moved in some way by the tragedy in question, the lawyer's finger would be our laugh for the day. But no one in the room cracks a smile. Judge Wimmer's face is like a stone wall. Out of the corner of my eye, I see Janis staring hard at her notebook.

Don Mullord, the second cross-examiner, reads to Dr. Yelland a portion of the testimony he gave at Tammy's trial eight months ago. Yelland has never looked at the trial transcript and says he doesn't remember making specific statements at the earlier trial about the length of time Kenny had problems with his bowels or the time it might take for his rectal injury to heal. It doesn't surprise me the doctor has scant recollection of what he said months ago, but it does surprise me that Mullord doesn't challenge him on it. Yelland's memory lapse is just that, not grounds for the defence to question his credibility.

Next in the witness box is Dr. Eleanor Anne McKenna. She also testified at Tammy's trial, though she'd examined neither Freddy nor Kenny, and restricted her evidence to the physical symptoms of child abuse in general. Here at the Sterling trial, she can be more specific, for during the police investigation last fall she examined seven of the child plaintiffs.

Fortyish, she is a stylish dresser. McKenna is an unusual woman, having trained both as a doctor and a nurse. Her specialty is paediatric medicine, specifically child abuse, and she has taught at the University of Saskatchewan for the past decade. During this time, she has seen more than 600 sexually abused children, all under the age of eighteen. With this much experience the doctor knows what to look for.

McKenna tells the court that a sexual abuser does not always leave evidence behind. When a girl is the victim, her symptoms may include redness, bruising, and tearing of the hymen, and cuts on the vaginal lips and the area between the hymen and anus. Boys who've been sexually abused have no visible symptoms on their penis or testicles. But they may have fissures or tears and redness in the anal area, and a slack sphincter muscle for as little as three or four days or as long as a year or two. If the abuse ceases, the muscle may return to normal. Sexual abuse can also cause constipation in both girls and boys.

McKenna tells the court she examined nine-year-old Bill on July 30, 1992. "I felt that his anal sphincter was slightly slack...but this is subjective." On the same day, she examined Anne, Bill's sister, and found nothing, and the same for Tommy and his sister Sandy. When McKenna examined their sister, Janey, she found a minor degree of non-specific vulvitis, common among pre-pubescent girls. A couple of weeks later she examined eleven-year-old Frank and his sister, Kathy. She found nothing in Kathy's case, but in Frank's anus she found an old scar which, she says, might have been caused by constipation. Even though she found few physical indications of sexual abuse, Dr. McKenna did not rule out the possibility.

When questioned by Don Mullord, she repeats that some children who've been abused have no physical symptoms. The reverse is also true — some kids who have not been abused do. Mullord has brought a study to court that indicates almost one out of every two non-abused children has anal dilation. He asks Dr. McKenna if she "adopts" the findings. She says that she needs to refresh her memory. Judge Wimmer calls for a short break to give her time to re-read the report. He dismisses the jurors.

McKenna sits in a seat vacated by a juror and begins to read the document while most of the public and journalists stay in the courtroom to chat and the Sterling trio stays in the box. Today Ron looks respectable in a charcoal suit and red tie, and jokes with his son Travis, dressed in jeans and suit jacket. His wife Linda doesn't join the merriment. She sits, stone-shouldered, and stares straight at the front of the room, where the lawyers chat and shuffle papers.

The nurse-turned-doctor looks up and says she has finished reading the report and agrees with it. Judge Wimmer asks the commissionaire to go and get the jurors. They file in, some chewing gum. It looks tacky, but maybe it helps relieve the boredom of sitting here listening intently to what every witness says. Fortunately, they get paid to do it. They get their $40 a day whether the court sits three minutes or six hours. To boost jurors' morale, which Wimmer perceives to be flagging, he gives them a pep talk. Like a friendly uncle, he says he's concerned about the financial burden the trial has placed on them. So concerned, he has talked to his employer, the Saskatchewan Department of Justice.

It's quite a change to hear the judge talk at length in this sympathetic tone of voice. His words reveal the mind of a man who spends most of his life thinking and weighing. Jurors, he says, have a civic duty, an obligation to do a good job. On the other hand, they have rights. And the state has a responsibility to uphold these rights because, without jurors, the justice system would collapse. There is a limit to what the state can expect from jurors. And when the state goes beyond the limits, or fails to mitigate the cause of juror discontent, such as during an unusually long trial like this one, it must find a solution to the problem. He looks straight at the twelve men and women and asks, What would be a good solution here? Though the Criminal Code permits a juror to be discharged, it must be with good reason. And financial hardship may not be a good enough reason. Besides, a "basic degree of financial security" is crucial. Therefore, Wimmer announces with a slight smile, he is ordering the Department of Justice to raise the daily jury fee to $100 a day, effective immediately.

Dr. Zillah Ann Parker, the third expert witness, also testified at Tammy's trial. The matronly looking woman with her hair in a grey bun is a child psychiatrist who has assessed and treated hundreds of children in the past twenty years, including many who were sexually abused. I wouldn't be surprised if Dr. Parker's own stress level has been elevated since her appearance at the first trial nine months ago. Recently, she was promoted to head of child psychiatry at Queen Alexandra Children's Health Centre in Victoria, British Columbia. She won't miss the snow-shovelling and the glare-ice sidewalks of Saskatoon, I'll bet.

Much of what Parker says is a repeat of her previous testimony. Still, it's pleasing to hear her soft, cultivated voice again and to have her remind us that she helps her child patients understand an experience, label the events, and put the events and the feelings together, so as to "externalize" the experience.

I could have used help from a warm woman like Dr. Parker when I was thirteen and my parents separated. Back in the 1950s, it was very unusual for a kid to see a psychiatrist. Most adults didn't have the opportunity, either. Those who did tried to keep it secret. Times have changed. Now therapy is chic in some circles, if not *de rigueur*.

For a sexually abused child, there is nothing chic about being in therapy. If the patient is very young and still in a "pre-language" stage, he or she will not even be able to talk about things. In the pre-language stage, a child stores everything in pictures, not words, according to Dr. Parker, and is unable to communicate the experience until older, when language and knowledge permit. Even then, the ability to sequence the events, putting all the parts together in the right order like blocks, is not something the child possesses. So the story may sound inauthentic to adult ears. In fact, a child's story may not conform at all to the adult expectation of a proper story — one with a start, middle, and end.

As Parker explains how the mind of a very young child works, I start to think of it as a still camera, and wonder if, as we grow older, the brain develops into a sophisticated videorecorder, abandoning the limited shutter-type way of snapping pictures. Even if a child's mind is limited, says Parker, the mental images children take are often vivid, although big gaps may exist between scenes and the pictures may not be in the right order.

My pictures from childhood are vivid, not just in colour but also in feeling. The earliest image is golden yellow because the late afternoon light is peeking through the thin curtain mother just closed on my bedroom window, in preparation for my nap. Though the only thing I still see clearly is the yellow light, the memory of lying in my crib fills me with sadness and longing. The next picture in my mental album is of me, about three years old, in my green hand-smocked dress with the matching socks, one of which refuses to stay up. The feeling that accompanies the scene is one of mixed annoyance and resignation at being dressed in socks that don't behave the same — one falls down as soon as I pull it up and teaches me early on that nothing in life will be easy. A slightly later picture is one of me in the kindergarten band, dressed in a red taffeta cape and hat that makes me look dorky — the frizzy perm doesn't help much either — holding a stupid triangle with a metal stick and smiling for the camera. (Because I was sick the day kids chose the good instruments, I got left with the triangle. This scene makes me feel rejected.) Then there is the one at the beach in my navy blue bathing suit that makes me look fat, and the brown and white plaid jacket that makes me look even fatter. These mental images of the perpetual fat girl inspire anxiety. But a feeling of adventure tinged with loss comes over me when I see the image of the black metal cow gates at Toronto's Osgoode Hall, and smell the musty law library where dad took me one day. These are snapshots of my childhood, fragments of vivid colour with big blanks in between.

Dr. Parker rests her hands on the witness box and sounds more like she's giving a friendly fireside chat than expert testimony at a criminal trial. Almost anything can jog a memory, at any age, explains the psychiatrist. Just as we can remember things, we can also forget, by accident or on purpose. A very important defence mechanism for a child who is sexually abused is called dissociation. The child dissociates himself or herself from what happened and buries the memories deep in the body. The child forgets in order to function. Forgetting certain details, or all of them, might explain why a kid doesn't tell his or her story. There are, of course, other reasons: guilt, shame, the fear of threats, or the possible loss of their parents' love. A child may change in the wake of sexual abuse and show any of the following symptoms or a "constellation" of them. Parker runs through the list of behaviours: The girl or boy may "act out" or become aggressive, fidgety or clingy, or suffer separation anxiety or lack concentration. The child may experience loss of appetite, sleep disorders and nightmares, abdominal pain, or fear of the dark. He or she may revert to bedwetting and thumbsucking or start to self-mutilate.

In a calm voice that belies the horror of the phenomenon she's describing, the psychiatrist explains why a child would do such a thing. It's as if one wants a physical pain that distracts from the psychological torment. It's also a form of self-punishment. And it serves to snap the child out of a state of numbness and back to reality. Does she mean that Kenny clipped off the balls of his fingers and rocked till he rubbed the hair off his head because he was in so much pain to start with?

As the court has heard, Kenny is not the only child with unusual behaviour. Now prosecutor Leslie Sullivan wants the witness's opinion about the "constellation" of symptoms presented by the others. When asking the psychiatrist questions, Sullivan must let her answer as an expert witness who is familiar with the symptoms of child abuse, though not with any of the children in question or their names. To avoid even saying their names, Sullivan has assigned a number to each of them.

Sullivan begins with the symptoms of Child Number One, who is six or seven years old and angry. The child bedwets, suffers nightmares, and has daydreams and stomach aches. The prosecutor asks, Would you, Dr. Parker, have concerns about that child? "I would be very concerned about a child that had all those symptoms, particularly if previously they've been well adjusted...that they'd had some experience that was upsetting them."

Sullivan continues: Child Number Two is nine or ten years old. He is reluctant to disrobe, repeatedly clutches his penis, has intermittent upset stomach, and wets the bed. "Again, I would be very concerned." Child Number Three. Child Number Four. Numbers Five, Six, and Seven. This one has nightmares and school problems; that one is clinically depressed, compulsively neat, and spaced out. Sullivan lists the symptoms of the children, and the psychiatrist labels some "vulnerable," others "anxious." Many of them, Dr. Parker believes, exhibit symptoms consistent with "threats to their security."

Therapist Rodney Franklin Butler takes the stand, looking and sounding the same as he did at Tammy's trial. From the witness box, he tells the court he has spent well over forty hours with Freddy in his office. With authority he can state, "Freddy has been traumatized in a way that his view of the world has been adversely affected...and his sense of trust of others has been damaged." Butler has also spent more than thirty sessions with Kenny, roughly half of them devoted to the boy's disclosures, the other half to the management of feelings and behaviour. Butler tells the court that "Kenny has been traumatized... He has a distorted perception...of his world...and experiences a sense of powerlessness and a major distrust...of people or relationships." Both boys, according to the expert witness, began therapy willingly. But defence lawyer Hugh Harradence is sceptical.

> Harradence: You encouraged Freddy and Kenny to make disclosures.
>
> Butler: I encouraged them if they had memories to make disclosures.
>
> Harradence: And you would suggest things to them, sir.
>
> Butler: I'm not sure what you mean by that.
>
> Harradence: Well, you would suggest things to them to see whether they could communicate anything to you on any given topic that you might suggest.
>
> Butler: I would suggest to them that — if they had memories — I would like them to talk about them, to share and try to get in touch with those feelings in relationship to traumatic moments...
>
> Harradence: Specifically, sir, what type of inconsistency would you challenge someone on?
>
> Butler: ...I am not doing an investigation. I'm a clinician. Perhaps if I was an investigator, I might treat that differently... But if I began to feel that...things were not adding up, I would begin to [challenge] after I'd developed a comfortable relationship...or felt the child was comfortable with me.

When Butler's testimony is finished, Dr. John Charles Yuille, expert witness for the prosecution, takes the stand. His specialty is memory, as we learned at Tammy's trial; in particular, he studies how children remember and disclose traumatic events they have eyewitnessed. After interviewing hundreds of children during the past fifteen years or so, including some former Mount Cashel residents, the forensic psychologist firmly believes that "it's not an easy task for a child to completely manufacture something that didn't happen." In preparation for the trial, Yuille has reviewed more than a dozen tapes of

Claudia Bryden and Rod Moor questioning the Martensville kids, and he has concerns about the job they did. In a nutshell, says the witness, the two officers asked the children too many questions of the wrong kind and too few of the right. Too many "leading and suggestive questions" and not enough to prompt the kids to "provide detail...their whole story." In other words, the officers lacked the proper experience and training.

I wonder, if the investigating officers had been properly trained, would they have interviewed the kids differently and heard different stories? Or would the stories have been the same, but richer in detail? None of us will ever know the answers to these questions. We have come to the point in the trial where the children and police officers have finished testifying and the prosecution's case is complete. Soon it will be time for the accused to tell their side of the story. Maybe then we'll get a fuller picture of what actually happened at the daycare.

The enemy expert

It's almost spring 1994, and we're nearing the end of the trial, which at six months is the longest in the history of Saskatchewan. Before going on to the case for the defence, where the three Sterlings get to speak for themselves, I want to turn back the clock to last spring, several months before their trial started, and just after Tammy's had finished. There was one event in particular that portrays the atmosphere in the community at that time and conveys the intense feelings the residents of Martensville and Saskatoon had about the events surrounding the trials.

On May 20, 1993, when Judge Albert Lavoie delivered his verdict at Tammy's trial, his finding pleased some in the community but angered others. Respecting Lavoie's ruling about the media ban, the *StarPhoenix* reported his verdict but not his reasons. The paper could not, the judge said, publish evidence that the court would hear again during the trial of the three Sterlings. Partially ungagged after four months of a total publication ban and not having been able to write a word about Tammy's trial, the reporter for the *StarPhoenix* heaved a sigh of relief at the judge's ruling. "Young Sexual Offender Gets Two-Year Sentence" read the headline that accompanied his front-page story, and the handful of local radio and television reporters who'd covered the trial composed and taped their scripts on the steps of the courthouse in time for the supper-hour news. I was a guest on "Morningside," and told Peter Gzowski I thought the trial was really about the difficulty of assessing the testimony of children. Still to come was the big trial, that of the Sterlings. Wedged between the trial of Tammy, the young offender, and the trial of the three adults was the trial of a policeman. For John Popowich, a Saskatoon officer, the court sat briefly and ended abruptly when Freddy, Kenny, and a third child plaintiff failed to identify Popowich in a police lineup.

The various decisions from the courthouse left residents as polarized about the children's allegations as they had been before, the only difference being that the allegations against Tammy had turned to convictions and the young woman was now facing prison. This was a big difference, especially for those in the community who believed she was not guilty.

It occurred to me that now the Martensville scandal had all the elements of a genuine potboiler: accusations of a witch hunt, allegations of child molestation, distraught parents, good cops and bad cops, and a convicted woman who was a natural blonde. All it needed to become a bestseller was a bit of holy water. Who better to bless the community and combat the forces of evil than an ordained clergyman, especially one who'd turned psychologist and looked like a cross between Colonel Sanders and Santa Claus?

A large man with the long white beard was invited to town by a handful of mostly middle-aged, middle-class women who called themselves the Community Awareness Project. They maintained that the children had fabricated evidence, and they were incensed that the judge had found Tammy guilty. They saw it as their civic duty to warn the community that the civil liberties of everyone were at stake, especially the three Sterlings, who were soon to go on trial. So the Project people went about town tacking posters on as many lamp posts as they could find. They also placed an ad in the *StarPhoenix* that said: "Public Meeting. Child Sexual Abuse: How to tell the difference between true and false allegations. Free Admission."

On June 18, Dr. Ralph Underwager, an expert in child-abuse allegations, came from Minneapolis for the meeting with his wife, Hollida Wakefield, also a psychologist. They liked to work as a team and billed themselves the "Number 1 Enemy Experts" of the U.S. Prosecutor's Office, because their views on issues involving child sexual abuse were frequently at odds with those of the state when prosecuting an alleged paedophile. By the time the pair arrived in Saskatoon, they'd already pitted their professional knowledge of child abuse against the testimony of hundreds of children in American courts. The his-and-hers photographs in the newspaper did justice to their looks, especially her young appearance.

But only a dozen people showed up for the Friday evening press conference presided over by Underwager and his wife. Only one local journalist was there, because what was the point of going to a press briefing if you couldn't file a story? Which you couldn't because of Judge Lavoie's publication ban. The CBC had obtained a formal legal opinion on the matter and gave no air time to the visitors so as not to be perceived as promoting "expert testimony" of any kind before the forthcoming trial of the Sterlings, or of being held in contempt for trying to do so. For their part, the Minnesota husband-and-wife team maintained they knew nothing about the Martensville case and said they'd come to Saskatoon as experts, not advocates. Maybe they believed they were impartial experts who would heighten the awareness of the local community. But I didn't, and neither did a lot of others in town.

If the Friday night press conference was a bust, the all-day Saturday session at the YMCA was a success, at least with regard to attendance. About 100 people decided to forgo the glorious early-summer weather outside in favour of squeezing into a hot, stuffy room beside the racquetball courts. It might not have been a big crowd by Toronto standards, but in a city of under 200,000, where the summer is shorter than a politician's memory, it's significant that so many adults deprived themselves of a whole day of summer. They undoubtedly felt the deprivation was worth the price, because being far from the black-robed sobriety and stodginess of the court, they could take satisfaction in expressing their real feelings about Judge Lavoie's verdict in particular and the Sterling scandal in general. For the first time since the scandal broke, members of the community could have their say. If venting their feelings was the first thing on their minds, heightening their awareness with the help of an American psychologist was probably the last.

By 9 o'clock Saturday morning, the daycare at the YMCA was crammed with adults gnashing their teeth and grinding their axes. Some citizens from Tammy's trial stuck name tags on their golf shirts, while a few of the expert witnesses helped themselves to coffee, and the lawyers from the trial, some of them good friends, patted each other on the back. Milling about the room were a few people accused of abusing the Martensville children but no longer under investigation, among them John Popowich, the Saskatoon policeman who had recently received a stay of proceedings.

While people took their seats in the hot crowded room, the experts themselves sat side by side on stage, patiently waiting for the commotion to die down. The invited speakers, Ralph Underwager, Ph.D., and Hollida Wakefield, M.A., looked just like their pictures in the paper.

While the men in the room loosened their shirt collars and women fanned themselves, Underwager began his awareness session. Child sexual abuse dredges up "very primitive, very atavistic feelings," he said, and every one of us has the capacity for savagery to kids. So far so good.

Underwager remained seated as he talked, fidgeting with his cane. "The problem [when interviewing children] is with the adults who have their own agenda and who pursue their own agenda." He continued: It is very serious to treat a non-abused child as an abused one. He or she might become a helpless victim or a psychotic. It's "like being raised in a war zone, like Beirut." Although I found the comparison to a war-torn country offensive, I got the message.

Underwager then turned to the topic of false memory syndrome and asked rhetorically, How can a child have a permanent memory of something that didn't happen? An adult may drive a child into the child's own fantasy life to find an answer. The fantasies include monsters, horrors and mayhem. To do that to a child is abuse. To which, his wife chimed in, "People can come up with actual memories."

Actual memories? That sounded like a contradiction in terms to me, since the word "actual" means real. How can a false memory be an actual or real one at the same time? Did Wakefield not know the meaning of the word actual, or did she mean that the person with the memory believes it to be real, even if it's false? I was starting to grow impatient with this psychobabble, as were others.

"Why did you come to Saskatoon?" asked a middle-aged woman in a red scarf, talking into the aisle mike with one hand on her hip. Underwager, sounding tired, answered her nasally, "We care about children." Just in case someone failed to understand that answer, he elaborated: The system now in place "damages more children than it helps... We've made the net so wide, they're scooping up some of the wrong fish." If there's an increase in abuse, we must find the cause of the increase, he said.

One woman stood up, doing a slow boil. She asked, "Are you qualified to tell us about medical evidence?" Hollida Wakefield coolly answered, "We're qualified to tell you about baseline research to date," sounding as though it wasn't the first time she'd heard the question. Probably no wiser but more sceptical, the questioner sat down, perhaps cowed by the word "baseline." But she deserved credit for asking the question. In Saskatchewan, direct questions like this are unusual.

But Satanism is not, according to the next man who spoke into the aisle microphone. Tongue-in-cheek, he told the crowd that Saskatoon seemed to be the "haven for Satanism and devil worship." The speaker was John Popowich. In response to the police officer's sarcasm, Underwager told his Saskatoon audience what he'd told millions of Americans months earlier on the Geraldo Rivera show: People alleging satanic ritual abuse are victims of "their mental health advisors." And the only place these accusers had ever been abused, he said, was in the office of their therapist, where false memories had been planted in their brain. I would have thought the matter was a little more complex than Underwager would have us believe.

The effects of sexual abuse are not nearly as serious as people think, said Underwager, hastening to explain to the fidgety crowd that a relatively small percentage of those abused, perhaps ten to twenty per cent, suffer serious psychological problems. That translates to between one in ten and one in five in the general population. I knew three people who'd been abused as children and remained emotionally troubled as adults. Mathematically, that's a high number of such people for me to know, if the incidence of long-term effects was as low as Underwager said. Could the numbers be wrong?

"They all stick together," shouted a man into the floor mike. He explained to the crowd that his daughter had once alleged he abused her, and her therapist believed it. Sphinx-like, Dr. Underwager responded, "The concept that rage is therapeutic, this is part of what is setting Western civilization on its ear because, until now, our society has been based on controlling rage." I wasn't sure if he thought the control factor had been good or bad for civilization.

A middle-aged man, a highly respected local lawyer, came to the mike and told the audience that rage was rampant. "We're no longer into attaining justice as much as we are into obtaining convictions regardless of the truth. Prosecutors dare not exercise judgement nowadays in sexual-abuse allegations. I think we've created a monster." Sensing a kindred spirit, Underwager nodded and agreed that acquittal "depends on your attorney, and how good he or she is."

The lawyer's condemnation of the legal system, and the guest speaker's concurrence, was just what police officer John Popowich was waiting for. The judicial system is contaminated, he said. Why was he denied due process? The charges [against him] were laid out of incompetence.

The heat in the room was overwhelming. One man called the therapeutic profession "a lot of semi-professionals," and one or two others said the legal system was just as suspect. The "awareness session" seemed to have turned into a free-for-all instead of the objective examination of the topic of children's allegations that the organizers had advertised. Given the tensions in town, I was not at all surprised. A man in an open-necked shirt and shorts left the room looking disgusted. I would have liked to leave myself and go downstairs to the pool to cool off.

One serious-looking woman, maybe a bit worried a mob might be in the making, tried to restore the meeting to its original purpose: "How can you tell when abuse has occurred?" she asked Underwager. There are no "magic bullets," he answered. If we knew how to answer that one simple question, some child sexual-abuse allegations might never reach the witness stand, the expert said unhelpfully. The woman sat down.

But this was the question that everyone wanted answered. Every adult in the room needed to know what clues to look for. A young athletic-looking man stood to rephrase the question, removing his glasses as he did. "How can you identify a child sexual abuser?" Again, Underwager failed to answer a serious question in a helpful way. He said there was no "one magic way" of identifying a paedophile, then launched into an essay about the pain an adult suffers when a false accusation is made. The young man sat down, shaking his head in frustration.

This meeting was sponsored by the Community Awareness Project. The crowd had come for answers, but there didn't seem to be many. But at 3 o'clock, Hollida Wakefield literally pulled a card from her sleeve. She said she'd got it at a convention of psychologists. The card, one in a set known as "projective storytelling cards," featured an altar with candles and a cross. She said that twenty per cent of allegations of child sexual abuse involve satanic elements.

And Ralph Underwager still had a couple of videotapes to show what bad interview techniques looked like. After the viewing, he told the audience that the theory and practice of interviewing had developed a lot in the past forty years, during the last thirty of which he and his wife had videotaped interviews of children. "There are no good reasons for not videotaping, only bad ones," he told the audience. I wondered if he knew about all the interviews that officers Claudia Bryden and Rod Moor hadn't taped.

After the tapes, a man grabbed the mike and spit his contempt for therapists into it: "According to the [interview] tapes we saw today, most psychologists couldn't pass their own tests." Underwager seized on this, saying, "The issue of competence for mental health professionals has never really been addressed, and apparently they are incapable of policing themselves."

Another man stormed out, probably as fed up with the whole thing as I was and without much hope of getting to the bottom of the Martensville mess. At 4 o'clock, those of us left in the stuffy room dispersed noisily, no more aware and just as polarized as before. Leaving the building, I learned from a lawyer friend that Dr. Ralph Underwager would be appearing, months later, as an expert witness for the defence at the trial of the three Sterlings.

The Defence

Expert witnesses

On a cold winter day in Saskatoon, the self-proclaimed "Number 1 Enemy Expert" of the U.S. Prosecutor's Office climbs into the witness box with the help of his cane. Dr. Ralph Underwager is here as an expert witness for the defence of the three Sterlings. The clinical psychologist is one of a number of witnesses, and one of a handful of experts, who will help the three-man defence team tell its side of the story, now that the Crown has had its say. Roles will now be reversed as the three defence lawyers conduct examinations-in-chief of each witness and the two prosecuting lawyers cross-examine them.

Besides having a Ph.D. in clinical psychology, Underwager has a Master's of Divinity and was a full-time Lutheran pastor until founding the Institute for Psychology in Minneapolis, where he has child clients as well as adults. With his heavy caseload, he doesn't preach much anymore, giving him something in common with Short Jim, the Anglican priest who comes to court every day now that he's retired. During a lull in proceedings, Jim whispers in my ear that Underwager reminds him of God, with his flowing white hair and beard. I write a note in return, saying he looks more like Moses to me.

Besides his professional qualifications Underwager has considerable experience, having dealt in his career with "well over 1,000" children alleging sexual abuse and having given expert testimony at 250 trials. When prosecutor Bauer challenges the man's credentials, Underwager admits that, in eight instances, the presiding judge disallowed some or all of his evidence, though no judge has ever disqualified him completely as an expert witness. Underwager says he is a scientist, a person who employs empirical study, quantifying and measuring. No one, he emphasizes, tells him what he can or cannot say.

After Underwager has been raked over the coals by Bauer, the court finds the witness qualified to testify in his areas of expertise: memory, suggestibility, and diagnosis and treatment of child abuse in addition to interviewing children and assessing the indicators of abuse. He publishes extensively, and one of his books is called *Solomon's Dilemma*. I imagine Short Jim sitting on the bench at the back of the room, designing a new spine for Underwager's book: "Written by God, Printed by Parchment Publishers."

Don Mullord, lawyer for Ron Sterling, steps forward to examine the psychologist on the topic of memory. The witness explains that memory is reconstruction, not recall. The mind does not work like a computer, he says, "We feel subjectively about certain memories." The problem starts when new ideas are mixed with old memories, like so much new and old paint. The fresh colour may be quite different from the original one, he says, and therefore false to the original event. Children are susceptible to having their colours changed, especially by adults, because their palette is less complex to begin with. Their mental images contain fewer details; they remember far less information than adults. Therefore, children have more room for new additions. They are more suggestible to misinformation and prone to false memories, not just about peripheral events but about central events as well.

Underwager's opinions weave in and out of the things we've heard from other experts, agreeing in some places and disagreeing in others. But the one thing all the experts agree about is the complexity of the issue.

The courtroom is packed, even the front-row benches, usually the last to be filled. Underwager continues: The use of anatomical dolls does not give "incremental validity," just the illusion of it. Therefore, their use can be positively harmful. People's liberties are at stake, intones Underwager, in a louder and louder voice. Judger Wimmer cuts into the monologue. "We don't need a lecture," he snaps.

Unperturbed, Underwager continues, pointing to the ceiling as though warning his flock of an impending storm. It's wrong to use dolls, he says, and rewards are wrong too, even verbal ones such as "good boy." The witness leans back in his chair, rests his hands on his stomach, and continues his recitation: Parents should not be present during a child's interview. Play therapy is of no value, and may even hurt the child. The interview itself should occur in a neutral and comfortable place, and there should be as few interviews as possible for the child.

Most of this makes sense to me, though I've always regarded kids' play as their version of adult work and animal hunt. Kids need play to develop, as much as eating and sleeping. Play is not frivolous. Kids know it, though some adults don't. I'm sceptical when Underwager says fear and anxiety are adult concepts. Does he mean that if it weren't for adults who offload their emotional burdens onto kids, children would never know fear? If so, I think the expert is trivializing the terrors that children face in their own world. I'd like to challenge him on this notion, and I'm sure a lot of parents in this room would too.

Repression — burying the memory of an event and dredging it up later, sometimes with help — is a highly suspect concept that can't be created in laboratory research, he continues. And there are no specific behaviours that indicate sexual abuse. Certain symptoms are stress indicators, but not necessarily indicators of sexual abuse.

Rod Butler, Freddy and Kenny's therapist, is taking notes at the back of the room. I wonder what's going through his head. What's going through mine is this: why does a child, out of the blue, show stress? Defence lawyer Don Mullord also wonders about this and asks. Obligingly, Underwager lists the possible causes of stress in a child's life: new school, new neighbourhood or sibling, death of a pet, illness, parental problems, being interrogated. Being interrogated? Mullord needs clarification and proposes the example of a hypothetical child who is, as the rest of us know, one of the daycare kids. Confronted with the constellation of symptoms, Underwager says that if the child in question suddenly became clinically depressed or angry, if he wet the bed or had nightmares and became compulsively neat, the symptoms might be the result of interrogation, not abuse.

Underwager probably knows the hypothetical child is a real one. In fact, he knows a lot about the Martensville daycare children, after studying almost two dozen of the police-interview video and audio tapes in preparation for his court appearance. And he doesn't think much of the interview techniques of officers Claudia Bryden and Rod Moor. He makes this clear for the court by describing their work as coercive, leading, suggestive, and contaminating, though not all in the same breath. Nor does he approve of some other things he saw and heard: dolls, parents, confusing instructions, repeated questions, selective reinforcement of a child's statements, failure to acknowledge a child's denials of wrongdoing, and encouraging a child's vengeful feelings and anger towards the accused. This is nothing I didn't already know, though it's a reminder of the serious deficiencies in the officers' interview techniques.

With Dr. Underwager's summary of police offences, defence lawyer Don Mullord has completed his examination-in-chief and prosecutor Bruce Bauer rises to begin the cross-examination. All of us who went to the awareness session Underwager gave at the YMCA last summer know that the witness is a controversial figure. Just how controversial he is comes as a surprise when Bauer asks him to identify a recently published copy of an issue of a Dutch journal called *Paidika, The Journal of Paedophilia*. The biannual publication has an international editorial board comprising a former Dutch senator, American professors, psychologists, a lawyer, and several writers and editors. It promotes paedophilia and carries advertisements for other organizations that do, too. One of these organizations, NAMBLA (North American Man-Boy Love Association), has an ad in the issue that Bauer hands to Underwager. In the same issue, Winter 1993, Underwager and his wife are interviewed at length about their views of paedophilia. Perhaps the most interesting thing Underwager says to the interviewer is this: Sexual orientation is learned behaviour, which means that every individual has freedom to choose, "courageously affirm what they choose," and "take personal responsibility for their own behaviour." They can say that what they want is to find the "best way to love."

I've never heard of *Paidika* and wonder how the prosecutors did. The defence lawyers must have been horrified when they heard Underwager would be questioned about the magazine interview. They wanted the witness to speak about the incompetence with which sexual-abuse allegations are frequently investigated and the poor interview techniques police officers use. His own interview will sidetrack this, maybe derail it. The "Number 1 enemy expert" of the American Prosecutor's Office is about to become the focus of this part of the trial.

Underwager tells the court it's time to have a conversation with the paedophiles of the world, to find out what makes them tick. Prevention programs aimed at kids don't work, he says, and neither have 2,400 years of punishing paedophiles.

It's been that long since the golden age of paedophilia in ancient Greece, when men loved boys with impunity and coined the word for intergenerational love. Curiously, while they were practising something this undemocratic, they were also developing democracy. And ordering their slaves about. Perhaps the men of ancient Greece liked making love to boys, but did the boys enjoy it? I seriously doubt that many boys in our modern world actively seek out sex with adults for their own enjoyment. Open your eyes in downtown Saskatoon or Regina at night and decide if kids do it with adults for fun. See if they are driven by lust rather than fear and need. Adults, on the other hand, gratify their psychological and sexual needs without regard for the rights of their young "lovers." Paedophilia is non-consensual sex, and I will continue to believe that until I get clear evidence to the contrary.

Bauer next grills the witness about statements he made during the Paidika interview. Is choosing paedophilia God's will? he barks. "I'm not privy to God's will," answers the witness. "I believe God's will is that we have absolute freedom. Therefore, we should take responsibility for our actions." He maintains that paedophiles have the right to say they are doing God's will and that it is "reasonable" for them to want to de-criminalize paedophilia. "I think any citizen has the right to address the state with respect to issues of justice." About the journal interview, Underwager asserts, "This article expresses my feelings and I still have these feelings." Later in the cross-exam, he says that "paedophilia is not a crime" as long as the fantasies about children remain in the adult's head. "The only hope we've got to reduce paedophilia is to persuade them [the paedophiles] that when they say they love children, that's not true." A case in point, he submits, was Lewis Carroll, the author of *Alice in Wonderland* and noted Victorian paedophile who justified the many photos he took of children and the stories he wrote about them by claiming he loved them. Underwager challenges the Victorian's claim, saying paedophiles are famous for "dumping" a child when he or she turns fifteen or sixteen and that paedophilia is a "travesty of God's love."

I'm confused. What ever happened to "Here I Stand," Martin Luther's manifesto of beliefs tacked to a church door in Germany 500 years ago? Luther, the founder of the faith that Underwager subscribes to, was a theologian who took his philosophical positions seriously. If the Lutheran theologian at the front of the courtroom takes a stand on paedophilia, I have difficulty determining what it is. Either he thinks paedophilia is primarily good in God's eyes, or not. If I were prosecutor Bauer, I'd ask Underwager to play one role, preferably himself, and stick to it. I'd ask him a few straightforward questions like: If you want a paedophile to take responsibility for his or her behaviour, when do you want them to do it? Before or after buggering a boy? Before or after fondling a girl? Before or after putting his penis in a boy's mouth? Before or after putting her finger in a girl's vagina?

The next question Bauer asks in cross-examining Underwager is why he's sceptical about anatomically detailed dolls. The psychologist answers: the dolls eroticize children the way *Playboy* eroticizes adults. Pardon? Does the witness know about the *Playboy* magazines police found during the raid on the Sterling house? I doubt he'd have answered that way, if he did.

Underwager's controversial interview in Paidika is entered as evidence so that Judge Wimmer can decide how much weight to give the opinions the expert offers in the courtroom. When the cross-exam is finished, Wimmer tells the witness, "We're done with you." Though Underwager looked at the jurors throughout his testimony, they didn't look at him. By now, some are glassy-eyed. After sitting and listening intently for so long they're probably exhausted, and recently they've begun whispering and writing notes to one another during testimony. Those who suffer from winter colds are sipping water from tumblers and sucking cough drops. Last week, after one juror had a prolonged coughing fit that drowned out the witness, Wimmer called for a couple of days' recess. I wonder if jurors are docked pay for those days, and whether they already got the raise the judge ordered the other day.

The second witness for the defence is Dr. Maggie Bruck, Ph.D., a psychologist who teaches and does research at McGill University. With her short brown hair and no-nonsense suit, she looks professional. Unlike Underwager, Bruck has not seen any of the police-interview tapes and admits to a very limited knowledge of the allegations. She is here because she knows a great deal about interview techniques. Bruck and her McGill colleagues perform experiments with children to find out how they think and remember things, when they tell the truth and when they don't. She has learned, for instance, that the longer the time lapse between the alleged event and the interview, the more forgetful the child and apparently the more suggestible. Children, she tells the court, are also susceptible to stereotype induction, which means that if you tell a child that someone is bad, the child soon starts to believe it, according to her findings. Bruck, like Underwager, has found that rewards are inappropriate in an interview and that the use of anatomically detailed dolls may lead to false allegations.

Bruck has labelled certain concepts for which I never knew there was a name. For instance, interviewer bias is something all journalists know about, though few would admit to ever having it. Bias is what you think and feel before an interview; it is the sum of your ideas about the person or the event in question.

Journalists used to think they could be completely objective, that "just the facts, ma'am" was a worthy goal, achieved with statistics and quotations. Then along came the "New Journalism" of the 1960s, which promoted subjectivity and encouraged journalists to admit they were seeing things with their own eyes (this book being a case in point). Maybe what's needed is a "New Psychology": there would be general acknowledgement that an interviewer, being only human, possesses natural bias before an interview and therefore finds it difficult to achieve objectivity during the interview. If everyone started from that point, perhaps everyone would be calmer about the interview process in general, and the professional sniping at people like Claudia Bryden could be put in perspective. What would Bryden say if she could talk with this expert witness now about interviewer bias?

One thing Bryden would hear is that when an adult leads a child to a particular objective, and barrels along without challenging the answers the child gives, the adult is guilty of "blind pursuit." Show me a person who has never been guilty of this. When you're in a hurry, blind pursuit is the quickest route, as every parent knows.

"Source attribution error" is another problem Dr. Bruck has studied in a controlled setting at McGill. As a working journalist, I sympathize with anyone, especially a child, who forgets who said what and who did what to whom. This can lead, explains Bruck, to "source confusion." The children in her experiments may be led to believe something happened when it did not. Even when told they're mistaken, they may still cling to their belief. Although I hate to admit it, I've experienced source confusion myself. That's why I take notes on the spot.

Then there's peer pressure. In Dr. Bruck's laboratory, this occurs when the interviewed child is told what other interviewed children have already said and is thereby encouraged to fall in line with the received information. She believes a child can be influenced in this way to think he or she was abused. She may believe this, but has she actually done research to prove it?

The question is asked by Bruce Bauer, the first in his cross-examination of the psychologist. No, none of her studies have involved kids who've suffered sexual abuse, she says. Bruck, who doesn't like to respond yes or no to Bauer's questions, gives him long answers, and sometimes the lawyer accidentally cuts her off in mid-sentence. On the other hand, she sometimes stops talking to let him speak, "I'll let you finish," she says once. This is an amusing turnabout in protocol. Bauer is very polite, addressing her as "doctor," even when she contradicts him.

State. Contradict. Disagree. Update. Revise. Restate. That's the nature of the academic world that Dr. Bruck inhabits. So it's not surprising to hear her say there is professional disagreement about the word "leading," which is like a sliding scale because what leads one child will not necessarily lead another. Because some kids are "amazingly resistant to suggestion," she says scientists have not yet arrived at a definitive conclusion about child suggestibility.

If scientists cannot agree on the matter, why have we been sitting in this courtroom for five months? And how will the jurors ever decide if the Martensville children were led by police to make the allegations they did? Judge Wimmer may wonder these things as well, for he tells the jurors that all the scientific research and expert evidence in the world is not going to help them do their difficult job.

Perhaps the third witness for the defence can shed more light on the suggestibility of children. Dr. David Raskin is a psychologist who teaches at the University of Utah and sometimes at the RCMP College in Ottawa. The court qualifies him to give expert testimony on interviewing procedures and the effects of suggestibility in adults and children. Over the years, Raskin has studied 1,500 taped interviews of children and has just reviewed some of the police tapes of the Martensville children. His assessment of them is scathing.

The small wiry doctor looks tidy in glasses, beard, and sombre suit. He's the kind of person I believe right off the bat, not because he has a professional résumé thirty-five pages long, but because he doesn't mince words.

"Extremely substandard" is Raskin's assessment of the police-interview tapes of the Martensville children. He says that what he saw violated all norms of interviewing and was sometimes "leading, suggestive, and coercive." In particular, the interviews Rod Moor conducted contain "some of the most serious violations" he has ever seen. "I was shocked," he says, referring to some of Moor's techniques, such as inappropriate pressure and selective rewarding, and he criticizes the officer for fear induction.

Raskin sees a big difference between the level of expertise in the interviews done by Rod Moor, the Saskatoon police teacher, and that of Claudia Bryden, the Martensville police student. He thinks the student did better than the teacher. Raskin knows what a good police interview looks like and says that the more times police interview a child the more opportunities there are for "cross-fertilization" and contamination.

The fourth witness is an American psychologist, Dr. Celia Fisher. She is in her early thirties, comes from New York, and wears a designer-label blue suit nicely fitted over an understated white blouse. Her long, straight hair and glasses give her a professional air which suits her job as director of developmental psychology at Fordham University. She also teaches and specializes in applying developmental psychology to the family setting. Dr. Fisher likes to look to the whole family for clues about an individual member's behaviour.

She does not diagnose, assess, or treat children and does all her research examining non-referred or average children. Though Fisher has had no direct contact with the Martensville daycare kids, she received a list of their symptoms to help her prepare for this court appearance.

When Earl Kalenith asks Fisher for her expert opinion on the possible origins of some of the symptoms, she goes through the list in a dispassionate way. She makes them sound far less serious to me than when the daycare parents talked about their children's behaviour. I guess that makes sense, since the daycare kids don't belong to Fisher, and she hasn't even met them. Dr. Fisher is commenting on the behaviour, not the children themselves.

Self-mutilation (such as Kenny's finger-clipping) would concern a professional, she tells Kalenith. Bedwetting and soiling are caused by stress. Separation anxiety, which Kenny's mom called clinginess, is normal at various stages in a child's development. Freddy's stomach aches and nausea may indeed be caused by abuse. A child's grabbing his own genitals, or someone else's, as Tommy and Janey's mother testified, proves nothing. A child's self-esteem is complex and depends on many factors. Anxiety is helpful and teaches children new things, such as watching for cars when they cross the street. It does not necessarily indicate sexual abuse.

Is psychology quantitative or qualitative? Is it a science, an art, or a combination of the two? Defence lawyer Earl Kalenith asks the witness if psychologists will ever develop standardized techniques to assess a child's behaviour and infer sexual abuse. No, answers Dr. Fisher. She also tells the lawyer that parents are not better than doctors, lawyers and psychologists at deciphering their own children's behaviour. When she says parents are not the best judge of their own kids, Judge Wimmer doesn't like it and interrupts the psychologist to say she's coming dangerously close to assessing the weight of the daycare parents' testimony. "I don't want this witness stepping into the jury's shoes," he cautions Kalenith. Dr. Fisher is paid her expert fee to speak as an expert, period.

Now that I'd listened to experts for the prosecution and for the defence, I knew a lot more than I did a few weeks ago, but I understood a lot less. Expert testimony had started to give me a headache, though not quite as sharp as the heartache I knew I'd feel sitting at the dining-room table for my second Christmas apart from my husband. I hate eating dinner by myself, even more than sleeping alone. My friends, who'd rallied to help me endure the pain of divorce and for whom I'd gained a deeper appreciation, had invited me to seven parties and dinners for the coming holidays. And my court-reporter colleagues had organized a pre-Christmas dinner for the dozen or so of us.

At that dinner, a journalist-who-shall-remain-nameless had three drinks and told the twelve of us he needed our help to start a pool. One of the jurors had worn a sweatshirt to court every day so far, and the reporter wanted us to bet how many different ones the juror owned. We were to put our signed bets and five dollars in the envelope he'd brought with him. The winner of the pool would be declared at the end of the trial, in a few weeks' time.

Everyone agreed it was a good idea to relieve the tedium of the courtroom and reached into their wallet — except Janis. Even though no one in court would ever know about the pool, she didn't feel right about mocking the man and said she was offended. Besides, she said, maybe he couldn't afford new clothes and sweatshirts were all we had. To tell the truth, I was proud of Janis and happy when the pool was nixed. I wouldn't feel right either, sitting in court betting on a juror like a racehorse. Even if we were about to enter the home stretch.

Ron Sterling testifies

Wimmer welcomes us back after the holidays, the regulars and a few new faces, about forty in all today. The jury files in. I can't help notice the bright red sweatshirt on one of them and wonder if it was an anonymous Christmas gift from a journalist. Two male reporters glance at each other and suppress boyish grins.

Don Mullord, Ron Sterling's legal-aid lawyer, stands to address the jurors in a faint British accent. He wants to get them on his wavelength with a show of human warmth. "You may be wondering how long you'll be here. If all goes according to plan, it should take three weeks. My office expects me back February 1, and I hope to return to my normal life then." He pauses, hesitates, and half smiles. Between now and then, he adds, it's the defence team's turn to tell what he calls the "other half of the story."

"Ronald Sterling will tell you shortly that he is innocent of these charges," Mullord tells the court in his soft, shy voice. The Sterlings are puzzled and amazed because they cared for the children properly at their home. Our position, he says, is that the children were never sexually assaulted and that any suggestions to the contrary result from the investigative process. The investigation was improperly handled from the very beginning, the fall day in 1991 when the father of Janey called Claudia Bryden. When a conclusion is reached too early, a police investigation goes in the wrong direction. "The children figured out what it was they were supposed to say" and tried to please the adults and do what they thought was expected of them, the lawyer emphasizes. The children are not lying *per se*, but have come to believe what the adults want them to.

Ron Sterling may look grumpy, Mullord says. That's because he has a lot to be grumpy about. But he is a warm and friendly person. His life has been committed to raising his family, to his work, community organizations, and his friends. Come to think of it, the forty-six-year-old does looks grumpy up there in the witness box, and no wonder. If he is found guilty of sodomizing any of the children or threatening them with a weapon, he may go to jail. Mathematically his chances of going there are lower than they were when the trial started in September, because the prosecution has just reduced the charges against him from twenty to sixteen. You'd think that would give him something to smile about.

But gone is the jack-o'-lantern grin, which used to spread ear-to-ear when anyone in the courtroom cracked a joke. No longer do the lip and cheek muscles rise or lift his skin to smile; now they sink and pull. And every now and then, a rebellious spasm ripples his lower jaw.

What Ron Sterling tells the court when he takes the stand is very matter-of-fact, starting with his life history. Born December 12, 1947, he grew up in Prince Albert. In 1966, he graduated from Prince Albert Composite High School and soon after started work and married his high school sweetheart, Linda. The following year their first child was born. Then Sterling and a friend — "him and I" — went into business. But the business went broke and he sought other employment, first at a garage, then at the Prince Albert Correctional Centre, where he worked his way up the ladder to assistant deputy director until he was suspended in early 1992 because of the criminal charges. In 1981, he and his wife and their three young children moved to Martensville. Six years later they built the now-famous house on Fifth Street, with the help of family and friends, among them the father of Sally.

Ron Sterling has made a contribution to every community he has ever lived in. Cub leader in Prince Albert, volunteer fire fighter for Martensville and nearby Rosthern, emergency medical worker, attending forest fires and highway accidents, sometimes in the company of RCMP officers.

Sterling's parents gave him his first gun, a .22, when he was twelve. It's still part of his collection, which now includes two .38 pistols, five shotguns, and a pellet rifle, which he uses to give cats and dogs "a snap on the rear end" when they rummage in the garbage. For birds and other animals, such as gophers and dump rats, he may use one of the other guns, depending on his mood. Sterling also has an unusual passion. He likes to collect guns made of glass and has built a collection over the years comprising more than 100 Avon cologne bottles — gun-shaped glass gifts from friends and family.

As for the Polaroid camera that police found during their raid, Sterling says he hasn't used it since the late 1970s. And the vibrator the police also found in the master bedroom? That was a "joke gift" to his wife from her sister one Christmas.

Mullord's examination-in-chief now takes Sterling back to 1988, and the original complaint Sally's father lodged with police. One day Ron Sterling received a phone call from Darryl Ford. When Mullord asks him, he acknowledges he knew Ford, and the lawyer doesn't ask when or how they met. Ford, then chief of the Martensville police service, told Sterling a complaint had been filed against his son, Travis, and that he was to bring the young man to the station. Sterling did as he was told, and he and his son met with the investigating officer, Ed Revesz. Travis signed a statement, then father and son left. Six months passed before Ron Sterling called the police to enquire about the status of the charge against Travis.

"Certainly I've got to know them all pretty well," Sterling says about the local police, several of whom were charged with sexual assault against the daycare kids. For instance, he and Jim Elstad have known each other for some time because Jim worked with Ron's brother, Bob, and has often been to the Sterling house. He and John Popowich have known each other for at least a decade, and once worked together. Popowich has never been to his house, unlike Ed Revesz who was there once.

Wimmer stifles a yawn. He looks as though he could use another holiday, but settles for a short break. I button up my purple Linda Lundström and run over to the Bessborough for tea and a muffin. Even though I don't need the calories, I do need the view of the river from the garden café, one of the great sights in Saskatoon. The South Saskatchewan, though not nearly as wide as the Niagara River where I grew up, is almost as romantic. Ice buries the river where it's shallow, and mist rises from where it flows free. At minus 40, the river that snakes through the middle of Saskatoon is the city's only natural feature that still moves in the dead of winter.

When I return to the courthouse to hear the rest of Ron Sterling's examination-in-chief, Kenny's aunt is leaning on the rail at the top of the stairs outside the courtroom. I know who she is because Janis pointed her out the day the woman was crying in the back row and Kenny's mom was crying in the witness box. Today the aunt is dry-eyed, but she looks fragile, as though it wouldn't take much to make her break down. She tells me Kenny still has frequent bouts of crying. The entire family is devastated by the boy's allegations, and even more by his behaviour. I think of my niece, my brother's only child, and how I worry about her safety. I know that if anything ever happened to her, my brother would never be the same and neither would my sister-in-law. She still hasn't completely recovered from the murder of her teenage sister, twenty years ago, in Toronto. I tell Kenny's aunt I'm deeply sorry and walk over to the courtroom, where Don Mullord is still examining Ron Sterling.

The room is silent. The witness is talking about the children who came to his house and how he always tried to make them feel welcome there. Freddy "was always a polite little guy," though sloppy and dirty — in short, a typical kid. He was respectful and did what he was told, except for the couple of times he played hookey and Ron had to drive him to school. I wonder what it would be like if Freddy were now permitted to cross-examine Ron Sterling in person, the way they sometimes do in European courts. The man and the boy could discuss the hookey incidents and their different feelings.

But Canadian courts haven't advanced to the stage where the alleged victim cross-examines the alleged criminal. No one is allowed this privilege but lawyers. Mullord asks Sterling if he ever put a pillowcase over Freddy's head in an old house or sodomized the boy, tied him to a pole, injected him with a needle, or threatened to kill him and his parents. To each of the allegations, the accused answers, "No, I didn't."

Mullord moves on. What about your relationship with Kenny? he asks his client. Sterling explains that Kenny came to the house once or twice, though never to be babysat. And never to watch a movie. I wonder if Kenny would insist he watched *Terminator II* at the Sterling house, if he were here.

Sterling is adamant. In reply to each of Mullord's questions, he answers, "No, I did not." He testifies that he did not shove the vibrator or the axe handle into Kenny, stick a needle in his bum, suck his penis, sodomize him, or lock him in a cage. When Mullord suggests that the allegations are false, Sterling asserts, "Yes, they are." It comes to light that not only did Ron Sterling get help building his house from Sally's father, but also from the father of Bill and Anne. And Linda Sterling used to have tea with their mother. "Yeah, they were friends," he tells the examiner.

I'm feeling very uncomfortable and wonder how these four adults handled their friendship after the children's allegations. According to Sterling, he and the kids' father have talked on the phone since then. I can only imagine the conversation, and the tone of Ron's voice when he told his old friend to ask his own kids, Bill and Anne, for the details of the alleged events.

In the Sterling house, Kathy was called "Gabby" because she liked to talk and her brother, Frank, was "Onion" because he "had way too much energy."

I wonder how their parents liked the daycare nicknames. I'd be very displeased if my babysitter found my daughter too talkative and my son too energetic and gave them nicknames. But later I'll learn Ron had his own nickname: Lumpy. I'm developing a mental picture of the kind of relationship he had with each of the kids. Besides chatty Kathy and hyperactive Frank and dirty, sloppy Freddy, there was Tommy, a boy who Sterling says "wanted to control." Maybe I'm expecting too much of this man, who was not the one responsible for the daycare kids' welfare. It was his wife's job. And soon she'll be testifying.

Mullord's examination-in-chief of Ron Sterling doesn't take long. Since neither Hugh Harradence nor Earl Kalenith has questions for the accused, the court is ready for the cross-examination. But the prosecutor is not. Sullivan tells Wimmer that things have moved more speedily this morning than she anticipated and she still needs time to prepare her material. Wimmer wonders aloud if it's time for a break. Ron Sterling, thinking Wimmer is asking him personally, answers, "It would be nice to have a smoke break." Wimmer, confronted by the breach of protocol in his court, merely says, "Fine."

Ron Sterling has finished his cigarette.

Not until Leslie Sullivan cross-examines Sterling does it hit me that he worked shifts while assistant deputy director of security at the Saskatoon Correctional Centre. Sometimes he worked all night and slept all day. Sometimes he had three days off in a row, sometimes four.

Ron Sterling kept magazines in the house like *Penthouse Variations*, which the court classifies pornographic. The magazines were gifts, though Sterling is not sure who gave them to him. Over the years he has received books from "all different kinds of people." He collects paperbacks, among them Louis

L'Amour westerns published by Bantam Books, which promotes L'Amour's 100 titles as the "best of the real west." I imagine Sullivan raising an eyebrow when she asks, "You would agree that the substance of [Variations] is quite a bit different than a Louis L'Amour novel?" The accused lowers his voice: "Yes, they are."

"Where would you read them [the magazines]?" she asks. "When I was in the bathroom," he replies. "Did you ever read them in the living room?" The answer is no. The bedroom? "I don't believe so." The kitchen? No. "So is your evidence that you would never have been reading a magazine like exhibit P-47 in the living room?" Sterling says yes, that is his evidence. Never? Never. "Your evidence is that the only place you ever did read them was in the bathroom off the master bedroom?" He replies, "I'm positive."

According to the Ron Sterling's evidence, his house had two bathrooms, an ensuite and the main bathroom. In the main one the porn magazines were always kept in a cupboard "seven feet in the air." When you have such items, Sterling asserts, "you put them away and you keep them away." Porn magazines are not the kind of thing you "hand about in the public when you got kids coming and going."

Sterling does admit that he let the daycare kids watch scary cartoons on TV. "Most of the kids...we've been in some of their homes and seen what they watch. Their parents have been in our home and seen what we watched... None of the parents ever told us that there was programs on TV that the kids couldn't watch." And Sterling never asked. Sullivan: "You felt that anything on TV the kids could watch because it was on TV?" Sterling replies, "Anything that doesn't have a rating on it." Sullivan sneaks the word "permitted" into one of her questions. Ron Sterling answers yes, he permitted the daycare kids to watch "normal TV" or taped cartoons.

I thought he said he never babysat them. I would have thought that all decisions about TV viewing would have been the responsibility of the same person who had overall responsibility for the children, his wife Linda. Either Ron Sterling had responsibility or he didn't.

In the next breath, Sterling acknowledges that he tracked Freddy down one day and drove him to school. He explains, "When the kids didn't get there [school] when they were supposed to, somebody went looking for them." In a lighter moment, he jokes that he used to play hookey himself when he was young.

I like to watch Sullivan cross-examine Sterling and compare her style with the four male lawyers in the room. I'd say she ranks second from the top with respect to aggressiveness. Throughout the cross-exam, her brown pageboy cut stays neat. Sullivan asks, Why did you wait six months before calling the police to see what they planned to do about Sally's complaint in 1988 against

Travis? Sterling replies, "Well, we were, basically we were told what they thought was going to happen." Does he mean the police told him they were going to do nothing for six months?

Knowing that neither she nor anyone else in the room will ever hear what the Martensville police said to Ron Sterling and his son that day, Sullivan focuses on another facet of Sally's allegation, "Did you tell any of the parents of the children your wife was babysitting about the allegations made by Sally?" No, replies Sterling. "Did it not concern you that they might be interested to know so that they could make a choice as to whether or not to remain with your wife's babysitting service?" Sterling answers, "I never thought about it at the time. It was something that...happened to us. We didn't spread it around."

If Sterling didn't talk to anyone about the first formal complaint against his son in 1988, he had to talk about the second one in 1991. Before anyone else could break the bad news to his boss, Sterling went to him right away and told him Travis had been arrested. Sullivan tries to refresh the father's memory of the occasion. Do you recall having a conversation that day with Wayne Whitford and Ralph Pistun about Travis? Yes, replies Sterling. She asks, Do you recall saying to those two individuals that "maybe if we would have done something about this three years ago, none of this would have happened"? Did you say that? He answers, "I don't recall those words, no." Sullivan sounds impatient. "Okay. Did you say something that was the gist of those words?"

Sullivan doesn't like his answers, and Sterling doesn't like her questions, this one in particular, which he insists on translating into his own words. Though different, they seem to add up to the same thing she just said.

It feels like obedience school. The accused is an old dog to whom the prosecutor can't teach new tricks, the first one being respect for authority. If only she could snap him on the rear with the leash and, when he paraphrases her questions, throw his own words back at him: "That's what I just got done saying." Instead of punishing him like a naughty puppy, she stays on the high road. Question: "So it's possible that you did indeed say the words that I quoted to you?" Answer: "I don't think so, no. I don't think I would have phrased it that way." If this were obedience school, Sterling would fail for sure.

The prosecutor keeps her temper and continues to cross-examine the accused her way. "With respect to the search on December 12, 1991, your evidence is that you had no knowledge whatsoever that it was going to take place?" Sterling answers, "None whatsoever." You hadn't heard the rumours rampant in Martensville? "No," replies Sterling. Not at all? "No." None of your friends took advantage of (the situation) to tell you about it? "No."

Sullivan, still trying to keep her cool, asks the witness, During the police search, is it true you turned on the VCR despite the fact that officers present requested you not to do that? "Yes, ma'am," replies Sterling, somewhat sarcastically. "It was my own home and I was not under arrest." Sounding as though he's still mad as hell about the search, he continues, "To put it politely, [the police] made a helluva mess of our house... It took us about two weeks to get it cleaned up and things back where they belonged... We had to clean the floors because they didn't have the courtesy to take their boots off."

It must be tough to be on one side of the law one day, and the other side the next. Yesterday you worked at the prison and kept the inmates in line; today you're on trial and face living in a cell yourself. One day you live in Martensville and run a babysitting service in your home; the next day you're told to stay out of town, live with your parents, and not go near any child unsupervised. One minute you're having coffee with your police buddies, next thing you know they're raiding your home.

Sullivan continues: Was there a reason the children were no longer allowed to go into the basement? Sterling treats the question with disdain: "Yes, because they were getting into stuff that they had no business being into."

I bet it's a strain to have other people's children in your home day in, day out. How does a babysitter handle the issue of boundaries? Kids need to explore. A daycare should be a special place, where kids are not restricted to the kitchen, living room, and bathroom the way it sounds they were at the Sterling house.

Sullivan: When did your wife, Linda, get the vibrator?

Sterling: A long time ago.

Sullivan: Did you ever use it?

Sterling is speechless. Don Mullord rises to object to the question and to protect the privacy of his client. Judge Wimmer, sounding weary, tells Sullivan she's going a bit far, and recommends she rephrase her question, relating the use of the vibrator to the children.

Sullivan: Did you ever use the vibrator in respect to the children?

Sterling: No, I did not.

Sullivan: How do you know where it was kept?

Sterling: Because [the dresser drawer] is where it was put. I know where most things are in the house. It was put in the dresser, and that's where it stayed.

Now the entire courtroom knows Linda's vibrator was kept in a nine-drawer dresser, and we'll soon learn that in the same drawer with the sex toy she kept her nightgown and wrapping paper. In the bottom drawer of the dresser Ron stored his military pantleg weights — the two "riddle ropes" Kenny talked about — beside his military beret and his Boy Scout beret and neckscarf.

Besides being sentimental about his possessions, Sterling sounds like a neat freak, and he was very upset that the search squad left his dresser drawers a mess. If Sterling believes so strongly that there's a place for everything, it's surprising he sometimes left his single-shot pellet rifle propped up against the kitchen wall in view of the children. "I didn't see any harm in it because it was never loaded," Sterling tells prosecutor Sullivan. However, he admits, Linda disapproved of this habit and gave him "heck quite a few times" for leaving it within reach of the daycare kids.

If the gun wasn't loaded, Sterling would have had to put the pellets in each time he wanted to shoot the cats and dogs that wandered into the yard to forage for garbage. ("Snap them on the rear end," as he poetically put it earlier.) To protect the sensibilities of the kids, he says he waited until dark to shoot at anything.

For all his concern about the children, Sterling did not have formal responsibility for them. Still, that didn't stop him from picking up Freddy the day he caught him playing hookey, giving him "heck," and driving him to school.

Sullivan: Can you think of any other reason why Freddy would want to take revenge on you?

Sterling: No.

Sullivan: Your explanation...for Freddy's allegations is not that he is lying, is it?

Sterling: I don't have an explanation for his allegations. As far as I'm concerned, his allegations are a lie.

Sullivan: Your evidence, then, is that Freddy was lying, is that correct?

Sterling: Whether he believes he's lying or not, I don't know. But I know that the accusations are not true. So therefore they must be a lie.

Sullivan: Can you explain to us how Freddy might have seen the *Penthouse* magazine in your house?

Sterling: I have no idea. I don't recall him ever being in our bathroom and the ones in the main bathroom were like...seven feet off the floor.

Sullivan: Is it not possible perhaps it was left out by someone other than yourself?

Sterling: No.

Sullivan: Not possible?

Sterling: Not possible.

Sullivan: Even when you weren't there?

Sterling: I don't believe it's possible, okay?

Sullivan: And I'm challenging you on that. I want to know why you say it's not possible.

Sterling: I know you're challenging me on it. I don't believe it's possible. People in our house, if they're reading a book like that, did not leave it around for any children to read, or get a view of.

Sullivan: Not even accidentally once?

Sterling: Why would you leave it out accidentally?

Judge Wimmer has had enough. "Excuse me, it's not very helpful to have an argument. I mean, he says he doesn't think it's possible. The jury will make of that what it will." At the mild reproof, Sullivan says, "Fine, M'Lord," and turns her attention to the topic of Kenny.

Sullivan: Your evidence is that you basically hardly knew the lad?

Sterling: That's right.

Sullivan: Your evidence is that he never got past the door?

Sterling: I know he came to the door lots of times to get Freddy, but he didn't come in the house.

Sullivan: Okay. And your evidence is that he never saw a movie at your house?

Sterling: Not the movie he said he watched, that's for sure. And besides that, I don't recall him ever being in our house to watch any video movie.

Sullivan: So your evidence is that he never saw a movie in your house?

Sterling: No.

Sullivan: And, likewise, your evidence would be that he certainly was never in your bedroom, or Tammy's bedroom or Travis's bedroom?

Sterling: He would have had no reason to be in any of those rooms.

I wonder: If Kenny was never in the Sterling house, how did he draw the floor plan for the court during Tammy's trial?

Sterling maintains that his personal dealings with Kenny were limited to brief conversations on the doorstep of his house. He tells the Crown prosecutor he cannot think of a reason for the boy to be vengeful towards him.

He told me the same thing when I ran into him accidentally the next day at lunch in the Vietnamese restaurant. When I asked him, Do you think this is all a conspiracy? he answered, Yes. When I asked why people would form a conspiracy against him, he said, "I've racked my brains." If nothing happened, I asked, why would Freddy need to see a therapist approximately forty-five times and Kenny twenty-five? "I've never seen the transcripts, so I don't know," said Sterling.

Sterling talked to me while I wrote in my purple notepad. He said his family had belonged to St. Alban's Cathedral for forty-five years, and that his minister had been helpful throughout the ordeal. He was also a member of the Masonic Lodge in Prince Albert, but had decided not to go to meetings until the scandal blew over. His back had been injured twice, once when as a firefighter he fell off a roof during a fire and once when as an emergency medical technician he tried to move a patient. I asked how he felt now and he said, "Pretty good," adding that he'd continue to feel good as long as Judge Wimmer didn't mollycoddle the "poor little cop" (Bryden). "She's one sick lady," he said, adding that there were enough real cases of child abuse without having to fabricate them. As for the other police officers involved in the investigation, they did an incompetent job. He was so angry about his arrest that, on the day they came to the house, he "probably would have ended up with assault charges" if two of the presiding officers had not restrained him. If he was still mad during our interview, his anger was tinged with a sense of helplessness. "I don't know what to say... How do you prove you didn't do anything?"

If he was convinced he'd done nothing wrong, Leslie Sullivan was not. During the afternoon sitting, she resumes her attempt to prove the case against him. She asks, What about the time you went to pick up strawberry plants at the home of Kathy and Frank? "We heard evidence that...the children really didn't want to have anything to do with you." Sterling replies, "I have to disagree with that evidence," adding that the kids were "friendly towards us." Referring to a minor incident, Sullivan asks: What about Tommy and the gardening-tools? Sterling explains: Tommy, for whatever reason, was upset with Linda Sterling and went outside. When Ron went out, he says, the tools were strewn all over the yard. "I mean, I can't prove that [Tommy] did it, but I have a feeling he did. He was that type of a child to me."

In his mind, Sterling convicted Tommy of something he can't prove. I hope jurors don't do the same to him.

If Sterling saw Tommy as the terror of the daycare, Sally was the darling. He liked her so much he once took her for a ride in his new car, from Martensville to Prince Albert. He let the other kids call him "Uncle" and sometimes took them on outings to the grocery store, the post office, the doctor, restaurants, and to see friends, though for the most part he can't remember whom he took where or when.

How he transported them is what interests prosecutor Leslie Sullivan, mother of two. Sterling explains that if the parents left a car seat, he used it; if not, he just belted them in. "Would you tell the parents in advance [you were] going to the grocery store?" No, he answers.

Sullivan's performance is so convincing that I can't decide if she's genuinely angry about what she perceives as sloppy management at the daycare or if she's just doing her job as the Crown prosecutor. But I am convinced she enjoys seeing Sterling squirm.

"Did you ever use foul language in your house...in the presence of the children?" she snaps. Sterling replies candidly, "Probably... Prior to this trial starting, or prior to us being arrested, I had a bad habit of swearing. Since it [the trial] started, I've been watching my language quite a bit."

Sullivan: You did not have a baby-gate at the top of the basement stairs, did you?

Sterling: A what?

Sullivan: A baby-gate.

Sterling: Oh, one of them sliding gates?... No, we didn't need one... The kids were taught not to go near the stairs.

Sullivan: And you're referring to children as young as a year, are you not?

Sterling: Yes.

Sullivan: Children who are crawling?

Sterling: M'hm.

Sullivan: Children who are just learning to walk?

Sterling: Yes.

Sullivan: And you taught them not to go near the stairs?

Sterling: That's right.

Sullivan: Well, how do you do that?

Sterling: The same way I taught them not to touch some of the stuff in the house.

Sullivan: How'd you do that?

Sterling: I'm not sure.... Somehow we taught them. I don't know how...

Sullivan: I'm sure every parent in the room would like to know, Mr.

Sterling. Can you not recall it for us?

Sterling: I don't know how we taught them... We had no problem with the kids going near the stairs.

Sullivan sounds sceptical, and so are some of us who stay in the courtroom during break to discuss Sterling's testimony. The ten-minute discussion ends when Wimmer opens his door, fixes his long black gown like a skirt as he sits, and nods for the commissionaire to let the jurors back in.

Under Sullivan's fire, the accused's face occasionally reddens and his jaw clenches when she asks a question he doesn't like, but he's obviously trying to keep the lid on his anger. If he didn't cooperate while in the witness box, it wouldn't look good and it just might affect the community's attitude towards him and the four police officers scheduled to be tried in the coming months.

Sullivan asks Ron Sterling about his relationships with these four officers, whom the children have accused of abusing them at the daycare and The Place. The first officer in question is Jim Elstad. Sterling says that Elstad worked for the Prince Albert city police while he worked at the Prince Albert Correctional Centre. Sterling left P.A. in 1980 and went to Saskatoon to start a new job as shift supervisor at that Correctional Centre, where he was one of four responsible for round-the-clock security of the facility. The following year he moved his family to Martensville, from where he could drive in less than twenty minutes to his new job in Saskatoon. In 1986, Elstad moved to Martensville to work with the Martensville Police Department. By that time, the Sterlings had built their home in Martensville and, besides their own three young children, welcomed other children into their house to be looked after.

Darryl Ford also worked on the P.A. police force. In the late 1970s, Ford left Prince Albert and moved to Martensville. By the time the Sterlings moved there in 1981, he was chief of police. When he was later charged with several counts of child abuse, the court ordered him to "not be within a five-mile radius of Martensville, except when travelling on Highways 11 and 16, and except when in Saskatoon."

In 1986 Ed Revesz joined the Martensville police force, while Darryl Ford was still chief. Ford and Revesz had grown up together in small-town Saskatchewan. Apparently Ford also knew both John Popowich and Jim Elstad from police college.

By 1986 Sterling, Elstad, Ford, and Revesz all lived in Martensville. As for the fourth accused, Darren Sabourin of the RCMP, Sterling tells Sullivan that the two of them occasionally worked together. He also worked briefly with the fifth officer, John Popowich, investigating drug possession among inmates.

Unlike the other four officers, Saskatoon policeman Popowich has already had his day in court. Since proceedings were "stayed," there's been a lot of public speculation that the trials of the other four officers will never take place. (Which, indeed, is what eventually happens.)

In a place like Martensville, everyone knows everybody else. In a rural community, people are governed by social rules, but the rules are flexible. You drop by if you feel like it. You pitch in if someone needs help, rather than waiting to be asked as you might in a big city. Many of the farmers have "off-farm" jobs in town and many of the townies have two jobs. Where else would you find a man like Rob Friesen, who was both the town mayor and owner of a general store with a liquor store in the middle of it? Where else would you find a policeman like Ed Revesz, who was a fireman too?

The police officers and firefighters of Martensville worked side by side, which made it easy for Ron Sterling to leave the firehall where he was a volunteer, walk next door and have coffee with the police and probably the accused "quite often." When not volunteering at the firehall or working at the Saskatoon Correctional Centre, Sterling was at home and "quite a few times" one of his police buddies stopped by to say hi or pick him up for a brief ride-along. He says that he has driven on official business in both Martensville police vehicles, the car and the van, and swears that no daycare child was ever in either vehicle with him. Though neither Darryl Ford nor John Popowich nor Darren Sabourin ever came into his house, Ed Revesz was there once and Jim Elstad came for coffee ten to fifteen times. On one occasion he brought Claudia Bryden with him. It was her first night on the job.

Sterling stayed on good terms with the four co-accused police officers throughout his ordeal. In fact, since the charges were laid, Sterling and the five constables are on friendlier terms than ever. "We have a lot more in common," says the accused without a hint of irony, since they share more than 100 criminal charges. These days the police come to court to help the Sterlings make it through the day, and perhaps get previews of their own trials. Sometimes Sterling and the officers go for coffee after.

I wonder if they talk about Sterling's trial, and his financial situation, and whether legal aid will cover their trials too. In the end, taxpayers won't have to worry about the cost because the Crown will soon drop all charges against the four policemen and none of the trials will take place. On the other hand, the City of Saskatoon will foot the bill for John Popowich's lawyer in addition to paying his salary for the months he was suspended. I wonder what the officers think about the Sterlings' defence team — Hugh Harradence, Earl Kalenith, and Don Mullord — whom the people of Saskatchewan are paying handsomely to defend the Sterlings' rights. I'd be angry if the daycare parents had to pay their lawyer out of their own pockets. Fortunately, Saskatoon lawyer Greg Walen agreed to do it for nothing. "Community service," he says modestly.

Lawyers and journalists share a passion for causes. When a couple of the trial lawyers tell me they're going for coffee after court today, I grab the chance to join them. There's little talk except about the trial. One lawyer tells me the case will never make him rich but it will teach him how to fight for clients' rights under the Charter of Rights. The trial is a balancing act of conflicting rights — the children's right to privacy, the Sterlings' right to a fair trial, the public's right to hear the story, and the media's right to tell it. Talk turns to the media's relentless pursuit to reverse the publication ban, the trial within the trial. Tomorrow, for the third time in nine months, a handful of lawyers will gather in court to argue the status of the ban. Some will try to overturn it; others will argue it's still necessary. The conversation comes to an abrupt halt with the invasive ring of a cell phone.

For more than 100 days, counting Tammy's trial and the publication-ban hearings, I've been sitting on a hard wooden bench. My back is stiff and so is my brain. When the media lawyers start to argue, for the third time, for and against the publication ban, I feel as though I'm in a time warp. This discussion is akin to a teenager asking for the keys to the car and, so far, being denied permission on the grounds that his right to drive is outweighed by the rights of other members of the family. A year ago, Judge Lavoie made a blanket ruling for the media: no keys. Several months ago, Judge Wimmer gave journalists conditional permission to drive. Now he must again listen to the reasons he should hand over the keys without condition of any kind.

Wimmer explains to the lawyers for the media, the accused, and the children that he ordered the ban in the first place, several months ago, to protect the children and the co-accused who had yet to stand trial. He did not want the testimony to gel in the public mind because that would be unfair to the alleged criminals. The lawyer for the CBC, himself a former journalist, argues that Wimmer re-think his position. The CBC wants the ban lifted from the children's evidence, and supports the *Saskatoon StarPhoenix*'s attempt to overturn the ban on the testimony of the other accused. I wonder if Wimmer feels a kinship with Judge Lavoie, trying to keep the waves from lapping his ankles. Surely both men see that budget cuts may soon wash over the courts of Saskatchewan the way they have in Ontario. There, the province's three most senior judges are resisting cutbacks as best they can and have just advised the attorney-general that proposed cuts may affect the "right of the public to have access to the courts." In a letter, conveniently leaked to the press, the judges say they don't want courtroom doors shut in the public's face and that the media's comments "add an important dimension." Justice officials of Nova Scotia seem to agree and are apparently embarking on a two-year trial project, no pun intended, during which television cameras will record courtroom proceedings for the public. I wonder if the judges of

Ontario and Saskatchewan feel left behind by their maritime *confrères*. On the other hand, prairie judges may be happy to stay high and dry.

In this courtroom beside the frozen South Saskatchewan, the media lawyers argue the ban should be lifted while the lawyers for the children and the accused-but-not-yet-tried adults argue it should not. The journalists sit on the edge of their seats and chew on the occasional pencil. When the media lawyers have finished their arguments, Judge Wimmer declares, "I am not prepared to reconsider the original order." No names, no faces, no clues about who the children are. Is that clear?

He reminds the court why he allowed the lawyers to use the police videotapes of the children in the first place: so that jurors could see how the police asked questions, not how the children answered them. If members of the public saw them, they might concentrate on the kids' answers, not the officers' questions. And then they'd see the children's faces. That would be intolerable. Therefore, he says, there are to be no tapes, or copies of them, allowed outside the courthouse. Likewise, there will be no reproduction of any photograph, drawing, or sketch entered as an exhibit during the trial. Journalists will direct all future requests to the court, on an item-by-item basis. Are there any questions?

No, M'Lord. Thank you, M'Lord. Court adjourned.

The publication bans imposed by Judge Lavoie and Judge Wimmer were there to protect the identity of the children and that of the young offender. Before Tammy's trial, Judge Lavoie ruled that the ban would be total because all the prinicipals were minors when the alleged events occurred. Months later Judge Wimmer ruled that the ban would be partial because the identities of the children were not for public knowledge, though the identities of the three adults could be divulged. Every journalist knew it would be a criminal act to divulge the identity of one of the children. Every one of us respected the ban, and no one slipped up.

Except the Saskatchewan Minister of Justice, Bob Mitchell, the province's chief lawmaker, who is himself a lawyer. He broke the ban during a hotline radio show when he inadvertently divulged Tammy's real name. An independent inquiry, undertaken by legal experts from outside the province, found Mitchell not guilty of malice, and the entire matter was dropped. To my surprise, there was little public reaction to the incident. Eventually Premier Roy Romanow switched Mitchell to a new portfolio; maybe the hotline incident had something to do with it, or maybe it was the number of apparent cases of "justice denied" that we seemed to be seeing a lot of in Saskatchewan. I wonder if a journalist would have got off so lightly for breaking the ban.

Linda Sterling testifies

The lines on Linda Sterling's face circle her eyes and etch her cheeks. She has no criminal record and, in fact, has never seen the inside of a courtroom before this case. In the witness box, she acknowledges in a soft pleasant voice that she's a bit nervous. Looking like a frightened though well-fed woodchuck, she admits to blood-pressure problems and hot flashes. She is forty-six and has been married to her high school sweetheart for twenty-seven years, and is the mother of three. To stay home with her kids when they were little and earn extra income she looked after other people's children too, thirty to forty over the years. She was originally charged with twenty-one sexual crimes against the children, ranging from simple assault to assault with a weapon and unlawful confinement. Five of the charges have since been dropped for lack of evidence.

Linda Sterling is relying on Hugh Harradence to defend her. He has practised law since graduating from the University of Saskatchewan Law School and built a solid reputation as a criminal lawyer. Harradence was almost disqualified from being Sterling's lawyer. Originally he represented both Linda and Ron Sterling, but this smacked of conflict of interest to Crown prosecutor Sullivan. Linda Sterling wanted Hugh Harradence to represent her at any cost, even after he told her about the implications of conflict of interest and explained to her that it might cost her the right to an appeal. To adjudicate the matter, the Crown called in an outside judge, who ruled that the lawyer was not in conflict after all.

Harradence is a strong lawyer. Despite a pronounced limp — or maybe because of it — he has presence. Linda Sterling, though dressed in a vibrant purple jacket, looks vulnerable, remote, shattered. Certainly not dangerous. There is a sharp contrast between solicitor and client.

It would be easy to criticize Sterling and ask what right she had to assume responsibility for other people's children without formal training in child development. But she must have learned something from raising her own three kids. So why not put the knowledge to work and make extra money looking after other people's? There's no law to stop anyone from babysitting, no training needed, no licence, no formal requirements, no systematic checkups. The Saskatchewan Child Care Association publishes a brochure called "Choosing Child Care," in which it describes unlicensed care as "unregulated" and subject to "few legal requirements."

Suppose all child care were regulated and subject to strict legal requirements. Imagine the impossible search for qualified caregivers. An ad might look like this: "Wanted: energetic, kind, mature person who can take charge; foresee the unforeseeable; is patient all day; consistent, even when drained of energy; has values to impart, and the unflagging will to do so;

never tires of answering questions, and reserves energy for play. You must love your work and the children you're caring for. Only serious candidates need apply." Few of us meet these requirements, certainly not all of those who are parents or babysitters. We take surprisingly few measures to prevent child abuse. When it occurs, we're shocked.

Harradence hobbles to the witness stand and begins his examination-in chief. Sterling says that her typical day began at 6: 30 a.m., when the children began to arrive. They'd have "quiet time" or sleep till 7 a.m., when she'd awaken her own family and feed everyone. Sometimes Travis would get up before her, though not very often. Her son is not a morning person.

When her own kids left for the day, she'd do housework while the kids she was babysitting played or watched TV. Usually they watched videos such as *Robin Hood, The Sword and the Stone, Teddy Bears' Picnic* or *Ninja Turtles*. She made lunch for as many as six or seven children, though the average number was four. How did she supervise them when they played in the semi-finished basement, as she initially let them do? Linda soon solved the problem by forbidding the children to go down there and, in the process, touching or breaking something.

Linda Sterling staunchly maintains that the alleged acts "never happened in our home. They are false accusations." She refutes all the children's allegations and denies that she or anyone else ever touched any child for sexual purposes.

Freddy was fairly quiet and polite, but liked to be in charge, she says. Kenny once swore in the house and peed outside, but was usually polite. Bill was a pleasant boy, though awfully close to his mother. His sister, Anne, was always smiling. Paul seemed to fit in well. Janey was a nice little person to have around. Kathy, nicknamed "Gabby," was talkative. Her brother Frank was a funny little character. There was a time the boy could make Linda laugh; today, on the stand, the memory of "Onion" makes her cry.

Harradence asks Wimmer for a break. As Linda and Ron leave the room, it occurs to me I've never seen them touch, not so much as a hand on the shoulder. Even now, though she's in tears, he walks stolidly beside her, as the roomful of middle-aged men and women tries to squeeze out the one narrow exit for a quick breath of air.

The trial resumes with Linda Sterling's testimony. "I think I'm a good housekeeper," she says. She took her job so seriously that on December 20, 1991, the day Claudia Bryden and two other officers arrived at the house to charge her with child sexual abuse, she continued to sweep and "finish my job." Recalling the moment that Travis learned of the charges, two days later, Linda again bursts into tears and Harradence requests a short break.

She returns to the stand long enough to tell the court that she thinks the daycare children were "a great bunch of kids." I wonder why she says that at this particular time. It strikes me as a bit of overkill, but then I'm such a cynic.

Nor is Leslie Sullivan easily won over. Before proceeding to cross-examine Linda Sterling, the prosecutor reminds the court of the importance of good daycare: "The babysitter often spends more time, more waking-hour time, with the child than the parent does." Sullivan stands before the court, not just the Crown prosecutor for Her Majesty, or the mother of two, but also as the voice of reason for everyone who sends their kids to daycare. In her gruelling cross-exam, Sullivan will focus on everyday errors and omissions committed at the Sterling house. Though these deficiencies are not criminal offences, strictly speaking, they are serious breaches of protocol with young children. When added up, the mundane offences of Linda Sterling will temporarily overshadow, at least in my mind, the sensational criminal charges against her.

Lack of judgement is the first. In the summer of 1988, when Linda Sterling learned that her son was charged with molesting Sally, she and her husband Ron sat down with Travis and asked for his side of the story. After hearing it, she concluded "the children were not in danger." She told no one of the allegations but her sister. "I wanted to keep it in the family."

Sullivan: And you were babysitting other children at the time?

Sterling: Yes, I was. I know I was babysitting Freddy at the time. I just can't remember what other children at that time in '88 I would have been babysitting.

Sullivan: And you did indeed continue to babysit after that, and took on new children in the fall of '89 and that sort of thing?

Sterling: Yes, I did.

Sullivan: And your evidence is that you, at no time, told any parent of any other child being babysat at your house about these allegations?

Sterling: No, I did not.

Sullivan: Can you give an explanation for that?

Sterling: Well, I suppose thinking back now that I certainly should have, and gave the parents the opportunity to make that decision. After talking to Travis, I believed in what he told me. I felt that the children were not in danger.

By doing so, Linda Sterling put her own son's welfare ahead of that of the children whom she was paid to protect. She told no one about the first alleged offence in 1988 and left matters in police hands. Nor did she alert parents after the second allegation and charge in 1991. From the sounds of it, she regrets her decision to remain silent.

But she doesn't regret other decisions. The cynic in me starts to wonder if she took in children like so much laundry, if she ran a daycare the kids conformed to, instead of the other way round. Why, for instance, did she accept her son's habit of wearing his bathrobe around the house at midday?

Sullivan: Did you ever suggest to him, "Travis, why don't you go get properly dressed?"

Sterling: No, because I figured he's just as covered up as other people. I didn't see a problem with that.

If she doesn't see the problem, the cross-examiner does: Did you not have a concern about that after the complaints by Sally that maybe now it was a good idea for Travis to start dressing more appropriately in the house?" Linda Sterling replies, "I didn't think it was inappropriate when it's in your own home."

Linda adopted the same territorial approach in April 1992, when her son set up a sign in the living room window: "Smile. You're on Candid Camera." Though Ma Sterling didn't approve of it, she understood her son's need to fight back at all the people driving by and "gawking" at the Sterling house.

Linda trusted her son and her husband, and tells Sullivan that she doesn't believe either of them would have ever left a copy of *Penthouse* lying around.

Sullivan: Now you indicated earlier that not to your knowledge did any of the children see any of the magazines in your home, such as the *Penthouse* magazine we have in court here. That's your evidence?

Sterling: That's correct.

Sullivan: I take it that they mostly belonged to Travis and your husband, or did you read them as well?

Sterling: I would say they belonged to Ron, not to Travis. Yes, on occasion, I have read those magazines also.

Sullivan: Okay. On occasion, is it not possible that one of the three of you might have left one lying around somewhere?

Sterling: No. That's not something that we would do. It would be kept in the privacy of our bedroom or our half-bath.

Sullivan: Okay. So your evidence is that — again — to the best of your knowledge, it's not possible that one of those was ever left accidentally around.

Sterling: No, I don't believe so.

Sullivan asks if Linda's husband's shift work interfered with her babysitting service. Linda says that if the kids played too loudly, they might on occasion wake Ron up. Did Ron get angry? "Possibly," answers Linda. I wonder if the kids whispered a lot, if they knew it was better to let "Uncle" sleep rather than wake him and possibly unleash a torrent of obscenities.

From the sounds of it, Sterling went outside as little as possible. She admits she never played with the kids, but did keep her eye on them, except for the ever-wilful Freddy. When Freddy got bored with the swing set in the backyard or tired of sitting on the front steps, he left without giving the woman a "phone number or a proper address." It concerned her, but not enough to find out where he was going or to stop him. And she did not check on Freddy when he frequented a favourite haunt, the spray-pool playground. "So you'd basically let him go and come back when he wanted to," summarizes Sullivan. "Yes, I did," answers Sterling without so much as a twitch.

"Freddy preferred to be outside a lot," says Sterling, and he frequently slipped out the side door without telling Linda where he was going. "A lot of the time he pretty much did what he wanted to do," Sterling tells an amazed Sullivan. Disappearing for hours at a time is not something I'd let a seven-year-old boy in my care do. Nor would I let him sit on the front steps for long periods of time, baking or freezing outside.

Linda Sterling didn't like Freddy's decision to sit on the steps either. "I didn't want people to think I had told him he was supposed to be out there sitting on the step for some reason." She spoke to Freddy's mother about the boy's odd behaviour. "They didn't seem too concerned about it at the time," she adds. Does that mean Freddy continued to sit on the front steps? "Like I said, he pretty much did what he wanted."

Linda had responsibility for Freddy but not for Kenny, who was "never" in her home. And she never took photos, so she hasn't a clue who took the picture of Sally found on the film seized by police. With the same certainty of tone, she denies that T-Mom, the mother of Tommy, Janey, and Sandy, ever asked about the need for a baby-gate at the top of the stairs.

Sullivan: Do you not recall T-Mom discussing that particular issue with you?

Sterling: No, she never discussed that with me.

Sullivan: You don't recall that, or you don't agree?

Sterling: I don't recall her ever discussing that with me.

Sullivan: Is it possible that she discussed that with you and you don't recall it, or is it your position that no such discussion took place?

Sterling: I actually don't think there was ever a discussion.

Sullivan: Do you recall her evidence? It might refresh your memory. Do you recall her saying that?

Sterling: I remember that it was brought up in court, but I don't remember it ever happening.

Sullivan: Just to be clear, you don't recall responding to her that you were always in the kitchen so there was no concern on your part about kids straying over to the chairs... or to the stairs.

Sterling: No, I don't recall that.

According to Linda, there never was a discussion and there never was a fall on the basement stairs. How could there be when she was in the kitchen most of the time? "Your evidence is that you didn't have a baby-gate because you didn't think one was necessary," says the prosecutor. "That's right," confirms Sterling. "And you agree that you did have, on occasion, children that were crawling or learning to walk?" Yes, the woman replies, explaining that if a child was in the walker and she had to leave the kitchen, she'd put a chair across the stairs.

Sterling stands by her husband's testimony, that just saying no was sufficient to keep the kids from playing near the stairs to the basement. "We just didn't seem to have a problem with them." Sullivan, waiting to trap the witness, pounces. "So you didn't really need the chairs there." Sterling squirms: "Well, when they're in a walker, yes." Judge Wimmer, growing tired of this, says, "You know she said they never really had a problem with it. How much more do you expect her to say?"

Linda Sterling never took the kids to the playground. How could she, when she didn't own a stroller? "And you didn't acquire one?" queries Sullivan. "No, I did not," responds Sterling. At her daycare she had no babygate, no stroller, one walker, one playpen, three kids of her own, three or four to babysit — sometimes more — three meals to make a day, and all the housework and laundry. How could she be everywhere at once?

For instance, she was in the kitchen the time Tommy was in the living room with his sister Janey and kicked her hard in the groin. Linda broke up the brawl, but neglected to tell the siblings' parents. "I have no reason for it. I just never brought it to their attention." Sullivan drives the point home for the sake of the jury: "I take it that, at the time, it didn't concern you that T-Mom might wonder why there were bruises in the genital area of her child." The accused coolly replies, "Apparently not, because I never said anything."

Why, I wonder, would Linda let Freddy wander off on his own? Why didn't she always know where Kathy was when her dad came to get her? Did she care more about the kids playing in the basement or the shape of the basement itself? Did she bawl them out when they made a "mess" of it, whatever that means, or did she quietly tell them they couldn't play there any longer? But I would have thought the living room would be the last place an immaculate housekeeper would want a bunch of rug rats after they'd trashed the basement. What would she do if they jumped on the furniture or fought over toys? She says she would have given them a "smack on the bum or the fingers." They'd also get the same for lesser offences: "The smacking of their fingers, I guess, would be if they were touching an ornament or a plant that they had been told not to touch before."

And I wonder why the word no wasn't enough to deter the kids from touching the lamp or the ficus if it was sufficient to keep them from going near the stairs to the basement? Did the parents approve of Sterling's slaps and consider them a "reasonable use of force," as defined in the Criminal Code?

If Linda eventually prohibited the children from going down to the basement where they liked to make a "mess" and kept them upstairs, what did they actually do all day from 6: 30 a.m. to 5: 30 p.m? "They watched TV...and they all knew where [the box of toys] was and they would bring it out and play in the kitchen and sometimes in the front room with them." She laughs briefly when the cross-examiner asks which toys the kids preferred. But not one woman in the public gallery even cracks a smile. Many of them are, or have been, mothers themselves. Two more women who look like mothers have just walked into the courtroom. They also look like sisters who are female versions of the McKenzie Brothers. The two middle-aged "hosers" have neglected to remove their wool toques and so are in contravention of courtroom protocol, which forbids headgear. But no one stops them. In fact, no one in the room even seems to notice. No spectacle, not even this True North special, is compelling enough to turn heads or make the woman one row over take her fingers from her pursed lips. No sound, not even the apocalyptic sneeze of that woman's neighbour, is enough to break her concentration on the witness box.

And nothing distracts prosecutor Sullivan. "You would agree that you had children of a whole variety of ages...Freddy being almost the oldest." The accused agrees. "And you'd agree that those children all have different interests and abilities." Again, the accused agrees. "You would agree that what would keep two seven- and eight-year-old boys occupied for an hour or two certainly wouldn't be the type of thing that an eighteen-month-old would want to do." Agreement. "So what would you do with the younger children to keep them occupied? Surely, they didn't just play by themselves." Disagreement: "On occasion, yes, they did." The toddlers played by themselves, and Sterling did not play with them. But she did watch cartoons with them and would sometimes hold, feed, and rock the younger ones to sleep. "I mean, they didn't just sit on the floor or in a walker all day."

Did Sterling have a spare second? With up to seven kids to supervise, four on an average day, she says that she cleaned on a continual basis: until late at night, at nap time, while tots played or watched TV. When she had time she watched TV herself, especially her favourite soaps: "Another World" or "The Young and the Restless," which Freddy dubbed "The Young and the Useless." It's hard to say how many times Sterling watched it while Freddy and the other kids played in the living room. But according to her evidence, "the children were in the front room with me." On the TV in the locker room at the YMCA, I've seen "The Young and the Restless." If I had young children, the last thing I'd let them watch are the skin-tight dresses and endless bed-hopping in that soap opera.

Occasionally, a friend would visit Sterling from out-of-town and the two would play cards, surrounded by kids and toys. From time to time she went to other friends' houses for tea, or drove to the post office to pick up her mail, or the store for groceries. Frequently she drove one of her own kids to school. On these local outings she'd take the daycare children with her, but "wouldn't probably have asked permission ahead of time" from their parents.

Once again, Linda Sterling's evidence has collided with T-Mom's, who testified earlier that one time Linda told her she never went anywhere, so she didn't need Janey's car seat. When Sullivan confronts the accused with this side of the story, she replies, "I don't recall that." Sullivan perseveres. "Did you ever take Janey anywhere?" No. "Never?" No.

This trial is nearly over, yet the truth is as elusive as ever. The criminal charges against the Sterlings may never be proved. On the other hand, some fundamental issues about the daycare are becoming clear. A couple of jurors have been madly taking notes today. I wonder what they think about the way Linda Sterling ran her business. Sterling acknowledges that she was the one in charge, though sometimes she called on her boarder Tammy for help. On occasion her husband or son would drive her to the doctor in Saskatoon if she had an appointment because she "did very little driving in the city." The daycare kids would go along for the ride and drive around with Ron or Travis in the car to do city errands till Linda was finished.

Back in Martensville, members of Sterling's family helped out as required. For instance, Ron once looked after a daycare child while Linda ran to a neighbour's to borrow a baby bottle. Her daughter Corinne, when she still lived at home, sometimes came straight home from school to give Freddy his snack. When Sullivan asks the accused if she ever left son Travis alone with the children, she answers, "No, I don't believe I have."

I'm confused. Linda Sterling testified earlier that, to her knowledge, none of the children ever saw a copy of *Penthouse* lying around. "It would be kept in the privacy of our bedroom or [ensuite] half-bath." Also stored in privacy, in a drawer in the master-bedroom dresser, was her vibrator, exhibit P-6. But the bedrooms were off limits for the kids. "I never saw anyone going through our drawers." The only times the children even went in the master bedroom were when they were enroute to the ensuite half-bath or going to sleep. That the children never saw a baby-gate at the daycare but did hear swear words is clear. Whether they saw a vibrator and girlie magazines, as they claimed, is not.

I'd like to believe Linda Sterling. Then I could stop losing sleep, turning over testimony in my head and tossing back and forth in bed at night. The dream last night was the worst one yet: I was driving an old car (as I do in real life) and came to the narrow Victoria bridge in Saskatoon (which I dread when my eyes are open). It's a sunny summer's day, no ice on the road. Suddenly, the bridge collapses and my car falls in slow motion into the fast-flowing South Saskatchewan. I panic and try to release the ancient seatbelt, but cannot. Then I wake up in terror. For the next week, I avoid the bridge and try to overcome my fear of it. If only I knew what the bridge stood for.

Another reason I'd like to believe Sterling is very simple: she's a woman. Women are the civilizers and men the warriors. Women aren't supposed to do the things she is accused of doing. I used to trust women much more than men, until I saw Karla Homolka on the front page, and read the things she did. Now I know no one is immune from committing the cruellest murder, torture, rape, or indignity. Now I think differently about women, including myself. I wonder if Linda Sterling has some creature she's trying to exorcize. Like me, she has lived half her life and come to the point where it's time to master the demons before the curtain falls.

Middle-aged woman like Sterling and me are supposed to be role models for the next generation, nurturing and protecting them, showing them the way, loving them. I feel guilty thinking that a woman my own age may have harmed these kids. So if I were one of the six female jurors, I'd probably try hard to believe Linda is telling the truth. I want fiercely to believe she committed no criminal act, for all her perceived civil faults and managerial oversights. I'd like to accept her testimony and close the case in my mind. But then the next witness arrives.

James Pearson is a tall, clean-shaven young man in his early twenties. He sometimes went to the Sterling house in the evening to visit his friend, Travis. He is a credible witness, and tells prosecutor Leslie Sullivan some of the same things we've heard from other witnesses: a few times police officers stopped by the house; Jim Elstad, in particular, sticks in Pearson's mind. He also tells the court that Travis "never had anything to do with them (the daycare kids)" except to play a video or get books for them. No, he swears, he never had any cause for concern about the way family members treated the children.

Prosecutor Sullivan has no time for small talk. She asks, Where did he and Travis usually talk in the Sterling home? He answers, The main part of the house. What did you do besides talk? asks Sullivan. Pearson says they looked at porn magazines together. Sullivan prepares solidly for the next question by planting her feet further apart: In what room did you read the magazines? "In the living room," replies Pearson.

Pearson, like the sixty or seventy witnesses before him, was not allowed in the courtroom till called to the stand. He did not hear the sworn statements Ron, Linda, and Travis Sterling made about where the porn magazines were kept and read. You'd think the testimony of Pearson would be like a breath of fresh air. After all, he's a man with little to gain or lose. But his answer knocks the wind out of everyone, and a suffocating silence fills the room.

I see a room of troubled faces. For the first time I understand what this trial is, and what it isn't. Even if something evil happened at the daycare, there is no one, not even the people who convicted the Sterlings before the trial started, who really wants to believe it. To do so would require proceeding to the next step: Not just the orderly conviction of the Sterlings, but the messy and demanding task of examining our own consciences.

Everyone can see there are discrepancies in the evidence. Having to deal with them, and move inexorably towards the conclusion that the accused committed crimes, is just the first half of the job. The second half, the much harder part, is believing that the accused actually committed crimes against children. Accepting that would amount to taking collective responsibility for letting harm come to the most vulnerable members of our society. Nobody in the room wants to tackle that troubling issue and admit we're all on trial.

Nor does anyone envy jurors their job. They have to choose the lesser of two evils: believing the children and convicting the Sterlings, or believing the Sterlings and denying the children. Win, lose, there's nothing in between, according to our system. The Martensville trial is what author George P. Fletcher calls a "political trial." A late twentieth century phenomenon, the political trial "expresses the grass-roots passions of groups who identify with victims." According to Fletcher's theory, the daycare children have rights and are a "symbol of social conflict." The Saskatoon and Martensville citizens who believe the children will accept no "apology for violence" nor tolerate "diminished responsibility" for the Sterlings. The perceived victims, writes Fletcher, must reclaim their rightful place in the court. And that's where the clash of rights occurs: According to the rule of law, the accused must not lose their rights in the process.

How can the twelve jurors balance these competing interests, especially when members of the community are banging on the courthouse door and plastering signs in their windows? According to Fletcher, jurors have two choices: either acknowledge the banging and be swayed by the posters and placards in the streets, or plug their ears and weigh the courtroom evidence. Easier said than done when you're dealing with the evidence of children and the thorny question of witness credibility.

According to the evidence of James Pearson, he and Travis sometimes looked at the porn collection in the Sterlings' front room at night; by day the kids played in the same room and, according to several of them, the porn was in full view. Odds are that Travis and James may have left the occasional magazine in the living room. It's easy to inadvertently leave secret possessions on display, even when you're a neat freak like me. I remember the day my birth-control-pill package circulated on the baggage carousel at Pearson Airport until a man picked it up and asked if I knew whose it was, and I wince when I think about the time I left my black fishnet stockings beside my toothpaste in the bathroom and my visiting five-year-old niece took them to the kitchen to ask her mother what they wereused for.

Travis Sterling testifies

The court clerk calls Travis Sterling to the stand. The twenty-four-year-old man enters the room, dressed in a purple turtleneck sweater, black suit, and cowboy boots. He looks a lot more court-worthy with his new blond brushcut than the old shoulder-length mop. Being on trial for allegedly assaulting children makes Travis nervous, he tells his lawyer, Earl Kalenith. But he hides it well.

Kalenith probably has a calming influence on his client. The wrinkle-free lawyer from Prince Albert looks like the perpetual student, earnest and untainted by the world, the kind of person you can trust. When he speaks, his thoughts emerge clear and organized. When he changes direction in the line of questioning, he prepares Travis with the warning: "I now propose to discuss with you." In other words, listen up. Like all good communicators, Kalenith has a knack for getting the attention of his listeners. But he is not a prima donna, so I imagine his ego doesn't often collide with that of his clients. Just as well, since some of them are quite irrational, and number among the province's most dangerous criminals. Last year, he defended Carney Nerland, the white supremacist who shot Native trapper Leo LaChance in the back. Kalenith negotiated a plea bargain for his client, successfully reducing a charge of murder to manslaughter. The Native community of Saskatchewan was incensed by the verdict, which led to a public inquiry. Now Kalenith is arguing the longest trial in the province's history, defending a young man charged with thirteen counts of sexual assault against children.

"Have you ever committed any sexual act in relation to any child?" Kalenith asks Travis. "Have you in any way ever physically assaulted any child?" The accused answers no to both questions. "Those things didn't happen."

According to his testimony, Travis Sterling graduated form high school in 1987. Since then he has worked off and on for various employers, never more than a year at a time. He lives with his parents because he can't afford to live anywhere else. He has managed to own four or five cars over the years and save enough money to go to Australia for six months.

Travis also owned several guns at one point. He and his father used to go hunting, but ten years ago he gave up the sport and put his guns away. He hasn't used one since. Nor has he used a vibrator on himself or anyone else, or tied anyone with ropes, as Kenny and Freddy allege. The accused swears he didn't even know such things were kept in the family home until the police raid in 1991.

Nor did Travis take photos of the kids. According to him, the Polaroid camera that the police seized was not used after the family moved from Prince

Albert to Martensville. He has no idea who took the photo of Sally that the police found, but it wasn't him.

Though his parents regularly socialized with the daycare parents, Travis testifies that he had minimal contact with Sally and the other daycare kids. However, his limited dealings did not prevent him from forming opinions about them. Bill was a quiet little guy; Freddy liked his snacks; Tommy was mostly quiet and well behaved. Throughout Kalenith's examination-in-chief, Travis repeats six or seven times that the children's allegations are not true.

Yes, over the years, he gave the occasional ride to one of the kids in one of his cars. No, it was never in a police car or van. Yes, he played videos for the kids, cartoons and Christmas stuff, never violent or horror movies. It's true he often walked around the house in a bathrobe, but always wore a nightshirt or underwear underneath. He tells his defence lawyer the reason he made the Candid Camera sign and put it in the living-room window on one of the occasions Claudia Bryden came to the neighbourhood is this: he was fed up with the attention the media paid to the daycare story and the relentless rubbernecking of passersby.

"Those are all of my questions," Kalenith tells Judge Wimmer. Since there are no questions from the other two members of the defence team, Hugh Harradence and Don Mullord, it's time for the cross-examination.

Prosecutor Sullivan approaches the accused. Her first task is to pit the credibility of Travis Sterling against that of Janice Brunsch, a witness who testified four months ago at the outset of the trial. Called to the stand as one of the Sterlings' neighbours for years, Brunsch swore she'd witnessed unusual, unsavory things from her window: police cars parking in front of the Sterling house every couple of days; Freddy frequently slumping on the front steps, even in the blazing sun; and Travis standing proudly by his yellow Candid Camera sign and giving her the finger when he saw she was looking at him.

"And did you do that?" Sullivan asks. Leaning back in his chair, Travis has a defiant look in his eyes and swears he did no such thing. "No, I didn't." You deny that you did that? "Yes, I do." So you disagree with that evidence? "Yes, I do." "Okay," is all she says to Travis, deciding not to beat things to death or bludgeon the jurors with the witness's lack of credibility.

The prosecutor shifts gears. Why, she asks, did you not follow up your conversation with the Martensville police, concerning your alleged assault on Sally in 1988? Squinting like Gary Cooper at high noon, Travis explains, "It's kind of like if someone threatened to beat me up at school one day and they didn't, I'm not going to remind them." I wonder what a psychologist would say about his choice of words, and what a psychological profile would reveal. Or what a public investigation under the Inquiries Act would reveal about the

Martensville police, who neither charged the nineteen-year-old Travis nor fully investigated Sally's complaint. The officers' lack of concern, evidently contagious, infected Sterling. "I figured if they weren't concerned that it was that important, then I wasn't going to bother with it." I would have thought a seventeen-year-old boy, as Travis was at the time of Sally's allegation, would be shaking in his boots. Even if you had nothing to hide, wouldn't you be worried the police might come to the door at any minute, cuff you, and cart you off in disgrace?

"Okay," is all Sullivan has to say to Travis again, and continues her questioning about Travis's dealings with the children. He says he didn't really have much to do with the daycare kids. When they made too much noise, he'd go to his room.

Sullivan: And if a child was napping in your room, you would have to stay out of that room?

Sterling: Yeah.

Sullivan: Okay. So did they ever get on your nerves?

Sterling: Well, sometimes, yeah.

Sullivan: Okay. What did you do about it?

Sterling: I'd either leave the room or leave the house, or just ignore them.

Sullivan: Okay. It's not a particularly large house, you would agree?

Sterling: No, that's right.

Sullivan: So it might be quite difficult to ignore them?

Sterling: Well, I could go to my room if no one was in there.

But sometimes there was. Perhaps the Sterling house seemed a little crowded, particularly on the days Ron was home after working nights and Travis was between jobs. On those occasions, Travis sometimes wandered around the house in his bathrobe and had time to watch cartoons and soaps with his mother and the kids. In the evening Travis liked to watch science fiction and alien movies — *Terminator* and *Star Wars* and *Star Trek*, stuff like that.

Sullivan: And you would rent those sorts of movies and watch them at home?

Sterling: Yeah.

Sullivan: And, on occasion, you would be watching those when the children were being babysat?

Sterling: I don't think so.

Sullivan: Why do you say that?

Sterling: Because they usually liked to watch their shows when they were there.

Sullivan: I see. You don't think children would be interested in watching the *Star Wars* shows?

Sterling: Oh, I don't know. They might be. None of them ever asked to watch any of them.

Sullivan: Does that mean they knew the movies were there?

Sterling: Well, if we rented them, they'd probably be sitting on the TV stand.

Sullivan: Okay. So if you rented the movies, then you're saying that you wouldn't even be watching them when the kids were in another room?

Sterling: I don't think so, no. I could watch them in the evening. That's usually when I watch movies.

What if Kenny were here to cross-examine Travis about watching Terminator? But he's not, and I despair of knowing if he watched the film at the Sterling house or merely saw the title on the box on top of the TV.

I wonder what the jurors think when Travis Sterling contradicts the testimony of his best friend, James Pearson.

Sullivan: And am I clear that you had your own collection [of magazines]?

Sterling: Yes.

Sullivan: Independent of what your father had in the bathroom?

Sterling: Yeah.

Sullivan: Okay. And these you kept in your dresser?

Sterling: That's right.

Sullivan: Did you keep them anywhere else?

Sterling: At that time, no. I think they were just all in the dresser.

Sullivan: And did you ever leave one lying on top of the dresser?

Sterling: No.

Sullivan: Never?

Sterling: No.

Sullivan: So...where would you read them?

Sterling: In my room.

Sullivan: Did you ever read them in the bathroom?

Sterling: I don't believe so, no.

Sullivan: Did you ever read them in the kitchen?

Sterling: No.

Sullivan: Living room?

Sterling: No.

Travis swears he did not read the magazines in the living room. His friend swore the two of them did. If Travis keeps this up, he'll make the jurors' job a whole lot easier. By my count, his testimony conflicts so far with that of his friend James Pearson, his neighbour Janice Brunsch, and with that of little Kenny.

Travis is also sure he never saw the vibrator before the police raid on his home in 1991. "I don't know whether my parents told me, or whether I'd seen it in pictures in disclosure, or whether it was actually in court." Interesting. When Freddy forgot certain details in the witness box, Hugh Harradence crucified him; when Kenny got confused about the sequence of particular events, Earl Kalenith pursued him like a bloodhound. Cross-examiner Sullivan could milk Travis's confusion for all it's worth, but she doesn't. She refrains from mocking the accused for not knowing if he saw the vibrator in person or just pictures of it, and questions him about the guns. Travis confirms that the pellet gun was sometimes in the kitchen, in full view. Sullivan asks: Did he ever look at any other guns in front of the kids?

Sterling: I don't believe so, no.

Sullivan: Okay. Well, you say "I don't believe so."

Sterling: I can't recall any time that I did, so I don't believe I did.

Sullivan: Is the answer no, but possibly. Or no?

Sterling: No.

What about transporting kids in the car? Travis remembers twice driving a daycare child, not one of the plaintiffs, while helping his mother run errands outside Martensville. But he doesn't recall driving Janey anywhere. "It didn't happen," he asserts. Nor does he recall the incident he heard Kenny describe earlier, which Sullivan now repeats for the court, when Travis and Ron Sterling once drove Kenny into the driveway of one of the Sterlings' neighbours, then Travis rang the doorbell. "I've never had any contact with Kenny at all," says Travis.

Once again, the court is faced with the question of credibility, Travis's denial versus Kenny's certainty. The driveway-doorbell story is unextraordinary, alleging no wrongdoing and indicting no one. But it could be the thin edge of the wedge. If Travis were to acknowledge that the incident occurred, he could not maintain he had no contact whatsoever with Kenny. I remember Kenny's portrayal of Linda Sterling peeling and coring apples for a pie while, in the next room, or so the boy claimed, Ron and Travis and several police officers assaulted him and other kids.

Travis does acknowledge the occasion he helped push Kenny's father out of a snowbank. "Well, that was the only time I ever had anything to do with them," he tells Sullivan. He admits his parents were on very good terms with many of the daycare parents, as he was. On one occasion, Bill's mother lent Travis a videotape. When he graduated from high school, Sally's parents gave him a gift. During the five years Linda babysat Sally, the girl was like a member of the Sterling family. That all changed when she accused Travis.

Sullivan: Do you agree with the evidence that she [Sally] would usually be arriving early in the morning?

Sterling: Yes.

Sullivan: And you recall her basically sleeping on the couch until it was time to mobilize for school?

Sterling: Yes.

Sullivan: And you would see her there?

Sterling: Yes, I guess on occasion I would.

Sullivan: And, in fact, would you not agree that there were occasions when you would be up in the morning before anybody else?

Sterling: That would be pretty unlikely. So I don't think so.

Sullivan: Never?

Sterling: I'm not saying never. I just don't recall any incident that I would have been.

Sullivan: So you're saying that it could have happened, but it wasn't a frequent occurrence?

Sterling: Yeah.

Sullivan: Okay. So you would agree that there would be times when you would be basically up and alone in the house with Sally asleep on the couch, and other family members would still be asleep. That's possible?

Sterling: I don't really think so. It's possible, but I don't think it ever happened.

Sullivan: Possible.

Sterling: I'm not saying it happened, I'm saying it's possible. I don't recall any time that that happened.

Travis says he is not a morning person, and that usually everyone else in the family got up before him. In fact, his schedule was flexible, especially when he didn't have a job to go to. From November 1988 to April 1989, Travis was unemployed.

Sullivan: And so, you would agree that during that time period you would have spent a good part of your day at home?

Sterling: Yes.

Sullivan: And so you would be there basically when the children were being babysat?

Sterling: Yeah.

Sullivan: Quite a bit?

Sterling: M'hm.

Sullivan: Especially during that time period?

Sterling: That's right.

Travis was unemployed from November 1988 till April 1989. In April he left for Australia, and did not return till fall. Sullivan asks: "After you got back from Australia...you would be home frequently when children were being babysat?" Yes, he answers.

During break, Janis and I try to reconstruct what Travis has done in the past seven years since graduating from highschool in 1987. According to his testimony, he started work in early 1988 and was employed until the end of the year. Then he was unemployed until April 1989, when he left for Australia. When he returned six months later, in November, he was again hired and worked for two Saskatoon companies, consecutively, until summer 1991. From then until fall, he was unemployed. Then we pieced together his work record using the time frame based on the children's allegations: ten-year-old Sally's complaint against Travis dates from spring 1988, and that of two-year-old Janey from fall 1991, when she told her mother that "Ravis and Uncle" had caused the red marks on her genitals. What Travis did during those three years to the other child plaintiffs, if anything, is still not clear. There are bald discrepancies between his testimony and that of other witnesses.

As one of the three defendants, Travis has the right to hear the testimony of every witness but not that of his co-defendants, his mom and dad. So he has not heard what his father and mother said on the stand. Nor, he testifies, has he ever discussed with his parents how he would respond to certain questions in court. It would constitute witness contamination, the same thing the police are accused of doing during their interviews of the kids. Travis does not know his parents testified independently that Jim Elstad was at their home ten to fifteen times during the period in question. In the witness box, he says Elstad came to visit a few times only, once to see Ron's brother who'd worked with Elstad years before at Corrections in Prince Albert and who was in town for the day. The only other time Elstad came to the Sterling house, says Travis, was the night he brought Claudia Bryden for coffee.

Travis testifies about the other police officers who visited the Sterlings' neighbourhood "quite a number of times." One officer in particular, not one of the accused, came regularly to visit the Sterlings' next-door neighbour on business. This policeman, Michael Swan, testified earlier that he visited their street between April and August 1989. Travis corroborates this and swears the man came to their street two or three times a week during that time. He saw the officer with his own eyes. "I'd see the van there or the car, or whatever he was driving."

Sullivan: You were in Australia.

Sterling: Yeah, I left at the end of April. I guess I saw him during the month of April.

Sullivan: Okay. So you're only talking now about a little bit of time in April?

Sterling: Well, I guess so. I don't know. I saw him there. I can't tell you exactly when he was there…

Sullivan: For almost all of that time you were out of the country, correct?

Sterling: I said I saw him there during that time.

Sullivan: And now you're saying it was just maybe a bit in April?

Sterling: Yeah. 'Cause I wasn't here for the rest of the time. How could I see him if I wasn't here?

Sullivan: Well, that's what I'm asking you.

Sterling: I didn't see him while I wasn't here. I saw him while I was here, during the month of April.

Sullivan: You didn't mention that, did you?

Sterling: You didn't ask that specific question.

Sullivan: So your evidence is that you saw... No, I'll leave it...

And she does. The cross-examination of Travis is complete and the case is concluded.

Summation and charge to the jury

Now that the jurors have heard all the evidence, Judge Wimmer dismisses them briefly so that the rest of us can hear the lawyers' estimates of the time they need to wrap up the trial. Sullivan thinks her closing address to jurors might take three hours. Harradence thinks his will, too. Hearing this, Wimmer quips, "I don't know if they can sit and listen to you for six hours at once." Just kidding, he smiles. Sullivan and Harradence force a smile at the judge's joke.

A few days later, we reassemble in the courthouse by the river and Wimmer looks pleased as punch. "We're almost there," he tells jurors, relieved that his job is almost over and the last part of theirs is about to begin. It is now the sixth month of sitting in this room. According to the court clock, today is Day 79 of the trial. Since Day 1, the warm fall day when the trial began, winter has come and almost gone. During the past five months, the jurors have trudged through deep snow, drunk their morning coffee and afternoon tea in the dark, and cursed the wind and their frozen cars. Their eyes are dimmed by cabin fever, and they know the only cure is warm air and sunshine.

But they know they can't escape until their work is done. Don Mullord, Ron Sterling's lawyer, sympathizes with them and musters a faint smile: "There may have been days when you wished you had not been selected for this responsibility," he tells them.

Mullord is the first to address the jurors. Speaking on behalf of the three-man defence team, he says their position is that "these parents and these children are really innocent victims of this investigation." The case presented by the prosecution depends almost entirely on the children's testimony, and that evidence is weak and improbable. Like a careful teacher prepping students for an exam, he now takes pains to remind the class what they've learned in the past six months.

The child plaintiffs are not so much lying as giving evidence "learned" from the police, their parents, and the therapists, who asked leading and suggestive questions, put them under "pressures" and gave them "rewards" when they said the right things. The interviewers had bias to begin with. The kids have adopted the interviewers' thoughts and recollections and believe the stories they've told in court. But, I wonder, if adopted recollections are one thing, natural-born feelings are another. How could Freddy imagine the sick-to-the-stomach feeling — "like doing a play" — if he hadn't felt so upset at the time? Being told you remember something is one thing; torturing your own body to distract your mind is another. What caused Kenny to clip his fingertips and bang his head against the wall? Why did he have perianal abrasions and why was he terrified to poop? The public debate about incest and child sexual abuse is at least a century old, yet we still don't know how to assess the evidence properly.

There's no evidence in this case, says defence lawyer Mullord. Not only were the children influenced by interviewers, but their parents were too — "quite early on in the investigation." In a low voice, made even lower by the beard he occasionally talks into and the eyes that sometimes focus on his notes rather than the jurors, Mullord reminds the six men and six women that T-Dad was skulking around Martensville, "pre-occupied" with finding the devil church and the person who'd hurt his two-year-old Janey. Meanwhile, T-Mom was at home "obsessed with this investigation," and reading books and articles about sexual abuse. On December 16, 1991, four days after the police raided the Sterling house and found the vibrator, T-Mom flipped through a Sears catalogue and saw a vibrator, which triggered Tommy's memory about the one at daycare. That was just too much of a coincidence, scoffs Mullord. T-Mom's evidence is not reliable. She and police officer Claudia Bryden "have shaved their evidence to suit what they'd wish to believe."

The children's courtroom testimony is shaped and full of discrepancies. Mullord distributes police photos to the jurors and asks them to pay special attention to photo 36, a picture of a vibrator that provided Freddy with his memory. The vibrator is really white, even though the picture makes it look blue. Freddy said it was blue. But how does Mullord explain that Kenny said the vibrator was peach-coloured? Mullord says the police photos also misled Freddy into thinking The Place had a basement when it didn't. But, by his own account, the then young boy was blindfolded much of the time. That's highly doubtful, in Mullord's opinion — no witness ever saw the kids either at The Place or being transported there, and no evidence was found.

The judicial system runs on evidence. There is no evidence, except what the police pressured the kids to produce, which the kids came to believe. "Empty allegation" is Mullord's description of Freddy's story about Frank in the freezer. I wonder what both boys' mothers would say. "Absurd nonsense" is Mullord's summarization of Freddy's story about Ron Sterling's sucking his stomach. Likewise, the boy's story about Ron's threatening him with a shotgun if he didn't suck his penis was "invented under pressure." Freddy couldn't even remember if his penis went in Ron's anus, or vice versa. And neither Kenny nor Tommy corroborated Freddy's story about being tied up in the basement of The Place. "As I've said, there's no basement there." Mullord says that Freddy's demeanour on the stand was not that of an abused boy. To help him remember alleged incidents, he brought a list to court that had no dates or times. On the stand he showed little or no emotion, and he looked bored.

So do the jurors. Mr. Sweatshirt has chosen red today. The three Sterlings have all chosen black. Ron's fingernails are more manicured than usual, and his Masonic ring looks shinier than ever. Judge Wimmer's fingertips rest on his mouth in concentration, broken only when he sees the need to give jurors a break.

In the hall, a lawyer visiting Saskatoon on business tells me why the Sterling trial is an all-or-nothing proposition: all the plaintiffs were younger than fourteen at the time of the alleged crimes. According to the Criminal Code, they were children. Sexual assault on a child is a crime, period. Once the prosecution proves it took place, there is no defence or excuse for it. On the other hand, when a person older than fourteen is sexually assaulted, the issue of consent is a legitimate defence for the accused. If jurors find the evidence inconclusive, the daycare kids are without recourse under the Criminal Code of Canada. Of course, the daycare parents could always launch a civil suit.

Our fifteen-minute break over, the visiting lawyer rushes to regain his seat in the back row and I take mine at the front. There are few spare seats today.

A crowd like this must give the lawyers a buzz. Mullord looks as though he's enjoying it, though for his sake and his client's I wish he'd make more eye contact with the jurors. They're just as susceptible as everyone else to human warmth, more so, given their task.

Mullord sticks to his oratorical style and his legal stance: The children's allegations, Kenny's for example, are bizarre and improbable. Among other things, the boy said the garage door at The Place was opened with a zapper; the owner said there was no zapper. Kenny's demeanour "was not consistent with sexual abuse," according to Mullord. I ask myself, How can he say that, when even the experts don't completely agree about what the symptoms are in the first place? And suppose the cops had adopted Mullord's assumption, or the converse. Isn't the officers' tunnel vision what the three defence lawyers have been harping about for the past six months?

Mullord argues that the kids had "more the demeanour of children who had been...coached to give evidence in court" than the appearance of minors who'd been abused by adults. And exactly what demeanour is that, Mullord? Are you criticizing the way they staunched their tears on the stand, answered questions till blue in the face, and held their own with lawyers like you? Did your boss, the Department of Justice, prepare the kids for trial and show them the accepted way to give testimony so you could scorn their courtroom demeanour?

He reminds jurors that even expert witnesses testified that the evidence was conflicting and inconclusive. One physician said scars like those in and around Kenny's anus could have been caused by constipation or penetration, and testified that as a medical practitioner he sees such things a lot, maybe several times a month. Another doctor testified she sees evidence like that once a week. In other words, perianal excoriation and anal scarring are not rare findings for physicians. And the therapists' opinions were just as inconclusive. One said that many of the daycare kids' symptoms appear among normal kids, too, while another expert witness believed some of the kids had experienced a stressful or traumatic event.

Stressful? I'll tell you what's stressful, Mullord says, cranking up the volume. It's a child being subjected to repeated interviews, getting ready for court, and living through the stress the investigation caused the parents. Nobody, I'm sure, disagrees with him on those points.

What is there for evidence? Nothing, not even a single photo. The allegations are absurd. They are unthinkable. They are far-fetched. In fact, there were no allegations at all until the police investigation began. "The evidence comes only from these interviews... The investigation created the case." Wait a minute, Mullord. The cops had nothing to do with two of the allegations. Have you forgotten that Sally went straight to her guidance counsellor and said Travis had abused her, but police dropped the matter for three years? And don't you remember that infant Janey told her mother, not police, that "Ravis and Uncle" caused the red marks on her genitals?

Finally, Mullord raises his eyes from the lectern and looks straight at the jury box. He asserts that the things his client Ron Sterling is accused of did not occur. In a very polite, British sort of way, he says, "I request that...you acquit him of all the charges against him."

Hugh Harradence takes his place at the lectern. Hearing his first words, one juror smiles and two others cock their heads like dogs listening to their master's voice. Masterful indeed is his voice and skilled are the movements of his black sleeves and long fingers. He's in charge now. This is his last chance to speak to the jurors on Linda Sterling's behalf.

"Ladies and gentlemen" is how he addresses them from time to time. (I hope I won't hear "ma'am" again for a long time.) "It is entirely your prerogative to decide the evidence." And, he reminds them, it is upon the evidence that jurors should base their decision. "This is a court of law, not of emotions."

Mrs. Sterling is presumed innocent, according to law. She doesn't have to prove a thing. The Crown does. The Crown says Linda "abused, attacked and confined" children in her care. If this is true, he asks, why didn't someone complain about her before the investigation began? "Don't be lost on insignificant details." The fact that there was no baby-gate in the house, for instance, is of no consequence when deciding if abuse occurred.

Harradence continues. Officer Claudia Bryden was young and inexperienced, though possibly well-intentioned. She lacked proper supervision, proper guidance, and proper support. And her boss, Inspector McGillivray, testified that he felt she was paranoid. When she undertook the investigation it spread, not only throughout the community of Martensville, but like wildfire throughout the province. Bryden proceeded on a determined course. It's one thing, he says, for parents to become fanatical about such an investigation, and another when police lose their objectivity. The investigation for this case lacks objectivity. The alleged crimes did not happen.

If they did, he continues, there is not a "shred of evidence." The LUMA-LITE test at The Place revealed nothing. And the owners of the property knew nothing about the things alleged to have occurred under their noses. The children's accounts are elaborate fabrications and their diagrams prove they were never even there. Maybe, I think. But even after scrutinizing the albums of police photos of The Place, I still couldn't draw a floor plan of any kind to save my life. Even Sergeant Gillis, though experienced in such matters, had trouble establishing the crime-scene grid for his computerized layout because the place was such a mess.

Ladies and gentlemen, the daycare children exhibited normative childhood behaviour. Kenny probably did have constipation, period. And, according to the testimony of Bill's parents, around the time their son started to act up they were having marital problems. "The observation and interpretation of behaviour is very subjective," he emphasizes. And he's right. That's what the experts taught us. So who knows what demons Kenny and Bill wrestled with?

"I suggest, Ladies and gentlemen, that you come to the conclusion that there is severe contamination," Harradence says about the police investigation, reminding jurors how expert witness Dr. Raskin condemned the interviews as the worst he'd seen of their kind. After such a bungle, he continues, it was impossible to undo the damage. By the time the children got to court, it was "far too late" to challenge them. If police hadn't contacted the kids in the first place, how many of them would have had to go to therapists? Harradence pauses to take a sip of water, and Judge Wimmer removes his glasses and stares at them, as though seeing them for the first time. There's not a peep from the mostly middle-aged crowd.

"None of this happened... It doesn't make sense," Harradence continues. There is no evidence that the children were ever ferried around in police vehicles. And why, that night at the Martensville police station, did Jim Elstad hand the file to Claudia Bryden, the rookie, if he himself was committing crimes against the children? "We're dealing with extremely serious allegations. The test here is: Do you have a reasonable doubt? I would like to suggest, ladies and gentlemen, that you return a verdict of not guilty...on all counts against Mrs. Sterling."

Harradence, as usual, is a hard act to follow. But to compare apples with oranges — the flamboyant style of Hugh Harradence with the low-key earnestness of Earl Kalenith — would be, well, fruitless. The "evidence proves nothing," says Kalenith, now addressing the jurors on behalf of his client, Travis Sterling. In the absence of irrefutable proof, he tells them, they will have to apply common sense. Struggling with a cold, he is determined to apply every ounce of his energy to keeping his client out of jail.

Normally, Kalenith asserts, the judicial system runs on the presumption of innocence. But the Martensville police already had a bias against Travis in 1991 because of the complaint lodged almost four years earlier by the child protection worker for Sally. Then Kalenith reminds jurors that the girl's parents took no particular measures to contact police and waited for officers to call them about the complaint. Surely, I think, Kalenith would not go so far as to criticize Sally's parents for expecting the Martensville police to simply do their job.

The case, he reminds jurors, must be decided solely on the children's evidence, much of which is inaccurate and unreliable. The improper investigation and repeated questioning led kids to say and believe what they did. On the other hand, "there is no reason to disbelieve the evidence of Travis." Travis is a young person who leads a normal life and testified before the court confidently and straightforwardly. None of the evidence proves Travis did anything, or that he was ever at The Place. For that matter, none of the children were there either. They knew nothing about The Place till police showed them photos. The notion that adults drove the kids there borders on the ridiculous. And the behavioural evidence is worth nothing. Indeed, many of the reported behaviours are normal, and none of the medical evidence proves sexual abuse.

Judge Wimmer folds his arms across his chest. Perhaps he's tired. This is at least the sixth time he has heard the evidence. I've heard it more times than you, M'Lord. You didn't sit through Tammy's trial, too. Buck up, old boy.

Kalenith knows the evidence inside out. He wants to make sure jurors do too. And he wants them to remember the gaps in the credibility of the accusers, the children. Janey, for instance, told her mother she was hit with a pink rope. She also told her mom she went with daycare personnel to a blue store with green elephants. Her testimony makes no sense and is not reliable. Her brother Tommy at first denied anything was wrong. But before long he was telling his father wild tales of abuse. Then he once said he'd made all his stories up. So the "whole thing is in doubt," concludes Kalenith. As for Freddy, he made no disclosures till police called. Then he felt pressured by his mother's questioning and, to keep his story straight, brought his "script" to court. Freddy has no independent memory, and none of the other children saw him being sexually assaulted by Travis while playing in the Sterling kitchen. Kenny told stories only when he had been informed by his mother that Freddy was talking. Kenny's evidence is troubling and problematic, and some of the details were wrong. For instance, he said a zapper was used to open the garage door at The Place. This is not so, according to the owner. Likewise, Bill's stories contained "obvious and straightforward errors." Yes, but what about the details that several children spoke of independently? For example, the cage and the freezer at The Place.

On the one hand, concludes Kalenith, you have the evidence of the children but nothing to corroborate it. On the other hand, you have the evidence of Travis, which is clear and credible. He concludes by reminding jurors that the Crown has already stayed five of the charges against his client and that they'd be doing the right thing to drop all other charges against Travis too.

Cough. Choke. One of the jurors is sputtering, his face getting redder by the minute. Wimmer, who can't afford to lose a member of the jury at this point, calls a break.

Leslie Sullivan, the last one to address the jury, has the most difficult job of all. Whereas the three defence lawyers have maintained that nothing criminal happened, her task is to prove that it did, beyond a reasonable doubt. Fortunately, she has two weapons in her arsenal the others don't. The first is makeup: blusher for the cheekbones, lipstick for the mouth, and mascara for the blue eyes above the grey bags. Sullivan looks in fighting trim.

Her other special tool is a mobile chalkboard. I feel like I'm back in Grade 6, and wonder what jurors think when it's wheeled in. "The picture as a whole" is what they must look at, says Sullivan, the "parallel nature of the children's evidence," and the kids' behaviour as supplied by the testimony of their parents and therapists.

The twelve men and women sit and listen in silence. Is it my imagination, or do they actually listen more attentively and look at her more sympathetically than they did the defence lawyers? Is it because of her message or her gender? I know there are times I'll smile at a woman when I wouldn't at a man, for fear he'd misunderstand. I never realized the converse till now, when I see the male jurors smile more freely at Sullivan than they did at any of the three defence lawyers.

Perhaps the occasional smile from one of the jurors reveals the state of his or her heart, which is the target of Sullivan's words. How could it be otherwise, when her sole objective is to speak, one last time, for the children and the wrongs she believes they have endured?

I hope the jurors will keep the promise they made to be fair, when challenged for cause, and to base their verdict on the courtroom evidence, not the media reports — such as they were. But is this possible? My guess is that a jury, like any other group, is composed of leaders and followers. I imagine that some would find it harder than others to forget the media coverage preceding the trial, and have more difficulty turning back their imaginary tapes to Day 1. But they swore they would base their verdict on nothing but the evidence, and that's why they were chosen for jury duty. Sullivan, by recapping the evidence, hopes to help them do their job.

She reminds the men and women that the children had a difficult task to do: face adult pressure, reveal private humiliations and give testimony in front of strangers. They coped with their feelings in different ways: Freddy took deep sighs and long pauses, and Kenny hung his head (a revelation for most of us, who've never seen the boy).

The children's word is pretty much all jurors have to go on. But, Sullivan reminds them, the kids did corroborate each other's stories and sometimes gave parallel accounts of events, though they've had no contact with each other for months. For example, both Freddy and Tommy talked about being taken to the house of RCMP officer Darren Sabourin; Kenny said he and Ron Sterling waited in Sabourin's driveway while Travis knocked on the door of the officer's house.

The adult evidence, too, sometimes corroborated the children's. For instance, Constable Keyes' floor plan of the Sterling house is remarkably similar to that of Kenny's who, according to the Sterlings, never stepped beyond the door of their house.

The children's language and imagery were spontaneous and authentic. Who can forget Kenny's picture of Linda Sterling making apple pie, or his description of Ron Sterling "nibbling" on his penis, or Tommy's tale about hiding behind the couch while Ron assaulted his two sisters?

Sullivan continues: Bill's story also had the ring of truth. Particularly memorable is the time he turned his head just enough to glimpse Ron Sterling sodomizing him and determined not to cry at that crucial moment. The boy still has trouble sleeping alone and needs to know the dead bolt is on the front door. Before testifying, he vomited and refused to eat.

Tommy is seven now. When he was four, he was allegedly assaulted at the Sterling daycare and became clinically depressed. In court, Tommy didn't even want to say the word "penis" and wrote it on a piece of paper. Also on paper he made a diagram of the Sterling house and the place he calls the devil church. His parents revealed how Tommy cried after a therapy session and begged them not to give him away for being a bad boy. On another occasion, his sister Janey sobbed, "Tell me I'm not a bad girl."

Freddy — here Sullivan's voice gets louder, and her throat tightens — Freddy was exposed to three years of sexual abuse. During this time, he wet his bed and suffered more than usual from his nervous stomach. Later, when discussing his experiences with the therapist he got erections, and told his counsellor he'd had pleasure from his encounters — as well as pain. He still keeps a baseball bat by his bed. In court Freddy stuck to his job of giving evidence, even when he got tired and fed up. "Would an adult have done better?"

Sally is fifteen now; she was ten when she told her guidance counsellor what Travis had done. Till that time, May 1988, she had excelled in school, but then her grades dropped. "There is no reason to make this (story) up."

Sullivan admits there are many unanswered questions in this case. The first one is why the Martensville police officers, Darryl Ford and Ed Revesz, did not, in 1988, charge Travis Sterling with Sally's allegation.

Then Sullivan — mother of two children, one a preschooler — gets everyone's attention. "I have one question which has not been answered," she says, pausing for dramatic effect that makes people sit up straighter. "How old were you when you learned about anal sex?" No one breathes. "Just as the kids were learning about school and sharing, they also learned about sex... They learned at the hands of Linda, Ron, and Travis Sterling." She has stunned the crowd to silence. For the daycare parents scattered throughout the room, it is a bittersweet moment.

By midmorning break, Sullivan has reached the "halfway mark" of her closing address, as she tells jurors when court re-convenes. It looks as though she'll take till noon, and she will now shift her point of view from that of the children to the adults.

First the police: Notwithstanding the mistakes made in the interview process and the "heavy-duty attack" subsequently launched, "I suggest that the officers were dedicated to doing a difficult job," trying to get the kids to tell them what they had already told their parents. Claudia Bryden did her job conscientiously. Once she'd spoken to Janey's father, and found the long-forgotten file on Sally, she had to investigate the two girls' allegations against Travis Sterling. Had she not, she would have been neglecting her duty as defined by the Criminal Code. The defence may think it strange that Jim Elstad handed the second complaint against Travis Sterling to Claudia Bryden if Elstad himself was assaulting the children. The prosecution does not find it at all strange, says Sullivan. "Who else would Jim Elstad give the file to but a part-time, short-term rookie?"

Then the parents. They did their best, says Sullivan, to cope with their kids' allegations. Paul's mother tried to get her son to talk by asking non-leading questions. Tommy's mother sometimes asked questions, and sometimes waited for her son to talk. Kenny took his mother to her bedroom, and closed the door. Freddy asked his mother, sometimes in the middle of the night, to write the details of his story in her notebook. Bill told his father, who then called Claudia Bryden. "The parents have to come in here and admit they failed." Not only did they fail to protect their children, they actually delivered them to the Sterlings. They were "naive... None of them was exaggerating for your benefit."

On the other hand, Ron Sterling was dogmatic and combative in his courtroom demeanour, Sullivan says. He proved to be inflexible, and on certain matters such as teaching the children to avoid the stairs he took an absolute position. The prosecutor doesn't mince her words: "This is the side of Ron Sterling the children got to know."

Sullivan continues: Linda Sterling was adept and cool on the stand. She is false, though she pretended to be a good provider of daycare. Travis was adamant about never reading the porn magazines in the living room, but that's not what his friend said. Travis is not a credible witness. He tried to mislead you, by talking about things he saw on his street when he was not even in the country. These small details, which contradict the evidence of other witnesses, should bring the rest of his evidence into doubt.

Sullivan spares no scepticism. It's true police found no sign of the children's ever having been at The Place. In fact, they found no sign of the owner's having been there either. No fingerprints, no hair, no fibres, and no animal blood though he'd slept and eaten and sometimes butchered livestock there. She suggests that, in a ruse to confuse investigators, "There was some sort of clean-up, which left the place looking messy."

The evidence raises questions in Sullivan's mind. If the children were never at The Place, how could they look at police photos and make elaborate stories from them? How would Freddy know the bedroom door opened to the left? How would Kenny know the floor was wood, when he couldn't see it in the photos? What about the people who said they saw the police van zoom back and forth down Power Line Road to The Place?

Sullivan shifts into parent mode and starts to use the word "we." She asks, How can parents be so oblivious to these atrocities? It's easy. We try to explain away our children's problems. We try to see our kids as normal. We do not even consider that our children may have been abused. "Ladies and gentlemen, child molesters need no motive... We didn't pick children to be the victims in this case. Someone else did." With these biting words, Leslie Sullivan concludes her closing address.

Then she turns from the jury to the judge. "Charges at 2 o'clock, M'Lord?" Correct, says Wimmer and, with a twinkling smile, advises jurors, "Pack a suitcase. From now on, we're going to feed and house you." The twelve of them file out of the courtroom, for home; the rest of us head for a nice long lunch.

Two o'clock. The room is packed with people of all ages, many I've never spotted before. I wonder if Wimmer sees anyone, so intent is he on the job at hand. Unlike Tammy's trial, where Lavoie was judge and jury, here Wimmer is the "judger of the law" and jurors are the tryers of the facts. Wimmer tells them they are supreme, in that regard. It is for them to weigh the evidence, consider the legal remarks or disregard them, and to have the final word. Like so many legal terms, the word "verdict" has ancient roots and means "to speak the truth." These twelve men and women will speak the truth as they see it, and decide the fate of Ron, Linda and Travis Sterling. To do it, they have worn their usual practical clothes to protect them from the cold. All except for the Fashion Plate, whose clothes I covet, and the Sweatshirt Kid, whose clothes I don't.

The judge and the lawyers are dressed, as usual, in the black vests and gowns that have changed little in the past 100 years, except that no longer in Canada are they accompanied by powdered wigs. All three Sterlings, who could have worn any colour they liked today, wear black too. To match the clothes, mother and son have selected sombre faces, though father has resumed his trademark jack-o'-lantern grin.

Judge Wimmer tells the jurors that, due to the complexity of the trial, he will supply them with a checklist of criteria they may use to determine the verdict for each of the remaining forty-six charges, according to the Criminal Code. By his count, there are 106 possible different verdicts arising from the charges. Wimmer knows how important his directions to the jurors are; if he misdirects them, it could be grounds for an appeal.

The presumption of innocence is key, he says. Jurors don't have to be sure that the three accused are innocent to acquit them. But they must be sure the accused are guilty before they convict them. They must digest the courtroom evidence and make it, not the media reports, the basis for their verdict. It is their job to analyze the known rather than speculate about the unknown, for example, where the children got their knowledge in the first place. This, he says, is an "exercise in logic, not fill-in-the-blanks."

Wimmer continues: Honest discrepancies in the witnesses' testimony are to be expected; blatant ones are not. No assumption should be made that a young child's evidence is different from an adult's, although "there may be need for special caution," when reviewing the children's evidence. If you see a discrepancy in any of the children's statements, ask yourself: Which statement is to be believed, the one made in court or the one made on tape? As for the tapes of the thirty-one interviews you reviewed here, you must not examine what the kids told the police, but the manner in which the police asked the questions. A young child's mind can be easily manipulated.

When assessing the testimony of the expert witnesses, you must use common sense and your own knowledge. "You were all children once," he adds. And, as you all know, a technician — a motor mechanic, say — may know more about what's wrong with your car than a theoretician. "Put everything into the mix" and try to capture the essence of the experts' opinions rather than concentrate on their differences.

This trial is about an investigation, not just the Sterling family. Sexual misconduct usually occurs in private. The fact that a person has no criminal record is irrelevant when assessing charges in a court of law.

On that note, Wimmer turns to the actual evidence, analyzing it piece by piece, child by child. The commissionaire distributes Wimmer's checklist of charges to the jurors, to help them assess each one and match it to the law.

Jurors stare at these long lists while Wimmer tells them how to use them. When assessing charge 21, for instance, which was brought by Paul, they have to decide three things: Did Linda Sterling assault the boy? Was it for sexual purposes? Did she use a weapon to threaten him? Once they've decided those three things, they must then decide four more. Is Linda guilty as charged? Not guilty as charged? Not guilty as charged, but guilty of assault with a weapon? Or not guilty as charged, but guilty of sexual assault? If this were a civil trial, jurors would not need to reach unanimity — a majority would be enough. But this is a criminal trial, and they have to be unanimous.

Eventually, the twelve men and women must agree on every verdict for every charge. If they can't, they will declare themselves "hung."

I don't envy the jurors their task, and hope they retire to a room without windows or other distractions. But if they're suffering from trial fatigue as much as I am, maybe a room without windows is the last place they should be sequestered. I wonder if petty rivalries have sprung up. More likely, some of the jurors have had time to discover they're friends of friends of their fellow jurors, or cousins several times removed. Such links would keep them on their best behaviour, worried that one of the jurors would snitch, sooner or later, over a display of bad manners or uppity behaviour. Till now these twelve people have sat together all day long and gone home at night to their families. Now they will live together at the Bessborough Hotel like family, until they come to a verdict. I wonder what they'll talk about at lunch and dinner, or dinner and supper as the two meals are sometimes called in Saskatchewan.

Wimmer plods his way through the children's evidence. Freddy's allegations have few details, even though he was allowed to keep his list with him in the witness box. His imagination and ability to blend fact and fiction are perhaps evident in the strange story he told about Ron Sterling throwing a hamster into a fire. Freddy's description of the cage differed from Bill's. On the other hand, his account of watching Frank being put in the freezer is plausible, considering the boy was small at the time. One time Freddy could remember what Travis did to Kenny; another time he could not. When the doctor examined Kathy, she found no evidence of intercourse, contrary to Freddy's testimony. And it wasn't clear if Freddy put his penis in Ron's anus, or the other way round. Peering over his horn-rimmed glasses, Wimmer tells the jurors, "It is up to you to decide." Hearing this, Ron Sterling grinds his chin into his tie, as though it's too tight, and his neck turns red.

During the break I catch a glimpse of a chocolate cake with candles on the coffee table in the witness room just off the court, and learn it's in honour of Travis Sterling's twenty-fifth birthday. A small sad circle of family members and well-wishers sings "Happy Birthday" to the young man inside the room, while outside many small groups mill around and gossip about the Sterlings' chances for acquittal. In the ladies' room, Leslie Sullivan has a bigger than usual scowl on her face and anger in her voice. Judge Wimmer's instructions to the jury so far are inadequate, she fumes.

Wimmer, I learn from a reporter, has his own problems: the instruction sheet, his checklist, has been misprinted by one of the secretaries. Finally, the chief jurist gets things righted and reconvenes court. From his high-backed chair, he tells jurors that the children's stories frequently lack context and suffer from frailties, which the Crown concedes. And "in the end, it comes down to the children." Are their anxieties the result of sexual trauma or of the police investigation?

Kenny's friendship with Freddy aside, it's a major puzzle, says Wimmer, why the boy kept going back to the Sterling house, especially since he wasn't babysat there and if, as he says, he was repeatedly abused. The boy drew a pretty good facsimile of the Sterling house for someone who was never there, as the Sterlings maintained. But does it prove Kenny was there, any more than any of the children's evidence proves anything, beyond a reasonable doubt?

Consult with each other, says Wimmer. Do not hesitate to change your mind. You must be unanimous. You have a right to disagree, but please try to agree. "I don't think anyone wants to do this again. You're on your own. Good luck."

With this, two security guards step forward and face the jury. The clerk reads the Jury Act, reminding them of their duty. One by one, each swears to abide by the Act and follows the guards from the room.

Not good enough. Sullivan rises to complain about the way Wimmer did his job: "I'm not sure the jury has been adequately instructed... You didn't repeat enough that would provide a balanced view of the children's evidence." She gives a couple of examples and says she disagrees, for instance, that Bill was unable to provide a description of The Place till he saw police photos. I am amazed when she tells the judge she wants him to instruct the jurors that they do not necessarily have to adopt his view of things. "I understand your difficulty, but the evidence is so vague," Wimmer says in a kind voice, agreeing to think about what she has said to him.

The next few days unfold like an unwieldy musical composition, composed of three surprise movements, each one bigger and more astonishing than the one before.

First Wimmer does as Sullivan asked, by re-convening court to give jurors further instructions. "It's confession time for me," he tells them. "I made some glaring errors." He admits that, in one case, he misinterpreted some evidence and that he left out things, such as the fact that Freddy sat on the front steps in the cold. "I want to remind you that any opinion of mine is of no consequence."

The twelve jurors look as though they're already hard at work. This morning they awoke thinking they'd spend the day holed up at the hotel discussing the evidence. Not expecting to be called back to court, they all dressed in jeans and sweatshirts, even the fashion plate. Is dressing the same the first step to reaching group consensus?

Wimmer adjourns the court. The jurors retire again. The RCMP officer locks the courtroom doors, and the public and journalists are forced to hang around the halls while the lawyers gather in their own room downstairs and the Sterlings play cards and drink coffee in the witness room.

Interminable hours go by, four straight days of jury deliberation, sunup to sundown. Then, from nowhere, word spreads that Wimmer intends to unlock the doors of the courtroom in a half hour. Everyone assumes the verdict has been reached.

Not so. We listen as Wimmer announces the second surprise: One of the jurors is too sick to continue, and the jury deliberations will continue without him. With the departure of the "heavy-set male juror," as the *StarPhoenix* reporter puts it on page 1, we are only one juror away from a mistrial.

If surprise number 2 isn't enough to set Wimmer's teeth on edge, I bet surprise number 3 is.

Publication bans are tricky things: for the minister of justice, the journalists, and the judges themselves. A few days ago Wimmer officially declared that the moment jurors were sequestered, journalists could report the "testimony of the complainants." To no one's surprise, he ruled that no information be published that might disclose the identity of any child or that of the four adults yet to be tried.

No sooner had Judge Wimmer made this fiat, no sooner had he hung up his black robe than Judge Marion Wedge put hers on. No sooner had the doors of his courtroom been locked than those of another courtroom were unlocked for the pre-trial of Jim Elstad, the co-accused police officer from Martensville. No sooner have the court reporters begun to lick their chops in preparation for the publishing frenzy they've been waiting to indulge in since Day 1 of the Sterling trial, than Judge Wedge rules we will have to hold our tongues till the Elstad trial in her courtroom is over, too.

A different judge has just stepped onto the stage, sat upon her high-backed leather chair, and struck a brand-new publication ban. It's like a Kafka play, a Woody Allen film, and a memo from the New Management all rolled into one. Naturally, no journalist wants to get hauled into Wedge's office for breaking her ban, but important stories are waiting to be written and Wimmer ruled we could write them.

The *StarPhoenix* plays it straight, in accordance with Judge Wedge's ruling. The reporter writes a just-the-facts-ma'am story for the front page: "The only thing reportable under Wedge's order is that there is now a ban and it remains in effect until the conclusion of Elstad's trial, or until further ordered." The short piece appears alongside a large colour picture of a smiling Judge Wimmer. I can only assume he was photographed smiling before he heard about the new ban. I'd give anything to be a fly on the wall of the judges' upstairs dining room, to hear what Wimmer and Wedge say to each other over catered cold cuts.

Meanwhile, in the downstairs courtrooms, the CBC lawyers are still fighting for freedom of the press. Now they have to sort out bans applying to three trials: the total ban Judge Lavoie slapped on Tammy's trial a year ago and the complete blackout Judge Wedge just imposed on the Elstad trial, which may or may not apply to all evidence previously given at the Sterlings' trial, which still has its own ban in effect from Judge Wimmer.

Even as one lawyer for the CBC stands before the Supreme Court judges in Ottawa this week, another lawyer for the "Mother Corp." stands in front of Judge Wimmer in Saskatoon, flanked by counsel for the *StarPhoenix*, and three other attorneys. Wimmer listens to the five of them for the better part of an hour, then rules that his original order, as he amended the other day now that the jury has been sequestered, still stands. "It is unimpaired, unabridged, and has not been suspended by any other order." In other words, his ruling takes precedence over Judge Wedge's.

It's enough to make your head spin and wish you were holed up with the jurors. They don't have to concern themselves with publication bans or many distractions from the outside world. On the other hand, they may feel cut off from everything, especially after being sequestered for eight days. And because they still haven't reached a verdict, Wimmer gets on their case, so to speak. He calls the eleven of them back to court for a pep talk and urges them to try harder. They must concentrate on the evidence, downplay their feelings, and try to reach unanimity. If they fail to arrive at a verdict, "it will be necessary to hold another trial." They look tired and grumpy. Who wouldn't?

The jurors sweat it out, and everyone else's life revolves around their deliberations. For eight days in a row, reporters stand guard at the courthouse, from the time jurors finish their breakfast till the time they go to bed at night. For fear of missing the verdict the moment it's brought down, the handful of journalists break to eat only when the jurors do. The rest of the time they read, gossip, use their cell phones and their laptops, file stories, eat, drink coffee, and act like expectant parents. The cramped space allotted us off Courtroom 1, which is more like a vestibule than a room, has no windows. Every now and then, more reporters want to sit than there are chairs available and, as the week wears on, the bickering has more of an edge. Here, we have no green passes as we did for Tammy's trial.

The small witness room, directly across from our vestibule, is reserved for the Sterling family and friends. Sometimes the door is closed, sometimes open. When it is, I catch a glimpse of the occupants sitting and conversing as though in their own front room. Through the door passes a procession of people of all ages, including children of friends and police officers still to be tried.

The main corridor on the second floor of the courthouse looks more like a maternity ward than a hall of judgement. Twenty or so people, most of them trial *habitués*, chat and laugh and knit. People of all description come and go from the floor, some stopping at the Sterlings' room to talk or snack. Superstore's Decadent cookies are popular with everyone, as much as the homemade goodies and chocolates that get passed around at regular intervals by none other than Ron Sterling. He is seldom refused.

Perhaps the only thing more astonishing than the offerings of our self-appointed host is the brazenness with which he makes his rounds. (The pumpkin grin is a given.) The first time Sterling offers me a treat, I don't know what to do. I think back to the day in the Vietnamese restaurant where he paid for my lunch, and blood rushes to my face. Inevitably, after three or four refusals I succumb to the Decadent cookies like everyone else.

From time to time, a lawyer appears, walking into the room where the Sterlings and their come-and-go entourage play cards, drink coffee, eat, chat, and laugh. Laugh? I can hardly believe my ears. Even if I were not guilty of abusing children, just being accused would make me hide my face. But I shouldn't impose my values on others. Besides, matters of morality are ultimately decided in a court far higher than this one.

The verdict and sentence

On the ninth day of sequestration — Day 91 on the trial calendar or February 2, 1994, on the real one — the jury reaches a verdict. Judge Wimmer is the first to know, then the lawyers and the Sterlings, then the rest of us. Everyone runs to the courtroom, where it's push and shove. There is not a spare seat, and a journalist from Toronto puts his hand on my bottom to prevent me from sitting in my usual spot, which he says is reserved today for someone more important. I won't repeat what I said to him or the icy way I stare him down. I am shaken by his boldness and struck by the irony of being assaulted in this particular way during this particular trial.

Wimmer arrives, looking sombre, and the jurors file in. Some look serious, others sad. You could cut the air with a knife. The premonition of the *StarPhoenix* reporter comes back to me, and I shudder to think he might be right — that someone in the public gallery might be packing a gun. After all, no one frisked us at the door.

Without fanfare, the clerk reads the eleven jurors' names and asks if they've reached their verdicts. "How say you?" The foreman stands and, clasping his hands in front of him for ballast, replies. "Ron Sterling: not guilty on all counts.Linda Sterling: not guilty on all counts. Travis Sterling:

From left to right, Linda, Ron, and Travis Sterling, January 28, 1994.

guilty, as charged, on six counts of sexual assault; guilty on one count of simple assault, and guilty of attempting to engage in anal intercourse."

Travis sits absolutely still. All I can see of him is his back directly in front of me. Wimmer calls a break, though few people leave the room. Here and there, clusters develop. Journalists run to and from the room, cell phones pressed to their ears. I leave for the ladies' and, on the way past the witness room, see Ron sipping a coffee. He looks relieved. He laughs and refers to the "dipshit from *Maclean's*," which I assume to be one of the journalists who wants an interview.

Ron, Linda, and Travis return to their usual courtroom seats. Mother's face is red and her eyes are puffy; father appears as feisty as ever, as though ready to enter the ring again. The two sit side by side in the dock, not flanking their son, who sits apart and alone. In the gallery, other parents, those of the daycare children, look dazed. Freddy's mother is staring into her lap, her husband's arm around her shoulder. Kenny's mother is crying as her husband pats her hand.

Wimmer looks straight at the Sterling parents. "I appreciate how devastating this has been for you. I hope you can put your lives back in order." Then he turns to the jury. "No [jury] has ever given more to help the justice system function than you. An individual judge is prone to error. You have provided tremendous service." He then reminds them not to discuss their deliberations with anyone, ever. Wimmer dismisses this court, for the very last time. Two RCMP officers approach Travis, handcuff him, and lead him away. The crowd funnels from the courtroom, buzzing as it goes.

"It's not ended, I'll tell you," Ron assures a woman in the swarm, sending his voice over the heads of two or three others. Then he stops obligingly in the hall, to answer reporters' questions in a scrum. He has invested twenty-four years of his working life in the justice system, and is not about to stop doing so now. "I want it back," he says about his job at the Saskatoon Correctional Centre. When I ask about his son, he answers, "I can't see how they could convict my kid and not us. I know in my heart that my son is not guilty of anything. It's a very hysterical type of crime. The first step is to appeal my son's convictions." On this note, Sterling excuses himself to feed the mob of electronic reporters pacing at the back door of the courthouse.

Next day the fifth co-accused police officer in the Martensville case is about to be tried. Jim Elstad is the officer who introduced Claudia Bryden to the Sterlings three and a half years ago, and then handed her the half-missing file containing the second complaint against the Sterling son. Some of the regulars from Courtroom 1 are here, as well as Ron Sterling himself and two other co-accused officers.

Ron Sterling breaks into tears after commenting about Travis to the media, February 2, 1994.

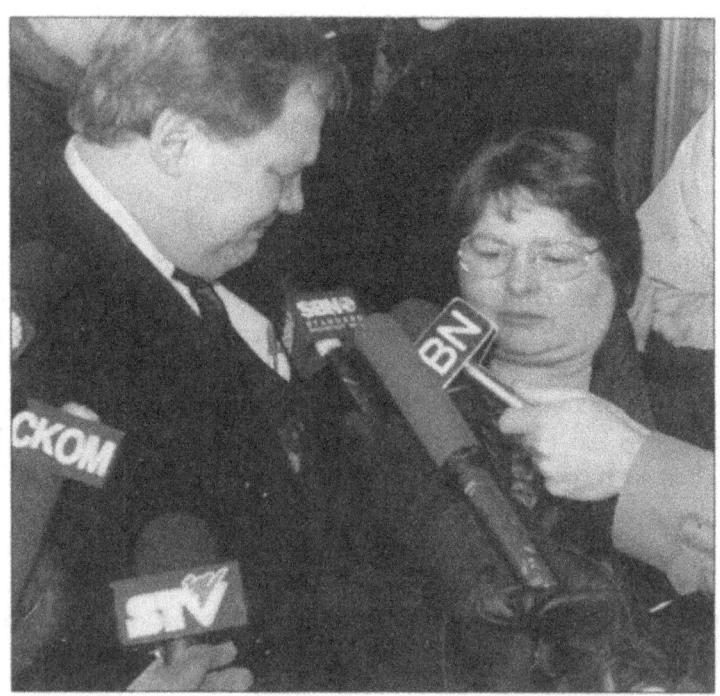

Let's put this fire out before it spreads, the lawyer for Elstad tells the court. The jury has spoken, acquitting Ron and Linda Sterling. Therefore, Jim Elstad, their alleged accomplice, must also be found not guilty. Automatically, and without a trial. Judge Marion Wedge responds, "I know less about the Sterling trial than anyone else in this room." Her admission causes snickers from the journalists in the room who are happy to be on the right side of Wimmer's publication ban rather than the wrong side of Wedge's. The judge needs a few days to do her homework and rule on the status of the Elstad trial. (Before the week is out, the Department of Justice will stay the charges against Elstad. Soon after, all charges against officers Darren Sabourin, Darryl Ford, Ed Revesz, and John Popowich will also be stayed.)

February 4, 1994. Courtroom 1 is SRO. Now that Travis Sterling has been found guilty of eight crimes against six children, the judge must decide the sentence he will receive for his crimes. Many of the regulars who've followed the case since Day 1 are here, the Native woman in the wheelchair, Short Jim and Tall Tim, the grandmother who wears her waitress uniform to court, the man who reads the *Racing Digest*, the Mackenzie sisters *sans* headgear, the daycare parents, Claudia Bryden, Rod Moor, several other officers investigating the allegations, and the children's therapists.

Ron and Linda Sterling are here. Found not guilty on all charges, they have crossed the courtroom bar that separated those on the wrong side of the law from those on the right side during the trial. They now sit with us, the public, behind their son, left alone in the prisoner's dock, dressed in a red sweatshirt and jeans. It is now the lawyers' job to tell Judge Wimmer what sentence befits Travis, and why.

Sullivan goes first, for the Crown. The principle of deterrence should be reinforced, she tells Wimmer. There's no hope of deterring others from committing such heinous crimes, if the sentence is not severe. The starting point should be three years because Travis has demonstrated contemptuous disregard for the personal feelings of the children. He should be sent to adult penitentiary. When sentencing him, Wimmer should consider three important things: the social disapproval of such crimes, the public confidence in the judicial system, and the rehabilitation of the young man. The Martensville parents took their kids to the Sterling house and trusted the family to look after their most prized possessions. Because the parents believed Travis was safe, the children automatically believed he was too. He betrayed their trust. He preyed upon six children, ranging in age from two to ten years. They were captive and highly vulnerable, and he used them like a revolving door. Sullivan continues: Travis was a serial abuser of the children placed in his mother's care. In 1988, the first complaint was made and the police talked to him about it, yet he continued to abuse children. He regularly threatened his victims. And now he shows no remorse. That's in the past. But what about the future? Sullivan reminds Wimmer that it is reasonable to expect that the children will suffer long-term emotional trauma. Indeed, it may be impossible for some of them to form loving relationships as adults. They may, indeed, become abusers themselves.

A chill runs through my body. What if she's right? What if the kids are so screwed up they hate sex? What if they think it's dirty and degrading? What if they have no more joy in life? What if they want to rob others of it, as they were robbed? Most of the abused kids were boys. And abused males are more likely to grow up and abuse others than abused females are, as we've heard in testimony.

Earl Kalenith, the prisoner's lawyer, looks untroubled by such questions when he rises to speak to his client's sentence. Travis has no criminal record, he says. He has the strong support of family and friends, and good character references.

Wimmer bursts with indignation: Character references? What evidence are you referring to? he asks. A chastened Kalenith continues: Travis was never in charge of these children and never in a position of trust. He does not believe Travis should go to adult prison and argues for a maximum two-year sentence, the threshold for a stay in a federal penitentiary. The Crown's recommendation is far too severe for what Travis did, and the sentence must not be disproportionate.

Wimmer, appearing impervious to Kalenith's words, asks Travis to speak for himself. The prisoner stands: "I maintain my innocence, and I'm not going to stop fighting."

The judge stands firm. "Mr. Sterling, I know you insist upon your innocence," but the jury has found you guilty. According to their findings, "you have boiled a nasty brew." Families are in tatters and children have been emotionally scarred, some with minds seemingly altered. There may be people who argue you alone are not to blame, but "your misconduct was certainly the catalyst... Your father was probably correct when he said, following your arrest in 1991, that if charges had been brought against you three years earlier, that would have put an end to it. Instead, lives have now been devastated in every possible way."

Wimmer sounds like a father himself who has thought long and hard about the crimes committed by the young man facing him. Throughout his scathing remarks, Travis looks straight ahead and stands at attention as best he can, but one leg twitches nonstop. The judge believes he must make the young adult an example for others that the penalties will be harsh for such offences. Just as important, he wants the sentence he gives Travis to reflect public denunciation, the outrage on societal values and the public's general abhorrence of revolting behaviour towards children. Nevertheless, there must be hope that reformation and rehabilitation will occur, and the sentence should not be so severe as to discourage the possibility.

Taking all these factors into consideration, Wimmer finally brings down the sentence. On count 1, the sexual assault upon Freddy, Travis Sterling will receive imprisonment in a federal penitentiary for three years. The judge then lists the seven other indictments and imposes various lesser concurrent sentences. But when he comes to count eighteen, the sexual assault of Janey, Wimmer's face sags and his voice drops. "I think this conviction justifies a different approach. This child was only two-and-one-half years old at the time of the offence... Any assault upon a child of this age must be viewed in the gravest light. She was little more than a baby. It is a loathsome crime. For this you will be imprisoned for two years, the sentence to be consecutive to the other terms of imprisonment." The total sentence, then, is five years in a federal penitentiary.

Travis's back stiffens and his head drops to his chest. His father, for once, does not smile. His mother looks as though she'll start to cry, but to my amazement does not, even when her son, the serial abuser, is handcuffed and led from the courtroom.

I run to join the swarm of reporters at the back door downstairs. Outdoor microphones and all-weather pencils poised, we wait in the freezing cold for Ron and Linda Sterling to leave the courthouse. Fifteen, twenty minutes pass, then a handcuffed Travis, flanked by police guards, walks through the side door. Janis thrusts a mike in his face and asks, "Do you maintain your innocence?" The prisoner replies, "Yes, I do." That's the last thing he utters, before being pushed into the back of the police van, and carted off to jail. No sooner has the van slid out of the courthouse parking lot than the back door of the courthouse opens and Ron and Linda emerge, she clinging to the arm of his suit. I don't know what surprises me more: seeing them touch for the first time, or seeing him coatless in minus-40 weather.

Mikes are thrust into their faces, and Ron's lips form a cooperative grin. As the reporters patiently make way for each other's questions, Ron and Linda look all too happy to answer them. Linda, wiping the corner of her eye, tells tomorrow's early-morning readers of the *StarPhoenix* that she hopes the parents of the children, and everyone involved in the case, will sleep with a clear conscience tonight, knowing they have convicted an innocent person. Ron, unfolding the lapel of his suit jacket to protect his ears from the wind, has his words taped for the supper-hour news: His son is innocent. The verdict is being appealed immediately.

Just as I'm about to put away my pencil and take out my gloves, the journalist from Toronto walks over and stands a little too close for comfort. Without the slightest bit of repentance for his earlier courtroom assault on my backside, he sneers, "That's a very small bonfire for you." Bonfire? If he's insinuating I'm angry that the so-called witch hunt has boiled down to the town-square staking of one young man and woman, he's right. I want a full-scale inquiry.

The trials seem to have resolved little, yet they have cost a great deal — as much in human terms as financial. And it looks as though they will cost us even more. Ron and Linda Sterling are suing for millions, naming the government of Saskatchewan in addition to prosecutors Leslie Sullivan and Bruce Bauer and investigators Claudia Bryden and Rod Moor.

Tammy is also suing the same parties, plus the plaintiffs' therapist Rod Butler. John Popowich and three of the other four police officers also plan to take the province, the prosecutors, and the investigators to court. In self-defence, Claudia Bryden has formally requested access to the MacNeill Clinic records to show where the stories the children told therapists matched what they told her, and where they did not match. So far, the daycare parents have declined to sue anyone or put their children through another long trial.

But the small soprano voices in my head have not faded, and I know they never will.

Ron and Linda Sterling leave court after a hearing about staying charges on others involved in the Martensville trials, February 10, 1994.

Afterword

February 1998

Truth or Justice?

The Sterling trial was the longest and most expensive in Saskatchewan's history, costing taxpayers close to $1 million. Though the eleven jurors reached a verdict, the 200,000 people of Martensville and Saskatoon continue to argue the case, harbouring feelings so strong you'd think it ended yesterday instead of four years ago.

The trial provided many lessons for those who participated directly in the fray, and even more heartache. When Ron Sterling stated publicly that some of the Martensville parents knew their children had not been abused, one Martensville woman, the grandmother of a boy who had testified, told the *StarPhoenix* she was extremely angry that the court had not believed the children and was mystified that jurors had decided the more than one hundred charges were worthy of only eight convictions. There was more disappointment to come for the families.

About a year and a half after Tammy's trial, the appeals began. Toronto lawyer Clayton Ruby, known for his successful defence of Donald Marshall, argued in the provincial court of appeal in Regina that the verdict against the woman was "unreasonable." After the three appeal judges heard Ruby's arguments, they deliberated and wrote a forty-two-page ruling in which they concluded that the eight convictions against Tammy violated the doctrine of reasonable doubt because they left "real and serious doubts as to the credibility of the evidence of the children and as to the guilt of the appellant [Tammy]." The three judges agreed that the entire matter turned on the credibility of the three witnesses — Freddy and Kenny on the one hand, and

Tammy on the other. Without the evidence of the children, they said, "there is no foundation for any conviction." Besides, the boys' testimony was full of inconsistencies and contradictions that Judge Lavoie "failed to consider."

As for the expert evidence, Judge Lavoie "seems to have made the error of elevating" what the medical experts said to the status of "proof beyond a reasonable doubt" that the boys had been sexually abused. By so doing, they said, he had made the "decision of who is to be believed a very one-sided question, weighted very heavily and unfairly against the appellant [Tammy]." If Judge Lavoie gave the experts' opinions too much weight, they said, he seems to have decided not to pay the faulty police interviews very much importance at all. He apparently failed to closely weigh not just the boys' answers but the police officers' questions, even though their interview methods "did not comply with the techniques recommended by experts to get accurate responses from the children."

The failure of the boys to remember Tammy's scars, said the appeal judges, was a factor Judge Lavoie should have given more weight to. "There was no onus on [Tammy] to prove anything." The burden of proof was on the Crown and when neither Freddy nor Kenny remembered the scars, the "proper approach" for Lavoie would have been to ask himself if such failure cast doubt on the reliability of the boys' evidence. Judge Lavoie, they said, failed to ask himself if a reasonable doubt existed as to Tammy's guilt.

In their ruling, the three went on to say that because Tammy's convictions rested "almost entirely" on the credibility of the boys, and because that credibility was called into question by the evidence, it would have been appropriate for Judge Lavoie to note that there was no other confirmatory evidence as to Tammy's guilt. But he did not and was therefore in "error."

In short, Judge Lavoie "treated the case throughout as being a matter of choice between the [boys'] evidence on the one hand and [Tammy's] evidence on the other hand. He failed to properly direct himself as to the law.... Thus, the verdict should be set aside.... It was not reasonable, according to the law, nor supported by the evidence. The three learned men signed the acquittal on May 2, 1995, almost two years after Tammy's sentencing. According to Judge Lavoie's ruling, Tammy was supposed to have spent those two years in closed custody. Before filing her appeal, she had spent approximately one week in a youth facility. Now, freshly acquitted, she was a free woman.

Six days after Tammy's acquittal, on May 8, 1995, noted Winnipeg lawyers Hersh Wolch and Heather Leonoff argued before a crowd of forty people in the same Regina courthouse that the conviction of Travis Sterling had also been unreasonable. The jury either failed to understand or receive proper instruction, according to the argument, and did not apply the doctrine of reasonable doubt. If jurors were not rational, they must have been "irrational" — so irrational that they found the Sterling son guilty but not the parents. How could they find anyone guilty when the children's statements had been so inconsistent and when it was clear that adults had "planted" memories in the kids' heads? With respect to preschooler Janey's evidence, some of which was given by her mother, its "reliability and credibility" were at issue. Because of a lack of corroborating evidence in many instances, Judge Wimmer should have told jurors that it would be "dangerous to convict."

Then the Crown rebutted, saying that Judge Wimmer directed the jury in an "exemplary" manner, reminding them of the "frailties of the evidence" when charging them. The jurors understood this, said the Crown prosecutor, then sifted through all the evidence and did their job properly.

On one of the eight convictions there was absolutely no room for appeal. The three judges told the packed room that, regardless of their decision about the other seven convictions, Travis Sterling would serve one year in prison for his very first conviction, that of sexually assaulting ten-year-old Sally in 1988. Accordingly, he was led from the room in handcuffs at the end of the hearing.

In front of the courthouse I ran into an acquaintance, a well-educated and well-meaning woman. She asked what I thought about Travis Sterling — guilty or not? Hoping we might discuss the matter in a nearby restaurant instead of on the courthouse steps, I said I knew only one thing for sure: the present system for handling cases of child sexual abuse was not compatible with the needs of children. Hearing this, she turned on her heel and walked away. From that warm day in May, it took the three judges six months to research and deliberate the trial evidence. In November, they delivered their written reasons for upholding the "Janey" conviction against Travis, and for quashing the six other convictions resulting from the allegations of Freddy, Kenny, Tommy, and Bill.

Their 124-page document began by saying that "children, as a class, are not to be viewed as inherently suspect witnesses," then went on to say that, as experts had made clear during the case, the reliability of children's recollections and statements may be "compromised or distorted" by a number of factors.

For instance, the three judges wrote, "We observe" that no allegations were raised until [the children's] parents began questioning them after being contacted by police. In each case, the child initially denied abuse. Only after repeated questioning by parents and police did the kids make allegations against Travis Sterling and others.

As for the interview techniques themselves, they did not comply with the techniques recommended by experts to get reliable information from the children. Further, the process was suggestive, leading and even hostile towards Travis Sterling. When photos were used, they were shown to the children before the children disclosed knowledge of such things. These practices were fraught with the "real danger of unreliable evidentiary results."

The children's evidence was, in many places, inconsistent and contradictory. For example, the only known cage at The Place is a fragile one used to hold chicks and not nearly strong enough to hold children. Whereas one or two contradictions in testimony might normally be expected, there were so many contradictions about certain things in this trial that the reliability of the children's testimony in question was undermined. On top of that, there were no independent witnesses — all of which raises a reasonable doubt about the guilt of Travis Sterling.

The expert medical evidence, the learned jurists said, was inconclusive with respect to sexual abuse. As for the evidence of T-Mom, Judge Wimmer may have admitted it out of necessity, but was it reliable, in view of the fact that two-and-a-half-year-old Janey could not be cross-examined in order to challenge the truth of the evidence? The three men concluded that, whatever frailties Janey's pink-rope story had, it was consistent with the redness of her genital area that T-Mom testified to in court. And it was "extremely remote" that a toddler with no knowledge of sexual acts would ever have invented the story. But, when all is said and done, Janey's statements cannot be said to suffer from the "frailties we have identified in other children's testimony." When she made the statements to T-Mom, she had yet to be exposed to improper interviewing techniques. And when Judge Wimmer instructed the jury, he did so properly. Thus, the three jurists' "judgement call" on count 18 — Janey's allegation — was that the guilty verdict was reasonable.

In quashing the other six convictions, said the judges, "We appreciate that these cases are extremely difficult to prosecute. However, the law prescribes certain legal tests that must be met to support a conviction. The concept of 'unreasonable verdict' must be applied on a case by case basis and admits of no easy application.... At the end of the day, this is a judgement call and not a precise science."

When interviewed by the *StarPhoenix* about the acquittals, the jury foreman asked that his name not be printed because of a death threat against him and his family after the Sterling trial. A second juror called for an inquiry, saying, "There are things people should want to have looked at. I've got my feelings on what went on." A third juror told the reporter, "[the appeal court judges] apparently have a little more power."

An inquiry. A little more power. Now you're talking, I thought, leafing through the newspaper. But the minister of justice hastened to scotch the idea, and told a TV reporter there was no need for a public inquiry.

Before the end of 1995, Premier Romanow announced the appointment of a new minister of justice, who, in turn, announced that the province would conduct, not an inquiry, but a review of the Department of Justice operations by two Calgary lawyers. When the report was unveiled at a press conference in April 1997, several journalists asked the minister how the report responded to public criticism of high-profile trials such as Martensville, and how the government of Saskatchewan hoped the bland review would help restore public confidence in the province's justice system. The new minister, John Nilson, replied that the "real value" of the report was that it would teach the public about the role of the prosecutor. "The public will see how the system works and how complex it is," he told the dozen reporters in the room. "Human beings run the justice system."

Only one page in the ninety-seven-page report dealt specifically with the Crown's handling of allegations of sexual abuse and, as far as I could see, didn't recommend much change in the prosecutorial procedure for handling them. Small wonder. According to Jack Hillson, a lawyer and MLA, the province's specific terms of reference for the two reviewing lawyers actually "forbade" them to look at why a high-profile case such as Martensville had become an "embarrassment." The way the review was conducted "guaranteed the process would fail." Hillson called the $150,000 report an "utter waste of money."

Around the same time it released the report, the Saskatchewan Department of Justice created the Saskatoon Child Centre for the city and communities within a one-hundred-mile radius. Now, a team of six prosecutors carefully investigates the court-worthiness of each allegation of child sexual abuse the Centre receives, in order to ensure that the requisite "pieces" of evidence are in place and the child plaintiff's "puzzle" is strong enough to hold up in court. This is an important change, and the Martensville trials had a lot to do with it, according to Diana Barr, executive director of the centre.

Barr says that, before the trials, many local agencies responsible for responding to allegations of child sexual abuse "could not help feel they were not doing the best job.... Martensville brought to the surface everything that everyone had been thinking about...and that people realized they could no longer walk away from," she says.

In its first nine months of operation ending December 1997, the innovative centre received approximately 360 children — all alleged victims of sexual abuse and most younger than seven years old. They were examined and interviewed at the one-stop centre by highly trained professionals drawn from a core team of fifty or sixty police officers, doctors, lawyers and social workers. Each interview, while being videotaped, involved at least two highly trained adults working together in an interdisciplinary way using the "best practice," which varied according to the child's age, attention span, cognitive development, language development and, in some cases, disability.

When interviewing, experts did not use anatomically detailed dolls, but they did encourage each child to draw pictures. According to Barr, the 360-odd interviews conducted during the centre's first months were "pristine and not contaminated." And the medical report for each child was filed immediately after the physical evidence was videotaped with state-of-the-art equipment (not photographed, as was formerly the case). To keep abreast of the latest research and interviewing techniques, team members receive regular in-service training in interviewing children and question-asking, and they learn how children think from experts and from children themselves who are drawn from the community for workshops. A local police official says his officers are pleased with the Saskatoon Child Centre because it's so child-friendly. During a recent reorganization of the city police force, a new unit devoted to sex crimes was created with six full-time investigators, who sometimes investigate allegations with the Centre's personnel.

According to Director Barr, it's "too soon" to say if the Centre will change things in the long run. "We hope we have created a better body of evidence," she says. "If the system is not going to change, we have to then work to assist the children.... Child abuse cases are here, appearing in court all the time... and bringing recognition to the need for change.... As we learn more about children, I don't think we will continue to hear children in court the way we do now."

The Last Word

by Sheldon Kennedy

In January 1997, NHL hockey hero Sheldon Kennedy stood in a Calgary courtroom and blew the whistle on his former coach, Graham James, for having sexually abused him hundreds of times when he was a teen. The game was up. James was led from the room in leg irons and later sentenced to three and a half years in prison.

I couldn't go to court until I was 27 years old because I was scared that no one would believe me. Even though I'm an adult now, and used to performing in front of thousands of people, I was very nervous standing in front of all those people in court. So it's gotta be very traumatic for a kid to go to court.

It takes a mountain of courage just to stand up there in the first place, without having to relive the abuse by telling your story in public. So I think an abused kid should be allowed to testify behind closed doors instead of being humiliated by a defence lawyer who twists your story. When it gets twisted, the jury might not believe you. I can't imagine how tough that must be. It just blows my mind.

When I "came out" a couple of years ago, certain people didn't think I was telling the truth. Some hockey buddies tried to convince me not to lay charges against James because of what it might do to my career. But I figured I had to keep going; not to speak out would mean that he still had power over me. Besides, I wanted to help other kids and set an example. Just because you've been sexually abused as a kid, it doesn't mean you have to be a victim all your life. So I just kept with it, and did what I believed in.

Fortunately, I was spared having to testify in court in person because my lawyer read my statement and James pleaded guilty. The hardest part wasn't hearing my statement read, it was hearing the defence lawyer make out that the abuse James had inflicted on me wasn't really all that bad. That was very hard for me to handle. Now I wish I had testified myself. If I had, maybe James would have got a stiffer sentence instead of a slap on the wrist.

You know, abuse hurts. It hurts a lot. Just because you can't see it — the way you'd see a kid's broken leg, for instance — doesn't mean the pain isn't real. In fact, the pain and depression of abuse kills. During my teens I tried to hide the pain — with booze and drugs and fast cars. I was scared everyone would think I was gay, or that I might lose friends or ruin my life as a hockey player. So I continued to put on a big show that everything was just fine. James was so intelligent that he fooled everyone in the community.

The emotional pain he inflicted on me was not something I can easily explain. All I know is that if I hadn't started to deal with the depression a while ago, it would have soon destroyed my life. I used to think about committing suicide, and just before the trial in January I took a knife and slashed my legs and my arms and face. If my wife hadn't found me and called the ambulance, I would have died.

So now I have physical scars as well as emotional ones to prove that abuse can kill you. If you are sexually abused as a kid, the best thing to do is tell someone right away. I know it's easier said than done, and I remember how scared I was when I was a boy and James raped me at gunpoint. Now that I'm an adult, I feel I have an obligation to speak out on behalf of all kids who are sexually abused, partly to show them they can speak out too and partly to convince adults to stop turning a blind eye to the issue.

Naturally, everyone's scared; it's a scary issue. And many people are naive. But the only way to conquer sexual abuse is to look it straight in the face. You have to be strong to deal with it. When a child tells you he or she has been abused, you have to try to listen with an open mind. Don't let fear hold you back.

There are no clearcut answers. That's why you have to ask: Why would the child want to make up stories about sexual abuse? How could he or she make up the stories if they've never even seen such things? On the other hand, I know it's not right to accuse an adult of doing something he didn't do. That's why you have to gather lots of evidence by listening to the child and watching for changes in behaviour. When I was a kid, I know some people thought I was screwed up. Maybe I was, but there were reasons for my behaviour. Now that I'm an adult, I'm trying to get to the bottom of my pain and heal it.

I have a daughter of my own, and I wonder how anyone could harm such a small and defenceless creature. I hope that by speaking out against the sexual abuse of kids I can help break the blinding spell that child abusers cast over adults and children. The two-year sentences the courts hand out to convicted child abusers — I'm including Travis Sterling and Gordon Stuckless — are a joke. If I can get people to open their eyes; if I can help just one abused kid; if I can prevent one suicide like Martin Kruze's — then my own uphill battle will have been well worth it.

Frann Harris grew up in Toronto, Ontario, and taught high school for five years before working at TVOntario and two educational publishing houses. For the past 15 years she has lived in the West, and has edited two national magazines and written articles for more than two dozen magazines and newspapers. This is her first book.

www.ingramcontent.com/pod-product-compliance
Lightning Source LLC
LaVergne TN
LVHW060925211025
823917LV00027B/174